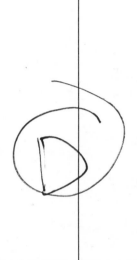

American Pimpernel

ALSO BY ANDY MARINO

Herschel: The Boy Who Started World War II

AMERICAN
PIMPERNEL

*The man who saved the artists
on Hitler's death list*

ANDY MARINO

Hutchinson • London

First published in the United Kingdom in 1999 by Hutchinson

The Random House Group Limited
20 Vauxhall Bridge Road, London, SW1V 2SA

Random House Australia (Pty) Limited
20 Alfred Street, Milsons Point, Sydney,
New South Wales 2061, Australia

Random House New Zealand Limited
18 Poland Road, Glenfield
Auckland 10, New Zealand

Random House (Pty) Limited
Endulini, 5a Jubilee Road, Parktown, 2193, South Africa

The Random House Group Limited Reg. No. 954009
www.randomhouse.co.uk

A CIP catalogue record for this book is available
from the British Library

Papers used by Random House are natural,
recyclable products made from wood grown in sustainable forests;
the manufacturing processes conform to the environmental
regulations of the country of origin.

ISBN 0 09 180053 6

Printed and bound in Great Britain by
Biddles Ltd, Guildford and King's Lynn

For

ANNETTE RILEY FRY

and for

DONALD CARROLL

a great editor and guide

and

CHARLES FAWCETT

whom so many have been privileged to call a friend

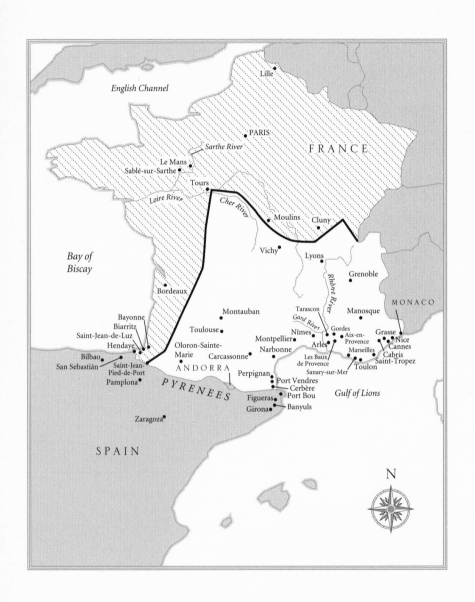

CONTENTS

PREFACE

THERE COMES A TIME following any remarkable event when memory inevitably fades into history. The story of Varian Fry's Emergency Rescue Committee turned this process around, in that after the Second World War it almost immediately became history—or rather one of its forgotten footnotes. True, the events this book describes were remembered by those who were involved and by those who benefited; but to the public at large, it was as if the extraordinary happenings in wartime Marseille had never occurred. Fry's own account, *Surrender on Demand,* was published in 1945 at a time when people wished to forget the recent conflict and get on with their lives, and it was soon out of print. The native modesty of all those people who worked with Fry stopped them from seeking the admiration and reward they deserved.

The prehistory of this book begins in London in 1965, where a brilliant young editor named Donald Carroll was working on art books at the London publisher, Thames & Hudson. "In the course of editing a book on Marc Chagall," he later recalled, "I found my curiosity aroused by a footnote mentioning, almost off-handedly, the fact that Chagall was one of the many artists who escaped to New York City early in the war through the good offices of 'The Fry Committee.' What, I wondered, was the Fry Committee? Nobody could tell me, despite the fact that at Thames & Hudson I had access to virtually every prominent art historian and critic writing in English. Eventually I gave up."

But the idea of an organization spiriting artists out of Europe from under the nose of the Nazis continued to appeal to Donald Carroll. It lay at the bottom of his mind while his career and travels sent him all over the world.

Finally in 1975, another clue prompted Donald to resume his research. "I was working as a columnist and broadcaster in Los Angeles," he said, "when I came upon another reference (I can't remember where) to the work of Fry and his committee. By now convinced that their work must have involved some kind of secret wartime operation that many people knew *of* but nobody knew *about,* I wrote to the State Department." All it could supply him with was an obituary of a man called *Varian* Fry, but the last paragraph mentioned that he was survived by his widow, Annette. After moving to New York with his German wife, Donald set about tracking down Annette Fry, and some months later discovered that she was living only a few streets away from him on the Upper West Side. "She turned out to be a most delightful and charming lady," and he was launched into a journey that sent him across the United States and Europe.

"I hit the road with my tape recorder, criss-crossing the country until I had interviewed every person I could find who had been in any way involved in Fry's operation: Marta Feuchtwanger in Los Angeles, Lisa Fittko in Chicago, Miriam Davenport in upstate Michigan, Albert Hirschman at Princeton, Harry Bingham in Connecticut, and of course many more in New York itself." Donald found Bill Spira in Paris, and cornered Gaston Defferre, who had been Fry's brave lawyer in 1940 and was by then famous as Marseille's powerful mayor. He also tracked down the mayor of Banyuls, on the French-Spanish border, who had been so vital to the escape operation. Finally, Donald sought out Fry's friends and collaborators whose testimony would now, regretfully, be impossible to obtain: that of Harold Oram, Anna Caples Hagen, Hans Sahl, and Fry's own relatives of a generation now departed.

The project of telling Fry's amazing story never came to fruition and languished for nearly another two decades. I had known Donald for half of that time, through my agent and friend Richard Gollner. In short, they both asked me if I would attempt to revive the story by picking up where Donald's research had left off. It goes without saying that if I had not benefited from Donald's invaluable work all those years ago, and his equally invaluable advice and guidance, this book would have been impossible to write.

Donald had already done much to publicize the exploits of Varian Fry, most notably with his essay, "Escape From Vichy," published in the magazine *American Heritage* in 1983. From then on, awareness of Fry's importance began to increase. Editorials in newspapers from New York to Los Angeles called for Fry to be honored for his work. A tree was planted in his name at Yad Vashem, the museum in Jerusalem dedicated to remembrance of the

Holocaust and its heroes. United States senators started to press for Fry to be awarded a Congressional Medal of Honor. A major exhibition, organized by the United States Holocaust Memorial Museum, began to tour the country. It was, argued Donald and Richard, high time the story was told.

Reluctantly, realizing the size and importance of the work, I agreed to take it on. Soon, though, the magic and heroism of the drama had infected me as it had done Donald years before. This is the result. Now, in the century's final year, when Fry's memory would be fading into history, it is apparent that many people are determined to keep it vividly in focus. My hope is that this volume might in some way contribute to such a worthwhile enterprise. Fry is an example to us all.

My thanks are due to many: Annette Fry, Professor Albert O. Hirschman, Dr. Miriam Davenport, Dr. Marcel Verzeano, Professor Justus Rosenberg, Lisa Fittko, Professor Walter Meyerhof, Pierre Sauvage, and of course Charles Fawcett. I have been generously helped by Susan Morgenstein, Elizabeth Kessin Berman, Anita Kassof and Marvin Liberman at the United States Holocaust Memorial Museum in Washington D.C., and by the staff (especially Bernard Crystal) of the Columbia University Rare Book and Manuscript Department at the Butler Library, home of the Varian Fry Collection, who have also provided photographs. Dr. Mordecai Paldiel at Yad Vashem deserves special mention, as do the staff of the Tate Gallery Archive, The Wiener Library and the Public Records Office in London.

Albert Zuckerman at Writers House in New York City, and Richard Gollner, Neil Hornick, and Anna Swan in London made the book a reality. Bob Weil, Becky Koh, Julia Pastore and Elaine Bleakney at St. Martin's Press have worked hard to make sure all went smoothly. In London Sue Freestone, Tony Whittome and Sophie Wills at Hutchinson have done the same. I am grateful to them all.

An extra benefit of writing this book is that fate put me in the way of Charlie Fawcett, one of the great personalities of this century, a real hero and perhaps the true protegé of Varian Fry. May his tribe increase.

ANDY MARINO

PART 1

THE LITTLE

PRINCE

CHAPTER 1

BEROLINA

RICK: *I stick my neck out for nobody.*
LOUIS: *A wise foreign policy.*
CASABLANCA

THE PENSION STERN on Berlin's wide, tree-shaded Kurfürstendamm was more hotel than boardinghouse. The hot and cold water and the telephone in every room were just what an American would expect in the better places back home, and Varian Fry took it as his due. He had arrived in Germany from New York in May 1935 and had chosen the Stern as the base for his travels. He was glad he did. It was cheap at only fifteen marks a day, and he had kindled a friendship with Michael Liebert, nephew of old Mrs. Stern, the proprietress. Fry's German, which was not as good as his French, had much improved. He now found himself speaking good colloquial Berlinese.

Fry always made it a point to talk to everybody he could when he traveled, and the clientele of the Pension Stern interested him. One such guest included a fellow American, the impresario Eugene Tiller, who had come from France to Berlin to recruit dancers for his troupe, the Tiller Girls. It was a prime time for such an enterprise, with the clubs and cabarets being shut down more frequently now. Fry enjoyed the unsurpassed musical satire of the nightlife Berlin had still to offer, but he sympathized with the desire of the performers to get out while the going was good. He knew that many of the most outspoken artists and writers had already fled to Vienna or Prague or Basle, out of reach (they hoped) of the Gestapo, which did not approve of their books or jokes or lyrics. Berlin—*Berolina* to the intellectuals and bohemians—was no longer the place for public displays of wit and irony, or for subversive ideas. People had begun to disappear.

Another guest with whom the young Fry was vaguely acquainted was Dr.

Alfred Apfel, the famous anti-Nazi lawyer. He was defending one of the men on trial for setting the Reichstag fire. The Nazis were attempting to blame it on their Communist opponents, but most of the world believed they had arranged it themselves, in order to gain unopposed control of the German parliament. Though the trial was proceeding well for Apfel, he was, in fact, a worried man, unsure of how he would make his own escape when the trial was over. With the foreign journalists and their protective publicity gone, he would then be at the mercy of his ruthless government.

The famous comedian Max Adalbert, another resident at the Stern, was downcast as well. For him there was not much to laugh at or joke about in Germany anymore.

Fry had no need to worry about the random incidents of terror under the Nazi regime. A knock on the door in the middle of the night simply meant room service had arrived with his cognac. But in two months he had seen enough of Hitler's brave new world to understand what was going on—enough of the gaily decked-out gingerbread towns and the wildly cheering crowds (*schwarmerai* was the word for it)—full of gleeful children waving their red and white flags with that sinister black spider at the center, their proud mothers smiling and waving to the bull-necked brownshirts strutting along.

Varian Fry had not been vacationing. No sane person would choose the Third Reich as a place for rest and relaxation. On the contrary, he had arrived with a mission, and a fat, empty notebook that was now entirely full. For a journalist there was no substitute for being on the spot. He had observed Hitler's economic miracle in action, it was true, with its new roads and railways, kindergartens and hospitals. Grown men who had never worked a day in their lives now had jobs in the Nazi Party. They had back their self-respect—from the look of it, perhaps too much self-respect.

All the dubious glamour of the uniforms and the ballooning nationalist uplift of Goebbels's propaganda was on display. The citizenry looked proud and prosperous. Germany was now a single-party state, and the Party defined its, and therefore Germany's, foes. The propaganda declared that the enemy lay within. Many who were excluded from Hitler's dreams of glory could not yet understand why. The atmosphere was disorientating, overwhelming. "Oh, Mother, Mother," one little girl was heard to say in a movie theater as on the screen a parade of storm troopers had marched stiffly past. "If I weren't a Jew I think I'd be a Nazi." In his own mind Fry was trying to resolve the paradoxes of terror and joy in the new Germany. Tyranny or not, and despite the latent opposition Fry had discovered, the feverish atmosphere of patriotism and racialism seemed to be the popular will of the people.

By the evening of July 15 Varian Fry had interviewed enough people, taken enough notes, and seen enough of the Third Reich to make for a thorough piece on the state of affairs in Germany. He was looking forward to a fine meal in celebration of what was almost the end of his task—just one more interview to go—before he returned to New York to take up the post of editor at the political journal *The Living Age.* He had struck the deal with its outgoing editor, who told him that if he thought it worth his while to take a couple of months off and see what was really happening in the cauldron of Europe's future, then the job would be waiting for him on his return.

Fry looked the very picture of the earnest young liberal. Smartly suited and wearing a bow tie, at twenty-seven years of age he appeared much less of a schoolboy now and finally more grown up. A dedicated, perhaps slightly prissy look was already etching itself on his features, tugging his mouth down at the corners and pursing his lips. It was a countenance that seemed to say, "I know I am right, and frankly I am astonished that you could think otherwise." His round, horn-rimmed spectacles added a certain owlish effect, but his dark wavy hair and a broad, friendly nose fought against an incipient seriousness.

Germany had both excited and depressed him. Fry adored the country but he was revolted by the injustices he had seen, the lies he had heard repeated. The place seemed to thrive on slander: it was "the Jews extort this" and "the Jews plot that," a set of falsehoods plain to anybody willing to use his brain. Yet people seemed to believe in them. Fry recognized a bullying crowd mentality that had left him clenched and angry, but had also liberated all the energy of his ferocious indignation. For indignation was Fry's lifeblood; and in a strange way he thrived on the exposure to evil he had experienced in Hitler's Germany. He was a man who supported good causes as a matter of course, but he wasn't content unless there were also bad causes to be defeated. Fry was not truly happy unless he was in some way outraged. For two months he had inhaled an atmosphere of repression like it was the scent of a flower; now he felt truly invigorated.

At about eight o'clock on that summer evening Fry left his hotel room to seek the broad and elegant boulevards of *Berolina.* What followed would change his life forever.

When he reached the hotel lobby he saw guests clustered at the door and windows, looking out onto the street with frightened interest. Somebody told Fry there was an anti-Jewish riot outside, and with a journalist's inquisitiveness he edged through the crush and out onto the Kurfürstendamm, where he saw people running along the road toward what seemed to be the source of the commotion. He decided to follow, and as he did the noise of cheering—or rather barking, as if wild dogs were fighting over a bone—grew louder.

The first sight that met his eyes delivered a blow of atavistic horror.

The old man's mouth was gaping and stringy with blood, screaming for help, but the plea was drowned out by the volume of the mob's blind fury. A pullulating circle of figures was flailing the elderly victim with fists and feet so that, already cringing and wet with their spittle, he was slowly sinking to the ground. Although he tried with all his might to remain upright, since falling meant certain doom, the man finally lost his strength and collapsed. The body of the crowd closed over him. An old lady who must have been his wife had been crying and clawing at the fringe of the unheeding gang of attackers. Now someone noticed her and smashed his fist into her face. Then she, too, was pulled into the blood orgy, kicked and stamped on until she went down as well.

Suddenly, Fry looked around him and saw other beatings taking place, and knots of citizens merging into larger groups as if by some magnetic attraction, until they were numerous enough to block the wide thoroughfare and slow the traffic passing through. A young man pointed his hand like a pistol at someone hurrying past. "Jew!" he shouted, and a section of the crowd surged away like swarming bees from some already motionless and crumpled shape, to converge on their new, terrified prey, pinning him against the wall and going through his pockets for his identity papers. "A Jew!" rang out the hoarse, gleeful cry again, and they were on him, sending his body crashing back over café tables before the boots and fists began to rain down once more.

On each side of the street the windows of Jewish shops and restaurants were being smashed, and the air sang with the shrill music of destruction. Oddly enough there were policemen standing guard in front of "German businesses," meaning non-Jewish ones, Fry supposed, while the mob sailed on its turbulent course toward the unprotected storefronts. Storm troopers were loitering about in obvious authority, their jodhpurs and brown mud-colored shirts straining to hold in big, hard bellies. They looked tough, all right, dumb but tough with bully slyness, redirecting the fleeing victims back into the fray with their fists.

Fry felt in no danger himself. It was like peering into a demonic slide show, unreal and grotesque, but intensely colored. People were running in all directions; he heard the slap of feet on the road. The tinny smell of blood was in the air. The pursuers went after their quarry unrelentingly, and it was as though a great good humor had taken possession of the mass. A young boy no more than twelve years old came up to him. "This is a holiday for us," he said breathlessly, and Fry looked at him, speechless. The boy meant it. He noticed smart, stout *burgerlich* couples of middle age, out for their evening promenade before supper or the theater, suddenly losing their senses and joining in a beating. Shop girls screamed with murderous fury at passing vehicles that the crowd engulfed, and from which they dragged the terrified occupants. Were they Aryan? They had to prove it, and if they couldn't, the spitting and kicking would begin anew, while the automobile rocked on its axles in the throng.

Still in a state of disbelief—not because he thought it couldn't happen, but because he was there when it did—Fry looked up toward the far end of the Kurfürstendamm. There, in towering majesty, stood the Kaiser Wilhelm memorial church. This was no time for irony, but what began to reach his ears now was evidence of another phase in the surging swell around him. The mob had begun to find its voice and it sounded, though surely it couldn't be, as if the rising notes were emanating from the church. A lone voice cried out, long and deep, like the lowing of cattle, sonorous and barely human, a line that would be repeated as slowly and deliberately by the crowd all along the boulevard. "Wenn Judenblut vom Messer spritzt," it intoned, and was echoed and multiplied by the still surging mass: *When Jewish blood spurts from the knife . . .*

Again the voice tolled out across the bobbing heads: "Dann geht's nochmal so gut. . . ." *Then things will go even better,* Fry translated silently, as once again this new line was repeated in the same funereal tempo. Other lines followed in mournful cadence, a solemn progression through an automaton's nightmare, so eerie amid this tempestuous brutality. Then Fry realized he was witnessing, loud and clear, nothing less than an inversion of the Christian liturgy. For all its dancing insanity, for all its murderous frenzy, he was sensible of a ritual aspect to this pogrom, some religious template underlying the chaos and channeling its anti-Jewish energy. The thought flashed through Fry's mind that this was not just a riot, but the beginning of a religious crusade against the Nazi devil of "Jew-Bolshevism." The high priest of this dark campaign was, of course, very near.

Fry gathered his senses and began to walk away, feeling as though he were swimming, slowly, in a dream. He was still too close to the macabre street theater to feel outrage, and he numbly entered the harbor of a café. There, Fry saw a sight that would haunt him, and which in later years he would retell only rarely and in a whisper. In a corner sat a man trying as hard as anybody could do to look invisible. Two storm troopers, ruddy faced and reeking of bull arrogance, had entered and walked toward him. The man, clearly Jewish, tremulously reached for his beer. As he did so, a knife flashed in the air and pinned his shaking hand to the table. The storm troopers laughed.

Fry walked back to the Pension Stern, past a poster outside the Ufa Palast movie theater that read WER VOM JUDEN KAUFT, IST EIN VERRATER!—*HE WHO BUYS FROM A JEW IS A TRAITOR!* In his hotel bedroom he took out his notebook, and on the last blank page began to write. When he had finished, he picked up the telephone and asked reception to put through a call for him. The next day his report, sent via the Associated Press, would make the front page of the *New York Times,* and America would have its first real taste of Nazism in action.

THE PREVIOUS NIGHT had not been just a bad dream. When Fry left the Pension Stern the next morning to walk the short distance toward the Brandenburg Gate and the government buildings, the victims were still there, many where they had fallen. They were now being tended to in the street and he saw bandaged heads, bandaged hands, and fresh, clean slings of plaster over their noses. Back in New York it was the middle of the night and the presses were already rolling.

Fry had already asked for and received an invitation to the offices of the Foreign Press Division at Joseph Goebbels's Ministry of Propaganda, where Ernst Hanfstaengel—"Putzi" to his friends—had been entrusted by Hitler with the mission to explain Nazism to the world. Fry suspected he had been granted an interview because of all Hanfstaengel thought they had in common. In fact there were only two things: they were both Americans, and both alumni of Harvard University, although Hanfstaengel had graduated ten years before Fry. The gregarious Putzi could never resist an opportunity to meet someone with whom he could swap memories of student life.

Fry was shown in, where he refused the offer of coffee. If Hanfstaengel noticed his visitor's tight-lipped disapproval, he didn't reveal it. Fry did not know before he met him whether the man was evil or stupid; he kept an open mind about it. Now, though, his mental dial was swinging in the direction of stupidity. Hanfstaengel began the conversation predictably by asking, as he settled his large frame into his seat, how Harvard was doing. Fry smiled stiffly at him but did not make eye contact. He replied that to the best of his knowledge their old alma mater was getting along just fine without them. At this, Hanfstaengel roared with laughter. "Without me, certainly," he said, hinting at past roguishness. Fry's mind was turning on the riot of the night before, and anger at this lightheartedness began to percolate through his system. Hanfstaengel had apparently forgotten that he was a journalist. He said nothing about keeping what they were going to discuss off the record. Very well, thought Fry.

He played to the bearish Hanfstaengel's obvious weak point—homesickness—chatting about America and lulling him into a warm feeling of nostalgia before introducing the matter of the Kurfürstendamm riot into the conversation. Hanfstaengel's face darkened with insincere concern as he agreed that it had been an unfortunate incident. An unforgivable one, corrected Fry, a wanton attack on people and property. Who did Hanfstaengel blame for it? His answer was civic indignation: a group of Jews had hissed a pro-Nazi movie at the Ufa Palast and set off the whole thing. At least, that is what he was told. It was, Fry must understand, difficult to separate out the sequence of events. Not all the Jews who were beaten up were to blame, of course, but a single spark may start a fire. . . .

As one old Harvard man to another, he went on, he had his suspicions that *fanatiker,* storm troopers, might have been involved. Fry, who had seen everything, simply sat there and let him talk on. There was a struggle, Hanfstaengel explained, between two principal factions in the Nazi Party. On the one hand there were the moderates. He smiled to include himself in this group. On the other, there were more radical elements who wished to be rid of the Jews once and for all—they didn't care how—and they wanted to show they had wide support. Last night's regrettable incident was provoked with that in mind.

The moderates believed that the Jewish problem could be dealt with in a more civilized manner, perhaps by designating certain areas Jews could be moved to in order to separate them from the German people, whom they antagonized. Not ghettos, Hanfstaengel added hastily, more like reservations, similar to those the United States provided for its native Indian population. The Jews would retain the benefits of German identity without experiencing their present difficulties. Or they could migrate. In fact, negotiations for the settlement of Jews in foreign territories like Madagascar were under discussion.

Fry pushed Hanfstaengel on what the so-called radicals wanted to do with the Jews. Why, they want to exterminate them, replied Hanfstaengel simply, offhandedly and off guard. Kill them all. This was the solution favored by Hitler, by Goebbels. Fry, even before last night's bloodletting, had attempted to extrapolate the logic of the Nazi movement, and such "ideology" as it possessed. His conclusion was that at the end of the road inevitably lay war and murder, and that this was in some way what it was all about, some mad Teutonic conflagration. But his image of it had been opaque. He read the things that were written, witnessed actions taken against the Jews. It was true one could almost smell the hatred. But to have the idea spelled out in plain

English by somebody who was as close to the font of Nazi power as Hanfs-taengel clarified everything.

What made Hanfstaengel particularly odious in Fry's view was that he should have known better. Germany had long suffered the worst, most inver-tebrate press in the Western world, and for centuries it had accepted an abysmal public education system. It was a sharply stratified society where one did not dare question one's superiors, and its worship of officialdom was practically a national cult, as the great but now banished German writer Heinrich Mann had pointed out in his novels written during the time of Kaiser Wilhelm. The true culprit of the Nazi phenomenon was German his-tory: when Hitler screamed at his people about their overwhelming need to obey, he knew what he was talking about. It was like they said of the Kaiser, when a generation earlier he ordered the German people into the mad slaughter on the Western Front, "The King makes war and the people die." And Bismarck, who hadn't wanted the war, said that all the people lacked was "civilian courage," the courage to take hold of their own lives and resist the will of the ruler. They would die unquestioningly in the trenches, but they re-fused to see that they could ever govern themselves. Their anti-Semitism was unremarkable: every country Fry knew of despised Jews to a greater or (nor-mally) lesser extent. But the conditions in Hitler's Third Reich had amplified a traditional feeling of surly distrust and turned it into government policy. Simply put, Germans no longer felt it necessary *not* to beat up Jews.

But Hanfstaengel was an American. He had grown up in a country with an egalitarian, individualistic ethos; he had received the best education money could buy. Now he was abusing that democratic inheritance and allying him-self with a base and vicious regime. The man's bluff good humor was an in-sult. Hanfstaengel's ancestors were German, and they had left Germany—like four and a half million others over the last century—precisely because of its narrow-minded chauvinism and its suffocating autocracy. Those who could not get out, or were content to obey their masters, never enjoyed the advan-tages that America had given Hanfstaengel. Now he had returned to lord it over them. In the end it was more than stupidity. By proclaiming his friend-ship with Hitler, in boasting of how the Führer liked him to play "Three Cheers for Harvard" on the piano, Hanfstaengel in his own trivial way had sunk lower than Hitler himself in the moral scheme of things.

Fry was a professional journalist, and if Hanfstaengel had made him promise not to use direct quotes, he would have assented and found a more general, unattributed way to announce his discovery of the genocidal plans being entertained in the upper echelons of the Third Reich. But it was 1935 and nobody would believe him. They probably wouldn't, anyway. But because

Hanfstaengel was talking—as he had said—as one Harvard man to another, Fry filed another report through the Associated Press as soon as he had left the country, quoting Hanfstaengel's exact words. It, too, made the front page of the *New York Times* that July. Fry could no longer visit Nazi Germany, but he didn't want to. What he feared was that Nazi Germany would soon be visiting everybody else.

CHAPTER 2

DON'T BE A GOOP

VARIAN MACKEY FRY in early life had been the proverbial sick child. But like everything else about him, this was more complicated than it seemed. For there was also a certain amount of make-believe to his infirmity. Fry had always been a consummate actor. By the time he was twelve years old he had mastered the art of duping his parents, Arthur and Lilian, into believing tales of suffering despite the fact that his ailments appeared with utter predictability. Whenever the weather turned bad, Varian was simply too ill to attend school. His complacent ruses always worked even though his young cousin Libby managed easily to see through him. Fry didn't care: his purpose was to fool his parents, and that he had done. When Libby pointed out that rain would provoke a cough, or freezing weather a headache, he merely shrugged. When she told Fry to his face she knew he was faking, he said he didn't see what business it was of hers. Varian was an only child, a boy in a world of indulgent women. In addition to his endlessly attentive mother, whose nerves were not all they could be, there were Aunt Da and Aunt Floss to fuss over him. There was simply nothing Libby could do.

Fry's candid attitude was that it was for the other boys, the herd, to trudge through mud and hail and be uncomfortable and bored in the dull prison called school. He preferred to lie in bed and be read aloud to by his mother. This was much more interesting than lessons, as were his daydreams. With only slight exaggeration of his status in the Fry household, he frequently imagined himself the son of a king.

In fact Fry's father worked on Wall Street for the firm of Carlysle and Mellick, and commuted fifty miles a day to his job as "office" partner in the odd-lot stockbrokerage. He managed the business, while the other partners traded on the floor of the exchange, or dealt with other brokers who traded there. Arthur was a solid domestic presence only on weekends. Even then he seems to have been a cheerful and credulous parent of exactly the sort a devious young plotter like Fry could take advantage of. In the way that some families develop, especially those with a single child, the little prince became the unofficial nexus of household policy.

Fry was born in Harlem, New York City, on October 15, 1907. The family was comfortable but not wealthy, "Certainly never 'wealthy,' as the wealth of stockbrokers is actually measured!" said Fry. Like many other middle-class families of the time, they soon moved from Harlem to the suburbs. In their case this meant Ridgewood, New Jersey, across the Hudson River. There, from the age of two, Varian grew up in the devoted feminine atmosphere that he could always snap to attention with a temper tantrum if need be. He led a little group of younger playmates, but was timid with boys his own age, and often chose solitude to their rough company. From early days, and by carefully choosing his territory, Varian grew accustomed to getting his own way.

There survive as a kind of family snapshot two verses of doggerel Varian's father wrote for his son based on a verse by Gelett Burgess. They sound almost like an admonition, but lack the sternness to serve as effective criticism. The precocious young boy may even have taken them as admiring encouragement:

GOOP POMES

This Goop bounces on the bed,
First on his feet, then on his head.
His mother tells him to get dressed,
For mothers always know what's best.
But he won't do as he's told,
He'll be a Goop and catches cold.
                    Don't be a Goop.

This Goop is Varian Mackey Fry,
Just watch him make his oatmeal fly.
It's on the cloth, it's on the floor,
It's even spattered on the door.
A boy of six is much too big
To eat his breakfast like a pig.
                    Don't be a Goop.

If the prospect of Goop-hood failed to strike terror into Varian's heart, the psychological boot camp of school was another matter. His first experience of the outside world poured like an unwelcome cold shower over the little prince. It was probably genuine distress that first added a nervous stomach to those fabricated ailments that changed with the weather. Long after Fry grew up he remained an excruciatingly sensitive individual. The stomach pain would regularly return, and although Fry watched what he ate, he was still rewarded with a duodenal ulcer by his mid-thirties.

The bliss of childhood never lasts, and the more blissful or at least insulated it is, the steeper the descent into reality. It would be wrong to assume Fry was a misfit, but he was never a "team player" and never had any wish to be one. Making good use of his strategic hypochondria, he retreated like many willful and bright young children into a more interesting, though perhaps lonely realm of his own making. The quality of Fry's observation and his interest in the natural world, especially in bird-watching, dates from early in his life and may have been an antidote to his isolation.

At school he displayed an alert intelligence and showed a great facility for learning. But in the roughhouse of grade school, the nascent intellectual is often (and sometimes wrongly) marked out as a sissy. Fry may have suffered from this common syndrome—it's hard to see how he did not—but characteristically he made it one of the pillars of his personality. He began to cultivate his aesthetic tastes, and from them eventually fashioned a source of resilience and even a feeling of superiority. A university friend remembered how Fry "held in lodged disdain the mindless games" of the sports jocks, although it would have been different if Fry had displayed any talent for sports himself. The competitiveness he missed on the football field he more than made up for in conversation. There he was an aggressive player, and always aimed to win.

Fry's isolation at the local school was uncomfortable and probably of his own making, but academically it put him far ahead of his contemporaries. Arthur soon enrolled his son in a private tutoring establishment to prepare him for the entrance examination to Hotchkiss—Lilian's suggestion—which had an impressive academic reputation as well as excellent social credentials. Lilian's social ambitions were curtailed by her nervous fear of entertaining and being entertained. But for her son she wanted the best, and Arthur was content to go along with her choice.

The prep school proved to be an awakening for Varian: "A whole new world," he called it. He was forced to work hard and enjoyed keeping up with the demanding regime of instruction. It was there that some of the groundwork was laid for the sharpness of Fry's adult intellect. Chief among his enthusiasms was Latin, the precision and complexity of which suited the grammar of his personality and gave him a means of privileged communication. Latin also gave Fry the chance to be incontrovertibly correct—and to correct others, of course, which was one of his main pleasures. Annette, his widow, remembers the mind like a steel trap, which may early on have found its spring loading in the ancient language.

He remained happily at the prep school until 1922, when he passed with flying colors the examinations that took him to the Hotchkiss school in Lakeville, Connecticut, just before his fifteenth birthday. But there things took a turn for the worse, for the student culture was dominated by the older boys, and in the cruel tradition of English private ("public") schools, the new arrivals were subjected to humiliation and physical abuse under the euphemism of "hazing." One of the ordeals, which with bitterness Fry never forgot or forgave, was to hang from a boiling hot steam pipe running the length of the dormitory, and proceed to the far end hand over hand. Fry let it be known that he thought this systematic tormenting of the younger students was pure barbarism. As a result he was singled out for special treatment, and his hazing continued beyond the traditional first year and right through the second. The pain and humiliation Fry certainly felt was compounded by the social violence it represented. For he didn't share with his persecutors their background of wealth and privilege. He was at Hotchkiss only on the strength of his academic abilities—a sign to him of his innate personal superiority, and an opening onto the next stage of Fry's self-invention.

By making use of his carefully nurtured manners and considerable learning, Fry began to reinvent himself as the perfect (or insufferable) young aristocrat. He would take inordinate care over how he dressed, and demand a knife and fork to eat a hamburger. He took to smoking a cigarette, because he thought it looked elegant in his hand, but he never inhaled. Choosing for himself qualities other than the dreary bourgeois fetish for money, he wrongfooted his peers and vaulted over their merely material advantages. "The first duty in life is to be as artificial as possible," said Oscar Wilde, and Varian took him at his word. He entered into a period of serious playacting through which he hoped to redefine and refine an unpleasant environment.

To others it may have appeared that Fry had simply retreated behind a wall of petulance. Despite his enjoyment of the intellectual rigors at Hotchkiss the taunts continued, and one day—there are contradictory versions of the event, but the conclusion is the same—he simply resigned from school. Family tradition remembers Arthur Fry driving to Connecticut to collect his son from the principal's office; but also recalled in one camp is the father's surprise at Varian turning up at his Wall Street brokerage one December day in 1924 to

announce that he would not be returning to Hotchkiss. Both Arthur and Lilian pleaded with their son over the Christmas vacation, but Varian remained
characteristically adamant. He was seventeen, and it was too late for them to
expect him to start taking orders now.

If Arthur feared that his son's singularity was in danger of overbalancing
into something more like rebelliousness, he did not show it. In the end an
agreement was reached: a school would be selected where Varian would not
be penalized for his sophistication. His parents reserved the right to name the
place, and chose Taft, a well-respected establishment in Watertown, Connecticut. This denied Fry his real objective, which was to be at the hub of the
action in Manhattan, with its jagged and colorful array of modern entertain-
ments. With all his sophistication it was where he felt he really belonged. It
was the jazzy twenties, and Varian felt he was missing out.

Taft not only proved a relief from the harassments he suffered at Hotchkiss, but he found the workload was lighter, too. Fry compensated for this by
educating himself beyond the curriculum and reading everything he could
lay his hands on. Nevertheless, by the summer he was restless in what he had
decided was a provincial backwater, and after a well-coordinated campaign of
persuasion he won out over his parents. They agreed to let him attend from
fall semester the Riverdale Country School in the Bronx, a mere bridge away
from his dream island, Manhattan. Varian's odyssey was at an end. He felt
wonderfully at home, and his last year of school was a triumph. His skills as a
linguist blossomed—as if in finding his place he had also found his voice—
and soon he could read and write in six languages. To top it all off, he passed
the Harvard entrance examinations in spring 1926 in the top 10 percent na-
tionally. Arthur sent him on vacation to Bermuda as a reward.

Nineteen twenty-six was also the year in which Fry formed his first real
adult friendship. Johannes Martens, a visitor from Scandinavia, soon fell
under his wickedly inventive verbal spell, and for his part Fry found the boy's
uninhibited and spontaneous behavior irresistible. Fry was a handsome and
well-formed young man by now, and also Martens's intellectual superior.
These things served to crystallize the foreigner's adulation. "You may know—
or not," wrote Martens much later, "that you played a decisive role in my
life—I was never quite the same after having known you!"

At the time Fry may have looked on Martens's adulation merely as his due,
but they quickly became inseparable, and he took the Norwegian with him
on his graduation trip to Bermuda. They cycled, swam, drank in the bars on
the island, and "devoured," Martens reminded Fry, "parts of *Ulysses* in that
forbidden magazine, what was it called—*The Little Review*?" Fry's graduation
trip lasted a whole month, but Martens soon had to leave to begin a job in

New York. "Yes," he wrote. "I only had a week in Bermuda, and I wept (in a toilet) because you were staying on." Already Fry had a charisma that could charm people and hold them under a spell.

By the time he reached Harvard, Fry had succeeded in stylizing himself. His friends at Riverdale and then at Harvard were attracted by Fry's certainty and his erudition—the apparent maturity—but they had to deal with the mannered arrogance that kept them at a distance. "I found him sympathetic," says one, "although I was wary of his covert disdain."

Outwardly Fry was the very picture of confidence, holding court in a small coffeehouse near the campus where he would discourse on whatever topic interested him (normally the superiority of everything French or the mediocrity of everything American). It was the style with which Fry addressed the subject that attracted his listeners. As for the substance, that was another question. Fry in his early twenties was hopelessly self-assured. When a classmate admitted that he was auditing a course in metaphysics, Fry dismissed the whole of Western philosophy with a well-turned aperçu. He, of course, acted as if he had it all sorted out.

Fry held an opinion about everything, and was interested in every subject but nothing in particular. The courses he took at Harvard seemed to reflect this: classics, history, physics, fine arts, political science, zoology, philosophy, English, French, German, Greek. Renaissance man or dilettante? Nothing, it seems, was quite good enough for him. As is the case with many talented but unfocused minds, secretly Fry felt unsure of himself. It was safer to stay on the outside, perhaps. It always had been so far.

Fry was bright and gregarious (on his own terms) but inevitably narcissistic, given how much time he had devoted to creating himself. At this stage his sexuality seems to underline that. He was attracted to those who were like himself (rather than the troublingly opposite), and he seems to have been open and even provocative about it. Martens wrote of "my two visits to Harvard, and a weekend at 'Westport' where your parents had rented a house and you had invited *three* boyfriends." Indeed, scandalous behavior was part and parcel of Fry's persona at this time. It fitted the spiky self-assertiveness he needed now that he was suddenly a small fish in a much larger pond. He was testing both the rules and himself, behaving outrageously but calling others "aesthetic hedonists." Such audacity reveals how wide a gap there existed between how he appeared to the world and what he must have felt like underneath his polished carapace. Fry looked and acted like a gadfly, but there remained the lonely seriousness.

In receipt of an allowance (and a four-door Packard convertible) from his prosperous father, Fry took rooms on campus in Gore Hall, overlooking the

Charles River. He lived upstairs from Lincoln Kirstein, a true devotee of Oscar Wilde and a man at the time "still trying on masks"—in short, the perfect audience for Fry's brand of performance. Kirstein remembered him as a "fair classical scholar with working knowledge of Latin and Greek, a good pianist, with old-fashioned courtly manners of a sardonic twist." Together they saw themselves as a pair of literary swashbucklers, and the prime target for their swashing and buckling was the *Harvard Advocate*. It was the student magazine and more of a social institution than a serious literary enterprise. Fry's feelings of inferiority and his wish for revenge, dating from Hotchkiss, stimulated a crusade against the upper-crust society students in residence at the offices of the *Advocate*.

The plan was to insinuate themselves into editorial positions and then hijack the journal for their own purposes, but Fry's "tart antagonism," says Kirstein, ended that. Instead, they began their own literary journal, naming it *The Hound and Horn* ("'Tis the white stag Fame we're hunting; Bid the world's hounds come to horn"), although it soon came to be known colloquially as *The Bitch and Bugle*. It was a sort of revenge on the establishment, and a very successful enterprise. So wide was its reputation beyond the undergraduate circle, that during the entire length of its publication, "unlettered sports fanciers sent in unsolicited advertisements for geldings, dachsunds, Airedales." Characteristically, though, Fry grew bored with it, and—also characteristically—he contrived a quarrel with Kirstein, after which he quit. This was the first of many such departures.

But Fry's confidence was brimming at the end of his sophomore year, and the high life continued. Margaret Scolari Barr, the wife of Alfred, director of the Museum of Modern Art in New York, wrote that "he lived in style and had planned his travels as though time and money would forever be available." And for a while they were.

The next summer, Fry boarded the SS *Sinaïa* for a voyage to Europe, and then on to Greece and Turkey. It was an idyllic vacation that whetted his appetite for archaeology and the ancient world. He brought back a small bronze bull and a fragment of (it would transpire) fake Attic pottery, that in good faith he presented to the classics department, where from now on he concentrated his time. The voyage through the Aegean had convinced Fry to follow—insofar as he followed anything—the course of the classical scholar. Eventually, it would be the subject he graduated in, despite being, as Fry admitted, "a very poor and very undisciplined student." It also implied a career: classics scholars become teachers, though at this stage the unconventional Fry did not seem quite like schoolmaster material.

Fry crossed the line separating risk from disaster one warm May evening in 1930. That was when his campaign against the staid respectability of Harvard went a stage too far and he finally got his comeuppance. It began as a drunken prank when he spotted a FOR SALE sign in front of a Chinese laundry. He uprooted it and replanted the sign in the dean's front lawn. Soon after, the forces of respectability struck back. Fry was suspended from the university and forced to repeat his senior year (something which still angered him nearly twenty years later). Added to the social humiliation was the dire practical consequence of graduating twelve months after his peers, just as the Depression was biting. Jobs were hard enough to come by even for college graduates. To have one's entrance onto the vanishing employment market delayed—and having blotted one's copybook so visibly—might have dealt a mortal blow to a promising career. Until now he had acted the part of an aesthete and sidewalk *philosophe.* Perhaps it was Fry's own plight that now alerted him to that of others, for the narcissist who awakes from his reverie will still try see his own image wherever he can. Fry's disgrace held up to him a mirror in which he saw the sufferings of the poor and unemployed, among whose ranks he clearly saw a place reserved for himself. Soon it would be Varian Fry, the iconoclast, the aloof non-joiner, the snob, the school drudge, who organized and led the Harvard contingent in a march for jobs down Broadway.

DESPITE THE SPLIT between Fry and Lincoln Kirstein over *The Hound and Horn,* there was no lasting enmity, and out of the association was to grow one of the enduring relationships of Fry's life. Lincoln's sister, Mina, was the best friend of Eileen Avery Hughes, who was the daughter of an old Bostonian family, not wealthy but respectably middle class rather like the Frys. She was seven years Fry's senior and nearly thirty years old when they first met. For the precocious young man still in many ways unsure of himself, she possessed both the glamour and the reassurance of the older woman. She was sophisticated, too, having been educated in England at Roedean and Oxford University. It is hard to see Fry having either the patience or the unironic simplicity of speech to attract a girl his own age, if indeed he was the least interested. But Eileen was a different proposition altogether. She was worldly and independent—when they first knew each other she was working as an editor at the *Atlantic Monthly,* a journal on which Fry had attempted to model *The Hound and Horn*—and moreover she was interested in him.

Fry was allowably flattered by her attentions, and Eileen came along at a time when if he wasn't actually changing, he was certainly open to change. It is probable that Eileen was responsible for his political awakening, though he eventually became the "specialist" in the relationship. Eileen was intelligent and unconventional, a gentle and tolerant woman who could also be as stubborn and bossy as Fry himself. Now he was boxing his own weight. Eileen often treated him like a naughty child and, perversely, he enjoyed it. She took him in hand and withstood what he called the "severe case of emotional maladjustment" he presented her with. In the early days of their relationship Fry tried both to impress and scandalize Eileen, and it seems he succeeded in the first but failed in the second, for he calmed down and married her on June 2, 1931. Eileen was a barrier protecting Fry from the cold world beyond the student's life, and it is no coincidence that marriage and graduation from Harvard came close together. But Lilian Fry was inconsolable, seeing herself so obviously replaced by the older woman Fry had chosen, and for years she would subject her son to hourlong crying fits on the telephone.

Fry's mischievousness in the whole affair, which pitted his mother and Eileen against each other, is difficult to gauge. His continued friendship with Martens would seem to be an outright provocation to Eileen, just as Eileen was to Lilian. But in a letter he wrote to his new wife, she appears also to have been his indulgent confidante:

> In the late afternoon Martens came in and I gave him tea and asked him to supper, and after supper, at his suggestion, I drove him up the Bronx River Parkway as far as Scarsdale, where we piddled against the wall of the RR station, and back again, and he seemed to enjoy it very much. He said that Greta Garbo was definitely a lesbian lady, and that she had a mistress in New York whom she came all the way from Hollywood to see very often, and that Arvid had taken them both to the *Bowl of Fairies* and they had enjoyed it very much and wanted to go again and that he had also taken them to a much worse place in Harlem, and that Victor Gilbert had a very sweet young blonde lover now and seemed very happy and that Arvid had gone back to Norway and he thought he would go soon, too. . . .

The tone is high camp and the voice strangely infantile, and it is interesting to wonder what Eileen was supposed to make of these exhaust fumes of adolescent deviance. It is facile to say he was looking for a mother-figure in Eileen, but here he seems to be testing exactly how much his relationship with her could take. The love Fry demanded from her at this time was clearly almost unconditional, of the same order as that he had received from his parents. Something of the Goop inevitably remains: he is still flinging his oatmeal, but now at Eileen.

For her part, Eileen tolerated Fry's showing off and the tantrums that went with it, because she so very much respected his intelligence. "I have always been proud," she told him later, "that I could see in you at the age of twenty-one, when your occupations and preoccupations were all so foolish, that excellent and unprejudiced mind of yours, so carefully concealed at the time!" That was not to say Fry was ever diffident or desultory. The first time they went to bed together Eileen made a reference to a work of Rodin's, and Fry replied with his usual brisk finality that the sculptor was sentimental and unworthy of attention. Eileen was hurt by his offhanded dismissal of her taste in art but she carefully remembered the remark and looked with fresh eyes at Rodin's work. Finally, she changed her mind in deference to Fry's opinion and never again spoke in Rodin's favor, though the particular statue she referred to still held considerable appeal for her.

In any event the marriage achieved a balance very soon. Eileen loved her young and good-looking intellectual, and Fry, discovering he was allowed to be what he wanted to be around her, lost some of the showiness of his carefully crafted personality. In short, he loved her back. He respected Eileen's superiority in certain areas and even allowed her to boss him about. According to friends, Fry had never been so relaxed, and never more consistently so than when he was with Eileen, whom he nicknamed, in a final flourish of infantile naughtiness, "Poo-Dog."

The summer of Fry's graduation from Harvard the couple moved to New York and had the triple good fortune to find an apartment on East Fifty-eighth Street, a job for him as assistant editor at *Consumer Research* magazine (dull, but it paid the rent), and a position as researcher at *Time* for Eileen. They knew they were lucky, and kept one eye on the ax until they watched it fall. The Depression was by now scouring from the American economy whatever scraps of nourishment had clung to it, and a double blow hit Fry in short order. First, he lost his job; then he lost his allowance when his father's Wall Street brokerage firm collapsed. Finally the modest Fry fortune, like that of so many others, was swallowed up in the economic black hole. The couple couldn't survive on what Eileen earned, and they were forced to leave New York.

Granville Hicks, the critic and writer, lent them his farm in Columbia County, north of New York City, where they lived on very thin rations. Fry claimed that at times all they had to eat was fried flour, and they huddled close for warmth on the freezing homestead. Because they were too poor to buy books, Eileen recited aloud the reams of poetry she had learned by heart. In spite of their affection, it must have been a cruel reminder to Fry of his childhood days, when in comfort and warmth his mother had read to him during his dreamy and fraudulent furloughs from school.

Fry's father adapted to economic disaster by unashamedly transforming himself into the whistling local handyman, happy to leave behind him the fifty-mile-a-day commute to Manhattan. But Fry's reclusive mother had been profoundly shaken by the financial and social reversals. To her natural antagonism for her rival, Eileen, was now added the distress of seeing her one safe place—the family home—threatened. She began paying frequent visits to Eileen and her son, and these would invariably turn ugly. Lilian wished to reclaim her one remaining valuable, and Eileen just as assertively refused to hand him over. There were fights between the two women, and the anguished phone calls from Lilian to her still-doting son continued. This put a terrible pressure on the young marriage, and luckily it was eased somewhat several months later when Fry landed a position teaching Latin at Wright Oral School in New York City. He disliked the job, but it kept their heads, and the relationship, above water that year.

Living with Eileen meant Fry did not have to spend all his energy maintaining the image he presented to the world, and during this difficult period his interest in politics continued to deepen. New York was by now a landscape of beggars and shanty camps, soup kitchens and unemployment lines. Like so many other young people, Fry and Eileen were fervent supporters of Franklin D. Roosevelt, to whose promise of a New Deal they clung. He was their only hope of transforming the desolate panorama of the Depression. At last, on January 20, 1933, Roosevelt was elected president, but by now Fry's interests encompassed more than just the domestic scene. Less than two weeks later he was disturbed by the news that Adolf Hitler had become the new chancellor of Germany. Fascism was rearing its head in Europe, and for some reason— maybe, after Hotchkiss, he knew a bully when he saw one—Fry took Hitler's ascendance as a personal omen.

At the end of the year, he enrolled as a student at Columbia University's Graduate School of Political Science, and he also found a job as assistant editor at *Scholastic* magazine, which required him to write as well, and which he preferred to the Latin teaching of the year before. When Eileen found work teaching English for good pay at the Brearley School they could afford to return to Manhattan, and took an apartment on East Eleventh Street. It seemed like FDR's election had been propitious. Little by little, the Depression was lifting, at least for Fry and his wife.

FRY'S WORK AT *Scholastic* went well, but in April 1935 he heard through friends that Quincy Howe was not only leaving his job as editor of the prestigious review of international affairs *The Living Age,* but had also been given the responsibility for finding his own successor. Fry applied for the vacancy, and Howe offered him the job on the spot, with just one condition. Fry had never visited Germany, which was now being rapidly transformed by its energetic Nazi government. It was essential that the new editor have some firsthand experience of what was happening—because nobody in America seemed to know exactly what *was* going on there, except that some sort of trouble was brewing.

A few weeks earlier, on March 8, Hitler announced as a fait accompli that he had established an air force. The next weekend he followed this by revealing the German army was being increased to over half a million men, in thirty-six divisions. Both these moves were in direct contravention of the Treaty of Versailles, the list of punitive and frankly unfair conditions and reparations imposed by the victors on Germany after the end of the First World War. It had limited the German army to one fifth of its new size, but so far the only national leader who had objected to Hitler's flagrant illegality was Mussolini.

Howe told Fry that if he agreed to tour Germany and find out what was happening, on the ground, the job was his when he got back to New York. Fry asked for some time to talk it over with his wife. Three weeks later, he was sailing to Europe for the second time in his life.

CHAPTER 3

SIGN OF THE TIMES

T HE PRESS WAS WAITING for the German liner *Bremen* when it docked at New York, and questions were shouted at Varian Fry even as he stepped off the gangplank. He had filed his reports for the *New York Times* in the heat of anger right after the events occurred. He hadn't expected, two weeks later, that interest would still be at such a pitch so many thousands of miles away. Fry repeated what Hanfstaengel had confirmed: that it was the brownshirts who had organized and provoked the bloody riot on the Kurfürstendamm. When the reporters asked if it could happen again, Fry said, "Definitely—there is a feeling throughout Germany that a bloody purge of the Jews is imminent."

Finally the reporters asked him what he meant by traveling back to the United States on a German ship, ignoring Roosevelt's boycott of German goods and services. At this, Fry's anger, easily piqued, flashed through his quotable reserve: "I don't believe in the boycott," he said. "Most Jews in Germany oppose it, too. They feel it hurts them more than it helps." It seemed to Fry he had accidentally become an international spokesman; it was a good augury for when he began his new job as editor at *The Living Age* the following week. In typical fashion, he was going against the standard liberal line, because he knew the stark reality of life in Hitler's Germany: if the country suffered from the boycott, Hitler would make sure the Jews were blamed, and he had seen the consequences of that.

Fry knuckled down to his new post and began immediately to editorialize on conditions in the Third Reich. He made good use of what he had discovered during his two months there, letting his readers know quite plainly that Hitler's aggressive foreign policy would lead to disaster. America had effectively withdrawn from the European sphere of influence after the First World War, leaving a power vacuum that with Britain it could have filled, helping to maintain and balance the peace. Now that very peace was under threat, and America's response had been to grow even more fervently isolationist. Like Europe, America dreaded another conflict; unlike Europe, it was situated well away from the danger.

If Fry's warnings failed to alert his compatriots to the need to halt Hitler immediately, the Führer himself helped reinforce this need by re-occupying the Rhineland in March 1936. This was a heavily industrialized territory annexed from Germany, as retribution, by the French after the last war. The troops Hitler sent to seize it back were poorly armed (in some cases unarmed) and heavily outnumbered by the French, Polish, and Czech forces garrisoned there. Such was the Allied antipathy to fighting, however, that they allowed in the German army without a shot being fired.

In truth, the Allies were spavined by their knowledge of how inequitable the Treaty of Versailles had been to the loser. Partly as a result of economic strangulation and national humiliation, Germany had undergone horrific turmoil, and every observer knew it had helped Hitler to rise to the surface. The Führer was everybody's fault, and a bad conscience had finally led the other powers to begin to have sympathy for Germany at exactly the wrong time: when she was preparing her revenge. Britain, especially, felt that Germany should be granted relief from the fiscal and territorial restraints. While Fry had been in Germany in June of the previous year, Hitler had sent his roving ambassador, von Ribbentrop, to London. There he had successfully negotiated the re-expansion of the German navy. Britain's misjudged foreign policy was also banking on Hitler being able to hold off the Bolshevik hordes in the East. It was certainly a part of what Hitler had in mind. But it was a shortsighted and lethal gamble to let him think that nobody was willing to oppose his aggressiveness.

The only man prepared to stand against the Nazis had been France's foreign minister, Louis Barthou. He had been a man after Fry's own heart, recommending stalwart resistance to Hitler's provocations, while easing the terms of the Versailles Treaty and drawing Germany into a mutual defense pact. But he had been assassinated late in October the previous year, in the southern French city of Marseille. Since then, France had signed an alliance with Soviet Russia, infuriating the British and further agitating the Germans. In fact, this was the excuse Hitler gave for re-occupying the Rhineland: it was only fair and equitable under the circumstances, he claimed, to consolidate Germany's own territory. In a plebiscite three weeks later 98.8 percent of Germans showed they agreed with him.

Throughout this period, Fry in New York was a Cassandra uttering unwelcome prophecies to a largely unresponsive nation. He was enjoying the work at *The Living Age,* but in July, four months after Hitler had snatched back the Rhineland, the Fascist General Francisco Franco attacked the young Spanish republic, plunging the country into civil war. Fry knew now that he had to do something more than simply present his thoughts on paper. Practical measures were needed. As an astute political analyst, he saw how this new conflict was more than just Fascists fighting Communists. Mussolini was pouring men and materiel into Spain, and Hitler was also supporting Franco's forces with elements of his new tank and air forces—blatantly using the Iberian peninsula as a war laboratory, testing weapons and tactics for what he was planning next. Fry noted the strategic element, looking at it from Hitler's perspective: with a three-nation Fascist alliance, France would be caught in a stranglehold, and Hitler would be safe from Allied encirclement.

IT WAS IN New York that various bodies sprang up in support of the beleaguered Spanish Republic. These groups soon agreed, in spite of their differing ideological colorations, to come together in coalition. The North American Committee to Aid Spanish Democracy (the Spanish Aid Committee) was born, and Fry immediately offered his services. It should be said at this point that among left-wingers in America, Fry was developing a reputation as a fierce anti-Communist, even being called by some a red-baiter for his outspoken denunciations of Stalinism—for in this, as in his revelations concerning the true nature of Hitler's régime, Fry was prophetic.

George Orwell wrote that Communism was the patriotism of the deracinated, of the uprooted and lost, but this might equally have been said of Fascism. By the thirties, in a century typified so far by giddy advance and calamitous upheaval, totalitarianism was gaining more and more adherents both to its left- and right-wing encampments. The numbers of card-carrying party members of either extreme may have been tiny outside Germany or Soviet Russia, but the general atmosphere of confrontation between one theory of living and its opposite was thickening. The ethos was one of religious fervor, certainty, and hatred. The thirties were not good years to be a staunch, grown-up, down-the-line democrat like Varian Fry.

While the left splintered into a hundred different sects and denominations, from mild socialism to anarchism to dead-eyed Stalinism, the capitalist right tended to sympathize with Fascism, which at least purported to uphold traditional Western values, like profit. In short, capitalism and Christianity both felt safer with Hitler than Stalin. In condemning both Communism and Fascism, Fry made himself unpopular with both sets of supporters; ordinary right-wingers simply assumed he was a socialist and Communist sympathizer for his opposition to Hitler and his support of the Republican cause. Communists denounced him for failing to acknowledge Stalin's essential saintliness and infallibility. Fry must have taken some comfort in the notion that if everyone is against you, then you must be doing something right. But in thirties America the suspicion that Fry was a Communist would return to plague him.

As a political independent, Fry proved an acceptable choice to the Spanish Aid Committee. He was put in charge of its public relations effort, which he happily accepted. But Fry was shrewd enough to bring in to help him a young man he had met through Eileen. Harold Oram had a brilliant mind and understood the mass media. He was perhaps one of the first true public relations geniuses, unafraid of such delicacies as putting a cash figure on people's conscience and morality. Thus, Oram's job was to raise money; Fry's was to spend it. He was now a very busy man, and the executive responsibilities suited him. The perfect remedy for the anxiety that afflicted him in dull times was to keep moving and be actively involved in large issues. If the Spanish Civil War and Nazi anti-Semitism kept Fry's indignation simmering, they also released in him the energy to be useful.

The mills of contradiction in Fry's character ground exceedingly fine. If he was an aesthete and a spoiled child who would quibble over an extra twenty-five cents for a restaurant meal, he was also the same man who cared for the survival of justice on the other side of the world and donated a large portion of his salary to the causes he supported. At this time he was giving to the Birth Control League, the American Civil Liberties Union, and the American League Against War and Fascism, among other organizations. Eileen did not object; her commitment had probably inspired Fry in the first place, and her own passion for liberal causes equalled his own. In fact, Eileen devoted her free time to assisting Fry in his work for the Spanish Aid Committee. Their shared ideals and the work they undertook together formed a large part of the comfortable arrangement that, after the difficult financial times, they had arrived at in their marriage. By making it a thing more of public and less of private constituency, they had strengthened their relationship. All told, it was not a bad marriage, and they lived together as they worked, side by side.

Fry's first real adversity with his fellow supporters came in January 1937, only five months after he had resigned from *The Living Age* to work full time for the Spanish Aid Committee. At this period in history, the strategy of the Communist Party in America, not yet demonized and forced underground by Representative Martin Dies's House Un-American Activities Committee (HUAC), was to fight open battles for control wherever and in whatever body it had an interest. Fry opposed this wherever he found it, on two grounds. First, because he loathed the theoretical arrogance of Marxism and saw it as anathema to true and humane democracy: "Marx was a very intelligent man, and . . . he made a very important contribution to economics and politics, but he certainly did not write a book which was the open sesame to all knowledge for all future time." Second, controlled from Moscow as they were, mentally if not materially, the Communists' tactics were nearly always detrimental, or at lest self-defeating, to whatever local situations in which they involved themselves. And without fail, the Communists always involved themselves. You just sat back and waited for them to act.

Sure enough, a struggle soon began for control within the Spanish Aid Committee, with the anti-Communists led by Norman Thomas. Thomas, who had been the Socialist candidate in the past three presidential elections in the United States, asked Fry to be his spokesman. In this capacity, Fry was supposed to be speaking up for the moderates on the committee in the developing tug-of-war, but he put the case against the Communists if anything too forcefully, and alienated himself in characteristic fashion from the Socialists. By June, Fry had divested himself of all allies and been ejected from the committee. He was devastated: Fry thought he had been on the side of righteousness, but had been sacrificed to expediency.

What he had done wrong was to allow his ideals to get the better of him. Instead of attempting to fight a workable draw with the Communists that would have allowed the committee to continue to do its job (the Communists were there and that was that; there was no way a committee helping the Republican side in the Spanish Civil War could not contain them), Fry had the bit between his teeth and decided the Communists simply must go. He believed they would wreck the committee, and that there should be no negotiation. That sort of starkness, in its own way more radical than either of the opponents, succeeded only in forcing them to cooperate with each other. The committee lived on, but Fry had effectively made himself the burnt offering on the altar of compromise.

He could neither see the irony of this situation nor conceive of how the actual politicking in such an organization might be about anything less than absolute values. To the extent that he never wanted to play team sports, literally or otherwise, Fry had remained somewhat unsocialized. He had the outsider's overview, an ideal picture, which was impossible to impose on the gritty reality of political roughhousing. The gap between words and actions in other people's outlooks had completely baffled him. Enemies and friends had made peace with each other at his expense, and it confused Fry profoundly. He felt betrayed, and his sentimentalism—that childhood inheritance that foreshortens emotions to either warm affection or tear-jerking stabs of self-pity—kicked in. This time it was the self-pity. His friends had deserted him, therefore friendship was empty and meaningless; with no friendship and therefore no loyalty in the world, there was no hope of change and no reason to do anything at all, except sit at home and brood about it.

This he did for over two months. And the more depressed and circular his brooding became, the more his natural reserve toward others turned to morbid suspicion. Prickliness became Fry's defining way of presenting himself to the world. On the rare occasion a friend or colleague knocked on his door or dialed his telephone number, he or she was answered with an exasperated, "Yes, what is it?" He was once again the little prince, except that this time his kingdom had been stolen. He developed a hypochondria of the senses. The slightest noise was like a hammer blow to his ears, and he went to the lengths of putting a towel in the bathtub to stifle the drip of the faucet; he removed a chiming clock from the mantelpiece to the far end of the apartment; and he kept all the windows closed and curtains drawn to keep out the brutal, mocking sunlight, even during New York's most stifling summer days.

Eileen was a practical woman, and she was less than impressed with her husband's reaction. Her attempts to snap him out of his gloom of funk met with predictable antagonism. Fry would speak of how the anti-Fascist cause was weakened by the petty self-interest that had undermined him at the committee, and how this sort of shortsightedness effectively strengthened the Fascist position in Europe and speeded its advance. Eileen agreed with him, of course, but preaching to the converted was the last thing Fry needed to change his insular state of mind. She decided in practical fashion to forget about changing the world and, in a phrase of the time, to change worlds instead, at least in a small way. To this end, she rented a new apartment at 56 Irving Place, near Gramercy Park. It was a larger, lighter, and airier dwelling that she thought just might have the effect of blowing a little fresh air and ideas through her husband's head.

Her tactic was one you might use with a child: changing apartments, the very act of filling and physically carrying boxes up and down stairs, short-circuits the self-consciousness required for a really effective sulk, and rejuvenates the body with the simple pleasures of movement and exertion. Installed at the new address, Fry was more cheerful, at least for a while. He was beginning to slip back into his interior monologue when world events came to the rescue.

In July 1937, two months after a new, military-dominated government had come to power in Tokyo, the Japanese invaded northern China. On July 30 they occupied Tientsin, and then the capital, Peking, on August 8. Japan, like Nazi Germany, was autocratic, belligerent, and viciously racist toward its neighbors. Unlike Germany, it was an island nation, not a nearly landlocked one, but it had much the same economic problems. Like Germany, it lacked many of the resources needed for "autarky" (self-sufficiency). It prospered by the import of cheap raw materials and the subsequent export of finished goods to open and pliant markets.

In this sense, populous, resource-rich China was seen by Japan's leaders as its milk cow; like their German counterparts, the Japanese saw a quicker route to wealth through conquest than through economic competition. Japan's ambitions in China had been a source of bitter conflict since the First World War, when she had seized German interests there. During the twenties, China managed to pulverize herself without Japan's intercession by suffering Chiang Kai-shek's National Party (the Kuomintang) on the one hand, and on the other local warlords who sprang up in opposition after the liquidation of the last Manchu emperors. Then, in the late twenties, Mao Tse-tung arrived from Paris carrying the Communist gospel, and China rapidly descended into an ungovernable free-for-all.

The Japanese had first marched into China in September 1931, and began to dominate domestic politics in the north of the country. Like Germany later, Japan had been condemned by the League of Nations, and like Germany it suffered no practical consequences. As if to recognize their common cause and behavior, Japan withdrew from the League of Nations a month after Hitler became chancellor, and then signed an alliance with Germany, known as the Anti-Comintern Pact, in 1936. Prefiguring the consequences of Hitler's invasion of Poland, Japan's seizure of Peking provoked fighting a few days later in Shanghai, and the Japanese suddenly found they had a shooting war on their hands. It would last until August 1945, when the Americans obliterated Hiroshima and Nagasaki.

In July 1937, Japan's actions meant two things for Fry. The events in the Far East were geographically distant from the arena of his consuming political interest, and took his mind off the painful personal events connected with the Spanish Aid Committee. Also, a little solipsism goes a long way: the feverish activity of his brooding mind had achieved a creative effect, in that he saw clearly how Japan's military expansionism offered so many parallels to Nazi

Germany. He quickly spotted a parable about what happens when aggression is appeased. That Japan's actions were at this time more advanced than Germany's suited Fry perfectly. He would write a book, he decided, and began it at once. His sense of moral outrage had found a new direction through which to flow, and he was galvanized with renewed energy.

The Foreign Policy Association, at 8 West Fortieth Street in New York, was the publisher of a series of pamphlets and books on "international problems of the day," under the imprint, Headline Books. Fry approached the FPA with his proposal for *War in China,* and was met with delighted approval. A sign of his boomeranging mental state was the brief time he took to complete the manuscript: only four months later he handed it over, again to the delight of the staff at the FPA, who were impressed by its incisiveness and the quality of the writing. Fry was asked to overtake editorial responsibility for the whole Headline series.

In many ways this was his perfect job. As a position for an aesthete with expensive tastes, it paid well—thirty-five hundred dollars a year. What's more, the post carried with it the metropolitan cachet of being in charge of a major research organization with innumerable political contacts at a time of growing international tension. Fry started to look back on the debacle at the Spanish Aid Committee as a mere triviality, and began to circulate within an expanding network of important people.

Fry's renewed enthusiasm made the following year equally productive and rewarding. In addition to expanding the Headline Books list, he wrote two more of his own: *The Good Neighbors,* a brief history of the United States relationship with the countries of Latin America, and *Bricks Without Mortar,* in which he detailed and explained the development of international cooperation; and he wrote a pamphlet, the *War Atlas,* that met with great acclaim. Fry also found the time to deliver paying lectures on what he was already calling, in 1938, the Second Great War. Cassandra-like, he was predicting its inevitability, and presently events hurried in quick succession to vindicate him.

In March German tanks rolled into Austria, to general celebration on the part of the Austrian public, which was even more enthusiastically Nazi in many respects than the German people. In the words of one writer, it was "clearly no national rape but a marriage in which the groom found himself overwhelmed by his bride's enthusiasm." A crowd of eighty thousand welcomed Hitler into Vienna following the *Anschluss.* It was an emotional occasion for him: he claimed he had received the gospel of anti-Semitism there in the early twenties. The response from the Allies was again apathetic. Although Anthony Eden resigned from the British cabinet, it took no subsequent diplomatic action; the French did nothing, and were in some quarters relieved to witness the demise of independent Austria. Vienna opened up the vistas of southern Europe and the eastern Adriatic to Hitler, and after the Munich summit at the end of September, the Allied powers forgot their obligations to Czechoslovakia. In the interests of "peace in our time," they handed Hitler the Sudetenland, a collar of territory around the western reaches of Czecho-slovakia. It contained about three million "ethnic" Germans, and was a piece of land the Führer coveted.

It was also the last territory to which the Third Reich had a semblance of a reasonable claim, and six months later, when Hitler occupied and dissolved the rest of the Czechoslovakian state, it was clear even to the most dilatory politicians of appeasement that German self-determination had gone too far. The seizure of Czechoslovakia had opened the high road to Hitler's next tar-get, Poland. From New York, Fry wryly observed his predictions validated yet again, and sat down to begin another book, *The Peace That Failed*. He knew Hitler's next move would be catastrophic.

CHAPTER 4

SOME CALL IT WAR

P AUL HAGEN wasn't his real name. Like many another individual, he had been forced to assume a new identity in the years following Hitler's seizure of power in Germany. Hagen was the advanced guard of a breed of refugee that America would before long come to know very well, and that Europe had already been acquainted with for the best part of a decade. The two things you noticed about Hagen—the two things Fry noticed—were that he looked like a boxer, with his heavy, forceful build and the powerful jaw, and that he also reminded you of a poet. It was in the eyes, their startling sadness; the saddest eyes Fry had ever seen. "He had a tragic face," said Fry, "handsome but drawn, like the face of a man who has been through a long and terrible experience." Hagen's speech was urgent, compelling, as if the Gestapo were breaking down the door and something had to be done right now.

In 1935, when he first came to New York on a fund-raising trip, possibly passing Varian Fry on his way to Germany, Austrian Karl Frank was already Paul Hagen. He had come from Prague, where he had relocated his headquarters after Hitler became chancellor, and the Gestapo had begun in short order to hunt down every political opponent in the country. Frank still had family in Germany who he knew would be used as hostages if he kept up his political work, so in Czechoslovakia he assumed the identity of Hagen, and continued his effort to reorganize the Social Democratic opposition to the Nazis. The old politicians had revealed themselves as vacillatory and weak. His new falange, which he formed in 1930, was composed of active and idealistic young German democrats and named *Neu Beginnen*, a fresh start, so to speak. Hagen was a man of fresh starts.

Like Fry's, Hagen's idealism had sometimes led him into avenues of eccentricity and self-sabotage. His political maturity had been hard-won, but his gambler's love of personal gesture had not entirely left him. It had begun early in his life, when he was conscripted to fight in the Austrian army during the First World War. The first thing young Karl Frank did to express his loathing for the imperialist adventure was to foment an uprising among his fellow soldiers. But "the King makes war and the people die," and Frank's revolution fizzled out. So the youthful conscript wrote directly to Emperor Franz Joseph demanding his abdication, and compounded this literary attempt at suicide by proudly showing his commanding officer the treasonous letter.

Luckily, this occurred just at the end of the war; had it been any earlier, Karl Frank would have been court-martialed and executed by his own side. The experience of the Soviet Revolution passing from Lenin to Stalin and transforming itself to state terror had revised his extreme views, as it had for other revolutionaries of that generation (such as the Russian novelist Victor Serge, then a teenage terrorist in Paris). Frank, no longer a staunch Marxist, had mellowed into democratic socialism, and completed the reordering of his sentiments in the direction of humane liberalism. By now calling himself Paul Hagen, his one extreme of hatred was reserved for the Nazis.

In New York he had made contact with the distinguished theologian Reinhold Niebuhr, and Fry's future friend Norman Thomas (later known as "the conscience of America"). Both were impressed by the shrewdness and energy of this man, no longer young, who was perhaps the most effective of the political leaders working to undermine Hitler in the thirties. While he was in the United States he also met and fell in love with a young American, Anna Caples. She followed Hagen to Prague, and two years later they returned to be married in New York. By this time, it was no longer "the good old days" in Germany that Fry had seen back in 1935. Matters were more serious, there were more refugees spread over Europe, and to the well informed the possibility of war was already looming large. While he was in New York for the second time, Hagen established an organization called the American Friends of German Freedom, and Reinhold Niebuhr agreed to act as its chairman.

After Germany swallowed Austria, Prague began to look unsafe in Hagen's calm and experienced view. He quickly moved his base of operations to Paris, both recapitulating and predicting the travels of many other thousands of refugees from Hitler's Reich. By 1938, Paris was crowded with German speakers, to the chagrin of the French, and after a few months Hagen transferred *Neu Beginnen* once again, this time to London. He found more sympathy there, and the support of Sir Stafford Cripps and Patrick Gordon Walker, who would both later become cabinet ministers in the British government. Eventually, thanks to his wife's American passport, Hagen completed his tour by landing once again at New York in time for Christmas 1939. There was no way back to Europe by this time; Hagen would stay in America forever.

IN THE SUMMER of 1939, Varian Fry took a brief trip to England. He returned to the United States a shocked and sobered man, having seen exactly how unprepared the British were for a war with Germany. In Europe there seemed to be a kind of schizophrenia, or at least a blind optimism, which dominated both politicians and policy—the maverick Winston Churchill an honorable exception. Everybody saw the inevitability of conflict, yet nobody was doing anything to prepare for it. Britain's lackadaisical rearmament was taking two steps forward and one step back. Frantic shuttle diplomacy threw British officials into Germany at the Führer's behest (for example, Neville Henderson, whose book on the subject, *Failure of a Mission,* Fry referred to as *Mission of a Failure*). It availed little, however, and matters had moved beyond crisis point. The brooding atmosphere was now revealed as the quiet before a storm.

On August 23, the Germans managed to surprise even Fry. It was announced that Hitler had signed a nonaggression pact with Stalin, and Fry knew what this meant. Hitler's strategic problem was obtaining raw materials; these, Soviet Russia could supply in return for badly needed goods from Germany's advanced, modern economy. The agreement between the two states, in addition to securing Germany's eastern flank, signaled the removal of the last economic barrier obstructing Hitler's military ambitions. The following week, just a day after Russia ratified the treaty, the *Blitzkrieg* on Poland was unleashed, and soon afterward most of Europe was at war.

Fry enjoyed a feeling of schadenfreude when he thought of all the distraught Communists left rudderless and humiliated by the fact that their leader had lain down with the arch devil. But he also appreciated what a master stroke of Hitler's it had been: those on the right in Britain and France had not wanted to fight anyway, while those on the Marxist left were now dazed and silent, technically obliged to support the Nazi invasion of Poland. Hitler had with genius split his enemies in half and bludgeoned unconscious their fighting spirit before a shot was fired. His foreign sympathizers would have the upper hand against the Communist "fifth columnists," and Allied defeatism would be exacerbated.

Fry reacted as he had done three years earlier at the outbreak of the Spanish Civil War, now lost to General Franco's Fascists. He again volunteered his services, this time to the American Friends of German Freedom. He was there when Hagen arrived from London, and was glad of an ally. The organization, to Hagen's dismay as well as Fry's, was already dissolving into the frustrating factionalism that the Spanish Aid Committee had suffered. This time there were one or two, like Fry, who thought the United States should do everything in its power, including waging war on Germany, to bring about Hitler's downfall. Opposed to him were the American isolationists, who were in a large majority. This body of opinion, ironically represented by Fry's old ally Norman Thomas, believed that every aid should be given to the refugees from Nazism, but also that the United States should on no account become directly involved.

Hagen, who knew the extent of Hitler's ambitions, and what the democracies were up against, saw and argued that only the total commitment of *all* resources could stop the Nazis and their allies achieving dominion over the entire civilized world. In this he agreed with Fry that what was taking place was not just another nationalistic war. It was, as Fry said, a "world revolution," in which the nature of humanity would either be upheld or hideously redefined. No country could abstain from the struggle unless it was prepared to forsake its moral right to call itself a civilized nation. Hagen and Fry, two quite isolated men, found a friend and soulmate in each other.

Throughout the spring of 1940, during the "Phoney War," the Allied and German forces in Europe faced each other in uneasy quiet. In New York, Fry and Hagen were only a city block apart, Hagen at Fifth Avenue and East Forty-first Street, Fry at the Foreign Policy Association on West Fortieth. They would often meet for lunch at Fry's favorite midtown restaurant, Child's, and discuss the situation. Both men wanted badly to do something practical, but their ideas and recommendations fell on deaf ears. The isolationist mood of the United States, bolstered by the pronouncements of Senators Vandenberg and Taft, and from popular figures such as Charles Lindbergh—an open Nazi sympathizer—meant that it was difficult, in the absence of immediate crisis, to rouse even the American Friends of German Freedom to drastic action. Hagen's call for America to declare war on Hitler was particularly inopportune, because he was "German" himself, easily seen as a citizen of a pariah state to whom no American would give a hearing.

In April, the British began to lay mines off the coast of Norway in an attempt to disrupt the supply of vital metal ores traveling from Scandinavia to Germany. It was an example of British overconfidence, and they paid the price when the Germans occupied both Denmark and Norway within twenty-four hours (although Hitler had been planning an invasion—

Operation *Weserübung*—since February). This disastrous development showed once again how easily Germany's armed forces could prevail, and further demoralized the Allies. In Denmark, there was hardly any fighting at all. An ultimatum was delivered by Hitler, and the weakly armed Danes gave in to it: "They took us by telephone," said the Danish prime minister. The British landed in Norway in an attempt to drive the Germans out, but their expedition proved ill thought out and badly supplied. Britain barely managed to evacuate its own troops shortly afterward. Throughout all this, Fry's dismay deepened.

The storm finally broke a fortnight later. On May 10, Holland was attacked, and fell in a mere five days. The British had been fooled into reinforcing Belgium, thinking that the Germans were following the same tactics they had in the First World War. While the Allies' best troops poured north to the Belgian border, German armor rumbled unopposed through the Ardennes forest to the south, into France, sidestepping the supposedly impregnable "Maginot Line" of concrete and artillery defense fortresses along the French-German border.

A telephone call from Hagen on Thursday morning, May 16, summoned Fry to Child's for an emergency meeting. Hagen was more agitated than usual. Much of the British army on the European continent, the "Expeditionary Force," was now effectively encircled. With the Germans to the rear and south already, there was no way the Allies could maneuver. They were going to be pushed into a pocket on the coast. Fierce fighting was taking place in France, but it already looked like disaster. Hagen wanted to know what on earth was happening. Were they fighting Hitler with bows and arrows? Pulling faces at the German Panzer tanks? By now Fry was jaded. It was becoming almost tedious to be proved correct in his predictions time after time. What transpired from his discussion with Hagen, though, must have been refreshing for him, because it concerned a subject on which Hagen was undeniably far more expert.

Clearly, if events continued on their present course, and Europe was to be ground beneath the Nazi heel, then they would have to forget all their ideas about organizing opposition from America. There would be no way of contacting anybody inside the Nazi fortress that Europe would soon become. As a refugee from Hitler who had fled from one country to another, Hagen had a very detailed knowledge concerning what had happened in Austria, Czechoslovakia, and Poland and what was about to happen in Norway, Denmark, Holland, Belgium, and France.

The Nazis always had a list, he explained. Every person designated as an enemy of the Reich—politicians, labor activists, artists, novelists, poets, scientists, musicians, journalists, intellectuals—every last dissenting voice, would be routinely hunted down by the Gestapo after the army had occupied a country, and either summarily executed or consigned to a slow death in a concentration camp. Since 1933, Europe had seen a group of highly qualified and talented refugees gradually increase. First, those who were able had run to Prague or Vienna or Basel. Later, those that could fled to Paris or Amsterdam, gathering new companions all the while.

Now, with France under imminent threat of being overrun by German forces, almost the entire active anti-Nazi population of occupied Europe found itself crammed into that chaotic and panic-stricken country. Paris was the bottleneck that had collected all the desperate, frightened fugitives from Hitler. Now, like millions of French people, they had taken to the road and were heading south, away from the enemy advance. If France fell to the Germans, said Hagen, those people would be doomed. The Nazis would be in a position literally to blow Europe's brains out in a matter of weeks.

Fry's immediate thought, when Hagen had completed his dire picture, was a good, American one—to raise money. With enough money, you could begin to bring endangered people out of Europe, one way or another. What came next was also Fry's idea. Harold Oram, the PR wunderkind whom Fry had taken on as his assistant at the Spanish Aid Committee, was contacted. The two had remained on good terms and shared the same outlook. Oram was the man to turn to if you needed to raise a lot of hard cash fast. He had the best contacts and the most persuasive line in talk. He would be able to arrange something.

The trouble would be to find the refugees that needed saving, but Hagen had the answer to this. War brings chaos and confusion, but paradoxically, veteran wanderers suddenly find themselves in a position of advantage. Their years of experience in crossing borders and relocating, changing countries more often than shoes, as Bertolt Brecht said, meant they were both adaptable and adept in crises and emergencies that required a rapid response. By now, the refugees were nearly immune to shock, if not despair. They could still act to save themselves and at least get to where they could hope to escape. That's where they would be found.

Then there was the "refugee telegraph," which Hagen knew a lot about. It was the complex system of communication within the shifting refugee population that enabled messages to be passed from one area to another and one person to another by travelers, who would often be a third or fourth party. Every refugee would inevitably collect in his head or pocket a store of messages. Many of these might be for people he didn't even know, but to whom he would be able to pass on an address, instruction, or piece of news, if a relevant name was mentioned. The endless gossip among the displaced (many of them German Jews, the world's best talkers) turned up endless items of information concerning the whereabouts of others, and constituted something like a "group-mind." In other words, you need not specifically search for a refugee. Pass the name out, stay put, and sooner or later he would find *you*. Hagen's second point was even simpler. The Gestapo had their list, of course; but with a little thought and consultation, it would not be beyond the arts of man to come up with a very similar list. They knew well enough who the Nazis' enemies were, and those same enemies had friends and supporters in the United States. You could never possibly help everybody, but maybe a few could be rescued.

Harold Oram was summoned to Child's restaurant, which was quickly turning into an unofficial headquarters. There, Hagen explained what he and Fry had in mind, and emphasized the urgent nature of the task they were asking him to undertake. Oram was a stocky, gruff man, always to the point and no-nonsense. His attire emphasized this: there was no thought given to style, only to the merest practicality of being decent, and his cheapish suit made him look like a ward-heeling politician. He was, though, a passionate idealist first and foremost. The career in networking and fund-raising at which he excelled was chosen only because Oram realized that to get things done, you needed money, or else your idealism was useless.

Oram wanted to know what they proposed to do with any money he managed to secure: people would not readily give away their dollars without knowing the exact purpose. Of course, at this stage that was a question it was difficult to answer. They agreed to say simply that funds were badly needed to help European intellectuals escape the Nazis, a broad and specific program. Oram suggested a fancy luncheon might be the best bet, but that some weighty names and a headline speaker would have to be roped in to attract an audience and the necessary publicity. In the thirties and forties, the radio stars in America were hugely popular personalities, far bigger attractions than today's television stars. Only movie idols were comparable, and they did not have the right appeal for the liberal- and artistic-minded crowd that would have to be gathered for this project. The most serious radio voice was obvious: Raymond Gram Swing, one of the biggest stars of the day. Oram reckoned he could get to him.

Other distinguished guests for the head table would still be needed, though, and this was left up to Hagen and Fry, using their own contacts and influence, to organize. Each had plenty of ideas, and set to the task straight away. Time was of the essence: each day brought the German armies nearer to Paris and the Allies closer to defeat. Once the battle was concluded, there would be no way to rescue anybody. Oram said he would take either eighty dollars or 10 percent of the money raised at the luncheon for his fee—he was a businessman, after all, but he was offering them a way to pay him very little for his efforts. Fry, Hagen, and his wife, Anna, and Eileen talked on after Oram left. By the end of the afternoon there was a list of ten names they all agreed would add luster to any occasion.

Reinhold Niebuhr, Hagen's collaborator and the chairman of the American Friends of German Freedom, obviously headed the list. He carried with him great dignity and a truly international reputation. There was Dr. Charles Seymour, president of Yale; Dr. Robert Hutchins, president of the University of Chicago; Dorothy Thompson, the first female foreign correspondent in the United States, ex-wife of Nobel Prize winner Sinclair Lewis, and a woman with the honor of being thrown out of Germany by the Nazis after she had lampooned Hitler in her account of an interview with him; Dr. William Allen Neilson, president of Smith College; Elmer Davis, the radio commentator; Mrs. Emmons Blaine, the philanthropist; Dr. George Schuster, the president of Hunter College; Dr. Alvin Johnson, head of the New School for Social Research in New York, an institution already known for employing German anti-Nazi intellectuals; and Dr. Frank Kingdon, the British-born, high-profile Methodist minister, author, and president of Newark University.

Hagen and Fry agreed on a date and a location: June 25 at the Commodore Hotel. Fry set about ringing the ten dignitaries on the list. One by one, they all accepted without hesitation. Frank Kingdon agreed to act as chairman of the proceedings, and soon after, Harold Oram called with the news that Raymond Gram Swing had also agreed. Now their task was to talk to those who would know the names of famous refugees who needed to be saved from the Gestapo, so that there would be a recognizable roll call at the Commodore. They went straight back to the telephone, working fast. Not fast enough, though. The news that Belgium had surrendered came through, and with the British and French armies encircled, it looked as if soon all their efforts would be in vain.

BY THE BEGINNING of June even Fry had to admit his shock at the way the Allied defense had collapsed. The British were surrounded at the coastal town of Dunkirk, the troops helpless on the beach under withering fire from the Germans. It looked as if the war would be over as quickly as it had begun, until suddenly, incredibly, deliverance came from the sea. Ships and boats of every size and description, from trawlers to pleasure craft, appeared over the horizon in the English Channel, and for days the motley fleet hove to in the shallows of Dunkirk, loading aboard the exhausted and demoralized soldiers. Under incessant attack from the Luftwaffe and from artillery bombardment, the hundreds of small boats plied back and forth across the water, and eventually the great majority of the British army was brought safely back home. "OUT OF THE JAWS OF DEATH," proclaimed the headline in the London *Times* on June 5; but if it was a miracle, it was certainly no victory.

Four days later, with the Germans approaching Paris, the French government decamped for the town of Tours, in such a state of panic that the Great Seals of State, without which no law could be enacted, were left behind. It was an omen of things to come. That evening, Italy announced it was entering the war, and Roosevelt responded to this blatant opportunism by announcing, in a speech at the University of Virginia, that "the hand that held the dagger has plunged it into the back of its neighbor." The crumbling French army was in no fit state to defend all its borders, but Mussolini's troops attempting to occupy the coast of the French Riviera still met with stiff opposition.

On Saturday morning, June 15, the news that Fry had been dreading was announced in the *New York Times.* "GERMANS OCCUPY PARIS," ran the headline, with the graphic subhead a little farther down the page: "REICH TANKS CLANK IN THE CHAMPS-ELYSEE." The next few days saw the battle turn into a rout. French soldiers began to lay down their arms, or wait in cafés and restaurants until puzzled German troops arrived to take them prisoner. The French government, like its army and its people, was coming apart at the seams. It fled Tours for Bordeaux, farther south, and the Premier, Reynaud, resigned. He was replaced by the nearest thing the French had to a national hero, Marshal Philippe Pétain, until recently France's ambassador to Franco's Spain. He was the commander who had turned back the enemy after the bloody stalemate at the battle of Verdun in the First World War. Then he had stood firm against the Germans. Now, Pétain was a doddering old reactionary, and he never had been a politician. He immediately set about suing for peace with Hitler, and so punched what wind was left out of the French forces. On June 18, Hitler and Mussolini met to discuss how they would divide up the spoils.

The shock of the French defeat was resonating around what was left of the free world. This was not Czechoslovakia or even Poland; France was not some dubious eastern territory no American had visited and would probably never want to. France meant Paris, home of the arts and democracy, cradle of the revolution, the spiritual sister of the United States. For the heartland of civilization to give up the ghost so quickly seemed to say that there had been nothing to defend, or nothing worth defending. Varian Fry could hardly contemplate it. Meanwhile the event at the Commodore Hotel was less than a week away, and now more than ever it looked as if the project was to be rendered purposeless. Both Fry and Hagen spent a tense week scanning the newspapers for any sliver of information that might give a sign that the massive steel door that was clanging shut on Europe had been left even slightly ajar.

On Wednesday the *New York Times* announced "AXIS CHIEFS TO SET TERMS TO CRUSH FRANCE," but those terms were not spelled out, and the tantalizing wait continued. Two days later, on Friday, June 21, the headline read, "FRANCE GETS TERMS AT COMPIEGNE TODAY." But still all Hagen and Fry could do was speculate. On Saturday came the unsurprising announcement, "HITLER DEMANDS FULL FRENCH SURRENDER," followed by the equally predictable news the next day that the French had signed what amounted to an abject, unconditional capitulation.

Forty French divisions and an entire British army had simply dissolved in the face of a determined aggressor. In an unprecedented military collapse, the very idea of freedom and democracy seemed to have been squandered, willingly handed over to the Nazis. On the other hand, one hundred thousand French soldiers had died in six weeks, twice the casualties the United States would suffer in nine years of involvement in Vietnam. But it seemed to have made no difference. Hitler had the whip hand, and Fry waited to see what he would demand. The Commodore luncheon was a mere forty-eight hours away.

ON MONDAY MORNING Fry practically sprinted to his office with a copy of the *New York Times.* He had registered the latest headline in a split second, and hadn't stopped to read on. All he could think of was to get to a phone and call Hagen right away. As he dropped the newspaper on the desk and began to dial, it unfolded to reveal a headline and a large map that was spread across three columns near the top of the front page. In it, France appeared to have been snipped in half by a drunken hand. A heavy black line undulated from a point near Geneva on the eastern border with Switzerland, all the way to Tours in the west. From there it turned sharply southward, leaving a corridor of land between it and the Atlantic coast, until the black line reached St. Jean Pied de Port at the Spanish border. It seemed roughly to mark the extent of the German advance. Fry couldn't believe it. The headline ran, "NAZI SHADOW FALLS ON HALF OF FRANCE."

Soon, he was back at Child's restaurant, awaiting Hagen's arrival. Fry tried to read the articles spread all over the front page, reporting the fate of France's large navy and the demobilization of its army, but his eyes kept being drawn back to the map. Mentally, he kept up a mantra that amended the headline: the Nazi shadow falls on *only half* of France. A back door to Europe had been left ajar, after all.

Hagen soon convinced Fry that the headline, and the map, really were too good to be true. The translation of the armistice agreement was spelled out, with its many terms and conditions, and he directed Fry's attention to the nineteenth article. "The French Government," it ran, "is obliged to surrender on demand all Germans named by the German Government in France as well as in French possessions, colonies, protectorate territories and mandates." There was a similar clause in the Italian document. If Germany had left the southern half of France unoccupied, it did not mean that unoccupied France was free. Hagen knew well how the Nazis worked: they would let the French do their dirty work for them, and act as a surrogate Gestapo in rounding up whatever enemies were wanted back in Berlin. "Surrender on demand" meant exactly what it said, and there would be plenty of demands very quickly. Once again, time was of the essence. The endangered refugees might not yet be in the hands of the Nazis, but if the French authorities had hold of them, they were nearly as good as. The only remaining hope was speedily to take advantage of the confusion and disorganization following the French defeat. If they were able to contact the refugees, they might be able to help them out of Europe before the net was pulled tight. Luncheon at the Commodore was now less than a day away.

CHAPTER 5

THE ACCIDENTAL
TOURIST

THE GATHERING AT the Commodore Hotel was a notable success. The dreadful terms of the previous day's armistice agreement had brought home to everyone the new perils into which the refugees had been plunged by the surrender. The banqueting room of the hotel was full, the tables crowded, and a specially printed blank check had been put at each place setting before the two hundred guests arrived. The big names at the head table each made short but eloquent speeches, before Raymond Gram Swing stood up and made a dramatic and moving appeal for financial help. Every guest wrote a check, and pledges amounting to thirty-five hundred dollars were made, an enormous sum of money for such an occasion.

Erika Mann, the daughter of the exiled German novelist Thomas Mann, stood up and urged that out of this one-time event, a new organization should be born. There had to be some way in which money could continue to be raised, and channeled to those who needed it in their attempts to flee the Nazis. And not only that. "We mustn't forget," she went on, "that money alone is not going to rescue those people. Most of them are trapped without visas, without passports that they dare use. They can't just get on a boat and leave. Somebody has to be there who can *get* them out."

Once it had been voiced, the idea seemed obvious. How else could any funds raised be successfully sent and usefully spent among an unknown number of people in obscure circumstances in a foreign country where they themselves were foreigners, amid the confusion and panic of defeat? Erika Mann's idea won instant approval; then and there it was decided to form an organization—and what else could it be called but the Emergency Rescue

Committee? There was an electric atmosphere in the room by now; for the first time in many weeks of hopeless news, here was a glimmer of action, of fighting against malign fate in some small but significant way. Everybody was eager to be involved and cooperate in whatever way they could. The speakers all pledged their continued support; Frank Kingdon, one of nature's chairmen, agreed to be chairman of the new committee; Fry offered his office at the Foreign Policy Association as a makeshift headquarters; and Harold Oram agreed he would continue to raise money for the rescue effort. Given the circumstances, he didn't think it would be a difficult task.

Later that afternoon, when the guests had left, some friends of Hagen's arrived. Herman Kesten, a German novelist and one of the first to leave Germany in 1933, had just landed in New York. With him was Ingrid Warburg, the attractive, Oxford-educated niece of the well-known Hamburg banker Felix Warburg. Ingrid was a veteran of the American Friends of German Freedom, and she volunteered her apartment that evening as a place where they could retire in order to plan the next stage of their operation. For the next few weeks, in fact, Ingrid's place at 25 West Fifty-fourth Street, tucked away quite aptly behind the Museum of Modern Art, would be the unofficial hub of activity. From this small apartment, the fates of hundreds of extraordinary and gifted people were decided, and the course of European culture was changed forever.

Deciding to help refugees and being able to act practically were two very different things. The complications appeared truly daunting, if not insurmountable. Little by little, though, solutions—tentative long shots, perhaps, but worth a try—presented themselves. For a start they had to compile a list of whom to rescue. Hagen, Warburg, and Kesten obviously knew some names, but also were sensible that beyond their personal experience and acquaintance, there were many others it would require a specialist's knowledge to identify. They decided that experts on and representatives of certain categories of refugees should be approached. These people could supply them with authoritative indexes of endangered artists, intellectuals, and scientists. Alfred Barr at the Museum of Modern Art was approached to draw up an inventory of painters and sculptors who needed urgent extraction from the war zone. His wife, Margaret Scolari Barr, would take charge of liaison between the artists and the Emergency Rescue Committee. The "Emperor of German Letters," Thomas Mann, supplied a list of writers and poets. He had been deprived of his German citizenship in 1936, three years after his brother, Heinrich, who was still somewhere in Europe.

On June 4, Mann, in California, had received a cable from France, signed jointly by several writers—the Czech Hans Natonek, and the Germans Walter

Mehring, Hertha Pauli, and Ernst Weiss—begging him to come to their aid and that of émigrés like them. Mann was eager to respond to their plea. Others chipped in from their own area of expertise: the émigré journalist Max Ascoli gave the names of anti-Fascist Italians; the exiled Czech leader Jan Masaryk put forward the names of fugitive and now stateless Czechs; Alvarez del Vayo and Joseph Buttinger did the same for similar Spaniards and Austrians; Alvin Johnson supplied names of more intellectuals, scientists, and composers. The French theologian Jacques Maritain and Jules Romains (whom Sinclair Lewis called one of the six best novelists in the world) filled in the gaps. Soon, the committee had an accounting of Europe's intellectual and artistic elite.

Only when all of the names were assembled did the truly terrible realization dawn on them that there would be too many people to rescue. Each name added by one member of the group was at the expense of another name on somebody else's list of suggestions. Inevitably there were harsh disagreements as the lives of those trapped on the other side of the ocean were bargained for. Professional, ideological, even nationalistic prejudices surfaced. Maritain accused Thomas Mann of favoritism to German writers. Max Ascoli told Maritain he was ignoring Italians and pushing too many French names. Paul Hagen accused Ascoli of ignoring radical socialist refugees. Jules Romains told Hagen he was forgetting about Jews. . . .

In addition to the personal disagreements there remained the fact that all of this planning was taking place in a vacuum: none of them could know for certain who had a chance of being saved. In a sense, almost all argument was academic; very few refugees had been able to provide fixed coordinates for themselves or an account of their circumstances. In truth, the Emergency Rescue Committee was in the dark, relying on often contradictory stories they heard from new émigré arrivals in the United States, or articles in the press. The very same day that the *New York Times* reported the escape of the novelist Lion Feuchtwanger to Portugal, for example, supposed eyewitness accounts of his arrest by the Gestapo, along with Thomas Mann's brother Heinrich, began to circulate in New York. Two days after the press had announced the Czech writer Franz Werfel's Gestapo execution in Paris, he was said to have been spotted in, of all places, Lourdes, probably praying for a miracle.

Neither was the next step in problem solving one that the members of the new committee could undertake alone. Importing foreigners to the United States, immigration by any other name, was the domain of the State Department. It was an open secret that the Ivy League officials and diplomats in residence there and at various Foreign Service establishments across Europe, were less than keen on allowing in anybody, never mind "Jews and Communists." In the mind of the average member of the American establishment, anybody who was on the run from a foreign government—Hitler's included—was almost de facto somebody who should not be allowed into the United States. Thus, refugees from the ever-expanding Third Reich had been doubly victimized during the thirties: first by the Nazis, who persecuted and in one way or another expelled them, then by foreign powers who saw them as criminals and troublemakers. All Western governments were anti-Communist and happy to tar anybody with that brush if they could; and all Western governments and societies were on balance passively anti-Jewish. It is easy to forget that before the Holocaust the taboo on anti-Semitism did not exist; on the contrary, to be anti-Semitic was almost a badge of one's membership in polite society. Persuading the State Department to issue visas for largely liberal and left-wing Jews from a belligerent foreign nation was the perfect job for, perhaps, an insomniac masochist with a martyr complex.

Luckily, America was large and contained contradictions. FDR himself may have appeared evasive so far on the subject of American obligations to refugees (in reality he was risking impeachment to help Churchill), but there were those in his administration whose sympathies could, with at least some optimism, be called upon. Eleanor Roosevelt was foremost among these, and Hagen had already had some contact with her through his work with the American Friends of German Freedom. On June 27, Joseph Buttinger and Paul Hagen traveled south to Washington, D.C., to petition her for help. Buttinger recalled that, while still in their presence, Eleanor Roosevelt telephoned the president in the White House. They sat, terribly impressed, as she attempted for twenty minutes to persuade her husband to grant the necessary visas for those on the Emergency Rescue Committee's list. After trying reasonable arguments she ended the conversation with a threat. "If Washington refuses to authorize these visas immediately," said Mrs. Roosevelt, "German and American émigré leaders with the help of their American friends will rent a ship, and in this ship will bring as many of the endangered refugees as possible across the Atlantic. If necessary the ship will cruise up and down the East Coast until the American people, out of shame and anger, force the President and the Congress to permit these victims of political persecution to land." Very quickly, a number of "Emergency Visas" were made available for "prominent" foreigners.

Three weeks after the luncheon at the Commodore Hotel, the Emergency Rescue Committee opened an office in the Chanin Building opposite Grand Central Station on East Forty-second Street. A wealthy young woman, Mildred Adams, well-known in philanthropic circles, became its secretary.

Buttinger advised the committee and, along with Oram, helped garner financial support. Anna Caples-Hagen worked tirelessly and proved herself a driving force—perhaps the most impressive and enthusiastic of all the volunteers. But what the committee still did not have was a suitable agent to send to France. The difficulty was in a sense obvious: anybody who knew the conditions and would be able to operate knowledgeably upon arrival was, by definition, someone whose life would be in danger and could not return to Europe. For who except an émigré already on the Gestapo blacklist would possess the vital qualifications of language and contacts? Yet all was not hopeless. An American might be preferable in some ways, and the Germans and French might at least treat an American citizen with a modicum of respect, or at least of legality. The drawback was that most Americans would literally be innocents abroad in the situation that now obtained in that part of France not overrun by the Nazis—the "unoccupied" or "free" zone. This area was now under administration by the reactionary and pro-German French government that had been installed under Marshal Pétain.

It was quickly growing obvious that Pétain's "Vichy" regime, named for the dreary spa town where it had established offices and ministries, was not going to help any foreign émigrés, least of all Germans and left-wingers, and would abide by the armistice agreement to the letter. At this moment the French police were busy rounding up refugees just as they had done the previous September at the outbreak of war, and herding them into unsanitary concentration camps. It was a depressing situation in France, with native right-wingers and their new landlords in power. One young French military commander named Charles de Gaulle had escaped to England with some elements of the French army. He opposed Pétain's capitulation and soon broadcast over BBC radio from London that he was in charge of the "Free French" forces that would continue the war against Germany from outside the country. He appealed to every true Frenchman to resist the invader, thus making himself and his supporters instantly illegal in France, and not only according to the Germans. In response to Pétain's acceptance of the German-drafted armistice agreement, de Gaulle said, "The country, the government, and you, yourself, are reduced to servitude. Ah, to obtain, and accept, such an act of enslavement, we did not need the conqueror of Verdun. Anyone would have served the purpose." Under these circumstances, not even a Frenchman could reenter France and undertake the sort of work the Emergency Rescue Committee had in mind: he would be marked out straightaway as a "Gaullist" enemy of Vichy and treated accordingly.

Fry had told Hagen confidentially that if nobody could be found for the job, he would put forward his own name. Hagen thanked him but really didn't think Fry was the man for the task. He knew from his own hard experience what was needed: someone who was tough and nerveless, clear thinking under pressure, adaptable to illegality and those who commonly practiced it; Fry, a neurasthenic intellectual and expert on the ancient Greeks, did not fit the bill by a long shot. Hagen liked Fry as a friend, and respected him as an idealist and a writer, but this was not a job to wish on your worst enemy if he was not exactly experienced and temperamentally suited.

It was only after two weeks of fruitless searching that Hagen reluctantly called up Fry to ask him if he was still willing to go to France. The paradox had died hard: nobody qualified to do the work was able to go because he would be too vulnerable. Hagen was prepared to sacrifice himself but he knew there was a chance he would not remain at liberty long enough to do anything useful. What decided Hagen that Fry was not such an outlandish choice after all was the plain fact that Fry had none of the essential "qualifications"—meaning those that would show up on Gestapo files. Fry could be usefully invisible for a while at least. As an American who could speak some French and German, he might even be effective in dealing with officials and policemen, as he would need to. Fry's stiffness and reserve, even his arrogance, might prove helpfully intimidating to petty officials. Other times, the French and Germans might mistakenly see Fry as a high-minded dumb Yank, and that too could serve certain purposes. More important, as an American citizen, Fry could be far more efficient than any European in his liaisons with the American consulates and embassy. They would, after all, be issuing the lifesaving visitors' visas on which authority the refugees would travel to the United States. It still seemed half crazy to Hagen, but there was no other solution.

The decision to send Fry to France opened up the next round of problems. Right away Fry had to get a passport valid for civilian travel into a theater of war where the American government was sensitive to remain uninvolved and rigidly neutral. Fry would also need some cover: he couldn't arrive at the French border, and in answer to the question "Business or pleasure?" reply that he had come to undermine the fragile French state by spiriting away the Gestapo's hated enemies from under its nose. This was in essence a secret mission that would have to appear transparent, innocent, and public. That would be Fry's protection—his only protection, in the end.

Representations were hastily made and warmly welcomed by the YMCA, which agreed to give Fry proof of affiliation. It was the perfect cover: the YMCA was a religious, politically neutral organization, and at the same time internationally recognized and of high repute. (It may be this connection that has led several writers mistakenly to refer to Fry as a Quaker, which he was not.) Similarly, James T. Nicholson, assistant to the chairman of the American Red Cross, promised Fry cooperation and help in Europe, and provided a letter of introduction to its director there, Richard Allen.

Thus armed, Fry's next task was to extend his passport. On July 8 Eleanor Roosevelt had written to Fry. She explained that the president was trying to get the cooperation of South American countries to give asylum to political refugees. Fry took advantage of this contact with her and wrote back on July 18, updating her on the development of the Emergency Rescue Committee in the three weeks since she had met with Hagen and Buttinger. He asked her in the same letter to help him get his passport endorsed for the French trip. Four days later he sent it to Ruth B. Shipley, president of the Department of State Passport Division.

By now Fry was working fast. He followed up his passport application with a telegram to William C. Bullitt:

PLANNING TO LEAVE FOR FRANCE EARLY NEXT WEEK SHOULD VERY MUCH LIKE TO CONSULT YOU BEFORE DEPARTURE CAN YOU GIVE ME BRIEF APPOINTMENT?

Until very recently Bullitt had been the American ambassador to France. He was relieved of his post for several reasons, and to examine them is to understand the rat's nest that Fry was getting involved in as he communed with personnel of the State Department. Under the Secretary of State, Cordell Hull, was the brilliant young diplomat Sumner Welles, a second cousin of the president, and a personal favorite. Hull was sixty-nine years old and an ineffective Secretary in some respects; the briefs he gave Roosevelt were often woolly and his ideas shallow and frequently outdated. The president had come to rely instead on the sharply intelligent Welles, and had a great deal of personal affection for him. Accordingly, Hull was deeply suspicious and jealous of his much younger assistant secretary of state. He also despised Bullitt, and was angry at the president because he thought he had dealt directly with the errant ambassador over his head. Bullitt in turn had conceived his own bitter enmity for Sumner Welles. It was one that would eventually spell the disastrous end of Welles's diplomatic career, as well as Bullitt's own, which was already in a rocky state.

Bullitt was a drinker with a loose tongue, and this had lately embarrassed the President. When the Germans attacked France and were well on their way to the capital, Bullitt had refused to abandon the embassy and follow the fleeing French government to Tours, as he had been ordered to do. He claimed this was on the grounds that no American ambassador had ever left Paris. (In

fact he cabled Washington on June 6 asking for twelve submachine guns.)
Roosevelt believed Bullitt cost America the opportunity to reason with and
encourage the panicking French administration to carry on the fight against
Germany. It is not clear anything could have been done, but Bullitt's obsti-
nacy certainly ruined the chance to find out. He was hastily recalled, and
when he landed at La Guardia Airport on Saturday, July 20, Bullitt further infuriated Roosevelt by holding an impromptu press conference calling for
recognition of the Vichy regime, which he denied was in any sense a Fascist
government; indeed, he heaped praise on Marshal Pétain. At Welles's suggestion, Roosevelt had sent a navy man, Admiral William D. Leahy, to France as a
replacement for Bullitt—and with good reason.

The American president had warned the French that if they surrendered,
they had better make sure the navy stayed out of Hitler's hands. So far this
had been the case, but the fleet's close proximity to German control was making the White House extremely nervous. Leahy may not have been, by any
stretch of the imagination, a diplomat; Roosevelt nevertheless hoped that as a
navy man he would be able to persuade the French admirals to sail to Britain
or, if that was impossible, for Canada, if it looked like Pétain was about to
surrender the fleet. Bullitt did not appreciate the subtlety of this consideration, or the clumsiness of his own behavior, and simply blamed Welles
(whom he believed to be poisoning the President's opinion of him) for his
dismissal. His angry mood and the wish to continue to "be involved" in the
French situation may have influenced his positive response to Fry. At any rate,
on the following Thursday, Delia Goetz, Fry's secretary at the Foreign Policy
Association, sent a telegram to her boss, who was in Washington, to tell him
that Bullitt had given Fry an appointment at eleven the following Monday
morning, July 29.

Fry was kept cooling his heels on the steps of the State Department for a
few hours, but was eventually shown into the office of the former ambassador, who was now forlornly scheming to become Secretary of the Navy. Fry
had scribbled down on the back of an envelope a series of questions for Bullitt, and noted down the answers. He asked what were the actual conditions in
France, and Bullitt told him a horror story. "How careful shall I have to be to
keep my real interest secret?" asked Fry. Extremely so, replied Bullitt, and he
also answered in the negative when Fry wondered if he could approach the
French authorities in Vichy and ask for their cooperation in getting non-
French refugees out. Bullitt supplied some information concerning transportation to Lisbon and Casablanca, but in reality the situation was very
volatile and subject to momentary alteration. Next, Fry made an inquiry that
would turn out to be crucial to the measures he was forced to take in France.

"How much refuge," he asked, "will consuls be able to give persons with visas whose lives may be in danger?" "None," answered Bullitt. "They have no immunity." This was indeed ominous. Fry's last question concerned the Allied blockade of Europe intended to cut off essential supplies for Germany's war effort. He asked whether he would be able to get out of Europe if conditions worsened and the blockade was extended to include Spain and Portugal, the only overland route in or out of France. Bullitt was only guardedly optimistic. There was the possibility, undeniable in such unpredictable times, that Fry was on a strictly one-way ticket.

Fry returned to New York to find two envelopes on his doormat. The first contained his passport, along with a letter signed by Ruth B. Shipley, which carried a dire warning on the dangers of travel in Europe. Fry's passport had been validated for European travel for exactly six months, to expire on January 22. That was fine with Fry; six months sounded like a very long time. Then he opened the second letter. Through Eleanor Roosevelt's good offices, Sumner Welles himself had provided an official State Department letter of introduction for Fry. This gave him, in practical terms, very near—and, it would transpire, extremely temporary—diplomatic status. He was nearly ready to go.

Officially, according to the job description drawn up by Mildred Adams at the Emergency Rescue Committee, Fry had three duties to carry out in France. The first was to prepare a full report on the conditions affecting the refugees. This included a survey of transportation, transmittal of funds (the émigrés' and German Jews' bank accounts had been frozen, rendering them destitute and liable to internment in concentration camps), and the attitudes of French and foreign officials. Second, Fry was to try to find certain named individuals and help get them to Lisbon or Casablanca, so they could more easily find their way to the United States. Last, he was to find and designate individuals who could in the future act as agents for the Emergency Rescue Committee.

Fry himself was to be in Europe for only three weeks or so; Mildred had sent him his tickets. He would fly out on Sunday afternoon, August 4, and return on August 29. The Foreign Policy Association had generously granted him a month's paid leave from his editorial post, and beyond that, the Emergency Rescue Committee promised to "make up the difference" if Fry was held up, as they put it, for any reason. But these funds would last only for another two months, until the end of October. That was fine with Varian Fry. He had no illusions about occupied France, but he was looking at one sunny month bicycling around Provence—in the "free" zone—and meeting up with the writers and artists for whom, he said, "although I knew them only through their work, I had a deep love; and to them all I owed a heavy debt of gratitude for the pleasure that they had given me."

Hagen had decided Fry should head first to Marseille, on the southern coast. As a port, it was a place from where people would try to leave the country. It had a rail connection direct to the Spanish border, five hours away. It was already a terminus for the refugees who had made their way south to escape the German advance. In fact, the ancient Roman city was groaning with the transient population of scared and desperate people whose last chance to escape Nazi persecution was to find a way, any way, out of Europe.

Meanwhile, things were growing frantic for Fry in New York. The deliberations of the committee had furnished not one but several lists. As Fry recalled, Mildred Adams had given him a list in the lobby of the Plaza hotel. Paul Hagen had brought one to Fry's office. Alfred Barr of MOMA had delivered a list of modern artists. Thomas Mann assembled a list of over one hundred German writers; a roll call of thirty French writers came from somebody else. Fry had over two hundred names. Finally he had to call a halt to all the individual requests he was being bombarded with—even the actor Charles Boyer wanted him to get the novelist André David, a friend of his, out of Bordeaux. What he did have was a hard core of names that everyone involved in the committee agreed were in the greatest danger.

There was Konrad Heiden, who had been a reporter for the liberal German newspaper, *Frankfurter Zeitung*. He had written the first biography of Hitler even before he came to power, and it was a devastating document that exposed the true character of the Führer and his Nazi movement. In fact, the word "Nazi" was bestowed by Heiden himself. Before that, Hitler's party had been called the "Nasos," for "National Socialists." Hitler was forced formally to adopt Heiden's "Nazi" to try to neutralize the term, which meant "bumpkin" or "simpleton" in Bavarian slang. So vocal and intimate an opponent was he that in the early days, it was said, Hitler refused to begin his political meetings until Heiden had arrived.

There was Hans Habe, real name John Bekessey, the witty Hungarian journalist who had called down on himself the Führer's personal wrath by revealing to the world that his true name was Schiklgruber. There was the intellectual Walter Benjamin; the poets Hans Sahl and Walter Hasenclever; novelists Alfred Polgar and Leonhard Frank; Angelus Gottfried (Golo) Mann, the historian son of Thomas Mann, and Peter Pringsheim, his brother-in-law and a leading European physicist; Rudolf Breitscheid and Rudolf Hilferding, the former leaders of Germany's Social Democratic Party; Giuseppe Modigliani, the Italian Socialist and Jew, brother of Amadeo, the painter; Hans Natonek, the anti-Nazi Czech journalist; the writers Ernst Weiss and

Hertha Pauli—also a literary agent and dear friend of Hitler's bitter foe, the poet Walter Mehring, who was on the list as well; the writers Alfred Döblin (*Berlin Alexanderplatz*) and Alfred Neumann, from Germany; the historian Valeriu Marcu from Romania; Dr. Otto Meyerhof, the Nobel Prize–winning biochemist, and his colleague at Heidelberg, Dr. Emil Gumbel, whose outspoken pacifism had once provoked a riot; Guido Zernatto, Austrian politician and poet; Largo Caballero, exiled prime minister of the defunct Spanish Republic; film critic Siegfried Kracauer; the publishers Jacques Schiffrin, Franz Pfemfert, and Kurt and Helen Wolff; André Gide, the grand old man of French literature; Nobel laureate novelist Josef Wittlin; the Surrealists André Breton and Max Ernst—the latter a German who was in fearful trouble for having refused to return home on Nazi orders, and for marrying a Jew; Jacques Lipchitz, the sculptor; and the painters Marc Chagall and Henri Matisse. Even within this core list, everybody agreed that the most endangered of all were, unquestionably, Heinrich Mann, Lion Feuchtwanger, Franz Werfel, and Walter Mehring.

Heinrich Mann was even more well known on the continent of Europe than his younger brother, Thomas. He had been a much more outspoken anti-Nazi than Thomas Mann, who had emigrated to the United States, and for years seemed to assume that the Nazis were an aberration that would disappear and could therefore be ignored. Unlike his brother's, Heinrich Mann's books had all been burned in the student conflagrations of May 10, 1933, and subsequently banned. The year before that, he had been put forward as a serious candidate for president of the German Republic; and Mann was stripped of his German citizenship as soon as Hitler took power—the first person to be so honored.

The second man to be told by Hitler that he was no longer German was Lion Feuchtwanger, a Jewish historical novelist hugely popular after the appearance of his phenomenally successful *Jud Süss* (published in the United States as *Power*). His later books dramatized the life of Flavius Josephus, a Jew in Rome at the end of the first century AD, and drew obvious parallels with the Nazi empire. His work was regarded by Hitler as pure anti-matter, and by the rest of the world as irresistible. He was a close friend of Dorothy Thompson, who had invited Feuchtwanger to be a witness at her wedding to Sinclair Lewis some years earlier.

It was Franz Werfel's popularity rather than his Jewishness (he considered himself almost a convert to Roman Catholicism) that primarily made him an outrage to Hitler. His novel about the heroic Armenian resistance to Turkish invasion, *The Forty Days of Musa Dagh,* was a brilliant allegory and repudiation of the Nazis, who banned it, and a worldwide bestseller in the thirties. Like Mann and Feuchtwanger, he was living under sentence of death.

Of the four, only Walter Mehring, the Berlin cabaret-poet, had gone out of his way to antagonize the Nazis; in a magazine called *Die Welthühne,* on the day Hitler became chancellor, Mehring published a long poem called "The Saga of the Giant Crab"—in which he made some grisly predictions:

> *If this Thing should leave the mire,*
> *Then its savage hordes will surge*
> *Over the earth with death and fire,*
> *A cruel, pestilential surge . . .*
>
> *A reign of unrelenting woe,*
> *Once the crab dictator's in,*
> *Will come upon us while we track*
> *Never forward, always back.*
> *Damn the crab and damn the Heils*
> *And damn the ghastly necrophiles . . .*

It resulted in the imprisonment and death two years later in a concentration camp of Carl von Ossietzky, the magazine's publisher, at the very time he was being awarded in his absence the Nobel Peace Prize. Ten of Mehring's books were publicly consigned to the bonfire; in 1935, he was also deprived of German citizenship. These men had all been trudging the refugee road for years. If they, successful and internationally famous, had been luckier and more comfortable than most of their fellow émigrés, they were also more visible and right at the top of the Gestapo execution list.

Now they were also at the top of another list: Varian Fry's.

IT WAS EXTRAORDINARILY HOT in New York over the first weekend of August 1940. *Rebecca* and *Dr. Cyclops* were playing in local movie houses; in the clubs people were dancing to the latest sensation, "Oh Johnny Oh." A few weeks before, Fry had been thinking quiet, domestic thoughts: should he take a house somewhere away from Manhattan in the fall? Would he buy a dog at last? He had no idea, he later claimed, of uprooting his life.

He had spent the Saturday afternoon hunting around Brooks Brothers for a couple of dress shirts to take with him. He thought he would need them in addition to the four suits, two light woollen ones, a natural color linen and a seersucker, that he was already taking along, together with a Burberry raincoat and some gray flannel pants. It was a light, summer wardrobe for the few weeks during which he hoped to enjoy the sunshine of the Mediterranean while he worked. "I think I am at last ready to go," he had written the morning of his departure to the staff at the Foreign Policy Association. "The last chores have been done and the last odds and ends bought. . . . Have a good summer. I'll see you in September—I hope!" One of the last things he did was to write the classics department at Harvard, to ask for the return of his bronze bull and Grecian vase. He explained that thoughts of death made him want to gather about himself his most valuable treasures.

UPTOWN IN HARLEM that weekend they were opening the fire hydrants so children could play in the icy spray; in Central Park people were seeking the shade; downtown, folks pulled on their collars and sniffed out coolness in dark cellar bars. But out in Queens the August heat was more bearable at the water's edge, where a small crowd was waiting for the big-bellied flying boat gently nodding in the offshore swell to tie up at dockside at La Guardia. Three figures stood apart from the rest and one of them, Eileen Fry, struggled to hold her skirt down against the breeze. With the other arm she pulled toward her the straight-backed young man whose round dark spectacles and short brown wavy hair made him seem to the disinterested observer at once attractive and serious. Her wifely embrace was returned by Fry, who bent toward her for the *au revoir*. The other man with the poet's eyes looked on, swaying a little in the breeze as if a heavy lunch with good wine had unsteadied him. Fry shook his hand, then turned to hand down luggage to the uniformed figures. Then he walked the narrow gangway over the lapping waves and onto the airplane, where he turned again to wave farewell.

Late Friday evening, two days before, Fry had welcomed an unexpected visitor to his apartment on Irving Place. It was a man, someone he knew, and he had come to make Fry an extraordinary offer.

The visitor, whom he never named, offered point blank to go to France in Fry's place. He told Fry they had the same build, and that they were roughly the same height. The customs men could be fooled. He said that Fry simply didn't know the people he would be dealing with. They were dangerous enemies, and would play for keeps. He said Fry had no experience of this kind of underground work, or what it really involved. He himself did, though, said the unnamed visitor; he could be far more effective.

Fry was astounded at the insane proposal. He replied that he wouldn't break the laws of his country by this fraud. He said he was unable to betray the trust that so many, including certain people in the government, had placed in him. It was an interesting offer, but one that he would have to decline. But the truth was that Fry wished to undertake the journey for himself, even above his sense of obligation to the committee that had elected him its representative, and to the people whose names were on the precious list he carried. Most of all (although he didn't say so), Fry simply wanted to go.

Perhaps the shadowy incident was a dream, with its nameless figure who so resembled Fry, outlining what were surely impossibilities. For of course the passport would be checked carefully, if not in Lisbon then at the Spanish and French borders: he would be traveling into a war zone, after all. And how would Fry explain his continued presence to his friends in New York after all the fanfare of farewell? What would Eileen have said? Would he have been prepared to go into hiding until the impostor returned to America? And what if, as his visitor hinted, the Gestapo did do its job effectively and having taken Fry's passport he never returned? Might Fry not find his life in some Kafkaesque way negated, his identity stolen and destroyed? Perhaps this was the real reason Fry wrote some years later about the strange meeting: because it signified for him the choice between finding or losing himself.

That summer of 1940, Fry was at a pivotal point in his life. It was the very normality of his existence, compared with the cataclysm of Hitler's victory in France, that was ominous to such a fervent and uncompromising democrat. In his own eyes, Fry saw the world suffering its most momentous and terrible convulsion for over a thousand years. "This is not just another nationalist war," he said. "It is a world revolution." As a trained classicist, his thoughts were drawn to the end of the Roman empire and the long Dark Age that ensued. Could he resist this opportunity to plunge into the maelstrom? Would he take the unexpected opportunity to leave New York and attempt to help turn aside the murderous juggernaut of the Nazis, the new Barbarians; or would he take up his anonymous visitor's offer and arrive at the Foreign Policy Association's offices again on Monday morning?

No, Fry would go to France, but he had first to see clearly what he was leaving behind, or what he could be forced to give up, if this new adventure really did take his life in a radically different direction: his job, perhaps his career, maybe even Eileen. This the late-night visit from the nameless man had shown him. Logical deduction points to Paul Hagen as Fry's prospective doppelgänger. Hagen had the experience, and the impulsive recklessness, to have made such a rash and impractical offer, and even to have made it sound, however momentarily, like it could work. But Fry's mind had already been made up: "In the end I volunteered to go," he said. "I still don't know quite why I did it. I had never had any experience in underground work, spoke French poorly, German even more poorly than French; Spanish, Polish, Italian and Russian, not at all." Now he was at La Guardia, and there was no way back.

THE FOUR-ENGINED SEAPLANE glinting in the sun showed the blue and white livery of the Pan Am Clipper Service, with its badge in the design of a winged globe, a beautiful example of thirties commercial artistry, elegant and exciting, promising distant exotic places made near. The plane was to break its eastward journey at the Azores to refuel, and then carry straight on to Lisbon, which in the summer of 1940 was the bustling point of embarkation to America for all those trying desperately to escape the nightmare that Europe had become.

Varian Fry glanced briefly out the porthole of the Yankee Clipper before he reached into his pocket for a small black notebook. During the last, tense meetings with the members of the Emergency Rescue Committee, all the disturbing, "What if . . . ?" questions had gone unresolved. All they had agreed on was a primitive, almost schoolboyish code so Fry could communicate by telegram with them without arousing the suspicions of the French censor. Money was to be known as "milk"; transportation became "clothing"; and boat, "warm-clothing." In Fry's notebook were the place names, together with their new designations:

> England = Ursula
> Africa = Leland
> Spain = Ernest
> Germany = Eloise
> France = Heinrich

He didn't know if it would fool anybody; Fry had no idea whether the Germans and the Vichy French were alert and efficient, or clumsy and foolish. He hoped for the former and feared the latter, but it was really too late to worry. He carried with him aboard the Clipper a large sum of money to be at all costs concealed from the customs men in Portugal, Spain, and France (and which was to remain strapped to his leg until he reached his destination), together with the Emergency Rescue Committee's lists of two hundred names, which he would attempt and fail to memorize before the flying boat touched down at its journey's end about twenty-four hours later.

Fry was traveling into the face of war, still surprised and even apprehensive at finding himself, of all people, moving in that direction. One of the most incredible rescue operations of the Second World War was about to begin.

PART 2

EXILES

CHAPTER 6

ON THE ROAD

And suddenly a completely ridiculous image came into my mind.
I thought of clocks out of order. All the clocks of France . . .
ANTOINE DE SAINT-EXUPÉRY, FLIGHT TO ARRAS

BY THE MIDDLE OF JUNE 1940, with the French on the point of defeat, Franz and Alma Werfel had all but given up their journeying in
search of safety. It had been a long haul, in terms of time as well as
distance, and it had taken its toll on Franz. When they at last arrived at Lourdes, the town of St. Bernadette, he was on the edge of emotional collapse.
Alma attempted as best she could, and as she always had done, to comfort her
husband and soothe his frayed nerves.

Many years ago when she was still a young woman, Alma had read one of
Franz Werfel's poems and immediately decided two things: first, that he was a
genius; second, that she would marry him. And she was not a woman who
was used to refusals. By the time they first met in 1917, she had long been regarded as the most beautiful and magnetic lady in Vienna. The career of love,
to which she had devoted her life, was an experiment in the nurturing of
what Alma regarded as genius. When she fell in love, the whole of Europe
knew about it; Franz Werfel was the next on her list.

The first of her famous *amours* to scandalize the continent began in 1897,
when Alma flung herself into a brief but intense affair with the painter Gustav Klimt. The flame-haired beauty depicted on the parti-colored canvas of
Klimt's masterpiece *The Kiss* is Alma herself, embraced as both lover and
muse. Five years later her marriage to Gustav Mahler crowned her queen of
Vienna society, even though it laid to rest to her own ambitions as a composer. Mahler simply didn't take her work seriously. Later, when he began to
neglect her romantically, Alma sought solace in the arms of the German ar-
chitect Walter Gropius. Devastated, the composer sought out Sigmund Freud

for help in pulling himself together. Alas, it was too late, and the fact that Mahler died only five months after she left him is testament to the power of Alma's devotion, which when withdrawn left her protégés bereft.

Indeed the artist Oskar Kokoschka, whom she admired enough to take to bed but not enough to marry ("I only marry geniuses, and Oskar is not a genius," she told a friend), was properly demented after Alma left him, and he went so far as to make a life-sized effigy of her, complete with sexual organs, that he worshipped as a love fetish. Although Kokoschka had continued to pursue her, she married Gropius instead in 1915. Her romantic campaigns were inflated by self-regard. In her diaries there is a record of a conversation she had with Gerhart Hauptmann, the German dramatist and poet:

"It's a pity," he said to me, "that the two of us don't have a child together. That would have been something. You, you my great love . . ."

"In another life," he once told me, "we two must be lovers. I make my reservation now."

His wife heard it. "I'm sure Alma will be booked up there, too."

Gropius was an odd choice as a husband, for architecture did not belong to Alma's breviary of truly spiritual arts, and the marriage foundered after two years when she came across the poem by Werfel. Gropius retreated into his work, and after some time emerged from the study with the invention of Bauhaus design, which took architecture into the realm of modern art, but did not win back Alma, for she had meanwhile moved in with Franz Werfel.

"This darling of the gods," she called him, proving that physically, at least, love really is blind. For Werfel was an unprepossessing specimen, with his sack-like rear end and bottle-bottom glasses that transformed his owl-sized eyes into runny eggs. His glistening, rubbery lips and accelerating baldness did nothing to lessen the effect of his squat stature, but to Alma he was merely "stocky," and the caricature face was for her blessed with "sensuous lips and large, beautiful blue eyes under a Goethean forehead." Basking in her adulation, young Werfel flourished, and under the maternal influence of his lover—she was twelve years his senior—he became over the next decade the leading "modern" writer in the German language, practically defining the Expressionist movement.

Perhaps it was the unlikely perfection of their union that delayed its formalization; it was 1929 before they finally married. Around that time Werfel felt an increasing need to escape Alma's lavish entertaining at their home in Vienna—he found her role as grand hostess interrupted his work—and he began to retreat to a small country hotel for weeks at a time. There he wrote the novel that would bring him international fame, *The Forty Days of Musa Dagh*. He finished it in 1933, and when he emerged, blinking, into the light, he found Adolf Hitler at the helm of the new Third Reich. The book was promptly banned, and the Werfels' troubles began. Two years later his German nationality was revoked.

Luckily for him, Werfel was in Italy at the time of the *Anschluss* in March 1938. Alma, though, was in Vienna, and only managed to flee over the border of Czechoslovakia after producing a baptismal certificate to prove she was not Jewish, and stripping naked to prove she was not smuggling out valuables. The Werfels were finally reunited in Milan after she had traveled from Prague through Budapest, Zagreb, and Trieste in order to avoid Austria. But the hope was forlorn that this experience would alert Werfel to the true danger of this situation.

The year before at the PEN Congress in Paris, he had delivered a speech that annoyed the fiercely anti-Nazi novelist Lion Feuchtwanger. Partly, this was because Werfel's advice to writers had stressed the "spiritual" side of existence, and he had castigated those who dabbled in politics, especially Communism. It had sounded to many like complacency, and he took the Austrian disaster perhaps too philosophically. Alma, though, having seen the troops and the rabid anti-Semitism of the welcoming crowds in Vienna, and having been unspeakably humiliated herself, was not so sanguine. She began to worry in earnest and plan for their future safety.

They traveled to Zurich and stayed with friends, then went on to Paris, where the realities of exile finally began to affect Franz. Isolation from friends and society, the fresh air of foreign languages, and an unfamiliarity of surroundings are prime ingredients of the perfect vacation; but if it is impossible to return home, they quickly grow oppressive. In June, Werfel suffered a heart attack, and although he recovered, his health was now fragile. He was ordered by the doctor to stop smoking, although it was the only thing that calmed his nerves. Worse, the heat in Paris that summer was intense, and with his obesity burdening a weakened heart, Alma decided her husband would do better elsewhere, in the company of colleagues.

They moved to a small fishing village on the south coast, between Marseille and Toulon. Over the years, Sanary-sur-Mer had developed into a writer's colony, and it had recently begun to attract exiled Germans, following in the earlier footsteps of D. H. Lawrence and Katherine Mansfield. Lion Feuchtwanger had blazed the Teutonic trail in 1933, followed by Thomas Mann, Alfred Döblin, Ludwig Marcuse, Ernst Toller, and at one point Bertolt Brecht. Five years on, several dozen writers were encamped in and around the village, including Arthur Koestler and Aldous Huxley. Thomas Mann's brother, Heinrich, was in nearby Nice. The Werfels moved into an old, taste-fully remodeled Saracen watchtower near Thomas Mann's "Villa Tranquille." Werfel worked happily and compulsively there, in a room right at the top, out of earshot of Alma's endless entertaining.

Their frequent visitors, Feuchtwanger and his indomitable wife, Marta, made another incongruous couple. She was a paragon of athletic prowess, and at the age of fifteen had been a top German gymnast. Later, she became a brilliant skier and swimmer, in addition to her other hobbies of running and mountain climbing. Calisthenics were her daily ritual. Feuchtwanger worked hard enough at his desk, but he was small, bespectacled and scholarly; not the mountaineering type. He was also older, with chronic stomach ulcers and a double hernia. Even so, in his younger days Marta had managed to coax him into a hike across the North African desert from Tunis to Hamamet, and they had climbed Mt. Etna in Sicily together.

The two men had overcome the disagreement sparked by Werfel's anti-Communist speech in Paris, which Feuchtwanger, recently returned to Moscow as a guest of Stalin, had taken personally. But they continued to argue about politics, and eventually the suppers they took together had to stop when Alma's fears about Werfel's heart condition (when agitated he reddened in the face and chain-smoked cigars) outweighed the pleasure she took in their conversations. The Werfels wintered in Paris but were back in Sanary during the summer of 1939, when their world came crashing down around them.

Suddenly, after the declaration of war on Germany by Britain and France, they were no longer distinguished exiles but enemy aliens. The French fundamentally refused to concede that those who had left Germany were opposed to Hitler's regime. With some justification, they assumed that there was a possibility of espionage and sabotage from Germans, and their mind-set was geared to a nationalist, not an ideological war. The French would not accept that some Germans were on the Allied side—even exiles like Werfel whose passports had been confiscated by the Nazis, or Austrians like Alma whose countries had been dubiously annexed. The Sanary locals were naturally suspicious of outsiders, and this was reciprocated by the aloof Werfels. When their persecution by the local police—with raids and searches—began, Franz managed to pay their way out of trouble, but after a light was seen glinting through one of their windows late at night, they were denounced and accused of signaling to German boats. At a stroke, the price of their liberty increased steeply.

With the threat of internment hanging over them, Franz decided that it was no longer any use bribing the police, and after paying handsomely for a few days' grace, they packed and departed for Paris to avoid arrest. They counted on the fact that there was a measure of anonymity and therefore safety in a big city, as did the other German émigrés who flocked there. By the end of 1939 Paris was swelling with frightened foreigners foretelling doom, but the nation itself was not in a particularly warlike mood. The anxiety that had followed Hitler's invasion of Poland had ebbed, and many French people were confident that the war would soon end in stalemate and negotiated settlement.

The French desire to avoid a fight was abetted by German propaganda, floating toward them in the shape of balloons trailing leaflets explaining the Führer's peaceful intentions. If that was the carrot, Goebbels shook the stick by distributing throughout unoccupied Europe vivid footage of Poland's brutal subjugation. Meanwhile, French troops along the border were serenaded by Bavarian brass bands, and at the same time loudspeakers barked at them about the likely unfaithfulness of their wives at home, the irresistible strength of the German armed forces, and the myriad advantages of accord. Huge billboards were pasted up all along the border: "The German people won't attack the French people if the French don't attack the Germans."

Nothing Hitler had ever done lent a sliver of credibility to his bare-faced lie, but a message of friendship was what the French most desperately wanted to hear. In late 1939 the Allies lost their chance of crippling Hitler's war machine by striking into the south of the country while Germany's armed forces were still occupied in consolidating their control of Poland in the East, and so winter slipped quietly into spring. In Paris, the unfortunate effect of Nazi propaganda and powerful native anti-Semitism made the exiles' shrill warnings about Hitler's true plans sound like warmongering. Germany's line was that only the Jews wanted conflict, and to many French people it seemed true. Here, after all, were thousands of mostly Jewish Germans idly cluttering up the streets, telling the French to fight on their behalf. The Werfels, like the rest of the exiles, were soon sunk in gloom. They knew an offensive was coming, and were waiting only to discover when and where.

Then, on the morning of April 9, news came through of the invasions in Scandinavia, and France was plunged into shock. Was it really possible that Denmark had fallen in only four hours? Only a month later their shock turned to panic. Hundreds of German airplanes blackened the skies of northern France, all but destroying the Allied air forces on the ground. At the same time, thirty German army divisions poured across the borders of Holland and Belgium in an unstoppable combination of motorized infantry, armor, and air power. Most armies of the time were equipped to advance at walking pace; Hitler's attack was proceeding at speeds of up to forty miles an hour, simply overwhelming every defense.

While the French and British sent their best troops north into Belgium to stop the German thrust, a massive wave of Panzers was sneaking through the Ardennes forest. The tanks were met with only token resistance, and a mere forty-eight hours later seven German armored divisions reached the Meuse near Sedan. Two days after that, on May 15, Rommel and Guderian broke through the collapsing French defenses and crossed the river; and at the same time to the north, Holland collapsed. It was a catastrophe; the Germans had split the Allied forces in two, and had isolated the British with their backs against the sea.

By this time, the population of Paris was terrified and many of her citizens were beginning to think seriously about fleeing south. But before foreigners could leave, they had to secure the necessary travel documents. In the Werfels' case, this would take two weeks, by which time the Allied defeat was well on the way to being concluded. The Germans themselves could hardly believe the rate at which their victory was being achieved. On Sunday, May 19, senior members of the French government went to Notre Dame Cathedral to pray for a miracle, but it made no difference. On May 21, the Germans reached the northern coast of France, and began herding the British into a pocket south of the Belgian border. Two days later, the port of Boulogne fell to the Germans, and after another three days, so did Calais. The British were now trapped at Dunkirk.

At last, on May 28, the day of the Belgian surrender, the Werfels received their papers. It took an hour for their taxi to travel the short distance to the Gare d'Orléans, down streets thronged with a population on the move, loaded with all manner of belongings and supplies. At the railway station a young man kindly helped the Werfels with their baggage. Franz realized, some time into the journey south to Marseille, that like many others he had seen around the station, the young man had not been in uniform. That meant only one thing: soldiers were deserting in large numbers. They had witnessed France dressed for defeat. At this point the possibility of death in the near future became horribly plausible to Werfel.

They had been lucky to find seats on what was probably one of the very last trains leaving the French capital. Defeat, the chasm into which France was plummeting, swallowed all the usual apparatus of civilized life and the invisible codes that keep society civil were being scrambled. As Saint-Exupéry wrote, defeat stops the clock of culture, and railway timetables quickly take on the status of quaint souvenirs. Panic was spreading, replacing the beliefs that keep people law-abiding and even altruistic with naked self-interest. There was fighting and squabbling and looting among the fleeing people, and the atmosphere was quickly turning to *chacun pour soi*, or "every man for himself."

It was not only the civilian population that responded to some primeval urge to scatter; the army had fallen apart as well. The young deserter who helped Werfel with his luggage was a benign example of the phenomenon that elsewhere revealed a different face. As French soldiers threw down their arms and fled, they also rioted and terrorized. Descending on towns like plagues of locusts, they looted and pillaged, personifying the characteristic inversion of order that defeat releases like poison gas. The French word for such unbolted men—*fuyards*—captured the sense of flight and threat perfectly. But the panic of defeat was also like a disease: the government collapsed, the army fragmented, the people were let loose on one another. Saint-Exupéry, who saw it happen, called it a "crazy contagion."

Where pockets of French troops attempted to stand firm and mount a defense against the invader (like those under de Gaulle's command at Montornet, then Abbeville, or the military cadets of the Saumur Cavalry School who died on the banks of the Loire, or the North African soldiers at Lille), they were not always thanked by the people they were protecting. At the towns of Vierzon, on the Cher River, for example, the citizens attacked the soldiers, fearing that they would be killed and their possessions destroyed if the Germans had to take the ground by force. There were few, though a good few, noble stands and inspiring examples. But mostly soldiers and civilians alike fought for the last piece of food, the last gallon of gas, the last sliver of space on the seat of a vehicle heading away from the Germans.

As their train made its way south the Werfels would have seen from their window a fair proportion of the ten million French people on the move. Most went on foot, and the rest were inching their way forward on anything that had wheels—bicycles, carts, tractors, autos, trucks, buses, prams, even resurrected tumbrels from an earlier age. They were laden and barnacled to within a straw's weight of collapse with bodies and possessions—those pathetic keepsakes of lost domesticity—which were both discarded as they lost their relevance to the new reality of unending heat, hunger, and danger. The roadsides were festooned with an honor guard of abandoned vehicles, their doors hanging open like the mouths of dead men.

And dead men too lay at the side of the road, and women and children, killed by the bullets of the German fighter planes that swept at low-level over the land to strafe the columns of tired and frightened people. Whenever an airplane appeared everyone would leap for the ditches at the edges of the road, but always there would be someone or something left in the path of the death-rattle cannon fire: a horse still tethered in its hafts, perhaps, or a weeping child atop a piled hay cart. Soon these would also be in the ditches, but permanently.

Before too long, there was no food left at the towns that the migrant hordes reached, and no water in the heat wave that was baking France in June 1940. Maddened by hunger and fatigue, the refugees turned on each other at the slightest provocation. The cry of *chacun pour soi* had delivered them into this living hell, and when the smoke cleared it would reveal the damage done not only to the landscape, but also to the very soul of France.

AT MARSEILLE the Werfels managed to find a room at the Hotel du Louvre et de la Paix on the city's main Boulevard, the Canebière. Then they began trudging the round of consulates to plead for a visa, any visa, that would allow them to leave France and the advancing Germans behind. The city was filling up with thousands of like-minded refugees, and daily bulletins of worsening conditions in the north were circulated by the waves of harrowed new arrivals. On June 10, the French government abandoned Paris and declared it an "open city" in the hope that, undefended, the Germans would not pound it to rubble. Sensing easy territorial gains, Italy declared war and attacked France in the South. On June 13, the French Prime Minister Paul Reynaud gave his final radio broadcast, from Tours, where the government had briefly rested on its chaotic flight away from the front line. He pleaded with the Americans to send "clouds of airplanes" to repel the invaders.

On June 14 the Germans entered Paris, and two days later, having reached Bordeaux, Reynaud gave up the ghost. He was one of the few French politicians who had any stomach for a fight, but he was surrounded by the unstoppable clamor of his defeatist ministers, and was also being importuned by his now hysterical mistress, Hélène, Comtesse de Porte. She had always dominated him, and demanded he surrender or resign. He resigned, handing over to the eighty-four-year-old Philippe Pétain, who immediately began negotiating an armistice with Germany. The battle was nearly over, but for the refugees a new nightmare was about to begin, and the Werfels embarked on another fruitless odyssey.

Realizing that at any moment the borders might be sealed by the Germans, and calculating that proximity to the French government was the safest place to be, they set off for Bordeaux in a taxi. Before long they were horrified to discover that they were traveling not west but north. The driver wanted to visit a relative, and knowing they were at his mercy, had taken what was for the Werfels an extremely dangerous detour. He told them they would be in Toulouse by sundown, but at eleven that night they had only reached Bayonne, barely two-thirds of the way there. They managed to find a place to sleep on the floor of a children's infirmary.

The next day the Werfels squeezed, with their fourteen pieces of luggage, onto a train destined for Bordeaux, and when they got there they found the city completely swamped with refugees. That night was spent, at full hourly rate, in a brothel, and the following day they discovered that their trip had been pointless. Not only were they still over a hundred miles from the Spanish border, but no visas were being issued in Bordeaux anyway. A taxi took them to the seaside resort of Biarritz near the frontier, where they found after several hours' wait that papers could be got only in nearby Bayonne. They also discovered that the Germans were already there and would be in Biarritz at any moment. In a state of numb horror, they made their way south to Hendaye, at the border.

For hundreds of years exiles from Spain—and there had been many—made their way over the Hendaye bridge into France, the haven of refugees, the country of tolerance. Now it was Spain, even Franco's Fascist Spain, that began to look relatively hospitable. The good news here was as fleeting as it was welcome to the Werfels. They heard that the Portuguese Consul was well disposed to those who came to him, and would generally be happy to grant a visa. But they had arrived too late: the strain of the situation had got to him before they could, and he had lost his mind. In a fit of dementia he had taken all the passports entrusted to him, and had thrown them into the sea.

The Werfels were just recovering from this latest shock when the terms of the armistice were announced, with its division of France into two zones. The Germans would have the northern half of the country and the Atlantic coast; the new French government would "administer" the rest. The panic they felt from suddenly finding out they were in the enemy zone was compounded by the sight of German troops arriving in the town. A lifetime of hailing taxis paid off, though, and with luck born of expertise they halted one and clambered exhaustedly inside. The border between the two zones, soon to be impassable, was not yet fully manned, and the Werfels managed to travel back up the coast to St. Jean de Luz, and from there inland toward the blessed unoccupied zone. On Thursday, June 27, they reached Lourdes.

Lourdes was the nearest town in the "free" zone to the border crossings through which fleeing refugees had hoped they would be able to pass into Spain. But without visas, they had almost all failed, and had fallen back in despair and fatigue to the place where the century before the peasant girl Bernadette Soubirous had seen a statue of the Virgin move and heard it speak to her. There the Werfels joined the other lost souls in the search for a place to stay, and they were at last successful in finding a tiny cell-like room in the Hotel Vatican, where the inconsolable Franz was tended by a very worried Alma. For a short time it looked like her husband had reached the limit of his endurance, but after a few days he recovered enough strength to remember a world existed beyond himself, and they began to go about the town together.

In the years since Bernadette's visions, Lourdes had become a giant Catholic shrine, the largest place of pilgrimage in France and a hub of spiritual yearning. Perhaps this invigorated the deeply Catholic-minded Werfel; in any case, he was soon visiting the grotto of the Virgin twice a day, and he grew convinced that water from the miraculous spring was having some supernatural healing effect. As life and optimism returned to him, Werfel gave thanks in the best way he knew how: he began to write again, a story about the humble girl who became a saint. He would visit the many Catholic bookshops and browse for hours searching for any material on Bernadette he could find. He was in one such religious souvenir shop, engrossed in reading a pamphlet about the shrine, when he heard his name called out.

Walter Mehring, the poet, and Hertha Pauli, the writer and literary agent, stood before him. He had not seen them since he had left Vienna two years earlier. Given all the circumstances, Werfel could be forgiven for thinking that the meeting was providential.

AFTER THE NAZIS had denounced him as a "cultural Bolshevik" back in 1933, Mehring had managed to escape to Paris. He had in a sense been the voice of radical Berlin, of its nightclubs, where his savagely satirical "violent songs" with their harshly beautiful lyrics had the verbal aim of a sniper. Mehring flung his opposition in the face of the brownshirts, but had lost the fight and was one of the first Hitler expelled. Now he was one of the first on the list of those sought by the German invaders to receive his due punishment, and it looked to Mehring very like the end of a lonely road that had taken him through his days in a succession of dreary domiciles. "Go up the groaning stairs," he wrote,

> And know they too, like you,
> And your peers
> Are doomed to end their years
> In little hotels . . .

Throughout the thirties Mehring had continued to sing his life as a lonely and stateless poet, and had become the unofficial laureate of exile.

After Paris, he had been drawn back by his own language to Vienna. He intended to stay a few brief days, but homesickness transformed that world capital of anti-Semitism into a paradise for him. And he met Hertha Pauli.

When she heard the poet Walter Mehring was in town, she called and left a message identifying herself as a representative of Austrian Correspondence. Mehring failed to return her call because the name sounded suspiciously official. It was a generally sound instinct but wrong in this case, for it was the name of a literary agency Hertha had recently started with a friend. She had telephoned in the hope of signing him as a client, as he found out when they met at a party several days after. In the end she got tiny Walter Mehring lock, stock, and barrel.

On the evening of Friday, March 11, 1938, the radio carried a fateful broadcast by Chancellor Schuschnigg. Mehring had enjoyed a fruitful four years in Vienna. It was true he had felt vulnerable in this nation infested with Nazi enthusiasts and agents, but he had produced some of his finest poetry, and had also been encouraging Hertha with her own writing. Earlier in the day there had been a large Nazi demonstration outside the State Opera House, with its choruses of "Heil Hitler!" but there was a positive feeling that the referendum on Sunday would decide to keep Austria independent, and not merge her with the Reich. Hitler did not want Austria to slip through his fingers due to the mere technicality of a democratic plebiscite. To this end he had sent an ultimatum to Schuschnigg that afternoon: either the referendum would be delayed for a month, or he would face the consequences. Schuschnigg had an hour to decide.

"This day has confronted us with a difficult and critical situation," came the chancellor's voice from the radio. "The federal President has instructed me to inform the Austrian people that we are yielding to force." After he had finished speaking, *Deutschland über Alles* was played. Mehring left his hotel and ran to Hertha's apartment. In the small hours of Monday morning, Carl Frucht, Hertha's partner in the literary agency, went by Mehring's hotel to pick up a suitcase full of clothes for him. But when he arrived he discovered the Gestapo had been there earlier, at two o'clock in the morning, to search for the poet. Obviously the chase was on.

After breakfast they set out for the Westbahnhof station, but when they found it crawling with German soldiers, Mehring panicked. Carl went and bought him a ticket for the Vienna-Zurich-Paris Express, while Hertha tried to calm him down, assuring him that she would soon follow and meet him in Paris. As they were about to put Mehring on the train an SS officer stopped them and demanded identification. Frucht distracted him and Mehring melted into the crowd moving down the platform. He hopped aboard the most distant carriage just as the whistle blew and the train began to pull out. It was a narrow escape, but Mehring was not safe yet.

At the Swiss border everyone was ordered off the train by German border guards, and told to form lines so that one by one their papers could be scrutinized. Beyond, there were two doors, one to the left and one to the right. When Mehring's turn came the guard checked his name against a list, and told him to go through the right-hand door. With the cunning that arises from utter despair, Mehring shuffled slowly toward it, until other passengers who had successfully passed the inspection obscured the guards' view of him. Then he darted with them through the door on the left and got back on the train. None of the people who had gone through "his" door emerged from the customs house. With a loud hiss that echoed his own sigh of relief, the train pulled out and crossed into Switzerland. Ten hours later, Mehring stepped down onto the platform of the Gare de l'Est in Paris. Now there was another little hotel for Mehring, the l'Univers in the Rue Monsieur le Prince, a narrow side street off the Boulevard St. Michel between the Sorbonne and the Luxembourg Gardens. This was the Latin Quarter, which by now housed so many exiles that wits had renamed it the German Quarter.

He had managed to reserve a room on the ground floor for Hertha, who arrived two days later. By now an author in her own right, with two books to her name, she and Mehring both quickly fell into the routine of the exiled writer. They worked in the mornings, and in the afternoons sat at a large table in a corner of the Café de Tournon, opposite the Luxembourg Palace, with a circle of émigré friends. These included some of the most famous names in modern German literature. The novelist Joseph Roth, the group's acknowledged leader, was there; and Ernst Toller, the radical poet and playwright whose work paved the way for Bertolt Brecht; the Czech novelist Ernst Weiss, who was a friend of Franz Werfel, and had been a close friend of Franz Kafka; and Odon von Horvath, a brilliant young avant-garde writer whose play *Tales from the Vienna Woods* had won a top drama award in pre-Nazi Germany. Sometimes Konrad Heiden, Hitler's "unofficial" biographer, turned up; and then, a month after Mehring's arrival, Werfel himself appeared. Around the same time came along a miniature young Viennese cartoonist called Bill Spira, who had renamed himself Bill Freier ("More Free") after his escape from Austria.

Conversation about the world they had all left behind was discouraged. Werfel once asked Roth if he missed Vienna. Roth replied that homesickness was the one imaginary ailment he had never suffered from. The subject was not mentioned again. More important was the exchange of information that could help in the daily struggle of living: which newspapers and magazines paid the best rates for articles; which hotels had the lowest rates for rooms; the tariff of bribes for officials and policemen; likely Nazi agents planted within the exile community; most of all where to obtain and keep updated the many permits and papers the law demanded in order for alien residents to remain legal, or, as the French had it, *en règle.*

This wearisome and circumscribed existence dragged on, always harboring the anxiety about what might happen next. The exiles found themselves in a tantalizing situation. On the one hand they were condemned endlessly to ruminate on their future prospects; on the other weighed the realistic fear that there was no future—that this, or the next day or week, might take them to the end of the line. Even fortune and chance seemed to have become their enemies. In June 1938, Odon von Horvath died in a freakish accident: he was walking back to his hotel through the Pantheon when lightning struck a tree and it snapped, falling on him and breaking his neck. The following year a harrowing double tragedy further thinned the ranks of the exiled writers. The political situation was already doom-laden with the notes of approaching war when news came that Ernst Toller, Mehring's childhood friend and fervent anti-Nazi ally, who had managed to get to America, had hanged himself in his New York hotel room. Next, Joseph Roth, an inveterate daylong consumer of the powerful plum-based alcohol called sliwowitz, collapsed. The attack was not fatal, but the treatment for it was. He was taken to a hospital, and the shock of being deprived of his drink for even a few hours sent him into convulsions, and he was strapped into a straitjacket. He was still wearing it when he died several days later at the age of forty-three. He was the leader of the Café de Tournon group, and without him it soon drifted apart.

War was declared after a few months, and Mehring was interned. The impossible had happened: things had suddenly grown even worse. While protestations at his inexcusable detention were lodged by writers' organizations, Mehring spent his days at the Falaise concentration camp, peeling potatoes by day and trying to sleep in a clump of bodies on a palette of wet straw by night:

> Our sleep, too short to blanket all of us,
> We take by pull and tug; we crowd, we fuss,
> Each one obtrusive on his neighbor's dream;
> Penned like pigs, we grunt, we squeal, we scream . . .

Mehring was released in November, after nearly three months in utter squalor, and he moved back into his old room at the Hotel de l'Univers, next door to a young American woman. He could not now, as an enemy alien, move about too freely on the Paris streets; but his Czech friends Ernst Weiss, from the Tournon crowd, and Hans Natonek, a journalist, could. They visited him frequently and discussed the situation, which Weiss was convinced was now hopeless. Natonek was more upbeat, believing survival a possibility; but this hope ebbed away after the *Blitzkrieg* began in May. Where was there left to run?

It was the optimist Natonek's idea to cable Thomas Mann, who had emigrated to America in 1938, to do something to come to the aid of his colleagues, now helplessly awaiting the coup de grâce from Hitler. Even the fatalistic Weiss was finally persuaded to add his name to the plea, along with Mehring, Natonek, and Hertha Pauli. They soon stopped worrying about what Mann's reply might be, though, when the Germans appeared seemingly overnight at the gates of Paris, and the French government decamped to Tours. Now was no time to think about securing the right permits: they had only hours to spare. Mehring and Hertha Pauli quickly gathered some possessions and squeezed into a car heading south. Natonek took to the same road on foot with some other friends. Ernst Weiss went to his hotel room and poured himself a drink he had prepared weeks earlier. When the poison began to take effect he picked up a knife, and opened the veins of his wrists.

The flight south of Mehring and Hertha Pauli provides another chapter of disaster and disorientation. The car was abandoned for want of gasoline barely beyond the suburbs of Paris, and they were forced to proceed *à pied,* like almost everyone else. But because the roads were so obstructed by millions of displaced French people in a thick soup of slow-moving panic, and such an understandable anti-German bias in the air, Mehring and Hertha decided to leave the endless column of misery and cut across country over field and through woods, sleeping under bushes and in barns, begging food from those they met on the way.

On June 16 they reached Orléans, and in eight days were in the Garonne, only ten miles from Bordeaux, where Mehring wanted to head because it was at least a port, and from there a boat might take them away somewhere, anywhere, away from France.

Hertha disagreed, because she thought that Bordeaux would already be under German control now that the armistice had been signed. She suggested they carry on south, aiming to get to Bayonne, about one hundred miles farther. She won on the flip of a coin, and almost at that very moment a French staff car with two officers pulled up beside them. They arrived in Bayonne two hours later, where they and many other refugees tried frantically and unsuccessfully to board the sole British ship. People were jumping into the harbor and trying to swim out to it, only to be dragged from the water and returned to shore. The ship left with the last British soldiers in the town, and after that, Mehring and Hertha began seriously to consider suicide. At one pharmacy after another they were refused poison without a prescription. Finally they collapsed into chairs at a café. There, somebody told them that the ship had struck a mine outside the harbor, and gone down with all hands. Perhaps an odd sort of luck still clung to them; at any rate, they decided to carry on.

At St. Jean de Luz they discovered the whole Atlantic coast was by the terms of the armistice now part of the German zone, so instead of making for the border at Hendaye, they turned toward the interior, and boarded a bus to Oloron. From there they continued eastward on foot, hoping that they were sufficiently distant from the sea to be in the free zone, but not knowing for sure, since the line of demarcation had not yet been finalized. After several days stumbling through undergrowth and over Pyrénéan foothills to avoid being seen, they spotted a procession. It was a pilgrimage to Lourdes and they eagerly joined it, relieved to walk along the smooth road without arousing suspicion.

They were passing a religious souvenir shop in the town when Hertha spotted a familiar figure inside. "Franz Werfel," she called. Mehring and Werfel had never been the closest of friends, either in Vienna or Paris, but here they greeted each other warmly, as do those who realize their lives are in jeopardy.

They stayed with the Werfels for several days in Lourdes, before deciding to try their luck at Toulouse, where there was an American consulate and the dim prospect of a visa, and perhaps a means of discovering whether Thomas Mann had replied to the cable they had sent him weeks before. Franz and Alma decided to stay where they were; they had had enough of dodging and hiding for the time being, and would wait to move until they were correctly en règle.

The American consulate in Toulouse was closed when they arrived in mid-afternoon, after hitching a ride on a French army truck. Mehring and Hertha wandered over to the inevitable refugee bulletin board at the city hall, where families separated on the flight south left notes, in the hope that their loved ones would read them and get in touch. This time it was Hertha's turn to hear her name called out, and she turned around in the act of pinning their names up to find Hans Natonek standing by her. He had been in Toulouse for twenty-four hours already, and suggested they find a café and eat something. This led to another reunion, for at the first place they tried, they found Konrad Heiden, sitting with the Paris journalist and former feature writer for Lumière, Charles Wolff. Heiden had been interned in a concentration camp in May, when the Germans attacked. On the eve of the surrender, the inmates

were evacuated south, on foot and under guard. He had given his French cap-
tors the slip when a German airplane had attacked the column, and was now
heading for Montauban.

With them was a thin young American woman with her hair done up in
two braids on top of her head. Mehring recognized her as a student of art history at the Sorbonne who had for a time taken the room next to his at the
Hotel de l'Univers. She introduced herself as Miriam Davenport, and said she
was leaving for Marseille in a few days. They pleaded with her to contact the
American organizations there on their behalf when she arrived, and Miriam
promised she would. Then, a week later, Mehring, Hertha Pauli, and Natonek
themselves squeezed aboard a train south to Marseille.

CHAPTER 7

A COLD MECCA

I T WAS HOT MIDDAY when a young soldier cycled into the square of a small village just off the main arterial road southwest of Bordeaux, dismounted, and looked about. The soldier was dark-haired and slender, and although his face was dusty and tired, his eyes were shining and alert. A smell of coffee wafted gently on the still air, and the village was ghostly quiet. He cocked his head, as if listening for something, then walked his bicycle across the street. There he spotted a group of equally young French officers slouching around a table on the terrace of a café. He approached and saluted them. The young soldier was unarmed, a sign that his company had probably been dissolved during the chaotic rout—the *pagaille*—in the face of the German advance. The officers around the table were also unarmed; they held only wineglasses in their hands. The soldier told them in perfect, unaccented French, that he had met some Germans on the road a little to the north. They ordered him to report to a nearby *caserne,* a barracks, to be made a prisoner of war.

"Wait here with us," said one of the officers. "We'll protect you. We consider ourselves prisoners."

The young soldier asked if they had already been made prisoners.

"No, but we consider ourselves prisoners just the same."

He told them there was a misunderstanding. He wanted to know the location of the *caserne* so he could be sure to avoid it. They just shrugged. The soldier declined an offer of wine and saluted the officers. Then remounted his bicycle and continued on his journey to the unoccupied zone. So far, all the way down from the town of Niort, he found French peasants who had sheltered, fed and hid him, and even given him the civilian clothes that were now in his kit bag. They had all refused to take a single centime for their kindness. The attitude of the officers angered him, but did not surprise him.

The soldier's name was Otto Albert Hirschmann, a German, born in Berlin in 1915. He was an enthusiastic francophile from an early age, and attended the French School there. He then left Germany for France, calmly but quickly, after a sequence of events sufficient either to make or break a young man. A few days before his eighteenth birthday, just after Hitler had come to power, his surgeon father had died of cancer. The Third Reich was no longer safe for Hirschmann. This was partly because he was Jewish, but more because he, like many other young Germans, had been active in the Democratic Socialist opposition to the Nazis. He arrived in Paris via Amsterdam, with one change of clothes and a volume of Montaigne's *Essais.* He studied there until 1935, when he spent a year in England at the London School of Economics. After that he traveled to Spain, where he fought on the Republican side for a short time, and was involved in the bitter combat in Aragon, before growing disillusioned with the infighting of the Communists. Late in 1936 he left Spain and joined his sister in Italy. For two years he had lived in Trieste and worked for the underground resistance against Mussolini. Hirschmann would smuggle documents for them across the Italian border into France, and back again, in a false-bottomed suitcase—or rather a false-topped one. He knew the customs officers—*douaniers*—would soon grow wise to a false bottom. So he simply switched. They never thought to look.

In Italy, he found himself impressed by the uncommon, vividly imaginative outlook of the anti-Fascists, including his brother-in-law, the philosopher Eugenio Colorni. They seemed to be an excellent model for Hirschmann's germinating ideas on the subject of the "democratic personality." Colorni and his friends did not pretend to have all the answers, or indeed any; they seemed to know only doubt, but somehow thrived on it. There was no set of imprisoning ideas, no overarching ideology needed to lend them the courage to act. "It was almost as though they set out to prove Hamlet wrong," Hirschmann later wrote. "They were intent on showing that doubt could *motivate* action instead of undermining and enervating it." They were cool under pressure and creative in their opposition to dictatorship. "Moreover, engagement in highly risky action was seen by them not at all as a price to be paid for the freedom of inquiry they were practicing; it was its natural, spontaneous, almost joyful counterpart." Despite Hirschmann's natural *Berolina* irony, this spirit—like a renewed surge of Renaissance *sprezzatura*—affected him deeply. It seemed like the basis of what he called "truly democratic politics." When the anti-Jewish laws of 1938 forced him to leave Italy, Hirschmann returned to Paris; when war on Germany was declared in 1939, he joined the French army.

His company, stationed at Sablé on the Sarthe River, southwest of Le Mans, was made up mostly of foreign volunteers, with some masons and shopkeepers from the Midi. Hirschmann had soon seen enough incompetence in the senior ranks to convince him that there would be disaster when the Germans attacked, as they were bound to do. One captain, for example, was a racist oaf. He read *Action Française* and *Gringoire,* extreme right-wing, crypto-Fascist French newspapers. He also made life miserable for his troops, but this was a common experience in an army riven with class antagonism and defeatist attitudes among its officers. Ordinary soldiers were often beaten down by contempt and injustice. "Vous considerez donc toujours la France," this captain, a colonial, said one day, "comme une vache laitière" ("So, you still think of France as a cow you can milk, eh?"). It was a grievous insult, especially to the Italians in the company, who had given up their country and left behind their families to fight for democracy. "Vous n'avez jamais fait autre chose et vous voulez continuer à sucer aux mamelles de la France," he went on ("All you've ever done and all you want to do is suck on the tits of France"). His outburst plunged the men into a nearly mutinous mood; after that morale was always low, said Hirschmann.

There were other disturbing incidents, as well. One day, his platoon was detailed to guard a train of cattle cars filled with Belgian "fifth columnists," spies caught attempting to subvert the war effort against Germany. But when the soldiers slid open the doors, they found not Nazis but cowering Polish Jews, terrified refugees who had been rounded up by the French and clapped in these foul, unsanitary conditions for three days. The soldiers—some Jewish themselves—were assigned to other duties when they tried to point out to their senior officers that a serious mistake must have been made.

The ordinary soldiers hardly ever received their rations of meat, cigarettes, or wine. Instead, these were delivered to the mess, which was reserved for the officers, and where proper cooks prepared lavish meals. ("Va, ce n'est pas perdu pour tout le monde," the soldiers would say: "Well, you can be sure somebody got it, at least.") Hirschmann and his comrades ate meals cooked by "shoemakers and blacksmiths," with whatever food was left over. They knew the officers were corrupt and hypocritical, and one particular occasion seemed to sum up everything perfectly.

The kitchen detail in the ordinary soldiers' quarters was cleaning out a large copper vessel, and it was brimful with dirty, soapy water. Suddenly, unannounced, a full general appeared in the doorway. He had stopped by to confirm the high standards of rations the soldiers were eating, and intended to do so by sampling them himself. Daringly, they handed him a ladle full of the tepid greasy muck from the pot, and he tasted it. After a few seconds, the general announced, "La soupe est excellente." Then he smacked his lips ostentatiously: *"Mais ex-cel-lente!"*

When they went into battle against the Germans in May, every French soldier was ordered to wear a heavy overcoat despite the warmth of the weather. "Faut pas chercher à comprendre," said the men ("There's no use trying to understand")—a phrase used by them so often it had been abbreviated to "f.p.c.a.c." But there was a reason behind this madness: the French army had suffered terribly from the cold on the retreat from Moscow under Napoleon, and they weren't going to get caught out like that again. One might laugh at the tendency of the generals always to be prepared only for old battles and not new ones, said Hirschmann, but he knew something more sinister was happening, as well. During the *Blitzkrieg,* he had witnessed too many French officers fleeing in high-powered cars, leaving their troops behind; he had seen too many wrong bridges blown up while the right ones were left intact for the Germans, to believe otherwise. The fifth columnists hadn't been the wretched people in the cattle cars, that was for sure, he said.

When the battle for France was all but lost, Hirschmann had managed to convince a sympathetic and understanding officer to issue him a new military pass under a false name. Otherwise, if he was captured by the Germans and they discovered his true identity, he would be shot as a deserter. The lieutenant agreed, and stamped it to certify the original identity papers had been "lost during the campaign." "Sauve qui peut, faut se débrouiller," said the officer: "Save yourself, look out for number one." ("Se débrouiller" would be a verb in great use under the occupation, giving rise to a whole range of outlook and behavior called "Le Système D.")

Hirschmann took the name Albert Hermant, after a French writer whose name resembled his own, and chose to have been born in the American city of Philadelphia on February 11, 1915. He supposed that would make it harder for the authorities—French or German— to check up on him through birth registers. It might even afford him, as an "American" by birth, a little extra protection. He buried his real identity papers in a coffee can, found himself a bicycle, and set off for "Vichy" France. He was on his way there when he met the young officers at the café, and didn't think of trying to persuade them out of their lethargy. They had never wanted to fight in the first place, and would rather cast themselves on the mercy of the Germans. So be it: Otto Hirschmann had done all he could to save France from the Germans; now it was time for Albert Hermant to look after himself.

He badly needed civilian papers, so, after being formally discharged from the army at a nearby military camp, Hermant traveled to Nîmes. It was there that Dr. and Madame Cabouat, the parents of his friend Jean-Pierre, lived. These were the only French people he knew outside Paris, and luckily they were at home when Hermant arrived and introduced himself in his new identity. They agreed to be witnesses for him at the local *mairie,* and Madame Cabouat swore that despite not having a birth certificate, the handsome young soldier was indeed who he said he was. That was good enough for the mayor, who exchanged the military pass for a civilian one. With a slight variation of Cartesian logic he confirmed Otto Albert Hirschmann's disappearance with the phrase, "We certify that Monsieur Albert Hermant is alive because he appeared before us today." Hermant had his priceless *carte d'identité;* he was now a Frenchman. It was lucky he could speak the language without an accent. In Italian and English, he sounded as German as they come. Hermant found a job at the local museum, but paleontology quickly bored him and a few weeks later he decided to leave Nîmes. Hermant had heard there was interesting work to be done in the port city of Marseille.

LISA SAW LOTTE running up the path; it was clear from her eagerness that she had been successful. Inside the barracks they huddled round to look at the purloined pile of white forms, valuable as gold dust. They were release certificates, and at the bottom it said "Le Commandant du Camp du Gurs"; only his signature was missing, but they would soon fix that. It wouldn't be foolproof, but it might just get them past the guards at the gate.

A few nights later there was panic and chaos among the concentration camp authorities; the organization was falling apart. The Commissioner of Police had been drunk for a week solid. Now he was a quivering jelly of fear as the rumors grew more urgent: they might just be *bobards,* piles of bullshit, but they might be true. It was said the German tanks were only hours away, and Lisa decided they should make their move. Over the years she had developed a sixth sense for knowing when to clear out of a place, and now the time was right. To wait one day more could be too long. About sixty of the women, each clutching a release certificate, made their way to the guardhouse. The first ones went through, then more, in twos and threes. She saw Marta, the wife of novelist Lion Feuchtwanger, escape through a hole in the barbed-wire fence. The guards were hardly checking the papers any more when Lisa sauntered past them. She had only been walking along the road for a few minutes when a car stopped and a French officer said, "It's okay. Get in."

When war was declared in September 1939, red placards had suddenly appeared all over Paris. Enemy aliens, they said, were to report for imprisonment in concentration camps. That meant all Germans, émigrés as well, not just the *Reichsdeutschen* who were caught by chance on business or vacation in France when the border was closed. It didn't matter that the émigrés might be Austrian or Czech, anti-Fascists or Jews—most probably Jews. Any male citizen of Hitler's Reich was now the enemy and had to be interned. Over the winter, some—usually the famous names and the rich—were released. Lisa's husband, Hans, volunteered for the French Foreign Legion as a way out of the terrible camp he had been thrown into. Some doctor friends fixed him a potion that made his breath sound like a death rattle and made sure he failed the medical. By this means he was issued a sickness certificate and released. He returned to Paris, and somehow Lisa and he managed to survive until the spring, scraping some food together and keeping quiet so their German accents would not be noticed.

But in May, when Hitler attacked, the red placards went up again. This time even the women were to be sent away in the shuttered railcars to destinations unknown. Lisa and her friend, Paulette, made a forlorn and almost poetic list of essentials they should each take:

> *Toothbrush*
> *A pot with a handle, a spoon*
> *Lipstick*
> *Razor blades (in case there was no other way out)*

Hans was taken away again, and Lisa was herded with thousands of other women into the Vélodrome d'Hiver, the big indoor cycle track, where they were kept for a week under the huge glass roof. When German planes overflew Paris, the antiaircraft flak sometimes came down, smashing into the crystal ceiling. The screams were deafening, and there were rumors of horrible injuries from falling shards of glass. Then came the train ride south, three days long, and the French threw stones whenever they stopped at a station.

They arrived at Gurs on May 25. It was a huge, flat barbed-wire enclosure on a muddy plain at the foot of the Pyrenees. Gurs had been hastily erected in 1939, after the Republican defeat in Spain, when hundreds of thousands of bedraggled soldiers fled across the mountains into France to escape the Fascists. When they arrived there was nothing, and the prisoners themselves had slowly hammered together the huts and other buildings, to protect them from the raking winds that swept down from the mountains in winter. No coats or blankets were handed out, and their clothes were soon rags.

Malnourished men froze to death in their sleep, here, a few miles away from Bordeaux. Even now the camp remained unsanitary and unpaved, and the rains turned the clay soil to freezing mud that reached over the ankles. Gurs was already overcrowded, and it was said that when Paris called the commandant in May 1940, telling him to expect 10,000 females, a dull thud was heard on the line—he had fainted away. On the first day they arrived, all the pregnant women among them spontaneously aborted. They lived on hard chickpeas in a thin gruel, and soon people were dying from dysentery. Lisa concentrated on surviving and looking for a way out. After a few weeks there were rumors the Germans had reached Paris, then that they were heading south. They would be coming for her soon; they always did. She wasn't going to wait for the French to hand her over. And she had to find Hans.

IN THE OLD DAYS Hitler was always a sick joke to Lisa Eckstein; Goebbels was "Joey the Crip," or "Wotan's Mickey Mouse." But after January 1933 it wasn't funny anymore. At the bank where she worked they knew Lisa was a Jew, and the kidding soon grew unbearable. One afternoon she walked out and never returned. After the Reichstag fire the Socialists began to be rounded up, and beaten to death, at places like the *Storm 33* headquarters on Berlin's Hedemann Strasse. If someone emerged alive it was only to serve as a terrible warning to others of worse to come. If you escaped the storm troopers there was the census. The order went out to be at your official address on a certain day. Then, squads of brownshirts would go from apartment block to apartment block with their pads and pencils. They knew who they were looking for. You could sit on a park bench for only so long before you were noticed.

Lisa was lucky. A friend of a friend knew an old lady who ran a candy shop on Gubener Strasse with a tiny living quarters in back. There was a door that opened onto the stairwell so you could enter and leave through the *Hinter-haüser,* the smaller apartments opening onto the courtyard, slipping onto the street without being noticed. She had told the police in her Berlin suburb of Kreuzberg she was leaving the city, and her name was removed from the residents' register. This meant Lisa was an "illegal," but it was safer than awaiting arrest for her record of anti-Nazi demonstrations. Lisa typed away quietly on her pamphlets and made sure to flush the toilet only once a day. Soon enough, though, the widow ordered her to leave. It was too dangerous, she said; the neighbors knew someone was there. At that point Lisa knew she had to leave not only the apartment but also Germany.

In Prague, to where she escaped, the émigrés slept five to a room and the refugee relief kitchens didn't provide enough calories in the soup, so she soon lost weight. The Jewish Committee wouldn't help Lisa because they said she was a "political." That's true enough, she replied, and why aren't you? Lisa always talked back. There exists a photograph of her from 1928, when she was nineteen years old. She looks cool and rebellious, wearing a beret, with a cigarette glued to her mouth. Her flashing black eyes dominate a soft-sharp face, actually quite beautiful. One exiled Berliner told Lisa he recognized her by her legs.

She had to register with the Czech police now, but they refused to speak German. People told her to ask them, "Parlez-vous français?" and *then* they would speak German as long as they thought you weren't one. It was the first time Lisa really felt on the run, but she found lots of company in the émigré community and met Hans from Berlin-Spandau, who was wanted for murder back home. He hadn't done it, but he had written an article for a newspaper, *Die Aktion,* and when a brownshirt was shot in the back (by his own comrades) some days later, Hans was blamed as the "intellectual author" of the crime. This was not uncommon; the famous photographer Philippe Halsmann had been similarly accused. It was one of those new laws that came out of the Nazi "realignment" of Germany, the *Gleichschaltung.* Hans Fittko was a tough one, "level-headed and always calm," she said, and he balanced out Lisa's fierceness with his analytical approach. In an old, torn fragment of photograph it is easy to see from a single glance what Hans was like: a defiant "come and get me" smile, narrowed eyes scanning the horizon, hair swept back as if in his own slipstream. They set up a counterpropaganda network, and Lisa Eckstein soon became Lisa Fittko.

Then the Gestapo found out through an informer where Hans was hiding, and they had to leave Czechoslovakia quickly to avoid his extradition. But the young couple never thought about giving up. Lisa and Hans simply continued to send their anti-Nazi literature into Germany from Switzerland instead. In Basle they lived on false passports, and Hans became "Stephan." If you were caught as an illegal, the Swiss sent you to France; then the French sent you back over the border after a spell in jail; then the Swiss deported you to Germany, and you were as good as dead. Sometimes, if they knew where a target lived, the Gestapo slipped in with a fast car and grabbed him just like that. "Stephan" grew a heavy mustache, and the Fittkos relentlessly kept up and even expanded their anti-Nazi resistance work. In the end they had a band of sympathetic truckers smuggling bales of pamphlets and posters into Germany, and smuggling back out everything from intelligence reports to munitions blueprints. But the human losses mounted, and the Gestapo eventually drew a bead on "Stephan." The Fittkos were forded to flee once more.

In Holland the gamble was even worse, for the police handed suspects straight to the Nazis. In a continent ruled by fear, appeasement of Hitler was the norm, and anti-Nazis were looked at by the countries bordering Germany as dangerous troublemakers. But the Fittkos' struggle to print newspapers and get them into Germany went on from Holland, too, until some contacts were caught over the border by the Gestapo, and the net began rapidly to close on them again. All through the thirties they shifted from one place to another, implacable enemies of Hitler, hunted fugitives. But the experience made Hans and Lisa strong and resourceful. They couldn't afford to make mistakes, and they developed a sense of impending danger that kept them one step ahead of capture. France, the ultimate destination on the list of free countries, was finally reached. But Paris was awash by now with stateless Germans, and French patience was wearing thin. Here, Lisa and Hans could do nothing but try to earn money for bread, and await Hitler's next move. Then war broke out, and the red placards went up. In the eyes of the French, the Fittkos were now themselves the very enemy they had fought against for seven years.

Lisa heard about Article Nineteen of the Armistice agreement, the "surrender on demand" clause, on her way to Lourdes, after the escape from the concentration camp. Vichy France wasn't safe for any German now, and she still had to find Hans. Lisa kept a notebook with her, in which she listed the names of all the refugees she met, and where she had met them. This meant that each day, and little by little, her network of incoming and outgoing information grew. Eventually a message on another branch of the "refugee telegraph"—relayed secondhand from her brother, as chance would have it—told her that Hans had been seen heading south to Montauban on a bicycle. Other émigrés on their way through confirmed the sighting, and Lisa wrote to some addresses they gave her. At last, a telegram arrived: "J'ATTEND LISE A MOUNTAUBAN." He was waiting for her there, and Lisa set out to find him straight away. The bus ride took forever, and she was exhausted when she arrived in Montauban late in the afternoon. Lisa found Hans waiting in the garden of an émigré safe house on the lookout for her. He had been standing there since dawn.

Hans told Lisa how Luftwaffe airplanes had been shooting down fleeing French civilians, claiming they were "illegal troop movements." She told him about Article Nineteen and what it meant for them. Luckily, Hans had been issued a military pass when he was released from his concentration camp as the Germans approached. If he had it warranted at a demobilization center, he would be given a travel permit to take him south. Lisa had miraculously managed to get a sympathetic official to stamp her release certificate when she passed through Lourdes, so they would have a good chance to get away together. They walked to a building packed with soldiers in the center of town. Officers sat at tables, processing the defeated men into civilian life. Hans stood in line for a long while, and eventually came away with the precious travel permit. He walked up to Lisa and showed her the *Route de Marche.* They looked at the officer's handwriting.

The words said, "Destination: Marseille."

IT WAS one o'clock in the morning, and the hospital ward was quiet and still. The only light sources came from beyond the small round frosted windows of the ward's double doors, and from an attendant's desk lamp. Within its glow, the shapes of sleeping figures could be made out in the beds lining the walls. They were British prisoners of war, and the Germans had placed them under French guard. Being wounded, though, they weren't very mobile, and now that Paris was occupied there was no place for them to run. So the guard was less rigid than it could have been; no self-respecting Nazi, after all, would be checking up at this hour of the morning.

Or so the guards thought. Suddenly there was a clump of boots in the corridor and the sound of a harsh German voice barking out orders. The sleepy French guards outside the ward snapped clumsily to attention, then the doors burst open on the slumbering British wounded.

"Raus!" came the shrieking command. Two tall German officers in greatcoats stood in the middle of the ward. "Everybody must get up. Quickly!" They were soon supervising the transfer of the British by frightened French nurses to a waiting ambulance, whose motor was already running. "Schnell!" barked the Germans. As the British limped down the corridor and out into the balmy night air, they exchanged surreptitious glances with each other. Was this it? they wondered. They had heard stories about prisoners of war being too much trouble for the Germans to take care of, of men being herded into barns and grenades thrown in. They were handed up one by one into the back of the vehicle. The vocal German officer "Heil Hitlered" at the guards and ordered them back inside. Then he climbed into the driver's seat. The quiet one wedged himself in back with the British prisoners.

Soon the wagon was speeding way from Paris. The German sitting with the soldiers took off his cap and ran a hand through his hair. There was a wide smile on his face.

"Gentlemen," he said, "consider yourselves liberated."

"You're a Yank," said one of the British.

"Never," came the soft, southern burr, "confuse a Virginian with a Yankee."

The American was twenty-one year-old Charles Fernley Fawcett. He was born in Virginia but was orphaned at the age of seven, and actually grew up with relatives in Greenville, South Carolina. Charlie had been traveling in Europe for some time, earning his living as a professional wrestler, and had escaped to Paris from Poland just before the Germans attacked in September 1939. He had attempted and failed to join the Polish army, and his rejection had probably saved his life. The French had not allowed him to join their army either, so he had enlisted Hemingway-style in the Section Volontaire des Américains—the ambulance corps.

There he met another American volunteer, William Holland, the man in front with his foot on the gas. Holland's mother was German, one of the aristocratic Stülpnagels. By chance one of his relatives, General Otto von Stülpnagel, had just been appointed as *Militärbefehlshaber*—Commander in Chief—of the new occupied zone of France. Through Bill's introductions to senior German officers, Charlie had already managed to supply important information to French underground fighters. Then Bill had told him of some wounded British prisoners under light guard in a nearby Paris clinic.

Charlie had been on the road for six years now, since he left Greenville nurturing an almost suicidal despair. A thirty-five-year-old society belle had finished the passionate affair they had kept up from when he was fifteen years old. Charlie had grown recklessly jealous of her powerful husband, and, fearing the consequences for both of them if this man discovered her unfaithfulness, the woman had left town and simply disappeared. Charlie's friends could not reason with him, and he left to crew out on a merchant boat to the Far East via the Panama Canal and San Francisco, keeping himself away from the guardrail in case his despair overwhelmed him and he jumped.

He spent time traveling through Hong Kong, Singapore, and the Philippines as a sailor on tramp steamers, before returning to the United States and a series of unlikely and eccentric jobs. He learned jazz trumpet and took a lesson from Louis Armstrong ("You take the horn *thusly,* put it to your mouth *thusly*—and blow, man, blow!"), and used his muscular physique to earn extra money: first from modeling for life classes, then from wrestling. The wrestling paid well, and after fighting the Australian middleweight champion, "Rough House" Nelson, to a draw, he found a Polish contact in one Count de Rosen. Soon, Charlie was fighting all over central Europe against opponents like "The Cross-eyed Cossack," despite the tuberculosis that had dogged him intermittently since he was a child. It was an interesting life for an open-hearted teenager, and his aristocratic contacts put him in the way of many elegant and obliging upper-class women. With them, Charlie was at least able to distract himself from his romantic melancholia.

Charlie was an aristocrat himself, one of the last real southern gentlemen. His family had been among the earliest settlers in Virginia, and his ancestors included Madisons, Randolphs, Bollings, Rolfs, and three presidents of the United States. His mother, Harriet Randolph Madison, had been a society beauty painted by John Singer Sargent; his father was a descendant of Lord Fernley. But one would never learn this from Charlie. His gentle speech, his feel for the underdog, and his politeness to all merely hinted at something uncommon. He was also a crazy, mixed-up kid with a secret, lovesick need to place himself in danger. So far, at least, it seemed the gods had taken pity on him. He had avoided disaster.

The ambulance now charged south through the night toward Vichy, France, and stopped only when it ran out of gasoline near a train station. Charlie struck a deal with one of the railway workers. The vehicle wasn't, strictly speaking, his to barter, but it was agreed that his passengers could board a freight train if Charlie handed it over. They duly clambered into a boxcar, and the journey toward freedom continued.

When Charlie and his band of wounded soldiers arrived at their destination the next morning, the lofty concourse of the Gare St. Charles was already bustling with people—many of them obviously nervous refugees. But he could see the police making arrests as newly arrived foreigners attempted to leave through the station's main entrance. Everybody's papers were being checked, and if they were not *en règle,* they were taken away and interned. Alas, it looked like it was impossible to maneuver the British past this last obstacle; Charlie's reckless luck had just run out.

Suddenly, he was aware of a waiter shouting angrily at him. "Jean, you stupid dope, I'm over here!" he said, grabbing Charlie's arm. The waiter made a big scene of welcoming his "brother" to town, and led him through the station restaurant and into the kitchen. There, at the back, was a connecting corridor to the Hotel Terminus, and an unguarded door that opened directly onto the street. In short order, limping British soldiers passed through the restaurant kitchen ("This way, gentlemen," Charlie ushered them along. "Single file please, there's people tryin' to cook.") and found themselves, one by one, on the broad stairway leading down to the sun-kissed Boulevard d'Athènes, in the middle of Marseille.

Charlie hijacked a truck and loaded the soldiers on board. Then they drove into the suburbs, where a dear friend of his from Paris was staying at her chateau. The Countess Lily Pastré was overjoyed when she saw him. "We'll have to do something about this," she said when she saw the British soldiers packed like sardines in the back of the vehicle. Over the following days and weeks, the British were dispersed around the area to the residences of her rich friends, while arrangements were made to spirit them out of the country and back to England.

THIS WAS the Old World, and Fry instantly felt it as the boat-plane ploughed smoothly to a halt in the island's harbor to take on fuel. He looked up toward the densely wooded, dark green hills above the town, and recognized the old whitewashed houses poking through. He saw erotic flashes of azaleas in the sun; and he remembered the last time he had put in at the Azores twelve years earlier, when he was still almost a boy and Europe was that shimmering unreal world where, for an American, the present drops below the horizon and the eternal past is revealed.

During the flight, Fry had given up trying to memorize the lists of names. After converting them into primitive code and succeeding only in confusing himself, he simply decided to chance taking the list over the borders intact. The many small worries he had in New York naturally evaporated as the event of arrival drew near; only the larger anxiety concerning himself remained. He was traveling, in the Pullman carriage-sized cramp of the aircraft ("I should not choose flying as the pleasantest way of crossing the Atlantic. . . . No deck to promenade on. No games to play. Nothing to do but stare out the windows . . ."), with a Rockefeller Foundation doctor, Alexander Makinsky, on his way to the Unitarian Mission in Lisbon. In Europe such dignitaries normally passed through customs with respectful ease, and Fry would make himself appear to be with him.

He took the risk and it worked; in fact the Portuguese customs officers had been a model of polite disinterest. Fry cleared the arrivals hangar and stepped out into the almost African heat and bustle, and expatriate social whirl, of Lisbon in the early days of the war. The giddiness in which he was swept up as a minor celebrity was the subject of his first letter to Eileen written on European soil. "I have been smothered in kindness," reported Fry,

> . . . and too busy to sleep. Portugal is full of notables, with many of whom I have struck up fast friendships—they come flocking to me at all hours of the day and night—and there has been a great deal to do also in preparation for my trip to France. Besides having a great many people to see and a great many reports to write, I have had to go through the endless formulas of European politeness, the excessive handshaking, the ceremony of the sidewalk cafe, the drive *en voiture pour voir la mer,* the *petite visite* etc., etc. All very exhausting, but none of it boring. The hotels are jammed, and business is booming. Everybody from the Archduke Otto down has passed through Lisbon in the past few months. . . . Living in Lisbon is ever so slightly like living in

Provincetown, at least one sees many familiar faces, and the names are mostly Olivas and Silvas. . . . There are all sorts of street cries, gotten off mostly by peasant women who carry their wares in baskets perched precariously on their heads (I say precariously, but I've never seen one fall). . . . But it isn't merely the street calls: it is also the bustle of an eastern bazaar—the life is terrific. Yet pleasant. It takes three quarters of an hour to change a travellers check. And yet one doesn't mind. I don't know why. One just doesn't. . . .

It is now five o'clock in the morning. I have been up all night, typing reports and letters and packing my bags. At half past five my bus leaves for the airfield, and at seven we take off for Madrid and Barcelona. I wish myself *bonne chance*. It's a Spanish plane!

Portugal was a neutral country, separated from the main European theater of war by being at the western edge of the Iberian Peninsula, buffered from shell-shocked France by the vast barren expanse of Spain. The mostly benign authoritarianism of Portugal's government welcomed the brief transfer to its own shores of the Mediterranean's traditional playgrounds. The "rich Europeans" were enjoying themselves while making arrangements to decamp further afield, to the Americas, north and south. After them there would begin to arrive another, more ragged and less welcome migration of haunted-looking people with tattered cardboard valises and dubious papers; and they would be shadowed by the "green fedoras," the plainclothesmen of the Gestapo. The streets of Lisbon would then become a place of terror, of disappearance and murder in narrow alleyways.

During the time he stayed at the Metropole Hotel, Fry kept busy making contacts and reconnoitering the aid situation. At the Unitarian Mission he met a very useful collaborator, the Reverend Waitstill Sharp, and quickly got to know personnel at the Quaker Mission, the YMCA, the American Jewish Joint Distribution Committee (JDC), and various other refugee relief agencies. He also met the sister of Franz Werfel, who confided that her brother and his wife were staying at Marseille, at the Hotel du Louvre et de la Paix.

Varian Fry found himself in a strange situation. He felt half on vacation, and half plunged deep in an enterprise that was too large and inchoate for him to grasp, but for which he alone had the responsibility of design and function. He simply did not know, beyond a vague notion of meeting some "names" in the flesh and giving them a little money and advice, what he was going to do. It was almost like work, but not quite: the carnival atmosphere of Lisbon, the heat, the eccentric glamour of European high society, the seductive confusion of African color and sound, all worked their magic on Fry's brain. It was difficult to imagine that a war lurked so close by, and that in a matter of hours he would be in it.

The train from Barcelona north along the Costa Brava to the Spanish border with France changed that somewhat. The civil war had been over for less than two years, and the already impoverished Catalan province, resolutely Republican, had been blasted almost into oblivion. There was less food here, and he saw a worn-down, stoical people, standing like milestones amid the twisted wreckage of Fascist victory. Fry's train, the ill-termed "Expresso," halting frequently at ruined little stations, steamed slowly through the charred and leveled moonscape, until it arrived at the border village of Port-Bou. Ahead lay France.

CHAPTER 8

PAGAILLE

MARTA FEUCHTWANGER KNEW the papers Lisa Fittko had given her would not have fooled the guards, so she dove through the barbed-wire fence of the Gurs concentration camp because she could not take the chance of being turned back. Her forged release papers, through some mix-up, claimed she was almost seventy, but Marta was only forty-nine years old. Her striking patrician face, with its sculpted cheekbones and black hair tied back, in fact made her look ten years younger. Hers was a face on which a policeman's gaze always lingered, a face incapable of conveying either compliance or fear, and so an irksome sight to petty authority. Once through the barbed wire, Marta began her search for her husband, whom she had heard was in St. Nicolas concentration camp just outside Nîmes, and by some miracle she made it there without being arrested.

St. Nicolas was a curious combination of vacation resort and death camp. It seemed set down in paradise, on a verdant Provençal hillside, full of the music of cicadas and birdsong. The gates to the camp were open, and inmates were free to come and go in the surrounding country, to forage in the woods for food, and to swim in the nearby stream. But there was no food to be found, and nowhere to escape to. Inside the compound there were no barracks, only rows of tents, and not even the rudimentary sanitation that the women's camp at Gurs had provided. The image of leisured bliss faded as one approached the camp and smelled the terrible ammoniac stink of impacted sewage, and saw the emaciated figures staring listlessly from behind the barbed wire. The French were allowing the inmates slowly to starve and were hastening the process by letting dysentery rule the camp, and typhus wait in the wings.

Marta simply walked past the guards into the compound and asked the first group of prisoners she saw where Lion Feuchtwanger was. One of them went to look for him, and soon a frail, white-haired man with a beak nose emerged from a tent. He was so malnourished that Marta blinked a few times before she managed to place him: it was Max Ernst, the famous Surrealist painter. He took her into the tent where Lion lay on the floor, almost dead from dysentery and starvation. The inmates, and one in particular named Dr. Leckich, had been nursing him around the clock. Feuchtwanger claimed he was over the worst of his illness, but he refused to leave with Marta. Without papers, one would merely be arrested again before long, and reinterned, quite probably in an even worse place. Fatalism alone, which was Feuchtwanger's lifeblood, would keep him at St. Nicolas until a realistic plan emerged—if it ever did.

Twelve years earlier it had been Heinrich Mann's letters to him that eventually persuaded Feuchtwanger to move from Munich, where he and Marta had settled after the First World War, to Berlin. Anti-Semitism was less prevalent in the German capital than in Bavaria, birthplace of Nazism. In Schwabing, the "artistic" suburb of Munich where the Feuchtwangers had settled, their friends included Bertolt Brecht, Lion's protégé. But he had recently left for Berlin. Thomas Mann lived across the street, but he kept to himself. So the Feuchtwangers moved, and joined the Berlin circle that included Werfel and Mehring, expatriate writers such as W. H. Auden, Christopher Isherwood, and Arthur Koestler, performers like the dancer Josephine Baker, and above all the phenomenon called jazz, whose rhythms the city was jumping to in its myriad vibrant nightclubs.

When Feuchtwanger arrived in 1928, Brecht had just enjoyed an enormous success with *The Threepenny Opera,* and Feuchtwanger himself soon began to be noticed in Berlin thanks to the series of satirical ballads about America that he published in the newspaper the *Berliner Tageblatt* under the pseudonym of J. L. Wetcheek—an English translation of *feucht* (wet) and *wange* (cheek). He had been inspired by his good friend, the American writer Sinclair Lewis, whose novel *Babbitt* was very popular at the time. Feuchtwanger himself soon published a new novel, *Success.* That year, 1930, he was widely tipped to receive the Nobel Prize for literature. When it was awarded instead to Sinclair Lewis, the American humbly announced in his acceptance speech that the prize should have gone to Feuchtwanger.

Success outraged the Nazis, who were by this time beginning to be a central force in German politics: a spirit of gloom was spreading among the German intellectuals well before Hitler became chancellor. In an interview with a Hamburg newspaper the same year, Feuchtwanger replied to a question about his future plans with the uncompromising statement, "I already see myself as an exile." As if to demonstrate this, he undertook a triumphant lecture tour of the United States at the end of 1932, where he met Charlie Chaplin and Eleanor Roosevelt, among others. The friendship he struck up with her would nearly a decade later set in train a series of events that would save Feuchtwanger's life.

In Washington, the German ambassador, Count von Prittwitz, gave a large banquet for the writer. Asked repeatedly what Hitler would do if he gained power in German, Feuchtwanger once again gave a stark answer. "FEUCHT-WANGER SAYS HITLER MEANS WAR" was the headline splashed across American newspapers the following day, January 30, 1933, and Feuchtwanger was awoke from slumber that morning by von Prittwitz telephoning him with the news that Hitler had just become chancellor. He hadn't supposed when he set out on his tour that he would never see Germany again.

Luckily, Marta was on a skiing holiday at the Austrian resort of Sankt Anton, and Feuchtwanger joined her there in her room at the top of a guest house. They soon moved out, though, in disgust at the jubilation over Hitler's election victory emanating from the room below, where the young filmmaker Leni Riefenstahl was staying. Brecht arrived and told them Heinrich Mann had managed to escape to France, and soon after, a news bulletin announced that both Mann and Feuchtwanger had been deprived of their German nationality. For them the siege of exile had begun.

"Hitler can always take away my citizenship," said Feuchtwanger, "but he can't take away my Bavarian accent." His defiance was tempered by fear of the Gestapo, whose tentacles were already reaching over the border into Austria. In the late summer the Feuchtwangers moved to a place of greater safety, a little village near Bandol called Sanary-sur-Mer, not far from Heinrich Mann in Nice, on the French Riviera. They found a primitive house, out on a promontory and surrounded by brush. There was a fireplace for a kitchen, a good big terrace along the front of the building, and some rudimentary furniture provided by the landlord. At the end of 1933 they moved to a larger residence where Feuchtwanger, who had wisely transferred his royalties to Paris, began to build up a library to replace the one the Nazis had destroyed when they raided his house in Berlin. He also began to stock a fairly serious wine cellar that soon became his pride and joy. Both Mann brothers were visitors, and Thomas was so taken with Sanary that he decided to move there, and stayed five years until he left for the United States.

Feuchtwanger worked steadily and well, and besides essays and short stories, he completed five novels at Sanary: he even rewrote from memory *The Jew of Rome,* the manuscript of which had been left behind in Berlin. The Feuchtwangers were comfortable, and Lion was comfortably one of the world's most popular writers. It was a process which had begun with his 1925 novel about a Jew in the seventeenth-century court of a German king (Goebbels travestied the narrative by filming a vicious, anti-Semitic version of it). In the wake of the success of *Jud Süss,* Feuchtwanger was invited to London to give a series of radio talks on the BBC, and he met the prime minister, Ramsay Macdonald, who came to his hotel. He was taken up by H. G. Wells, John Galsworthy, and George Bernard Shaw. The world, it seemed, was at his feet. But later in his career he nearly threw away his popularity with the public and fellow writers alike, when he accepted Stalin's invitation to visit Moscow. On his return Feuchtwanger wrote a book, *Moscow 1937,* which was derided as shallow propaganda by everyone outside the Communist Party. "In the Western civilization there is no longer clarity or resolution," he wrote, at the height of the Stalinist terror. "One breathes again when one comes from this oppressive atmosphere of a counterfeit democracy of hypocritical humanism into the invigorating atmosphere of the Soviet Union."

He had an ego, there was no denying it. To him, Stalin was a genial man who obeyed when Feuchtwanger asked him to put out his pipe. He failed to realize the contempt in which the Soviet leader held him and every other artist in the world; he failed to notice the murderous purges and deliberate starvation practiced on the Soviet peoples; and he failed to notice that he was being used as a propaganda tool to divert attention from the show trials. Perhaps he was unworldly: Henrich Mann, a more political player, had refused the same invitation, just like Brecht, who was more left-wing than both of them. Werfel delivered his condemnatory speech at the PEN congress, and Goebbels took the opportunity to make a broadcast in which he declared, "Now the German people must finally rid themselves of the idea that Feuchtwanger is one of the best German writers." For a time he almost eclipsed the kudos of his anti-Nazi credentials without realizing that in France, at least, the Communists were even more unpopular than Hitler.

When war was declared the Feuchtwangers were subject to the same harassment and intimidation from the local police as the Werfels. Its flavor was sharper in the case of the Feuchtwangers, perhaps due to the actions of a former Soviet agent. It was rumored (probably by his former Stalinist colleagues) that Willi Muenzenberg was expelled from the Communist Party when Stalin grew weary of his lavish expenditure of the funds sent to him from Moscow. In need of a new way to earn a living, he began to denounce people as Communists or as anything else that was suitable to interested parties high up in French political circles. He might have fingered Feuchtwanger, who was then briefly imprisoned at Les Milles concentration camp near Aix-en-Provence, before international protests had him freed. After that, Feuchtwanger was bound in red tape; he couldn't even travel the short distance to Toulon for a shopping trip without completing a brick of official forms. His application for an exit visa from France was ominously rejected.

Then Germany launched its offensive against France and Feuchtwanger found himself, at precisely 5:01 p.m. on May 21, 1940, walking once again through the gates of Les Milles. Like every other German under the age of fifty-five, he had been ordered to report for detention; he would not turn fifty-five years of age until that July. At first the prisoners were optimistic about the future: they were not criminals, after all, and French justice would surely free them before long. But following an almost inevitable outbreak of typhus—there were three thousand men crammed into this old brick factory with no sanitation and one water faucet for the entire population—they were put in quarantine. Then came news of the German advance south, and things began to look grimmer. Enduring stomach cramps and hopelessness with his usual fatalism, Feuchtwanger remained calm and thought the situation through. Others were not so relaxed. One night, the poet Walter Hasenclever, one of those names Fry would soon attempt to memorize, crawled over to where Feuchtwanger lay. He was very upset, and asked the novelist what he thought their chances were. Feuchtwanger answered, "No better than fifty-fifty." The next morning Hasenclever was found dead of an overdose of sleeping pills.

There were those who criticized Feuchtwanger's behavior in the camp. A fellow inmate, Franz Schoenberner, recalled that Feuchtwanger threw away cables addressed to him but which contained valuable information applicable to all; Schoenberner actually protected Feuchtwanger when the other men discovered what he had done and tried physically to attack him. Possibly it was part of Feuchtwanger's fatalism: if he was to live, the chances were they all would, and nothing he could do would make any difference. Certainly, there was in himself an element of the same *je m'en fiche* ("I don't give a damn") attitude that he saw and criticized in the camp guards.

Feuchtwanger did think he would live, in fact. He told his fellow writer Alfred Kantorowicz at this time, "I still have fourteen books in me which I am determined to write, come what may. I can't possibly imagine that something would happen to me, or that I would be killed, before I have written those fourteen books." He would often wander around the camp, just thinking things over. One day he looked up and saw someone on the other side of the wire who was taking a photograph of him. He was not pleased: he felt like a beast in a cage. But that photograph would indirectly save his life when it was brought to the attention of his old friend Eleanor Roosevelt. Shortly afterward she was visited by Paul Hagen of the Emergency Rescue Committee, and was thus disposed sympathetically to listen to his plea for help in arranging visas for writers and artists in peril in France.

Meanwhile, circumstances worsened. When the inmates of Les Milles were transferred to the camp of St. Nicolas on June 12, they went somewhere still more fetid and primitive, but at least more spaciously disposed and rural than Les Milles. The problem was that by this time the men were so worn down by the double blow of malnutrition and dysentery that the beautiful countryside did not count for much. The sick got sicker. At one point Feuchtwanger told Max Ernst he was looking forward to death. But that would be impossible while there was still breath left in Marta's body.

At the start of the German invasion Marta had been ordered to report to Hyères, a small town east of Toulon. From there she and many other women were transferred to Gurs, the worst camp in terms of its death rate, and where the female guards, who were taken from their normal employment in the French prison system, enjoyed humiliating their prisoners, most of whom were innocent except for the fact that fate had made them German. After Marta had escaped and made her way to St. Nicolas to see her husband, she tried to carry on to Marseille in order to look for help to get him released. But when she arrived at the Gare St. Charles, the police were there arresting those without papers, as usual. She reboarded the train now heading east to Nice, and jumped off when it stopped to take on water at Aubagne, about twelve miles away. Then she walked back to Marseille, far from defeated.

DURING THE First World War Heinrich Mann in Germany had been considered a sort of literary and spiritual twin of D. H. Lawrence in England. Condemned and persecuted by their countrymen, both held fast to their denunciation of the jingoism and militarism that led to the muddy *untergang* of the trenches. Mann was rewarded with recognition in peacetime once the war fever had been broken and the wisdom of his positions accepted. He was welcomed back into the bosom of his German audience. His novel, *The Underling*, perhaps the first modern German satire, had been banned in 1914, but was republished after the war to great acclaim. Only the feud with his brother Thomas, who had called Heinrich a traitor for his pacifism, continued.

A man of great gentleness and avuncular formality, heavy, jowly, with sparkling blue eyes and rimless spectacles, Heinrich Mann looked like a perfect figure of reassurance, like a family doctor or a beloved uncle. His kind-ness, humanism, and anti-Fascism were inalienable, and when he fled into exile in France in 1933 he was quickly dubbed "our secret emperor" by fellow exile Kurt Hiller. Mann was an old man of nearly seventy when war came, so internment posed no threat to him. Even when France was so swiftly beaten, he cleaved to his stately routine. He continued to write all day in his third-floor apartment on Nice's Boulevard des Anglais, until, at exactly five o'clock, he would repair to the Café Monnot in the Place Massena. There, almost alone in the war-deserted resort, he read the day's edition of *Dépêche de Toulouse,* the only newspaper he ever looked at. After an hour he would re-turn home to his new wife, Nelly. She was the latest in a procession of volup-tuous nightclub artistes that he could not seem to keep away from. The weakness for a little class comedy in his private life was possibly the most lik-able thing of all about Heinrich Mann.

Nelly Kroeger was a fisherman's daughter, vivacious and unpretentious, with a ribald vocabulary she would unleash during literary dinner parties while her husband pretended to be shocked. She was also emotionally unsta-ble, and had once attempted to commit suicide. Mann fell in love with her in 1929, but it took the declaration of war against Germany to prompt an offer of marriage, just as the beginning of the First World War had engaged his sense of chivalry and led Heinrich to wed his first wife, Maria Kanova, a plump Czechoslovakian actress. Between these had been his affair with Trude Hesterberg, a full-bodied cabaret singer. It lasted a year, until he met Nelly, at the very time when *The Blue Angel,* with Marlene Dietrich in the lead role, was released in movie theaters. The film was based on Heinrich Mann's early novel, *Professor Unrat,* in which a middle-aged teacher falls in love with a cabaret singer. Thomas Mann won the Nobel Prize for literature the same year. Yet all in all, it was probably more fun being Heinrich than Thomas.

After fleeing Germany in 1933, however, Heinrich Mann's life was hardly one of comfort and joy. He had been an ardent lover of the French way of life, especially its republicanism, since his youth; but he felt cut off from his Ger-man audience, who were now forbidden to read him. He broadcast to them over French radio, and smuggled his anti-Nazi polemics into Germany, some-times on tissue paper hidden in tea bags. But it was not enough. The pain of exile was the pain of amputation for him. He gratefully accepted honorary Czechoslovakian citizenship, and one of his only two trips away from Nice in his first years in France was to Marseille, to pledge his oath of allegiance at the Czech consulate there. The Czech president, Masaryk, arranged to have his li-brary transported to safety from Munich to Prague, in exchange for the dona-

tion of his letters to the national museum. Mann, ever courteous and digni-
fied, said it was "more an honor than a payment."

As the thirties dragged on, Mann realized he was growing old yet having to
paddle harder than ever, like all the other exiles, just to stay afloat. "I would
like to live," he said, "just one month the way Goebbels thinks I live." He held
fast to his belief that the Nazi regime could not survive—"The use of power
which is not filled with goodness and kindness will not last"—and only
slowly accepted the necessity of leaving France after war was declared. His
nephew, Golo, a son of Thomas, contacted him in July 1940, when Heinrich
was still managing to keep his daily routine in Nice. Golo had been in an ambulance corps before escaping the German advance and finding his way to
Toulon, near Sanary, where he stayed at the house of a Mme. Behr. It seems
that Henrich Mann was oblivious to the fact that he was liable, under Article
Nineteen of the armistice agreement, to be handed over to the Nazis. Or perhaps he could not bear the thought that he would have to abandon his
daughter, Goschi, trapped in Czechoslovakia—not that there was anything he
could have done to help her. Golo told him of his own escape from the concentration camp of St. Nicolas, and revealed that he was in hiding at the villa
of Hiram (Harry) Bingham, an American vice-consul at Marseille. Come to
Marseille, urged Golo, and come quickly.

LION FEUCHTWANGER HAD a fan at the American consulate's visa section, which had recently relocated to the Marseille suburb of Montredon.
Myles Standish had even once visited the Feuchtwangers while they were living at Sanary. People described the tall, good-looking Standish as a playboy,
but he was in fact a serious reader of literature. At the limit of her energy,
Marta had at last reached the consulate. There she found it in a state of siege,
for by July 1940 every refugee in France wanted a visa for America, and many
were converging on this building. Waiting in line would be hopeless, but
Marta persuaded a guard at the door to hand Standish a message she scribbled down on a piece of paper.

At St. Nicolas Dr. Lekich had told Marta that Lion had passed the crisis of
his illness; he was still very ill, but he could be moved. Standish, when he was
told this, suggested without hesitation that he should borrow the red Chevrolet belonging to his boss, Harry Bingham, and drive directly to the concentration camp. Bingham was already involved in such illegalities, as the secret
presence of Golo Mann at his residence attested. He would be happy to cooperate. The difficulty lay not in the security surrounding the camp, which

could be described as almost lax, but in finding an accomplice who could enter and leave without attracting attention. Standish, as a representative of the United States government, could on no account be seen leaving St. Nicolas shortly ahead of the discovery of an important prisoner's disappearance. Marta's suggestion was that he should go there in company with Dr. Leckich's wife, who lived in Nîmes and regularly visited the camp, taking in whatever supplies of food and medicine she could lay her hands on. She would be known to the guards and would not arouse suspicion. Standish asked Marta to write a message he could pass to Feuchtwanger, in order that his mission be understood, and that he would not be mistaken for some more sinister visitor.

They waited nearly all day for Feuchtwanger, who had first been swimming in the river Gard, and after that felt well enough to walk to the nearest town for a meal with some other inmates. It was nearly five o'clock when he returned to the camp. Just as Feuchtwanger was leaving the road at the spot where it overlooked the river, in order to take the path back to St. Nicolas, Leckich's wife emerged from a bush. She handed the novelist a slip of paper, on which was written, *Frag Nichts! Sag Nichts! Geh Mit!* "Ask nothing! Say nothing! Go along!" Somewhat confused, he said farewell to his companions and followed Madame Leckich to the shiny red automobile parked a little way along the road. Standish greeted him and handed Feuchtwanger a woman's coat and headscarf to put on. The story would be that Standish was out on a drive with his wife and mother-in-law if the auto was stopped by a gendarme—which it was, at the first town they passed through. Standish, with the envious status of an American in war-wracked Europe, pulled off this charade, and had successfully brought the novelist to Bingham's villa by nightfall. So it was that Myles Standish rescued Lion Feuchtwanger from St. Nicolas.

PART 3

THE SECRET

CITY

CHAPTER 9

THE SECRET
CITY

All is kept underground.
All is secret.
The story of Marseille remains a secret.
BLAISE CENDRARS

MARSEILLE, SELF-ABSORBED and businesslike, is different from the other towns on the south coast of France. It is the country's oldest city, Roman in its roots, but nautical since the seventh century B.C. when Phoenicians, wearing their purple woollen caps, plied the waters of the Mediterranean and first fetched up there. Marseille is also the southern capital, and arguably the toughest place in France, with its transient human traffic from Africa and the Orient, and its solidly established Corsican gangsterism—earning for itself the sobriquet, "the French Chicago." Even the weather and the light are distinct from elsewhere on the coast; at Marseille they lack the distinctive softness of Provence. Encircled by the mountains of the Vaucluse to the north, the bitter mistral wind sweeps down out of season, making the Marseille summer rather shorter, and its winter rather longer, than those in Nice, St. Tropez, Monaco, or even nearby Toulon.

As for its inhabitants, the Marseillais themselves remain a breed apart. They are willful and at odds with things—in a fishing port, for example, they are famous for spurning fish as part of the diet, except for the ubiquitous bouillabaisse. They are attuned to living, in great ways or small, outside the law: "Half of them were gangsters and the other half wanted to be," said Charlie Fawcett. In the Vieux Port, a questionable but picturesque quarter, the most ancient part of Marseille, there existed a system of caverns hollowed out within and beneath the medieval warren of streets and buildings. An entire, invisible netherworld of secret warehouses and hideouts, of gambling dens and killing floors, nestled undisturbed as it had done for centuries. Into this zone even the police dared not venture. Its denizens knew which sewers led into the waters of the harbor, and into these they would toss the severed heads of their enemies—a favored conclusion to disagreements among the inhabitants of the Marseille underworld. The Nazis dynamited the whole area in late 1942 as a "hygienic measure," revealing for the first time in 1500 years the Roman docks buried below.

On the surface, in the slanting sunlight, was the wide, busy façade of a thriving international center of trade. But the city remained turned in upon itself, neither boasting of its status nor confiding its secret to outsiders. The city had existed for well over two thousand years, and in that time its inhabitants had not erected for celebration of place a single monument; no such impulse of civic pride had united or moved them. The city on which Varian Fry first gazed, on the morning of August 15, 1940, looked back at him with studied indifference. It was, when all was said, a romantic, dirty, hard-edged city, the Casablanca of the northern shore. The French academician Louis Gillet described Marseille as the "cesspool where gathers the scum of the Mediterranean." Hitler had called it an "asylum for the international underworld"—by this time it had certainly become an international asylum—and "the ulcer of Europe."

Marseille would make no allowances for Varian Fry, either, and would turn its back on hope and sympathy, even as, geographically, it turned its back on the French Riviera, facing away from the vacation coast, westward across the Golfe du Lion, aloof and sidelong. "A city on the northern shore of the Mediterranean ought to face south," Fry wrote soon after he arrived, "and when you walk down the Canebière you walk toward the water, so you think you are walking south. But you are really walking south by south-west, and if you continue along either side of the Vieux Port you are walking due west, or very nearly so." For an outsider, it is a disorientating experience.

The night before, he had eaten supper at Cerbère on the French side of the border. Then he had to wait until the early hours of the morning for a train that wound its way along the coastal track, heading east, and which arrived at the Gare St. Charles in time for breakfast. Fry took no heed of the barricades where police apprehended those lacking the necessary papers, for he was an American, a privileged citizen of a neutral nation. But he was also dirty and tired. A station porter attempted to earn his first commission of the day by leading the newcomer to a smelly little family-run concern, the Hotel Suisse. Fry demurred and insisted on the place that been recommended to him, the Splendide, one of Marseille's finer hotels. The middle-aged, Jewish desk clerk apologized and explained, as the porter had also explained, that the city was bursting with refugees and that there were hardly any rooms to be had. Fry asked to be informed as soon as one came up, and gave his address as the Suisse, to the delight of the hovering porter.

There, the smell of "drains and garlic" assailed Fry's epicurean nostrils until lunchtime, when he felt sufficiently rested to go about his business. He walked out into the stunning midday heat, and made his way down the main "north-south" boulevard, the Canebière, then turned left toward the American consulate at No. 6, Place St. Ferréol. The strangest thing about the sight that met his eyes, before he had adjusted himself to the new condition of defeated France, was its apparent normality. "Life here is very different from what we imagined it would be before I left," he wrote to Eileen. "There is no disorder, there are no children starving in the streets, and there are very few signs of war of any kind. The people of Marseille seem to have resigned themselves to defeat, and even to take it rather lightly—as they take everything. . . ." But all around him, in the shade of the café and restaurant and at the windows of every hotel and boardinghouse, were thousands of refugees, scanning the street with worry and fatigue. Fry was oblivious to them just as a novice hunter in a jungle is oblivious to the abundance of wildlife watching his every move.

Fry's first day was to provide his first disappointment. The queues of shabbily dressed people snaking around the block would have identified to him the building that housed the American consulate even if he had not known where he was going. He entered and walked up to the second-floor reception, where a curious young woman with bleached hair and blue-mascaraed eyes told Fry that if he wanted to speak to the consul, he needed the visa section. She redirected him to the suburb of Montredon. Something about her made Fry think all was not well with the United States Foreign Service. "She smirked and squirmed coquettishly as she talked," he said, and her eyes had an "unnatural sparkle." Clearly, she was high on something, either drugs or sex; but Fry did not know at this point her true story.

The trolley ride out of town was airless and soporific. The vehicle rattled due east along the Avenue du Prado for about one and a half miles, and Fry, in his sleep-hungry state, drifted in and out of consciousness. The landscape of gray, tufted limestone hills dotted with umbrella pines and date palms reminded him of the coast around Athens he had seen over a decade earlier. When he arrived at Montredon and the big brick villa—loaned recently to the consul by the heir to the Noilly Prat fortune, Countess Lily Pastré—which now housed the visa division, almost the entire trolley-load of people disembarked and made en masse for it. Fry walked, as any confident American citizen on official business would, through the entrance and into the building, past the lines of visa applicants and official notices tacked to the walls. "APPLICATIONS FROM CENTRAL EUROPE CLOSED," read one of them. "QUOTA TRANSFERS FROM PARIS DISCONTINUED," and "PASSAGE FROM LISBON SOLD OUT FOR MONTHS," they continued as he walked down the hallway. At a quick glance, one would believe there was no way out of France at all. Surely the drawbridge could not have been raised so quickly.

The misgivings aroused by the woman at the consulate were confirmed when a clerk walked into the office where Fry was waiting. What struck Fry was the change from imperious to obsequious in the young, "dog-faced" man who accosted him and shouted in French what on earth he meant by daring to walk in ahead of the queue. "Go back to your place and wait your turn!" he ordered, but soon became oily and deferential when Fry answered him in his own language, with the well-modulated tones he reserved for moments of quiet fury.

It was an inauspicious beginning to perhaps the most vital relationship Fry would need to cultivate on his mission in France. Visas were the key to the success of the Emergency Rescue Committee's mission. Washington authorized them, but the Foreign Service on the ground issued the visas. Thousands of miles away from the center of decision, and in a war zone, the helpfulness, efficiency, and sympathy of young men such as this would be vital.

Hemorrhaging apologies, the man showed him through to an inner office, and carried Fry's card to the consul, whom he promised would soon see him. Fry waited there, gazing out of the window eastward toward the lawns of the Château Pastré, where probably at that moment Charlie Fawcett was unloading his British soldiers onto the warm hospitality of his friend Lily, the Countess. Ten minutes later another young man appeared, this time a vice-consul, and an identical scene was played out. This time, however, when he was asked what he thought he was doing, Fry kept silent and simply walked back into the waiting room. He sat there for the next two hours, watching how little was being done by the American staff to see, let alone help any of the hundreds of French and Germans who sat waiting. Then Fry got up and left. He rode the trolley back to the center of Marseille, the heat slightly subdued by the lengthening day, turning over in his mind the experience of what it was like to be treated as a refugee, if only for an afternoon. Fry's interim conclusion was that it might not be wise to rely too much on American help. In the meantime, there was a lot of work to be done. He had his list, with the names at the top heavily underlined, so to speak. Before he went on his tour of southern France by bicycle (which was already starting to seem fanciful), he could at least begin to follow up the lead he had from Lisbon. And top of those was to make contact with Franz and Alma Werfel, at the Hotel du Louvre et de la Paix, on the Canebière.

BY THIS TIME, Heinrich Mann was comfortably ensconced at the Hotel Normandie, opposite the Splendide. Lion Feuchtwanger was in hiding at Harry Bingham's villa, along with Mann's nephew, Golo. But not all the refugees were so lucky. Walter Mehring was cowering, some distance away from the center of Marseille in a suburb called Pointe Rouge, a stone's throw from Montredon. Every refugee with a "face" lived in terror of being spotted, either by the police or by fellow countrymen. Even those who were friends or fans of the famous exiles were potentially fatal threats, as an enthusiastic but loose word in the wrong ear ("Guess who I saw today?") could give away an exile's location and unleash the Kundt Commission, which would duly sniff him out. The commission consisted of German diplomats, military officers, and secret police, together with a smaller Italian contingent. It was the body set up at the time of the French surrender to oversee the implementation of Article Nineteen (number twenty-one in the Franco-Italian document), dealing with the "repatriation" of Reich citizens—in reality turning them over to the Gestapo, with the wholehearted cooperation of the Vichy government.

Mehring in particular stood out like a sore and rather grimy thumb. His appearance in good times was best described as on the shabby side of rumpled. Add to that the circumstances of the past few months, including the arduous journey south, and he had the appearance of a ready-made *clochard*, a bum, just the sort of fellow the police might take for a pickpocket or petty thief. Walter Mehring was an easy arrest. It was not safe for him to be seen on the streets, so he spent most of his days sitting with his fellow exile Professor Emil Gumbel in the Bar Mistral, next to his hotel, squabbling about who was in most danger (it was Mehring). The one time Mehring had ventured into the center of Marseille, a compatriot had recognized the famous poet and cried aloud in joy. Already half paralyzed with nervousness, he panicked and ran off down the street, away from his admirer and directly into the arms of a gendarme, who asked why he was traveling so fast, and demanded to see his papers. Mehring claimed he had none, so he was arrested and taken to the police station.

In fact, he did have papers, but not any he wanted the police to examine. Mehring had recently taken advantage of the help of the local Czech consul, Vladimir Vochoč, who was distributing ersatz Czech passports on his own authority to whoever wanted them. Vochoč was an old-school diplomat and a former professor at the University of Prague, and such illegality did not sit easily with him at first. But he recognized the dire situation, and understood that unless he helped the fleeing anti-Fascists, the liberation of his country would be even more of a dream. Czechoslovakia, technically speaking, no longer existed, but even brand-new Czech passports were still recognized by the Spanish and Portuguese, making them a perfect means of travel under false identity for those the Gestapo was hunting. Mehring added to his new passport a visa stamp he procured from the Chinese consul, as had many other refugees, at the low price of one hundred francs. It was a beautiful stamp, and on it in ideograms unintelligible to any *douanier* in the western hemisphere was the instruction, "Under no circumstances is this person to be allowed entrance to China." It didn't matter: simply to leave France halved a refugee's worries at a stroke. So near, yet so far; Mehring had been waiting in line at the Spanish consulate for an interview that would get him a precious Spanish transit visa, when he was identified.

At the gendarmerie he asked to visit the toilet, and in the cubicle flushed away his precious documents. Mehring calculated that to be caught with none was better than to be caught with false papers. He also gambled that policemen did not read much poetry and would therefore know neither his name nor his fugitive status without specifically checking. So he revealed his true identity to the inspector (the Frenchman's face remained blank), and added that Harry Bingham, the local United States vice-consul, would certify that he was *en règle*. Bingham came around directly after he was telephoned, and agreed to take responsibility for the sprat that had flapped into the Vichy net. Then he drove back to Pointe Rouge with a very depressed and fatalistic Mehring, who by now was convinced he could do nothing but wait for the Germans to come and collect him.

As it was, the Germans were briefly preoccupied in securing the military buffer zone of northern France, and planning their continued campaign against the British. They were also at this point more interested in expelling Jews from Reich territory than rounding them up and deporting them to concentration camps. As a result, in addition to all those refugees who had traveled south of their own volition, Jews were being herded onto trains in Poland, Germany, and elsewhere, then sent to France and dumped over the demarcation line into the unoccupied zone. There was a nightmarish absurdity to the situation. In July, for example, the enthusiastic Vichy authorities handed over twenty-one people they had arrested, in accordance with the "surrender on demand" clause. But the Nazis were not impressed with this unasked-for cooperation, and actually forced Vichy to take them back, because they didn't want Jews coming into their zone. At this moment Mehring had more to fear from the French than the Germans, although that would soon change once again.

Instead of allowing the thousands of unwanted foreigners to flee France, the Vichy regime, with disturbing eagerness to please its conquerors, penned them in. This meant, first of all, that Vichy was keen to apprehend those on the Gestapo lists so they could be handed over when Germany requested. Second, it meant there was no way out for any man between the ages of eighteen and forty-two, no matter what his nationality: he might leave only to join the British or the Free French forces under General de Gaulle, who was now in London. Franco was just as keen to keep them out of Spain. General Kleber, the Polish Ambassador at Madrid, was in charge of evacuating the remnants of the Polish army. He ordered one of his men still inside France, who was actually about thirty, to shave a bald spot on the top of his head. This would hopefully make him look old enough to get past the French and Spanish border controls. But somehow the Spanish were suspicious. They detained him at the frontier until half an inch of stubble had grown over his bald patch. Then they arrested him.

The bureaucratic man-trap was very simple, yet almost wholly effective. A refugee had to apply directly to the Vichy authorities for a French exit visa to leave the country. As soon as he did, his name was handed over to the Kundt Commission—to the Gestapo, in other words. This ensured that those in dire need of escape would be rounded up first, and that to apply for an exit visa was roughly equivalent to signing one's own death warrant. The Pétain government, having agreed to "surrender on demand" anyone that Hitler might be looking for, was now making sure that he would not have far to look. France was effectively a stockyard. Soon it would be a slaughterhouse.

Few nations have ever been so abruptly and thoroughly closed to the outside world as France was in the summer of 1940. With the Germans to the north and west, and the Italians in the east, the only escape route was the Mediterranean Sea. But this was patrolled by warships and restricted in its passenger traffic by Vichy. To buy a ticket one needed an exit visa, which few could risk applying for. For the refugees, Marseille was a blockaded port. They were well and truly trapped. Only the Pyrenees remained as the possible route of escape.

The head of the New Vichy government, Marshal Philippe Pétain, took more than a page out of *Mein Kampf*. Racial purity and moral puritanism soon became insistent themes of government policy under his leadership. As early as August 27, the "Marchandeau Law" (outlawing racist libel) was repealed, marking open season for press attacks on foreigners and Jews. Vichy was an energetic legislator, piling up statutes aimed at "purifying" the French nation. And they had not been ordered to by the Nazis; everything was done on Vichy's own initiative well before any pressure was put on the puppet government by Hitler. "The Vichy ideologists threw themselves into an orgy of penitence and abasement," wrote one American who witnessed their actions. In fact, the Nazis were surprised at the abject prostration of Pétain's administration—and surprise would quickly turn to contempt.

In the shock of defeat and the recoil of occupation, the French were haunted by the slogan that had delivered them over to the Germans: *chacun pour soi.* Now they yearned for a return to order and stability, even if it involved moral as well as economic slavery. As a result, a series of peculiarly French contradictions were resolved in favor of the racists. Anti-Jewish feeling grew stronger in the wake of defeat, but the serious matter was the freedom of expression now granted these feelings, which was hijacked by the extreme right and adopted as policy by the Vichy government. France had previously been the most tolerant of Western societies; it had repealed its anti-Semitic laws in the 1790s, soon after the Revolution and long before any other state. It had opened its doors, a little like the United States in the nineteenth century, to welcome the oppressed and wretched of the continent. France was seen as the heartland of liberty and freedom, but this had brought some unforeseen consequences.

On the one hand, French Jews, and foreign Jews in France, were the most assimilated in the world by the 1930s, except perhaps for those in Germany. In the "Anglo-Saxon" countries, like Britain and America, they were more socially marginalized and suffered clearer discrimination. But in Britain and America, the exponents of progressive anti-Semitism were almost always on the fringes of politics, their voices minority ones, and their followers few and disorganized. In France and Germany, on the other hand, anti-Semitism always enjoyed a substantial and vociferous constituency, always had brilliant spokesmen, and a voice in mainstream politics backed up with organizations and media power.

People act meanly when they feel poor, and the French had felt poor in all sorts of ways throughout the Depression. During the 1930s, refugees had flooded into France: at the beginning of that decade there were already three million immigrants resident within her borders, 7 percent of the mainland population. In a period of prolonged unemployment, this began to rankle with the native right-wingers, and soon they were not alone. By 1937 even the Communist Party of France quietly changed its immigration policy in the direction of keeping out foreigners. During this time, the French government had been assembling lists of names of aliens—the infamous "Carnet B," which had ensured the expulsion of three thousand immigrants going back to 1935, for example—so that Vichy was well prepared to act as it did when it came to power.

Laws had already been passed in the previous decade setting quotas for foreigners in certain professions and occupations. These had led to many absurdities, such as the ruling that a Russian balalaika orchestra could contain no more than 15 percent Russians. A decree of November 1938 made it much more difficult to be naturalized French, and even allowed for citizenship awarded by the government to be stripped away. Such legislation Vichy did not invent: it had no need to, it simply used "with extreme prejudice" what was already on the statute books. When war with Germany finally broke out, refugees and many immigrants could hardly feed themselves any longer, and this led, of course, to further claims that they were bleeding France dry. The cultural temperature during the thirties had been steadily rising, and anti-Semitism was its symptom. The scapegoat mechanism that the Nazi Party in Germany had exploited so masterfully was also at work in France, though not as efficiently or malignantly, or perhaps simply not as widely. It took the horror and trauma of defeat in war to change attitudes fully, and when it did, the facade of tolerance fell like a ton of bricks.

On July 17, 1940, a law was passed that barred entrance to the civil service unless an applicant's father was born a Frenchman; a month later, the day after Fry arrived in Marseille, the same rule was applied to the medical profession, instantly throwing out of work the many doctors among the refugees: they could even be arrested for going to the aid of somebody suffering a heart attack. Less than a month after that, the same restriction was placed on the legal profession. On July 22, a commission called the Revision of Naturalizations was established: it sought to revoke the citizenship of those people naturalized French since 1927. Immediately, fifteen thousand foreign-born Frenchmen and Frenchwomen found themselves without a passport or any of the rights of citizenship they had enjoyed the day before. In time, this would be one of the most powerful weapons in Vichy's battle to rid France of "inferior breeds"—namely Jews. And these were just the beginning. When Fry left the Hotel Suisse to walk the short distance to the Werfels' hotel, he was stepping into the streets of a nation undergoing a sea change of spirit.

French people, shocked, numbed, confused, and frightened, looked to their social superiors for leadership not just in morality but in order. Like all conquered peoples, they also looked at their conquerors to see what qualities they themselves lacked. Add to this shame and self-loathing, which soon turns to recrimination, and the zealousness in harassing the Jews begins to make sense. By persecuting them, Vichy could be seen to be restoring stability, and could also convince itself that it was working with—and so was respected and treated as an equal by—the Germans. Tormenting the Jews gave Vichy a feeling of potency. It was an almost perfect self-deception.

Already a vigorous campaign was being mounted to counter the old "immorality" that was fast becoming associated with the "Front Populaire" administration (a liberal, "New Deal" French coalition government of the late thirties) and its ex–prime minister Léon Blum, who happened to be Jewish. It was planned that Blum himself, and other politicians held responsible for France's "decline" and its recent military disaster, were to be placed on trial at the town of Riom. (Blum eventually wound up in a German concentration camp, which he survived.) In its current mood of servile abasement the weaknesses that led to France's defeat were additionally being blamed on loose living and general flabbiness. As a result, the drinking of alcohol was strictly curtailed: drinks stronger than thirty-two degrees proof were banned, and on three days a week—*jours sans alcool*—no wine was allowed to be served in public places. Women were forced to wear more "modest" bathing costumes at the beach, and dancing was forbidden. If France had been a person, it could have been described as suffering a neurotic collapse. Or as one German exile, Theodor Adorno, put it, Fascism is psychoanalysis in reverse. France was repressing itself.

The attitude of the Vichy regime was graphically summarized in one of the many propaganda posters that suddenly appeared on walls everywhere. It bore the slogan of Pétain's *Révolution Nationale*—"Work, Family, Country"— and depicted two houses. The one on the left, lopsided and tempest-tossed, was labeled "France & Co." There was a Star of David on the roof and above it a hammer and sickle. Beneath this rickety structure lay a series of foundation stones, each one labeled for a sin of the old France: RADICALISM, CAPITALISM, DEMAGOGUERY, LAZINESS, DEMOCRACY, PARLIAMENT, EGOISM, JEWISHNESS, FREEMASONRY, AVARICE, WINE, DISORDER, ANTI-MILITARISM. The sunny and stately residence on the right was by contrast solid and upstanding. It was endowed with the firm pillars of the new order: SCHOOL, ARTISANRY, PEASANTRY, LEGION. The bases of the columns read, in turn, DISCIPLINE, ORDER, THRIFT, COURAGE. The whole structure was topped with a fluttering tricolor.

These sinister banalities were endlessly trumpeted by Vichy radio, which also declared daily its one political message: the Germans are our friends, the British and Jews the traitors and architects of national humiliation. Weak people lash out at their friends, and ordinarily, Vichy's would be an interpretation of recent events so transparent that a child could see through it. But it was the official version, under a state of emergency, and it had a certain effect. The newspapers followed up with crude anti-Semitic cartoons and ecstatic headlines announcing the imminent destruction of Britain. "NOW IT'S THEIR

TURN," hollered one headline, expressing the hurt and fear that the French felt, and which instinctively they sought to pass on to their erstwhile ally.

The hypocrisy of all this went unnoticed, at least publicly. But in private, the land of Voltaire had not been completely eclipsed, and many French people looked with contempt and wry humor at the behavior of its government and press.

Recently, in reply to a question about how many French were involved in resisting the Germans, an elderly former Resistance fighter sarcastically replied, "Maintenant, tout le monde." Now, everyone. His answer was a comment on the collective amnesia that grew in France about what really happened in the war. But it was also the case that many Frenchmen loathed Vichy from the outset. "Only a few days ago," Fry wrote wryly to Eileen soon after his arrival in Marseille, "a French newspaperman told me that France is full of people who are only waiting for the signal; that nobody believes the propaganda in the papers . . . here he is not quite right: I have met one person who does."

ALERTED BY FRANZ'S SISTER, the Werfels had been eagerly anticipating Fry's arrival. It was Fry's first experience of putting a face to one of the famous names on his list. Part of the problem he had in preparing psychologically for the trip to France was that he was supposed to contact a roster of the most well known and acclaimed cultural figures in Europe. He had read their books and poems, enjoyed their paintings and music, and they loomed as large and as unreal in his mind as movie stars. Now, at last, reality would intervene and shrink the mental image to human size. But there was also a risk: in awe of them, and unimportant by comparison, Fry was appearing in their midst as a savior. The refugees themselves were not used to asking for help— the Werfels, for example, were Viennese cultural royalty. Most were artists and intellectuals used to freedom of expression and considerable deference, and they might well probably act the part.

Reality had certainly shrunk Werfel to size, as Fry observed when, after considerable confusion and delay, he was shown into their hotel room. The great author, "pallid, like a half-filled sack of flour," was wearing a silk dressing gown and sitting "all over" a small gilt chair, said Fry. Alma was already drinking plentifully of Benedictine, which she practically forced on him. In a curious effort at subterfuge, the couple had booked in under the name of Mr. and Mrs. Gustav Mahler. Perhaps they assumed the police were ignorant of music, as Walter Mehring thought they were of poetry.

The three best restaurants in Marseille were La Brasserie de Verdun, the gangster-run Beauvau, and Basso's. They dined at the last, where Fry was bombarded with entreaties for help ("You must save us, Mr. Fry." "Oh, *ja*, you must save us!") and hair-raising accounts of the Werfels' recent travels. The Werfels were stuck. They had now been granted American visas and had picked them up from the consulate. But an American visa was not enough to leave France. For that, an exit visa was required—the same exit visa that ensured your name was given to the Vichy authorities, and then passed on to the Gestapo. The Werfels had applied for exit visas. They had heard nothing.

Back at the Hotel du Louvre, Alma insisted they drink champagne, perhaps in defiance of the situation. Without an exit visa, and with an imminent need to leave France, there were few options. Crossing the border with Spain illegally was dangerous, since capture by the French led back to a concentration camp, and from there to the Gestapo. Merely getting to the border without an impossible-to-procure travel pass (a *sauf conduit*) was liable to produce the same result, since there were random checks of papers everywhere. But sitting still was just as risky, and once the police had cracked the "Gustav Mahler" disguise, they could easily arrest the Werfels at their hotel.

Fry had no idea what to do next. In fact he must have been nearly as terrified as the Werfels, for the difficulty of his own task had just been exposed. Here he was, a preppie young journalist, a "paper tiger," suddenly pushed in at the deep end. If escape for such favored celebrities as the Werfels was a depressing round of dead ends, then what of the many other less glamorous cases whose American visas would not be handed to them with a smile? Suddenly, Fry felt unsure he could do anything at all to help. He didn't even know how to find the people on his list, let alone begin the interminable bureaucratic process of evacuation for each one of them. He was completely on his own, suffering "the shock of my own inadequacy." His advice to the Werfels was to stay where they were: he would be in touch. It was a very agitated Varian Fry who walked back to the Hotel Suisse that first evening in Marseille. Had he not been so utterly exhausted by his journey from Barcelona, sleep would not have ambushed him.

There were several other Americans in France whom Fry had been told about, in strictest confidence, back in New York. One of them was Dr. Frank Bohn, who worked in the same "export-import" business Fry was about to enter. Bohn was in Marseille—with a room on the third floor of the Hotel Splendide—courtesy of the American Federation of Labor, who had sent him to extract various labor leaders, union officials, and democratic politicians whose lives were now endangered. Inevitably, the exiles had eventually slid into that bilge of hope, Marseille. The Gestapo, Franco's Seguridad, and Mussolini's Ovra would all be hunting down these people, who had converged on

France from Germany, Austria, Czechoslovakia, Spain, and Italy during the past few months.

The United States had been extremely reluctant to issue entry visas during the lead-up to war. The logic, issuing from the State Department, and quietly assented to by Roosevelt, had been that if these people were in trouble, then they must be troublemakers—probably "Reds" or Nazi spies—and not the kind of immigrants that America wanted. Some undoubtedly were Communists, and the law was that such people could not under any circumstances be admitted to the United States. One or two were perhaps spies. But most were simply democrats, and brave ones who had been fighting the losing battle against Fascism for over a decade. And many were Jews, of course. All in all, they comprised what the United States Minister to Portugal, Herbert C. Pell, complained were seen by the State Department as "the least desirable elements" to be kept out at all costs. "There is a fire sale of brains going on here," he told Fry, "and we are not taking full advantage of it. Our immigration laws are too rigid and some of our consuls interpret them too strictly."

As a result of this attitude the exiles were in the process of being delivered into the hands of the Nazi enemy by a democracy (in fact by all the remaining democracies) that refused to aid them because they were guilty of having defended democracy. It was another paradox that the new war was fashioning. The West was still, fatally, thinking in terms of old-fashioned nationalistic conflict, not the international revolution Fry had described, where often your best allies were from the enemy states. "Everywhere we are making the test of nationality, of present, or former citizenship, the crucial one," he wrote in the *New Leader*. "But this is not just another nationalist war. It is a world revolution. Even in the enemy countries we have friends." It was not a message the State Department wished to hear.

Throughout the thirties in America the uptake of visa quotas had been sluggish where non-English speaking countries were concerned. (On the other hand, the quotas for Britain and Ireland were vastly increased, even though they produced far fewer applicants.) Immigration to America overall was actually undersubscribed. It was not for lack of desperate refugees that visas were rare in being issued, but rather a "go-slow" on the part of the State Department and the American Foreign Service. The slogan of Assistant Secretary of State Breckinridge Long had been "postpone and postpone and postpone" where refugees from the European continent were concerned, and his Ivy League staff for the most part happily complied. Jews weren't allowed in their country clubs, after all, and the reasoning was easily extended to the country itself. The fiction that Communists and Nazi spies formed the great majority of visa applicants suited many in the American government.

But the summer of 1940 produced a convulsion that could no longer be ignored. The American public's desire to stay out of the war almost kept pace with its sympathy for those suffering before Hitler's onslaught. The American Federation of Labor, along with many other labor organizations in the United States, did all they could to cajole, reason with, and embarrass Roosevelt's administration, until the president gave way to the pressure on his public image (and threats from his wife) and granted a number of emergency "visitors'" visas—not for permanent residence in America, but sufficient to bring the refugees into the western hemisphere and out of danger. Hence Frank Bohn at the Splendide. The next morning, Friday, August 16, Fry went to call on him.

It was to be Fry's second disappointment, not as ominous as his experience at the Consulate, but salutary. The Splendide was infested with uniformed officers of the Italian Armistice Commission, which should have urged caution, yet when Fry knocked on the door of Bohn's hotel room, it was flung wide without hesitation. A warmhearted Yankee greeting pulled him inside, where a man and a woman sprang to their feet. "This is Comrade Fry," announced Bohn in booming tones, eliciting more comradely felicitations, this time in thick European accents. It sounded as if Fry had stumbled across a convention of Soviet tractor salesmen.

It was soon apparent that Bohn was representative of a type of "underground" worker that Fry would meet frequently in France. He was dismayed to learn that Bohn, involved in the illegal traffic of refugees into Spain over the Pyrenees, had arranged no cover for his operations, and was organizing everything from his hotel room. Bohn kept the illegalities of false passports and mountain passes secret, of course, and held the attitude that the police could not possibly object to what looked like straightforward refugee aid, as indeed they did not. But there was precious little security to his operation, and the "Comrade" display seemed to summarize the essential theatrically in Bohn's approach. He had arrived in France earlier in the summer when disorganization still reigned in the aftermath of defeat and border controls had not yet been coordinated between France and Spain. In other words, Bohn had enjoyed the good old days of a few months back when the doors of France had not yet slammed shut. He assumed wrongly that it would continue this way, and was enjoying his role as Humphrey Bogart, acting the hero in his own spy movie.

Fry was unimpressed with the loose talk and attitudes that had greeted him. Bohn had taken Fry's word for who he was without further ado, and was talking openly in front of two Germans in the room. Fry may have been new to the business in hand, but his instincts told him there should be more caution. The Germans were introduced as Bedrich Heine of the Social Democratic Party, and Erika Bierman, the Secretary of Rudolf Breitscheid, who had for years led the opposition to Hitler in the Reichstag. They were acting as Bohn's assistants. They told him that Breitscheid was in Marseille with his colleague Rudolf Hilferding, and Fry knew those men were very high up on the Gestapo's list, because they were also on his own.

Fry learned from Bohn that Konrad Heiden had been spotted in Montauban, and that Lion Feuchtwanger had been rescued from St. Nicolas by Myles Standish. This was good news: Fry had read an article in the *New York Times* back in July that reported Feuchtwanger's arrest by the Gestapo. Until this moment, he had heard nothing else. Bohn dragged Fry into the bathroom and continued talking in a loud stage whisper: it was part of his repertoire of cloak-and-dagger affectations. "Bohn was naïve," said Charlie Fawcett; so was Fry, of course, but he was serious-minded and not—to use a word that would become part of the Marseille vocabulary of Fry and his friends—a *mythomane,* a fantasist. Eileen was more blunt: she called Bohn "an unctuous ass."

Those refugees Bohn had been getting out had for the most part been on the original State Department list of emergency visas, so he had enjoyed fairly unproblematic relations with the Foreign Service and could not recognize the imperiousness Fry had encountered. Perhaps Bohn's had been the more typical experience. Perhaps there was something in Fry that elicited opposition; perhaps he went looking for it—his life after all had been a tapestry of major and minor disagreements. Bohn was the sort of glad-handing team man who would glide over incidents where Fry would inevitably generate friction.

"Or maybe Harry Bingham was out," said Bohn. That name again, the byword for help and cooperation. The consul general, John P. Hurley, was a different proposition, Bohn added: he was no help at all. The idea that success at the consulate was a matter of potluck and who was in the office on a particular day was not encouraging. Still, Fry looked forward to meeting Bingham.

His conference with Bohn solved two major problems, though. First, it was obvious that the political names on Fry's list should really be Bohn's responsibility. Likewise, the artistic and intellectual names that Bohn had accumulated should be taken care of by Fry after they had shifted the backlog of German and Austrian political activists. This suited them both, and Bohn offered places on a boat he was organizing to take his refugees away. It solved the problem of the Werfels and Feuchtwangers at a stroke. And Bohn managed to get Fry a room, number 307, at the Hotel Splendide.

CHAPTER 10

AN AMERICAN
IN MARSEILLE

T HE IMPORTANT THING," said the man to Fry, "is that once you're
over the border and into Spain, you go to the Spanish customs and get
the *entrada* stamp in your passport. Then it's okay."

That morning Fry had been awakened by children's voices, and he opened
the louvered doors onto his shallow balcony at the Splendide to discover the
courtyard of a girls' school. The sun shone brightly, and the picture postcard of Marseille lay stretched out before him. His reverie was ended by a
knock on the door, and the entrance of a young Austrian who thrust his
hand toward Fry in a gesture of grateful friendship. The first refugee of the
morning.

Later, another refugee handed Fry a map, crudely drawn, of the border at
Cerbère. A wavy line marked the sea. Some box shapes were the buildings of
Banyuls, and to the left, a row of crosses indicated a cemetery. Above that, a
zigzag represented mountains, with a line of "x"s threaded through: the bor-
der. Snaking around it was another line, or arrows, showing how to avoid the
French customs post and its lines of sight.

Fry gave the man some money from the thick wad he had brought into
France with him, and wished him luck. They continued coming up to his
hotel room all morning, sent by Bohn. Fry had needed some encouragement,
and these young men, many of whom were Paul Hagen's German associates
from the exiled Social Democratic Party, gave it to him. They weren't much
like the refugees haunting the American consulate and hiding in the cafés and
maisons closes—the brothels, which were safer than hotels because there was
no register for the police to inspect. These men were eager and optimistic and

vigorous: once they had been given funds for the journey to Lisbon, they took their chances and headed for the border, then hiked over the Pyrenees to safety. So far, Fry was told, everybody had got over successfully. Now that he had a map, there might even be a chance of using the route for his other clients. He had started writing to them, the ones whose addresses he already had and those Bohn had given him, as soon as he had moved into his small room at the Splendide the night before. Little by little Fry was beginning to understand the intricacies of the visa situation. Happy were those who had received an American visa, but even for them difficulties remained. Fry knew already of the potentially lethal danger of applying for a French exit visa. These men, being of military age, would never be issued one anyway. Luckily, he now discovered, the Spanish border guards did not care if a passport lacked one. They only wished to see a transit visa. That was a piece of very welcome news. Also to the good was the fact that both the Spanish and Portuguese consulates were still issuing such transit visas—which allowed through-travel en route to a final country of destination. All the Spanish wanted to see was a Portuguese visa. The Portuguese in addition required a preexisting "onward" visa, which guaranteed that the refugee would not simply arrive and "settle in them with like bedbugs." For those without American visas, Fry learned, the Chinese "fake" visas substituted perfectly. So did the Siamese, which were real, but impossible to make use of because there was no way to get from Portugal to Siam. Perhaps the Portuguese were unaware of this; at any rate it had not been a problem so far.

Meanwhile, Fry busied himself making contacts with others in Marseille who could help him track down the names on his list and offer other kinds of support. Bohn had told Fry about Richard Allen of the Red Cross, and Howard E. Kershner of the Quakers. Most important among these, though, was Dr. Donald Lowrie, the local representative of the international YMCA. Lowrie was a seasoned relief worker without any of the stage-struck *faux* heroics some of them cultivated. Not only was he experienced, and a great source of advice for Fry in the beginning, but he was also known as a good friend of the Czechs. He had been in Prague when the Nazis invaded Czechoslovakia, and had helped a lot of people to escape then. It was Lowrie who introduced Fry to Vochoč, and they soon agreed to cooperate on the matter of false passports: Fry would pay the printing costs and Vochoč would supply documents for all the anti-Nazis he recommended. "The work was actually done at Bordeaux, in the occupied zone, under the noses of the Germans," Fry recalled. "It was a very nice job. The covers were pink, whereas the old Prague passports had been green, but otherwise you couldn't tell one from another."

On the afternoon of the Friday he met Bohn, Fry caught the same trolley car to Montredon that he had taken the day before. He intended to see Harry Bingham and give the man a piece of his mind, but it didn't turn out that way. Fry was greeted warmly by the tall, bespectacled vice-consul. Bingham's father was the late Senator Hiram Bingham, who had also been a historian and found fame as the discoverer of the legendary lost city of the Incas, Macchu Picchu. Bingham was a cut above the usual employees of vice-consular rank in France. He had the sort of kindly face—as befitted a former theology student—that Fry could not remain angry at for long. Around forty years of age, he was also older than most of his vice-consular colleagues and wiser in his outlook, and very sympathetic to refugees. The two men quickly discovered they had a lot to talk about.

Bingham explained to Fry that the Marseille consulate was notoriously slow in issuing visas, partly because of the contradictory orders it received from Washington—whose general directive was best summed up as "issue all the visas you want, but not to those people who apply for them." There was also the problem of Bingham's boss, Consul Hugh Fullerton, who was not an evil man but a nervous one, and keen to do nothing that might antagonize the Vichy authorities. Bingham himself actively worked to speed up the process of getting visas to refugees, but it meant disobeying direct orders. He and his deputy, Myles Standish, were doing all they could, but they were outgunned.

Fry was impressed that Bingham did not mention the fact that he was hiding Feuchtwanger and Golo Mann: it seemed to prove that he was serious. There was nothing in Bingham's conversation that glamorized himself, and he seemed genuinely embarrassed and chagrined to be associated with the behavior of the other consular staff. Bingham invited Fry to visit him at his villa, midway between Montredon and the center of Marseille, and that was how Fry met Feuchtwanger and persuaded him to ship out on Bohn's boat. Soon, Fry would be regularly taking the streetcar along the rue Paradis for about a mile and a half, then getting off and walking the long block of the rue du Commandant Rollin, to the steep Boulevard Rivet. There in the evening, in Bingham's three-story, yellow stucco villa with its large overgrown garden, the men would swim in the shallow pond and then eat together, talking over the day's difficulties and planning to cooperate however they could. Fry had found another collaborator, and a true friend.

"HE LOOKED LIKE an attractive person, and he seemed interested in me, and my story," said Albert Hermant. Speaking English with a Berlin accent, he introduced himself to Varian Fry near the end of the first week. Besides the confusing discrepancy of his accent, the thing that struck Fry about the man who stood at the door of his hotel room was his serious and almost pouting expression, that turned to a wide beaming smile whenever an interesting thought passed through his head, or whenever he heard an idea he liked. Fry pointed out to him that he shared his name with a French poet, and "Hermant" admitted the truth about his nationality. Fry quickly latched on to the fact that Hermant-Hirschmann was a very useful fellow to have around, and welcomed the young man as his first employee.

Hermant had been given Fry's name by another refugee. Already Marseille was buzzing with the rumor of his presence. "Like the first bird note of a gloomy morning," Hans Natonek wrote, "a rumor ran through the cafés of the Vieux Port and Canebière. It was said that an American had arrived with the funds and the will to help. . . . It was another distraction in a city in which black-market operators sold hysterical men berths on ships which did not exist to ports which, in any case, would have denied them entry. But the rumor persisted and grew. It was said that this American had a list. . . ." In fact, Fry's fame had already spread beyond Marseille by means of the "refugee telegraph." At the Gare St. Charles, a man was selling Fry's name at fifty francs a time to refugees arriving in the city.

For his part, Hermant was also interested in the list, and in what he could do to help. He had an offer of a fellowship in economics from the University of California (he already had his Ph.D., from Trieste in 1938), and his chances of being granted an American visa were consequently better than average. In the meantime, he was *en règle* to a tee. Taking no chances, Hermant had little by little furnished himself with every conceivable form of identification and membership that could vouch for his new persona. He had joined every club and organization he could think of as "Albert Hermant" in the effort to bury Otto Hirschmann well in the past. It suited Hermant's sense of irony to be so extravagantly walleted with cards and papers—although, as he admitted, any self-respecting policeman would suspect him right away just because of it.

He was also, Fry discovered, seeing the strange peroxide-blond woman, called Camille Delapré, from the American consulate. The woman's deceased husband was a journalist who had been killed in the Spanish Civil War while covering the conflict for the *Paris Soir* newspaper, Hermant told him. Some Communists had thrown the man from a train as it sped through a tunnel. It had been the shock, perhaps, which had turned the young widow violently anti-Semitic and reactionary. She now blamed all Jews and Communists for her husband's death, and was taking refuge in cocaine, plentifully available in Marseille. She had no clue that the good-looking young Frenchman she had begun an affair with was really a leftish German Jew.

Hermant may have had an ulterior motive for cultivating that particular intimacy: what better way of getting to the head of the queue for a visa than to have a devoted contact on the inside of the consulate? The mercurial Hermant had a way with doors; he was elusive and always one step ahead. He claimed that he was *"un peu dans la lune"*—which means roughly that he had his head in the clouds rather often. But that description was most likely a smoke screen. He was an intellectual Berliner, always sizing up the situation, always several moves ahead of the game. For certain he was using the young widow to line up an escape route for when he might possibly need it in a hurry.

But more important to Fry than Hermant's private life were his qualifications for the job. Beyond doubt, the young man was intelligent, resourceful, daring, and courageous. He was German, and an exile himself, so he would know the scene very well. As he was *en règle* as a Frenchman (with no trace of an accent) he could move around with relative ease. And at the age of twenty-five he already had two wars under his belt and a wealth of underground experience. He had even actually crossed the border into Spain once, undetected.

Soon after they met, Hermant was again re-christened, this time by Fry, who called him "Beamish" in recognition of his brilliant smile. It was the beginning of a beautiful friendship.

BY THE END of the first week, with the émigré grapevine spreading word of Fry's presence well beyond Marseille, refugees began to arrive in significant numbers at the Hotel Splendide. From his small room, Fry and his young companion launched one of the most audacious undercover operations ever conceived, much less carried out. It was done under the noses of the Gestapo, arguably the most efficient instrument of terror in the history of mankind. For there were German as well as Italian officers in residence at the Splendide who came and went through the hotel lobby all day long, or sat drinking and laughing at night in their rooms. Perhaps it was the unthinkable audacity of what Fry was up to that led the enemy never to question the steady stream of people walking up and down the stairs, and jostling outside room 307.

Fry and Beamish were soon joined by another collaborator, Franz von Hildebrand, scion of upper-crust Catholic-monarchist Austria, who spoke perfect English like a country gentleman, and mixed it with fruity American slang he had picked up at college in the United States. Franzi's advantages were threefold. First, he had worked for a refugee committee in Paris, so he knew about relief work. Second, he was the holder of an authentic Swiss passport, bestowed as an honor on his family generations earlier. To be, like Fry himself, a citizen of a neutral country was a great boon, and it meant he could cease to be Austrian except for when it suited Fry, for example in advising him on the Austrian Catholics who should be helped. This was Franzi's third useful function, together with the fact that he gave the office an air of diversity, so that if the police became suspicious, it would not look as if Fry was running an illegal socialist operation.

The Austrian socialists who came to room 307 and saw Franzi there were initially appalled. Before Hitler marched into the country, they and the Monarchists—Franzi among the most conspicuous of them—were on the way to fomenting between them a civil war. It was a ridiculous and stupid struggle, said Fry, since it blinded the Catholics in Austria to the real threat of Nazism. But after the socialists found Franzi treating them like his best friends, and recovered from their shock (many Catholics were now properly contrite for their terrible mistake in 1938), Fry noticed that they got along "beautifully."

Each day proved busier than the last in room 307. The refugees would begin to arrive about eight o'clock in the morning, and the last one would be sent back downstairs at sometime around midnight. The conditions were cramped, but the men soon worked out a system. There were two desks: one, the little writing table, the other, an unscrewed wall-mirror placed facedown on Fry's bed. It was a miniature and more benign replication of what went on at the American consulate. When a refugee knocked on the door, Fry would conduct a brief interview to see if he could be classified in any way as somebody the Emergency Rescue Committee was interested in.

Already Fry was widening the scope of his operation. His first duty was to effect the departure from France of the two hundred names he had brought with him. But he saw he could also help a wider circle of refugees with their visa applications and the myriad bureaucratic tasks involved in emigration and staying clear of concentration camps.

If the refugee seemed like a prospect for assistance, Fry would pass him or her on to Beamish and Franzi, who would ask more detailed questions, and also seek to establish what the applicant knew about the overall situation. In this way Fry discovered which of his so far uncontacted "names" was where, and which hadn't made it. He found out about Ernst Weiss's suicide this way, and Walter Hasenclever's. He heard about Willi Muenzenberg's murder (it is thought he was killed by communists, perhaps for denouncing the Nazi-Soviet pact)—his rotting corpse had been found hanging from a tree—and several other disasters. But on the whole the luck and resilience of the refugees so far gave him hope that he would at least be able to get in touch with most of the people he needed to.

Fry quickly became aware, uncomfortably so, that he had been placed in a godlike position. The three men were diligently executing their duties, minutely sifting the claims of the anxious people who ascended the stairs of the Splendide. But they could never help them all: it was an inexorably rising tide. For the lucky few it could be like having a private army on your side. But Fry knew the plan was not perfect: "Some names had been put on them which ought not to have been there. Others had been left off which ought to have been on."

At the end of the day's work, which was more often than not stuffy in the August heat, and filled with the suppressed hysteria of the refugees, the three men would get together and compare the white file cards that had been generated by the interviews. The comparative merits of each claim for help would be weighed, and the names of those Fry decided should be included in the priceless visa quota would be cabled each night to New York. After that, it would be the New York committee's responsibility to begin to pursue the lengthy process by which the State Department would eventually transmit instructions to the Consulate at Marseille, or Lyon, or Toulouse, to issue the relevant visas. Fry waited to hear from New York, and then would contact the refugee in question with the good news. Some of them, in long-term danger but not on the Gestapo list, could afford to wait. They needed only subsistence money so that poverty did not conduct them to some scabrous camp, as was Vichy policy. This Fry could help with, although his money would not hold out for long.

Others, even after they had their American visas authorized, were unwilling to leave. They were scared to stay in France, but even more terrified about what would happen to them if they tried to leave. Often they madly insisted on waiting for an exit visa, but such were uncommon. Mostly, Fry recalled, he would shake the hand of a newly visaed exile and say, "I'll see you soon in New York." They thanked him numbly, in bewilderment and disbelief. Who was this man who had appeared out of nowhere, and like an angel promised them life when they had thought only of death? Who was this tall, rather awkward young man who put his arm around their shoulders and said, "Don't worry, you'll be all right," when they were ready to jump from the high bridge over the Marseille harbor ("a certain enough method" wrote the novelist Victor Serge)?

Fry said that the saddest cases were those whom the French called "apatrides"—people whose citizenship had been revoked by Hitler, and who had no passport. It also meant, almost inevitably, that the Gestapo was after them. Some Fry could assist, since an American visa was seen by the Spanish and Portuguese as a certificate of pedigree. With it, in the absence of a passport, came an "affidavit in lieu," which acted as a passport, and which provoked a response of overwhelming respect from petty officials. The stateless refugee might as well have been American if he had one of these. Meanwhile, yet more refugees arrived at the Splendide. There was hardly any time to write to Eileen, but when he managed to, Fry attempted to sound cheerful: "It is a crushing job," he wrote. "I have never worked so hard in my life, or such long hours. Strangely, though there are a dozen harrowing scenes every day, I love the work. The pleasure of being able to help even a few people more than makes up for the pain of having to turn others down. . . ." But really it didn't. He wanted to save them all.

When the day's cable had been prepared—the details often discussed in the bathroom attached to 307, with the faucets opened wide and roaring to foil any listeners in the next room, or at the other end of a microphone— Beamish and Fry would stumble through the blackout to the police station behind the rue Colbert, and go through the rigmarole of cabling New York. The apathy of the policemen was remarkable. Eventually one would arise in response to Fry's rhythmic tapping on the wooden shutter of the telegraph bureau, and would peer in mock expertise and official suspicion at the words he could never understand. Then, according to the typical doublethink of Vichy, Fry would sign a paper that promised he was not sending a coded message. Reassured, the policeman would drift off and lazily transmit the cable, before returning to whatever game of cards was just about keeping him awake.

Streetwise Beamish escorted Fry back to the Hotel Splendide every night, along the dark and threatening rue des Dominicaines. He insisted on doing this because he knew there was a chance they were already being watched, and that Fry could easily "disappear." And if the Gestapo was not that well informed, this was still Marseille, after all.

FRY, THE PERFECTIONIST, was already unhappy. The refugee problem was clearly far more extensive than the small portion of it he had been sent to address. And American policy was not making the situation any easier. As a ham-fisted economic measure against the belligerent nations, all moneys in the United States had recently been blocked from moving to and from Europe. Unfortunately, this succeeded only in worsening the situation of the refugees. "I wish everybody in America could be made to realize just who suffers most from the policy of blocking funds," Fry wrote to Eileen. "It is not, certainly, the Germans, nor even the French, but the non-French refugees. They are being crushed in one of the most gigantic vises in history. Unable to leave France, unable to work, and so earn money, unable to obtain funds from Paris or London or from New York, they have literally been condemned to death here—or, at best, to confinement in detention camps, a fate little better than death."

He talked the situation over with Beamish, the doctor of economics but also, as Fry discovered, a denizen of the bars and brothels of Marseille's Vieux Port—which was just as well, considering the solution they eventually formulated.

There was a problem, both men agreed. Back in New York, the tireless Harold Oram was raising money at the fantastic rate of almost twenty thousand dollars a month. With that kind of money coming over, Fry could keep all the refugees out of the camps, and arrange for all the false papers and passages on ships out of Lisbon that he needed. But he couldn't wire for a single nickel to be sent because of the latest obstructive government measures. The problem was replicated on the French side, but in a twofold manner. First, there was an official exchange rate that bore no relation to reality, so even if one possessed dollars, Vichy basically stole them when they were changed into francs. (The Germans were charging France four hundred million francs *a day* for "administering" the country—about 60 percent of gross domestic product. It was extortion on a scale that had murdered the currency and would soon begin slowly to starve France to death.)

Also—a specific problem relating to Fry's line of business—the authorities would have a record of any transaction on the official exchange. If one's criminally overvalued francs were spent on forged passports and other illegal fare necessary for helping refugees, the expenditure had to be concealed from the police, or there would be the job of explaining discrepancies in the account books. These could be seized and examined at any time—indeed, it was a favorite means of harassment by the authorities of the refugee aid organizations. If it was discovered that irregularities had occurred, an operation like Fry's would be shut down without further ado: he would be sent back to New York, and the refugees would be at the Gestapo's mercy. So an alternative to the official exchange had to be found. Also, a way of importing dollars from the United States to France that evaded international embargoes had somehow to be contrived. Beamish was already considering the possibilities.

Another German Jew soon turned up who was to solve the problem of evading the official exchange rate and hiding dollar expenses. Heinz Ernst Oppenheimer ("Oppy") was an engineer who had escaped from Germany when Hitler came to power. He fled to Holland and had run a relief agency there. But he was also a bookkeeper of some talent. Oppy beavered away on the accounts, "disguising the illegal expenses in various ingenious ways and preparing beautiful statistical charts, all utterly legal and above-board," said Fry. "Instead of entering the grants to departing refugees as 'travel expenses,' which would have implicated us in illegal departures, he put them down as 'living expenses.' . . . Oppy translated all the dollar payments into francs before entering them in the books. Thanks to him, we were always ready for the police."

Oppy's work made it possible entirely to bypass the official exchange rate of 43.5 francs to the dollar. This was an estimable advantage, for in late 1940, paper dollars were really worth between 40 and 90 francs. Later on, as the French economy was strangled, the dollar would rise to around 125 and eventually 180 francs, making Fry's funds go many times as far as Vichy would have liked—and 50 francs higher again if Fry cold lay his hands on gold. The dollars he already possessed were thus taken care of. But there remained the difficulty of transferring to France all the money piling up in the Emergency Rescue Committee's bank account in New York. Beamish had been working on it. His face split into a wide electric grin as he explained to Fry how things were.

The Montagues and Capulets of Marseille were two Corsican gangster families, the Guerinis and the Carbones. As if tailor-made for a five-act tragedy in the circumstances of the war, the Guerini brothers headed the crime syndicate that supported the British cause, and the Carbones were on the side of the Fascists. When Fry wrote his account of the war, he obviously planned on revisiting Marseille one day, so he changed all the names. In *Surrender on Demand,* Charles Vinciléoni was Jacques, the owner of an "almost completely respectable" restaurant called Les Sept Petits Pêcheurs. It was really the Dorade, on the corner of the rue Sainte and rue Fortia, just back of the Quai de Rive Neuve. Charles, who sat there all day sipping bicarbonate of soda and surveying his customers with a lizard eye, ran the restaurant as a front for his truly profitable business enterprises. These, despite his admirable political views, remained the traditional ones of girls, black market goods, and *coco*, for Charles was tied into the Guerini gang.

Vinciléoni's competitor, Sabiani, on the other hand, was a bad guy allied with the Carbones. "The restaurant Beauvau," said Fry, who later moved to the hotel that housed it, "was kept by the Fascist gangster Carboni [Sabiani], dealer in drugs, women, contraband of all sorts, corruptor of the police, election frauds, political muggings, etc. . . . and a great admirer of Pétain." The advantage of eating at the Beauvau was that no food coupons were required, just large amounts of cash. Usually, waitresses in Vichy France walked from table to table with a pair of scissors dangling from around their necks on a piece of string. They would serve the dish, then clip the little printed squares from one's ration book. Not at Sabiani's joint. A reporter from American *Vogue* was duly impressed when she visited in late 1941, and she also noticed the long queues outside. But many refused to eat there on principle: Carbone owned the infamous Doriotist (French Fascist) newspaper, *Midi*. Marseille was rotten with graft and extortion, as it had always been. The gangsters had already weakened the social fabric by 1940 by systematically corrupting, then brutally controlling, the entire scene of municipal politics (it had been their duopoly between 1926 and 1934). The war had made them even more powerful, preeminently because they could lay hands on supplies of scarce goods, and they were cutting deals not just with the police, but with the Germans and Italians as well.

Ironically enough, it was an American Foreign Service employee—the bleach-blond widow Delapré, who probably knew the scene through her *coco* connection—who proved Beamish's initial contact with the underworld around the Vieux Port. She introduced him to a Corsican "businessman" named Malandri. Ordinarily, a healthy survival instinct would be to stay away from such people, but Beamish needed an "in" to the local rackets for the good of the rescue operation, and one or two facts about Malandri seemed to vouch for him. To begin with, Malandri was a friend of an anti-Nazi German banker called Frankel, who had bankrolled von Papen, an opponent of Hitler's at the time of the fateful elections in November 1932. Frankel made a bad bet and backed a terrible candidate, and he subsequently fled to Paris where he financed an anti-Nazi journal, the *Neue Tagebuch*. Frankel had certificates that supposedly proved he had been stripped by the Nazis of his Reich citizenship.

What was more impressive, Malandri had managed to provide for this old enemy of Hitler a set of papers that allowed Frankel to travel virtually unhindered throughout the unoccupied zone. This was unheard of for anybody, much less a German whom the Gestapo must have been looking for. It was an impressive set of credentials for Malandri, who, being Corsican, said Beamish, would not be working for Mussolini's secret police: all Corsicans hated the Italians. By extension of the same logic, it was unlikely the man was in the pocket of the Gestapo, either.

Beamish got close to Malandri, and began to talk of the money troubles he and Fry were experiencing. Soon enough Malandri introduced Beamish to Charles Vinciléoni, the inscrutable *patron* of the Dorade. Vinciléoni, who had many contacts of the sort Beamish was looking for, was uninterested in doing business with America himself. He had traveled there several times—illegally, of course, on illegal business—and had returned to France with the sour opinion that American criminals were all crooked. Vinciléoni hated to miss out on a share of the profit Beamish was dangling before him, though, and he was impelled to help out of self-interest. For this reason he introduced Beamish to a character who would prove fateful to Fry's mission in more ways than one.

Kourillo—Fry called him Dimitru—was a Peter Lorre character. He stood at barely five feet tall, and his handshake felt like an empty glove. Kourillo claimed that in the old country he had been landed gentry (like many other rich "White Russians," his family presumably fled during the 1917 revolution) and said that in Paris he had been a member of the most select society. He had the manners and excessive politeness that made this seem both plausible and suspicious: Kourillo was a classic Marseille *mythomane*. Fry found out he had worked in the American Express office in Paris, from where he was fired for stealing money, and was warned against relying on Kourillo in financial matters. The Russian had the usual minor-underworld weaknesses for women and liquor, but he did possess one redeeming quality: Kourillo knew many people in Marseille who wanted to make large amounts of money disappear from France.

For a commission, split three ways with Vinciléoni and Beamish, Kourillo would act as an agent between the Emergency Rescue Committee and his own Marseille clients. For example, if one of Kourillo's customers had 150,000 francs he needed spiriting out of France, this would show up in a matter of days as several thousand dollars in his New York account, and Fry would simply collect the francs from Kourillo in Marseille. All it took was two cables: one from Fry telling the committee how much money to deposit, and the account number; and another from the committee back to Fry to confirm that the deposit had been made. Beamish had to take a commission on each transaction, or else Vinciléoni and Kourillo would simply have split it between themselves. But he unfailingly handed it over to Fry.

With a cash flow established, Fry was set to carry on his work indefinitely. Events were moving so fast that he hardly remembered his return ticket on the Yankee Clipper was from Lisbon on August 24. He had missed it without even noticing.

"YOU SEEM TO HAVE DISAPPEARED into a vacuum," wrote Eileen soon after Fry had arrived in Marseille. She had left the stifling heat of Manhattan for Provincetown and was enjoying the late-summer weather, and reported that her garden was bursting with tiger lilies. But she worried that she had not heard from her husband. The letter she had posted while Fry was aboard the flying boat on his way to Europe would not turn up in France until the following summer; his letters back were as likely to be delayed. And if that was plain bad luck, there was still the usual three-week delay and the French censor to contend with. This time lag would put a strain on relations between Fry and Eileen, in addition to the usual worries of separation, and the fact that Fry was involved in real danger and adventure in which Eileen could participate only vicariously. And there was much that obviously he could not tell her at all. Lastly, and most seriously, there was the realization slowing dawning on Fry that he was in no hurry to go home.

CHAPTER 11

IRREVERSIBLE

I T WAS THE LAST THURSDAY in August when Fry heard the bells of the police van—known locally as a *panier à salade* (salad bowl)—outside his window. A few days before, the management of the Splendide had complained to Fry of crowds in the corridor outside room 307. Sensitive to this, he had asked the refugees to wait downstairs in the lobby so he could call them up one at a time. But it was too late, and the shiftless group had pricked the interest of the police. Such roundups of refugees, called *rafles,* were un-announced and common in Vichy France, especially in overcrowded towns like Marseille. It was a serious development, for they would naturally connect Fry's presence in the hotel with the motley collection of foreigners they had just arrested for questioning.

Fry had been expanding his operation and taking on more staff, and in the last few days he had found three more employees. The first was the young Virginian, Charlie Fawcett. Since the time he delivered the British troops to Countess Lily, he had been shuttling between Marseille and Paris carrying out orders from the nascent French underground. It was a personal connection that led to his introduction to Fry. Back in Paris before the war Charlie had befriended a young couple, both foreign students and refugees. He had been in a café one day when another student sitting with them had called the girl a "wop," and Charlie had turned the table over on the man and kicked him onto the street. The student couple had never forgotten Charlie's gallantry, and when they spotted him in Marseille, led him straight to Varian Fry, who—despite their obscurity—was already helping them escape France. Charlie was soon running low-level errands for Fry, and decided to make

Marseille his base. He was impressed with what Fry was doing, and it seems the footloose and reckless Charlie—"He was a nice, utterly crazy youngster," Fry said—had stumbled upon a mentor.

Two or three days after Charlie had joined the crew, Fry and Beamish were sitting amid the wreckage of breakfast on an unmade bed in room 307. Without warning, the door opened and a pretty young woman marched in. She shooed them into the corner and, with great efficiency, began to tidy up. The men were impressed with her presence as well as her energy. She introduced herself as Lena Fischmann, and explained that Donald Lowrie of the YMCA had recommended that she see Fry about a job. Lena's story of transit to the secret city was another hair-raising tail. Before the war she had worked in Paris at the Liaison Committee for the High Commissioner for Refugees, and continued to help the stateless until the Germans were at the point of entering Paris, when she fled with four friends in the direction of Bordeaux. When she arrived there, the American consulate gave Lena, who said she was Polish, a particularly stiff refusal to her request for a visa. Undaunted, she carried on toward Spain, only to be turned back at Hendaye, like everybody else without papers. As usual, the next stop—the final and only stop—was Marseille. Lena found an abandoned Packard automobile on the road and took off in an easterly direction. Gasoline was almost unobtainable, but before Lena had traveled very far, she had an idea. She clipped the Red Cross insignia from a box of cotton wool and taped it to the windshield. Then, usually after midnight, she would stop in small villages and noisily awake the groggy mayor. Declaring she was on official business, she would wave her rejection letter from the American consulate in the face of the confused man, and demand some gas. It worked every time.

She never told anybody this, not even Fry himself, who called her "our smiling Polish friend," but Lena was not Polish at all. She was only traveling on a Polish passport. Really, she was Russian, but as she spoke six languages, gaily mixing them all into her sentences, it meant nobody could tell. Because she was multilingual, and fast with shorthand, Fry quickly found Lena invaluable as a stenographer and secretary. But these were the least of her useful accomplishments. Above all, she was always gay and utterly unflappable. It was wearing for them all, holed up in the hot and claustrophobic space of the hotel room, to be assaulted daily with the panic and desperation of the refugees. Lena was the perfect remedy. For every outburst of tears she was a joyful equal, dismissing hysterics with her characteristically gentle rebuke, "Il ne faut pas exagérer!" (Don't exaggerate!) Nothing ever got to Lena. One night a sailor was murdered noisily right under her window at the seedy

Hotel des Postes. When Fry showed alarm at the dangers she faced in that rough area, Lena replied, as usual, "Il ne faut pas exagérer!"

The third new member of Fry's growing staff was American, and she arrived via her acquaintance with Walter Mehring. Fry had sent word to Mehring that his name was on the New York list, and that help was at hand. The paranoid poet had been due to show up at the Splendide for an interview, but when the time came he was too scared to travel into town. So when Fry answered the door at the appointed time, he saw standing before him instead a beautiful slim young lady with big blue eyes and two braids of hair done up on top of her head. She said Mehring had sent her.

The woman's name was Miriam Davenport. It turned out that she was from a Boston family, like Fry's wife, and had studied art history. After graduating from Smith College with high honors in 1938, she traveled to France to continue her studies on a scholarship from the Institute of Art and Archaeology at the Sorbonne. She fell in love with a Yugoslavian art student Rudolf Treo, and decided that she would stay on there to complete her graduate work. When war broke out she went to Yugoslavia with Rudolf and supported herself by teaching English, and when the Germans launched their spring offensive against Holland and Belgium, she returned to Paris alone. There she met Mehring, who was living in the room next to the one she took at the Hotel de l'Univers. Her final exams were disrupted by the entrance into Paris of the German army, and Miriam just managed to catch the last train south to Toulouse (the line was bombed the day after), where she had arranged to sit the exams instead. It was there she met up again with Mehring, and with Hertha Pauli, Heiden, and the Werfels, who had converged on the city by various routes.

Miriam smoked almost nonstop, and had a hacking cough to prove it, but one that would blend seamlessly into ribald laughter at the bawdy language with which she embellished her many anecdotes. Here was another tough, and tough-minded, not to say talented and intelligent young person. After she left, Fry thought it over. It was physically impossible to fit any more people into room 307. To handle the work he needed larger premises, but finding larger premises implied expanding the scope and length of his work in Marseille—something he had not asked permission of the Committee in New York to do. Expanding the job also meant he himself would have to stay on indefinitely, at least until a replacement could be found and sent to France. There was an inexorable logic to the work that made it seem Marseille was reeling him in.

Secretly Fry knew it would be difficult for New York to send a replacement.

Conditions were growing harder and more complicated every day, as the new regime in unoccupied France consolidated its organization and sorted out border controls and various other repressive measures against the foreign population. Fry was well involved by now, had experienced several lucky breaks already, and found trusted collaborators. He was getting to know the ropes. His was one of those jobs that are just tailor-made for the man, and he was already a veteran compared to anybody the committee could send over. To stay could mean he would lose his job at the Foreign Policy Association, and an important link with his New York existence would be severed. But the work in Marseille seemed so essential and vivid—he couldn't imagine leaving yet. That night he wrote a letter to Miriam at the inaptly named Hotel Paradis Bel-Air on rue Madagascar: "Do you do typewriting?" he asked. "If you can, will you show up at my hotel tomorrow? I very badly need help."

FRY WAS FURIOUS with himself. If only he had thought things through more carefully it need never have happened. A couple of days after the *rafle*— it was the last day of August, a Saturday—his breakfast in room 307 was interrupted by the ringing of the telephone. Bohn's hoarse stage whisper told him that the police were at the hotel and wanted to see both Americans to find out what they were up to. Fry had failed to contact the police in any formal capacity since his arrival in Marseille a fortnight before, which was naive at best and arguably plain stupid. The police would have expected it as a courtesy, and probably required some informal registration as a matter of course. Whether Fry had been lulled by Bohn's complacency or had simply been too busy to remember this is unclear. The fact was, the police now wanted to see him downstairs, immediately.

Fry loosened the mirror on the inside door of his closet and slid the map with the escape route and the list itself behind it, tightening the screws again, taking care not to scrape them with his pocket knife. Then he destroyed some incriminating papers, including the addresses of safe houses for refugees and sources of forged documents, by tearing them up and flushing them away. The telephone rang again, and Fry descended to the lobby. There he found a police inspector in the hotel's writing room. If it was the case, as Fry reported, that most French people were embarrassed by the direction in which the Vichy government was dragging the country, this was less true for the powers of law enforcement. Most police had the professional love of their own powers like police the world over, and to some extent approved of the new measures designed by Vichy to clear the streets of what they saw as human garbage. But many officers were able to discriminate between criminals and poor unfortunates like the refugees; and not all of them were anti-Semitic. Some would even offer passive resistance to the more draconian measures handed down from above, and would attempt to help, if only in small ways that were certain not to compromise themselves (giving warnings of planned arrests, for example, or turning a blind eye to certain activities). Inspector Gaillarde, it seems, was such an officer.

Gaillarde had a soulful face and wore a dark blue business suit. He informed Fry that disturbing reports concerning his activities had been received at the *Evêché* (the police headquarters, known as such because it was housed in a beautiful old building that had been the local bishop's palace). Fry hastily denied any wrongdoing but he still had to explain the exact nature of his business, and as he did so, a very respectful Gaillarde took notes. Fry explained how he was affiliated with the YMCA, and was handing out aid to certain refugees while he arranged visas for them to travel to the United States: surely the French would not disapprove of his efforts to lighten the refugee burden they were under in this difficult time? The evidence suggests that Gaillarde knew very well that Fry was involved in illegal activities. Forged papers and illicit black-market money exchanges were common: the latter, as a charge, was even regarded by the police as a joke ("C'est de la blague"). Illegal escapes over mountains was another matter. Gaillarde must have known about the Austrians, but he must also have approved, for he ended the meeting on a note of cordiality that was loud enough for most of the lobby to hear, and he shook Fry's hand warmly, just to let people know it would no longer do any good to provide anonymous accusations against the American in room 307. Fry could breathe again, and he was impressed by the policeman's sympathetic attitude. "The French people are no more ready for fascism than the American people are," he told Eileen. "Rather less so, I should say, because they are the most urbane and cosmopolitan people in the world, and fascism is neither. . . ." But this visit was not the end of his troubles, only the beginning.

The visit alerted Fry to danger, and to the importance of maintaining at least a semblance of cordial relations with the authorities he was trying to outwit. To this end, he made an appointment to see Roger Homo, Secrétaire Générale de la Préfecture des Bouches du Rhône (rather like a commissioner of police in a political capacity) at the Prefecture in Marseille. Fry hired a young lawyer, Gaston Defferre, to go along with him (Defferre would be the longtime mayor of Marseille in the postwar years, and François Mitterrand's Minister of the Interior in the 1980s). Fry also asked the American consul-general, John P. Hurley, if he would kindly accompany them. Hurley, who had no time at all for refugees, refused. The secretary-general, said Fry, "was very correct, but very frigid," and it did not help that Fry had trouble concealing his frustration with the situation regarding the refugees: he found it very difficult to lie, even to the extent of injecting into his speech a more diplomatic turn of phrase. The lawyer, acting as interpreter, was placing an impressive legalistic gloss on Fry's invective. The high official sat behind his desk, impassive, then turned to Defferre and said, not in French, "You know, Maître, I speak better English than you think." Fry came away from the meeting relieved that he had permission to continue his work—but with the strict proviso that absolutely nothing illegal would be attempted. Fry had naturally appeared scandalized at the very suggestion.

MEANWHILE, ILLEGAL ESCAPES had been proceeding at full speed.

Not long before the police roundup at the Splendide, Fry and Beamish held a conference in which they attempted to sort out who—apart from Heinrich Mann, the Werfels, Feuchtwanger, and Walter Mehring, whom they nicknamed "Baby"—was in the most danger of being caught by the Gestapo. They whittled down from the overall list over two dozen names, among them Konrad Heiden, a personal enemy of Hitler, Professor Gumbel, Hans Natonek, Leonhard Frank, Hilde Walter, novelist Alfred Polgar, and Mehring's friend Hertha Pauli. Heiden was top. Nobel Prize winner Otto Meyerhof had been spared the concentration camp because of his status, but it was not clear how long even he would be safe.

It was Beamish's role in the evolving rescue operation to be out and about, meeting people like Guerini and Kourillo, and testing arrangements for sending those whom Fry was beginning to call his "protégés" out of the country. Beamish had been down to the French border at Cerbère with the map the young Austrian had given Fry, and investigated the escape route over the Pyrenees. This had to be the way into Spain because without exit visas there was no way for the refugees to pass legally through French border control. Beamish discovered the mountains were not that high just above the sea, in fact only about three hundred meters. But it was difficult terrain: they were steep, with smooth slopes and few handholds. The winds were treacherous and at so steep a gradient could easily knock a person off his feet. Above all, there was the difficulty of ascending in full view of the town, while managing to avoid the attention of police and customs. But it was possible—and it helped that Monsieur Cruzet, the mayor, was a socialist who was willing to help. It looked as if they would have to try it out with Heiden as a guinea pig.

As far as documents were concerned, Heiden's case was exemplary. Fry had fitted him up with one of Vladimir Vochoč's Czech passports he had received from Donald Lowrie at the most recent of their biweekly breakfast meetings at the Hotel Terminus. Using this, and the false identity—"David Silbermann," a businessman—that was on it, Fry had also obtained Spanish and Portuguese transit visas for Heiden. Heiden himself already had a United States visa, and the document that came with it that served as a temporary passport: the "affidavit in lieu of." As these were in Heiden's real name, and would obviously be needed to get him into America, he would have to keep them hidden for his entire journey. In fact, he could reveal his true identity only when he arrived at the passenger dock at Lisbon. Having passed through Portuguese customs as David Silbermann, he would then present himself to American officials at the gangplank of the New York–bound liner as Konrad Heiden less than a minute later.

At least, that was the plan. Heiden would still have to undertake the five-hour train journey from Marseille to Cerbère without a *sauf conduit* (travel permit) and this could lead to his arrest if he was inspected en route and asked to produce a *carte d'identité*. The solution was to catch the relatively safe first train from the Gare St. Charles at five o'clock in the morning, before any policemen were awake. At Cerbère, he was to leave the railway station and walk to the cemetery, climb over the wall and up the slope. Once Heiden was over the mountain, he was to go directly to the Spanish border post at Port-Bou to receive his *entrada* stamp. Then he could continue on to Barcelona, Madrid, and Portugal. Fry told him to meet in Lisbon one of his contacts, Dr. Charles Joy of the Unitarian mission, to help with lodgings and passage on a ship to America. Then he handed him a paper bag containing six packs of cigarettes—some Lucky Strikes and Gauloises—for which Fry had been assured the Spanish guards were always demonstrably grateful, and told Heiden he would see him in New York.

Heiden took this leap into the unknown rather well, for he knew the cost of remaining in France could be his life and that this plan at least gave him a chance of survival. In fact Fry was more nervous than Heiden: if things miscarried he would be responsible for his protégé's death. There was no higher authority in this mischief than Fry himself, and he had to make the fateful decisions alone—and take the consequences. It was once again the feeling that he was playing God, and although he didn't like it, he also felt invigorated: here was the real game of holy poker. If he brought it off, then by the same token it would be by his own doing and decisiveness, and he would have saved a man's life. Fry would, in some small way, be a hero.

Silence followed Heiden's departure. There was no announcement of his arrest, and no desperate message from any concentration camp near the border, so Fry had to assume—but only assume—that Heiden had crossed the border successfully at Cerbère. There was no time to be lost, and over the next few days, Beamish hastily summoned the rest of the most endangered refugees to room 307 to receive their instructions from Fry. Some, like Emil Gumbel, were sent down to the frontier singly; others went as a group, like the party composed of Natonek, Norbert Muhlen, and Hertha Pauli. Heinrich (Henry) Ehrmann was a young economist, a friend of Beamish's from his Paris days. Beamish had persuaded Fry that Ehrmann was also in danger, and Fry agreed to add his name to the list. It was the first in an historic expansion. Each escapee was handed by Fry a supply of the magic cigarettes—they smoked them at their peril—and Fry dispatched them all with confident good humor. He was a good actor. Whenever he would say, "Have a good journey and I'll see you in New York," he looked as though he believed it. But each time he wondered whether he was sending these men and women to their deaths. It was like playing Russian roulette repeatedly for two days with each group he sent over. The odds were in their favor on any given click—the train to Cerbère, the border crossing, the Spanish customs, Madrid and the Portuguese frontier. But Fry did not yet know the chances of surviving every squeeze of the trigger.

There was also a savage irony in the exile's situation, for these were people who had made their living from what they wrote on paper. Now, suddenly, their lives depended on what *others* had written: there was Fry and his list, the Gestapo and its list, the false names on fake passports, the young Austrian's primitive map, the wording of the U.S. visas; and then in turn the future of those still in France hung on a brief and enigmatic telegram. By the time Fry, sitting in the office at the prefecture, assured the tight-lipped secretary-general that he would never countenance any illegality, most of the twenty-eight refugees on the danger list were on their way to Lisbon. Fry had been in Marseille for just over two weeks.

ONE OF THE CONSEQUENCES of Fry's discussion with the secretary-general was the establishment of a proper office, and the formal incorporation of Fry's enterprise under the name of the Centre Américain de Secours (The American Relief Center), accomplished with Defferre's help. It was rather a grand title for what amounted to three people who had been operating out of a hotel room, but that was exactly why Fry chose it (in fact, it was Oppy's suggestion). The more respectable-sounding the enterprise was, the happier the police would be. From now on, it had to look as if everything was legal and aboveboard. The whole point of undercover operations, Fry wrote, is that they should look completely and transparently innocent. For this there had to be a plausible cover, and Fry did not see why he should not set himself up as an aid agency like the several others operating in Marseille. In fact he could probably do better, since with funds from the United States blocked by Washington, their work had effectively ceased for the present time. A large "Closed" sign, for example, hung on the door of the office of HICEM, the Hebrew relief agency. It would stay there for several months, as long as money was difficult and the French refused to issue exit visas. Fry by contrast was unhindered because he was prepared to use the black market in currency to finance himself, and was learning to scorn the very idea of an exit visa.

There had been another lucky break during the search for office space. A French-Jewish businessman was looking to sell up and get out as fast as possible, before Pétain's government expropriated his company. Laws were soon to be passed in France, just as draconian as those in Germany, which would force Jewish traders to sell their property and everything else to a (gentile) French "trustee" for a fraction of its value. It was nothing less than legalized robbery. This man had a leather goods business at 60 rue Grignan, a nondescript little street near the American consulate, running parallel to the lower part of the Canebière. He offered his premises, and even waived the rent until January because of the work Fry was doing.

The Centre Américain de Secours came quietly into existence on a Monday morning in early September. On the principle that the wider a road is, the more traffic will be generated, so the Centre Américain experienced an upsurge in its own refugee traffic as a result of moving into a proper office. Again, events conspired to bless Fry's progress. Dr. Burns Chalmers at the local Quaker aid agency, the Friends Service Committee, had bumped into Miriam on the street. As chance would have it, this was the very man who had been the chaplain at Smith College when she had studied there. He donated to the Centre Américain a number of meal coupons, which meant that Fry could now mix in some regular relief cases to mask the real business of illegal emigration. Upstairs, in the second-story office, Lena and Miriam sat typing and conducting interviews. Beamish sometimes attended, but more often would be away, engaged in shady business, or enjoying some quality time in one of Marseille's many picturesque brothels—probably Madame Coste's place on the rue Dumarsais, where he was well known. Downstairs, on the street, Charlie Fawcett acted as doorman and genial bouncer. He spoke very little French, but it did not matter: the warm, reassuring tones of his lilting Virginian accent spread good humor among people who were otherwise frantic.

Charlie in Marseille was beginning to discover that, as he recalled, the greatest aphrodisiac in the world was an American passport, although this did not stop women pursuing him from purely amorous motives. One Polish girl called Lili dogged his every step. Her young husband was stranded in North Africa, and Charlie was chivalrously attempting to bring him back into France before the inevitable occurred. Lili was not impatient for her husband's return, and by the time Charlie succeeded in reuniting them, he had given way to her insistence. Charlie was stricken with what to tell the man, especially when he was almost asked straight out what the situation had been. "I hope you managed to entertain my wife while I was away," inquired the man tactfully. "I'll tell you the truth," said Charlie, untruthfully. "One time I tried to entertain her at home, but she wouldn't have it." Charlie was also conducting a minor emigration initiative on his own time. He himself had been in touch with Gaston Defferre, and with his help had begun to marry Jewish women trapped in concentration camps so that, being wed to an American, they could leave France with an automatic United States visa. A woman who worked at the Lisbon consulate told him after the war how puzzled she had been at the stream of applications from "Mrs. Fawcetts" turning up in her pending tray. Charlie was to marry six women over the next three months, and not even Fry knew about it.

In the early days of the Centre Américain on rue Grignan, when the leather-goods merchant was still in the process of removing his stock, the conditions were especially chaotic. For this reason, Fry and his staff would retire to his room at the Splendide (he had just managed to move into a larger one) to hold their evening conferences on the day's applicants once the doors of the office were closed. It was a very hot summer in France that year, and the press of bodies in Fry's room would add to the stultifying atmosphere. Miriam remembered how it was around this time that Fry began to lose some of his characteristic reserve. In all the horror and danger of Marseille in September 1940, Fry was actually loosening up. He kept his poker face and outward seriousness, but little signs showed that he was growing comfortable with the people around him—that they were becoming almost like a family.

At the hotel and in the company of his most trusted collaborators, after a day in the formal guise of director of the Center Américain, Fry would finally take off his tie and loosen his collar. After a while he would detach collar from shirt and roll up his sleeves. Later, the shirt itself would come off, and he would begin to *lounge* in his singlet. At last, as the heavy evening grew even closer, the boxer shorts would be revealed when Fry discarded his trousers. Miriam said they were a Black Watch tartan, perhaps in honor of Fry's Scottish ancestors.

During this time, Beamish continued searching for new contacts to solve the major problems confronting Fry's operations. Kourillo the money changer seemed to have been sent from heaven, and there was, said Fry, no shortage of people in Marseille who wanted to transfer their funds to America. Now, though, establishing reliable supplies of forged documents was a priority. Vochoč's passports could not be relied on indefinitely, as it would only be a matter of time before the Spanish authorities grew suspicious. More urgently, if the Gestapo caught a refugee with false Czechoslovakian papers, they would simply issue instructions to arrest anyone in possession of such a passport. In the clandestine travel business it was good to spread one's bets, and Beamish soon succeeded in securing a similar supply from the Polish consulate in Marseille, and the Lithuanian Consulate in Aix-en-Provence to the north.

He also tracked down a corrupt and—to use a Marseille oxymoron—principled army sergeant at nearby Fort St. Charles who was prepared to issue bogus demobilization orders to refugees for a price of two hundred francs. The order stated that a French soldier's home was in North Africa, so that he was given a thousand francs and a free boat ticket to Casablanca. For an extra five francs a photograph and official stamp could be added. It was a way of making refugees vanish from metropolitan France in short order, and worked like a dream until the officer was caught and court-martialed soon after. This meant the police now had in their possession a list of all those refugees who had bought the false papers—which caused yet more panic. That was often the way with practical outlets for helping those in danger: windows of opportunity could slam shut at a moment's notice and leave people dangerously exposed, and it meant that Beamish stayed very busy and ever on the move.

His real coup was to discover a diminutive Austrian cartoonist whose experience of exile had trained him in the art of forgery. He was the artist of fake identity cards *ne plus ultra,* and his name was Bill Freier. This was the same man who had been part of the Café de Tournon group with Mehring and Feuchtwanger in Paris. He had fled Vienna when, from his upstairs window at the newspaper where he worked, he saw the Gestapo entering the building (*before* the *Anschluss* had taken place). Freier decided he had better take a coffee break. "I'm still on my coffee break," he told Fry. He was in Marseille with his equally miniature fiancée, Mina, and he was painting portraits outside Basso's brasserie down on the Vieux Port: three francs for a small one and six for a large. Mina was pregnant, and Freier was doing his best to get some money together so they could escape. He explained to Fry that Hitler and Goebbels would not be displeased if something happened to him: the year before, one of his cartoons was printed in the British journal, *London Opinion.* It depicted Hitler the former painter and decorator with a bucket and brush. He had signed it, and Hitler had seen it. So Freier was looking to get out of France.

Fry was more interested in Freier's unsigned work. The *carte d'identité* blanks could be bought at any street corner *Tabac,* but they lacked the official stamps saying "Commissaire de Police," and the Commissaire's signature. One filled in the form, then took it to the prefecture with a birth certificate and got it officially warranted. The *carte* was the single most important piece of identification for anybody living in France, but it was impossible for a stateless refugee to obtain one, leaving the individual open to arrest and detention. Freier said he could produce a perfect forgery on one of the blanks in a matter of only two to three hours, and would be happy to do so.

Bill Freier only charged Fry for materials—about fifty cents per—and to watch him at work was an inspiration. He had a tiny glass that exactly matched the size of the official circular stamp. Carefully Freier would wet the rim with ink, then press it down on the virgin document with a minor rotation to imitate precisely the slight blurring that occurred when the real rubber stamp was banged down. Next, he would use a two-hair brush to match the filigree and wording on the original he used for comparison. The signature of the bureaucrat was the easiest part. Freier always made sure that the place of issue was somewhere deep in the occupied zone, like Metz or Strasbourg, so the police in the Bouches du Rhône Department (where Marseille was) would find it tremendously difficult to check out the authenticity of the *carte.*

When he had finished, Freier would drop the perfect identity card to the floor and perform a little dance on it. Thus scuffed, said Charlie, it "looked as though you'd had it in your back pocket for a couple of months." Freier labored at a desk in his garret room at the Hotel de l'Esperance in the rue du Musée, his drawing board propped at an angle and his feet dangling free to the floor. Everybody loved Bill Freier, but Mina loved him most of all.

There were other, less savory demimonde characters in the world of forgery. One was an Austrian called Reiner, an amiable sociopath who sold everything including forged exit visas. Beamish found him, but it was Fry who ended up suffering his insidious attentions. Reiner was always showing up unannounced, uninvited and definitely unwanted at the office on the rue Grignan, and even at Fry's hotel room. Fry caught him one day in the office typing up a false demob paper on Lena's precious typewriter. Perhaps Fry was being paranoid or at least overimaginative, but he was responsible for his staff and the well-being of the refugees in his care. Reiner did not care that the form could be used by the police—in the event that they got hold of it and identified the typewriter—to close down the Centre Américain. Reiner clearly didn't give a damn about anyone but himself. "He protested indignantly when I threw him out of the office and told him never to come back again," Fry said.

Before his ejection, and to Beamish's silent horror, Reiner had introduced the endlessly smiling Frederic Drach, who happily referred to himself as an old criminal, and he looked it. Fry's word for him was "louche"—actually more a whole concept than a word—and he had a career similar to Willi Muenzenberg's, except that Drach had so far evaded revenge from former colleagues. Drach began as a German Socialist in the twenties, although he was probably a mole for the Communists or the Nazis (both were equally likely). Later he turned up in Paris as a stringer for two Moscow-financed weekly newspapers. Then he managed to attach himself in an advisory capacity to the head of the German section of the French CIA, the *Deuxième Bureau*. The Frenchman's name was Lemoine, and he was responsible for gathering information on the German military buildup. Manifestly, Lemoine had enjoyed a spectacular lack of success in his task, and it was a reasonable assumption that Drach had something to do with it. Beamish was certain Drach was in the pay of the Gestapo now. He was living in a big house on a hill outside of town, where he had a chest of drawers crammed full of passports—mostly Dutch and Danish—for sale. Fry was interested until he learned that they would cost $150 a piece, and Beamish breathed a sigh of relief: his belief was that Fry would simply have been turning refugees over to the Gestapo. He didn't trust Drach any further than he could have thrown him, and was glad to see his back—although in the end Drach turned out all right. One could never trust to appearances in Marseille.

"THANKS. DAVID." Konrad Heiden had made it. The two-word telegram confirmed the success of his escape, and soon afterward, other brief cables began fluttering their way to the Centre Américain from Lisbon announcing the staccato arrivals of the other original two dozen or so refugees from Fry's list. When Ehrman's cable came through Beamish was especially pleased, and took this opportunity to persuade Fry how painless it would be to send other refugees, whose names had not been on the original list, to Portugal. Beamish had in mind particularly a young German writer called Hannah Arendt, and her husband Heinrich Blücher. Arendt, said Beamish to Fry, was "a woman who will someday be famous." This was the dilemma quickly growing apparent as the days went by. The original list naturally contained the names of those already considered distinguished, but it also held few names of those who were to be the "next generation" of cultural leaders in Europe. They were out there, desperately needing to be saved as well, but there was no mechanism for doing so. Fry didn't need much persuading, of course.

The stream of escapees clambering over the cemetery wall at Cerbère continued. It was risky, though, to send them all down to the border town without any chaperone—many could not speak French, and they were all novices at finding their way over the mountain. And it was only a matter of time, Fry believed, before something went wrong and a refugee was arrested. That would effectively close down the route. What was needed was a guide, somebody *débrouillard* who knew the way and could sweet-talk any difficult border guards that turned up. Charlie Fawcett came to the rescue when he introduced to Fry one of his friends from the Ambulance Corps, an American named Leon Ball, who called himself Dick.

Ball and Charlie had a lot in common. Both were easygoing, good-natured, and patient. Both were keen to do anything they could to help. They were also matching opposites. Charlie had the soul of an artist—in addition to playing the trumpet he had studied sculpture while in Paris, and met Matisse and Braque—and the rugged good looks of a cowboy truck driver. Ball, on the other hand, looked like an artist but spoke like a truck driver. "A rough diamond, a knight in overalls," Fry called him. He was born in Montana but had become "Frenched" to the extent that his fluency included the local patois and a full range of obscene slang. He had such a dirty mouth that he could make the Marseille stevedores blush. Ball claimed to own a lard factory outside Paris (it may have been a pig farm) and before the war he worked as a traveling salesman. That was good: he knew all the routes and layovers and friendly faces in much of southern France. Fry employed him to take a couple of refugees down to Cerbère three or four times a week, and Ball would see them safely over the mountain and on the path down to the Port-Bou border station before returning to Marseille. The first refugees that Ball took over were Otto Meyerhof and his wife, whose exit visas had expired. By a lucky chance they met Consul Hurley at the border—he was being recalled to Washington—and he helped the Meyerhofs at the customs post. "Without his pleading with the Spanish frontier guard to give me the entrance stamp, we would not have gotten it," wrote Meyerhof to Fry of his escape.

At the Centre Américain the spiral of expansion wound inexorably outward, and Fry knew he would soon need to take on even more staff. The pandemonium at the office was compounded by the nature of the emigration Fry was attempting: "We are in effect a deluxe relief bureau for a special type of client, the intellectual who has never before had to ask for help of this kind, who is embarrassed to have to do so, and who cannot be asked to take his place in the lines which wait outside the ordinary relief agencies." This failed to stop "ordinary" refugees from claiming to be such intellectuals or—more often—artists (and many did once the word was out on the street about Fry's Centre Américain). Some were genuinely talented but unknown—whom Miriam called the "near misses" and whom Beamish thought they should begin to take care of—and they arrived always carrying under their arms a portfolio or a manuscript: anything that could prove they too were worthy of saving.

Others were simply pretending. Here, it was Miriam's training in art history that proved useful. If a potential client came to 60 rue Grignan claiming to be a painter, she would send him down to the harbor with the request to make a sketch of it. When the refugee returned, Miriam would appraise the drawing and either place him on the list of Fry's clientèle or express her regrets. Those who arrived claiming to be poets were dealt with in much the same manner, except the rejection process was usually quicker.

For all of the staff, though, it was a heartbreaking situation. To turn away people on the basis of their talent (or lack of it) seemed to everybody a bloodless method of judging human worth. Yet Fry could could only apply for United States visas where a refugee was famous in his field, or of "outstanding quality," besides satisfying a host of other immigration requirements. Above all, anybody could be rejected whom Washington officials decided, in a catchall phrase, was "liable to become a public charge" (the infamous "LPC" clause). In other words, any refugee needed either rich relatives or friends to sponsor him, or the promise of a paying job in America, before a visa was awarded. Only famous artists and writers, such as Henri Matisse or Heinrich Mann, who could clearly earn their own living were self-evidently exempt (and even Mann was later forced to rely on his brother's largesse in California). Back in Washington, the State Department's decisions remained not just discretionary but disturbingly haphazard. There was no appeal process following a rejection, and if a refugee through no fault of his own had been subject to internment in France, as many had been, he was classed as a criminal by Washington, and invariably turned away.

The committee was doing what it could—and Fry himself, much more. If he was able to obtain United States visas for a refugee, he would. If not, or if he knew it was useless to try, he would attempt to procure an immigration visa for another country (Latin America was looking hopeful); if this was a failure, he would try next to send refugees at least away from the French mainland to North Africa or the Middle East, where they would have a better chance to hide from the Germans. And if he could not even do this (no mean feat from a blockaded port), he added the "painter's" or "poet's" name to an auxiliary list—which eventually numbered nearly four thousand—for many of whom the Centre Américain provided a subsistence allowance for food and accommodation.

Saving refugees from destitution was the one method of keeping them out of concentration camps for as long as possible. When the Vichy police started to round up Jews and send them to camps anyway, Fry launched an in-depth study of camp conditions and attempted to bring them to the attention of both the Vichy government and the State Department in Washington. He was roundly ignored by both. Assistant Secretary of State Breckinridge Long and his cohorts dismissed the tragic reports of daily death tolls in French camps that occasionally Fry managed to persuade a diplomat to send to America: "I am enclosing some 'fryana' which somebody up there may care to read, and which we were left with the other day" was a typical comment.

By the end of August, Fry had made a decision. He did not yet know how important it would prove, and what consequences it would entail for himself. The human suffering was having a profound effect on his austere nature: here was the greatest outrage he had ever seen, and therefore his greatest challenge. He could not turn away from it. "This job is like death—irreversible. We have started something here we can't stop. We have allowed hundreds of people to become dependent on us. We can't now say we are bored and are going home."

CHAPTER 12

TROUBLE

Late one evening, despite Beamish's warnings not to go, Fry took a walk down to the waterfront to see what he might find. He walked along the Quai du Port right out to Fort St. Jean, the prison at the entrance of the Vieux Port. Then he turned right and began to walk westward, toward the commercial docks—the *bassins*—stretching away from the center of town. In the distance he saw several large ships tied up, and carried on toward them, intrigued. When he got there an amazing sight met his eyes. They were all being unloaded in the dead of night, and *what* they were unloading was stunning: whole flocks of live sheep, bleating wildly as they were shooed down broad gangplanks extending from the bowels of the vessels, thousands of barrels of Algerian wine, which were being stacked on the quays; great trundling contraptions on which were hooked hundreds of sides of beef; endless crates of dried figs and dates. It was a cornucopia, the more remarkable because Marseille—in fact the whole of France—was now on meager rations.

Fry could not help noticing that Vichy propaganda about the shortage of food, gasoline, soap, and a thousand other essentials was very effectively channeling French resentment against its preferred targets. On the one hand the British were to blame for their naval blockade of France. It was almost open war. On July 3, the Royal Navy had sunk a large part of the French fleet just outside Dakar (at Mers-el-Kebir) to stop it sailing for German-controlled ports. Over two thousand French sailors had died, and the Pétainists were foaming at the mouth, although Fry said he saw "no sign of indignation" on the streets of Marseille. On the other hand, went the propaganda messages, the shortages were also the fault of foreigners and refugees (namely Jews) who were "not fond of work" and were taking food from rightful French mouths. As the Pétainist newspaper, *Gringoire* put it: "How long shall we house and feed these undesirables, more accustomed to using a revolver and a bomb than a pick and a shovel, while our children, our women and our invalids lack milk, meat and bread?"

Ration cards had been introduced on August 4, the very day Fry caught the Yankee Clipper to Lisbon from New York. For that month people had to survive on one pound of sugar and half a pound of pâté each, two hundred grams of margarine (there was of course no butter), and one hundred grams of rice. "Milk and cheese were free for sale (if you could find any)," Fry noted. "In restaurants if you had meat you could not also have fish and cheese." There were still some private reserves at this point, and food was more plentiful in the countryside than in town. But the shortages would slowly become exacerbated to the point where vitamin deficiency would lead to widespread disease.

But here at the *bassins* was evidence of all the milk, meat, and bread France could want, and it looked like a regular delivery. None of it was staying on the docks for long, though: under the close supervision of Italian soldiers, the goods were being quickly loaded onto the boxcars of a long train. Fry knew all of it would be in Italy by the morning. So this was where France's food was disappearing to after it was unloaded from the "ghost ships," and if any of this delivery did find its way to the Marseille market, it would be requisitioned at dawn by German officials who had "priority of purchase" on all food, at a ridiculously favorable exchange rate of the franc to the mark that made it a "purchase" in name only.

NOBODY WAS FEELING the official pressure piled on refugees more keenly than Walter "Baby" Mehring. In fact, he informed Fry that he was determined to leave France forthwith. He had another false passport by now, and although Fry and Beamish tried to persuade him not to set out for the border, Mehring was convinced there was more danger in Marseille. He was awaiting a false *carte d'identité* from Bill Freier, but in the meantime his residence permit was about to expire, and to apply for a renewal would be equal to turning himself into the police. Mehring wished to go right away and not even hang on for Leon Ball to return from his latest excursion to Cerbère. Reluctantly Fry showed him the map, gave him some money for the trip and the name of Dr. Joy in Lisbon, and wished the small poet in the greasy suit the best of luck. Mehring set off on the train for Perpignan on the morning of Wednesday, September 4.

A matter of hours after Mehring had departed, Ball returned to report that his latest expedition had been a complete success, and that security at the border had been relaxed in the late-summer drowsiness. Fry was pleased, and secretly even a little relieved to have Mehring off his hands: the little poet was exasperating out of all proportion to his size. It was a strain when Fry was dealing with dozens of frantic individuals each day to have persistent "pests" insist that they had to come first in everything. But Mehring was not so easily gotten rid of. The next morning when Fry arrived at the rue Grignan and checked the overnight cables, there was one from Mehring. He had been arrested near the border, and was now interned in St. Cyprien, possibly the worst of all the concentration camps in France.

Typically, Mehring had swung directly from wide-eyed paranoia to greedy overconfidence. Fry's instructions had been a model of simplicity: disembark at Perpignan and wait for the connecting train to Cerbère on the station platform. Do not under any circumstances leave the station because of the danger of police patrols checking identity papers. When Mehring saw that there was no police presence at Perpignan station, he promptly walked through the barrier and out onto the street. Then he settled himself down in a café. Perpignan was not Marseille, though. It was a small, sleepy town and strangers stood out—especially those as scruffy and suspicious looking as Mehring. A plainclothesman arrested him before Mehring had finished the first glass of wine. "I suppose the poor *flic* thought he had found the explanation of all the purse-snatchings and petty thefts of the previous six months," said Fry.

There was another furtive trip to the toilet, this time on the train to St. Cyprien, and another flushing away of priceless false documents. Now Mehring lost his American visa, too. Discovering that he was an *apatride* and had no travel permit, the police simply did what Vichy policy told them, locked up the prisoner and threw away the key. As he read the cable, Fry realized that once again Mehring had managed to monopolize his time. Now he must go and find a lawyer to try and spring Mehring from this latest trap. Defferre was unavailable at such short notice, so Fry went to another just around the corner at 30 rue Paradis. Maître Murzi was a Corsican who wore the nails of his pinky fingers extra long as a sign of elegance in his culture. He was a low, wide, volcano of a man who never ceased to talk at full volume. Of course he could help, shouted Murzi, and he promptly telephoned a colleague at Perpignan, who said he would find out the circumstances of the case straight away.

Next, Fry went to see Howard E. Kershner at the American Friends Service Committee, whose offices at 29 Boulevard d'Athenes were right next door to the Splendide. Fry knew the Quakers had an office in Perpignan, and Kershner promised to cable his colleagues there to see what could be done. If it was a matter of a financial guarantee, Fry told him, he should tell the authorities he would pay it. All that mattered was to get Mehring out of the camp quickly, because the Gestapo officers of the Kundt Commission were now patrolling the camps, and would be sure to snap up the poet without further ado. After seeing Kershner, Fry trudged wearily back to the Centre Américain. He comforted himself with the thought that at least the troublesome Mehring had not been arrested as he struggled over the cemetery wall at Cerbère; at least he had only destroyed his own chances of escape and not those of other refugees.

SATURDAY CAME, bringing not a relaxing weekend but a shock and a disaster. A postcard arrived from Spain, bearing the stamp of the Spanish censor, indicating that it had been officially noted. It came from three refugees who had been arrested inside Spain, and they were now pleading with Fry to help them. The disaster was not just that they had been caught—and were now in prison at Figueras—but that they had so publicly associated Fry and the Centre Américain with their illegal escape. The rumor was that Franco's Seguridad was increasingly working with the German secret police, and that Himmler himself was due to meet with Franco in Madrid. What if the Spanish were now cooperating directly with the Gestapo? Fry's head was swimming. If that was the case then the Centre Américain could be closed down and all of them thrown into prison for what the postcard revealed.

Possibly even more perplexing was the fact that the cry for help contained no explanation of why the three refugees were arrested. Figueras was very near Port-Bou, so maybe they had just crossed the border. But did they go directly to the Spanish customs post for their *entrada* stamps as instructed, or had they foolishly thought they would carry on their journey without risking contact with officials of any sort? If that was the case, the refugees had merely ensured they would be arrested at the first interior checkpoint. Yes, and that would have been at Figueras. These intellectuals were not always the brightest people in practical matters.

That was not the end of Fry's unwanted weekend mail. Arriving like a stream of certificates guaranteeing the insanity of their senders came other postcards from Lisbon arriving at addresses all over Marseille. In theory such postcards should have been good news in themselves, for they meant that refugees had made it through Spain and were now awaiting ships sailing for America or Mexico. Actually the refugees were writing not only to thank Fry, but also to announce to their friends, in incriminating detail, the success of their escapes. Those in Portugal wanted to share details of their illegal journeys, advising how to follow routes over the mountains and avoid guards, for example. Now not only was the Centre Américain under direct threat, but the refugees in Lisbon had effectively greased the rails for whoever was to come after them by alerting the authorities. Fry was dumbfounded. Such selfishness and stupidity he had never experienced in his life. What were these idiots thinking of?

With such nakedly clear instructions on the escape route from Cerbère now available to the French authorities courtesy of some thoughtless exiles, Fry couldn't trust to using it indefinitely. He thought of who was most endangered and found himself worrying about the original party of exiles. The Feuchtwangers, Manns, and Werfels had not been sent over the border earlier partly because of the practical difficulties of their age and condition, and partly because Frank Bohn had assured Fry that there would be a boat for them. Now more than ever he needed Bohn's boat. Fry also had to begin thinking of an alternative route out of France over the Pyrenees to keep the main escape traffic flowing. In the meantime, the *débrouillard* Leon Ball could carry on with the Cerbère route, and they would just have to be extra careful—conducting refugees under escort all the way to Lisbon if necessary. Fry felt his own ship was suddenly leaking very badly, and was only partly reassured by Bohn's promise that everything was almost ready.

Then, late on the afternoon of Sunday, September 8, a train pulled into the Gare St. Charles. A very small, shabbily dressed man sprinted from the platform into the entrance of the station restaurant and seconds later emerged from the front of the Hotel Terminus. He bounded down the wide stairway onto the Boulevard d'Athenes and disappeared into the Hotel Splendide. A few moments after that Fry answered a knock on his door. Mehring had returned.

Probably it had been Kershner's good offices rather than Maître Murzi's that had secured Mehring's release. A few days after his cable to the Quakers at Perpignan, the camp commandant had called Mehring into his office. The poet was handed a release order, unsigned, and the commandant said that of course it had to stay that way unless Vichy was informed of the matter, but that the police probably would not bother to check it in detail. Mehring took the hint, took the release form, and then took himself straight back to the railway station and caught the next train to Marseille.

"Not again!" cried Fry, when he was told about the second set of papers the poet had flushed away. This was not the end of Mehring's troubles, though, for his residence permit (*permis de séjour*) had now expired, and without it he would soon be back in another camp. Fry managed to get Mehring a small room on the second floor of the Splendide by paying a month's rent in advance, and the next morning, Monday, September 9, he went back to Murzi's office. Murzi was a man of extravagant promises, but he seemed certain there would be no trouble in this instance. He took Fry to Marseille's Department of Aliens (*Bureau des Étrangers*) that dealt with such matters as residence permits. It was headed at this time by a man called Monsieur Episse, and his second in command was a friend of Murzi's named Georges Barellet. As a government official in Vichy France, Barellet stands as representative of the mixture of greed, opportunism, and half-buried decency that gave the unoccupied zone its bureaucratic character.

Barellet's father owned the imposing Hotel Bompard, a twenty-five-room, two-story building perched high on a hill overlooking the city. What made it useful to Barellet in his current powerful position was that the property was surrounded by a high wall, and suitable for holding interned refugees. In short, he had turned it into an unofficial detention camp for women and children, while nearby Les Milles, where Feuchtwanger had been and where Walter Hasenclever had committed suicide, housed the men. There were from fifty to seventy women residents there at any one time (they could not be released until their husbands were first let out from whatever camp *they* happened to be in), and half again as many children.

The setup was a lucrative cash cow for Barellet. He received a daily allowance of around fifteen francs for every woman imprisoned at Bompard, and instead of using the money to feed them, he made even more profit from the canteen he had set up there, which sold them food at more than double the market price. Adding insult to extortion was the fact that it was their own food, for at the same time as he overcharged, Barellet confiscated the inmates' ration cards and used them to secure supplies for the canteen. In another moneymaking sideline, Barellet accepted cash to secure the release of illegal refugees picked up by the police. The going rate for the release of a refugee picked up in a *rafle* was two thousand to three thousand francs. Barellet had made his brother his chauffeur, and all bribes were paid to him. The proportion kicked back to the police remains unknown. Barellet may have been a shameless opportunist, but as Maître Murzi pointed out, he was a friend of anybody with money, and was well disposed to help refugees. It was better than finding a rigid Vichy ideologue in such an important position at the prefecture, after all.

When Murzi and Fry arrived at Barellet's office they found him in a state of high dudgeon. Two Gestapo agents had just left, after lining up his staff and bombarding them with questions about their boss's politics and competence. The Germans had gone through files and drawers as if they owned the place, which in a way they did. Nevertheless, it shocked Fry that the Gestapo was no longer trying to disguise its activities, and was instead carrying on in broad daylight. It said volumes about Vichy's lack of resolve, and the Nazis' growing contempt for the armistice they had negotiated. Before they left, one of the Gestapo agents gave Barellet a slip of paper with three names on it. "We want these and you will find them for us," ordered the agent, before he turned his back and walked out.

Barellet was not about to suffer mutely such a slur on his independence and incorruptibility. In his opinion it was not his job, or that of France, to do the Gestapo's dirty work. Somehow Fry managed not to laugh his head off, and Barellet handed him the paper. Prince Ernst Rüdiger von Starheim, an Austrian aristocrat who opposed the Nazis, was the first name. Max Braun and Georg Bernhard were the two others. Braun was a politician who had led off against the Nazis in Saarland (part of Germany annexed to France after the First World War), and Bernhard was the editor of the German émigré newspaper all the exiles had read in Paris during the thirties. The fact that Fry knew Starheim and Braun were in London while the Gestapo did not was almost encouraging. It was too easy to assume that the Nazis were all-seeing and that struggle was hopeless; perhaps in reality they had only a partial knowledge of whom they sought. As Beamish said, "One always tends to overestimate the tentacles of a totalitarian regime." Bernhard was still in France, though, and Barellet told Fry that if he knew where Bernhard was, to tell him to scram ("filer").

Warnings such as Barellet had just given were a benign aspect of Vichy officialdom, and always welcome when they came—especially when they were free. Barellet also said that there were others the Nazis wanted, whose whereabouts the French police knew very well. For example, there were Rudolf Breitscheid and Rudolf Hilferding, the two German Social Democratic Party politicians from the late Weimar Republic. These men sat about openly and complacently in Marseille, holding court in a café next to their hotel, the Normandie, and almost challenging the police to apprehend them. The fact was, the same sort of blinkered arrogance that had led Breitscheid and Hilferding to underestimate Hitler, and so deliver the German state into the hands of the Nazis, still governed their outlooks and actions.

Fry already knew about these two troublesome fellows, who behaved like spoiled brats. More accurately, there was one ponderously self-important man, Rudolf Breitscheid, and one servile underling, Hilferding, who "seemed to resent Breitscheid's authority over him, but to assent to it nevertheless," said Fry. It was hardly a winning combination. Their careless talk so alarmed the other refugees that they approached him and asked him to have a word with the ex-statesmen. Fry tried reasoning with the two Rudolfs, but nothing in his experience had prepared him for the condescension and imperious naïveté of the pair. Breitscheid was still confidently waiting for the return of the Weimar Republic, when he would be welcomed back in Berlin, carried through the streets shoulder high and hailed the returning hero. Hilferding was a mere bumbler in his colleague's shadow ("Breitscheid tyrannized him," Fry believed), and had been the Minister of Finance during the period of inflation in the twenties. When he was finally forced from office the German mark was valued at around four trillion to the dollar, give or take a few billion. These were not men to be reasoned with easily, and they refused point-blank to escape. "To tell you the truth," said Fry, "the behavior of Breitscheid and Hilferding was the despair of all their friends." Charlie Fawcett was more blunt: "They were a couple of sons of bitches."

So was Giuseppe Modigliani's stubbornness the despair of his friends. As a former member of Camera dei Deputati (the Italian Congress) and leader of the Socialist Party, he was in direct danger from the Italian Armistice Commission. But he insisted on remaining as recognizable as he always had been, with the trademark beard he refused to shave off, and the heavy, floor-length fur coat he insisted on wearing even in the dog days of August. Modigliani was outraged when Fry suggested he take it off in order to make himself a more difficult target. Local 89 of the Garment Workers Union of New York had presented it to him, and to discard it would disgrace the honor of the labor movement, he declared. Modigliani had decided to leave France, but thought it beneath his dignity, and the position he thought he still occupied in Italian politics, to attempt anything illegal.

At least Fry and Barellet had their annoyance in common, and paradoxically Fry had caught the corrupt official at a good time, while he was still boiling with self-righteous indignation at the intrusion by the Gestapo agents. When Fry mentioned Mehring, Barellet gave him the name of a friendly doctor. He told Fry to get him to sign a certificate stating that Mehring had been too ill to attend the prefecture to apply for a renewal of his *permis de séjour.* Mehring would then be on "sick leave" from being a refugee, at least for a time.

"It worked beautifully," said Fry. Mehring was put to bed at the Splendide; the laconic doctor came and filled out an impressive document valid for two whole months—four times longer than the standard sick note given to refugees. On the strength of it, Barellet issued a two-month *permis de séjour.*

His motives in this matter must remain inscrutable. Why he momentarily set aside his money-grubbing to help Fry may be put down either to whimsy or farsightedness. Vichy officials had thought the war was over at the beginning of July, and that the British would collapse. Now the future was no longer absolutely certain. For Barellet it might one day be worth standing out in the memory of somebody like Varian Fry as a friend of the refugees and an enemy of the Nazis. Fry himself was growing cynical about the French authorities. One day they would help, the next hinder. Clearly they were under pressure from the Germans and could not be trusted: "Most of them couldn't see that the honor of their country would be involved if they arrested their former guests and handed them over to the Germans to be executed." But honor in defeat can only be got at high rates on the black market, and as Ibsen wrote, "With the best will no one can/Be an official and a man."

AFTER THE DISTURBANCES of Mehring's arrest, and the potential catastrophe of the careless postcards, things seemed to settle down in Marseille for a day or two. Fry was told "Pish and nonsense" by Rudolf Breitscheid when he delivered Barellet's warning. "Hitler wouldn't dare ask for our extradition." There was nothing else he could do. When Bill Freier wasn't busy forging documents, he was on the sidewalk outside Basso's, sketching portraits. One day a tall, well-dressed man sat for him while Freier skillfully rendered quite a flattering likeness. "Six francs, monsieur," said Bill to the very satisfied customer when he had finished. The man gave him a ten-franc note and walked away. Mina, who had been sitting at the café, came over. "Did I see him give you ten francs?" she asked. "Yes," replied Freier. "You see, his French was not too good and when I said *six,* he thought I said *dix.* He was Gestapo."

Heinrich Mann relayed an anecdote that amused him and horrified Varian Fry. One night, on his way home from dinner in a restaurant with his friend, Alfred Kantorowicz, where they had tried and failed to cheer each other up about the prospect of leaving Europe for America, Mann was stopped by two gendarmes. They demanded to see his papers, and in a rare moment of anger, Mann lost his temper. "Don't you recognize me?" he shouted at the surprised policemen. "I am the Prefect of the Bouches du Rhône!" Incredibly, they believed him, and Mann went on his way.

Leon Ball returned from another successful frontier crossing on Tuesday, September 10. The route was holding up, but he had heard about a disturbing amount of German military activity just across the demarcation line in the occupied zone. Columns of panzers and troop transports had evidently been moving toward the Spanish border, and rumors were rife about Hitler planning to invade either Spain or the rest of France. Again, Fry thought of opening a second route over the mountains in case the Germans came too close for comfort at Cerbère. Beamish had already been investigating the possibilities, and he told Fry he was attempting to arrange a meeting with some interesting people at a little bistro called Cintra on the Vieux Port. The Cintra was relatively safe, as one of the waiters was trusted to tip them the wink if the police showed up. They would make a fast exit through the rear of the building with whatever illegal refugee was with them, just as the police were coming in the front.

The interesting people Beamish mentioned were a married couple, German exiles and active ani-Nazis, who had managed to find a residence near the border to the north of Cerbère, at a sleepy little town called Banyuls, famous for the sweet wine that bears its name. They had made contact with the Socialist mayor of the town, a man called Vincent Azéma, who knew a route over the mountains that was effectively a "back door" to the Spanish customs post. "One walked west," recalled Fry, "until one could no longer see the spire of the Banyuls church. Then one turned south and walked through the vineyards to the barren Pyrenees beyond them. After crossing the frontier, one turned east and followed it closely, on the Spanish side, all the way to Port-Bou." Azéma insisted that the émigrés organize the route themselves, because he was in enough danger already from the right-wing Vichy authorities, who were systematically removing political enemies like himself from office all over France. The exiled couple—Hans and Lisa Fittko—had taken up his challenge.

It was a longer crossing than the one Leon Ball was using, between three and seven hours, depending on one's age and degree of fitness; the advantage was that there were far fewer border guards and *gardes mobiles*—the motorized police—patrolling in that area. The mountain path was known as *La Route Lister,* after the Spanish Republican general who had used it to good effect in the recent civil war, and it had been—still was—a well-trodden smuggler's track. Already the sculptor Aristide Maillol, whose studio was in Banyuls, had helped one or two refugees across with the aid of his shapely young model, Dina Vierny. But Beamish saw the potential for something more organized and systematic. Fry eagerly assented to the suggestion that he meet the young German couple. He desperately needed something to happen, because he had just been forced to face another catastrophe.

On the morning of Friday, September 6, Fry had awoken early, and eaten breakfast alone in his room. Even as an American with dollars, Fry was not immune to rationing, which had by now extended to the hotels. He was just finishing the meager fare when an almighty hammering began on his door.

Instinctively, he leaped toward a pile of incriminating papers, but the door flew open before he reached them. It was not the police, though; such reckless noise and lack of caution could mean only one thing. It was Frank Bohn, giving an Oscar-winning performance in a movie called *The Jig's Up!*

"They've got it, old man," he cried. Fry knew already what the hysterical Bohn meant, but asked anyway. Breathlessly, Bohn told the story of how, the night before, his trawler had been impounded by Italian soldiers. There was now a guard posted on the quay and no way for anybody to get near it. The entire gambit, upon which at least thirty lives depended, had vanished. In the next few minutes, as Fry listened to Bohn's hoarse exclamations, his shock turned to cynicism, and then to stark horror. The boat was effectively sunk, and Fry suddenly realized he had never had much confidence in it. He had assented to including the Manns, Feuchtwangers, and Werfels on the passenger list party because he had been in Marseille for less than twenty-four hours when Bohn made the offer. Fry hadn't known any better, and if since then he had learned, he had simply been too busy to revise his plans. Now he was kicking himself. There had of course been the customary lack of security and camouflage in Bohn's preparations: "Half the refugees in Marseille had known about it days before the Italian Armistice Commission woke up to it," Fry later commented. Worse, although he had nothing to do with the arrangements, the police would naturally associate his activity with Bohn's, which meant he was in at least as much danger of arrest as his reckless collaborator. For the second time in a week he thought that this could well be the end. Expulsion from the country was almost too mild a penalty to hope for. Here was a concrete disaster, not a speculative one like the incriminating postcards. He could only pray that, as Beamish had reassured him, the police were not as knowledgeable as one instinctively feared. For the first time Fry felt a flash of the true panic that comes with the intuition of the infinite blankness of death.

CHAPTER 13

GOING UNDERGROUND

I T W A S N ' T A V E R Y B R I L L I A N T I D E A to meet in a small, rather grimy *bistro* in a side street near the Old Port," Lisa Fittko recollected. Beamish had been the marriage broker in this exploratory meeting, but she and Hans were not very impressed with the prospects they were confronted with. Fry and Bohn, worried men, "were completely out of place here . . . they looked so conspicuously neat and nice," she said. Bohn couldn't even speak French, never mind German. Hans cast Beamish sidelong looks, wondering how such an experienced and *débrouillard* resistance worker like him could have mixed himself up with these ingenuous and therefore dangerous Americans.

The Fittkos were back at Marseille from Banyuls for this meeting, and had already exposed themselves to considerable risk merely by traveling on public transport. If this was a waste of time there would be trouble for sure. Hans Fittko thought Fry wanted to have the "General Lister" route explained to him. He and Lisa were about to leave for Portugal, so it did not make much difference to them if they shared their knowledge; indeed, it was a duty among underground fighters against Nazism to help each other in whatever way they could. Fry coughed nervously when Hans made clear his simple assumption. He told the Fittkos that what he intended was to establish some organization at Banyuls to help a steady stream of refugees across the mountains. Lisa was somewhat impressed: they had hoped to be able to leave behind them some system to keep the route open and steadily useful. But it would take personnel and money.

"The money is no problem," said Fry. He coughed again and looked down at the table. "This all centers around finding the right person with border experience, someone who is prepared to do the job and on whom we can depend. . . . Would you, for a few months—?" Hans refused point-blank. He almost got up from the table. He pointed out that they had been on the run, fighting rearguard actions against the Nazis as they went, for over seven years. Now, at last, after ever more precarious close shaves, they had a chance to save their own skins. If out of the blue some natty American adventurer appears to ask them to lay down their lives for even more strangers, were they supposed instantly to obey? Helping men of military age across the border carried the death penalty—didn't this American even know that? No, they had done their duty. "I promise you," said Fry, "that if you remain here during the border project, we will help you get out." Now it was Lisa's turn to be angry; she had heard so many promises from people who were in no position to guarantee anything—it was the white noise of an exile's existence, the *bobards* one had to step over every inch of the way—that to hear it from this fresh-faced naïf was almost too much.

"Combien?" said Fry.

". . . What?" Hans could not believe his ears.

"Combien voulez-vous?" *How much do you want?*

Hans turned to Beamish, anger flooding his face. Did this Varian Fry think they could be bought? Didn't he understand the word "conviction," that what they had been doing for the past decade was not running a business but maintaining a set of moral and political principles? Beamish tried to save the situation. Speaking in German, he hastily admitted that Fry was inexperienced, but swore he could be trusted, that he wanted to help and had money, connections. Fry meant only that he would supply whatever funds were needed for transport, headquarters, food, clothes, bribes, whatever. Fry's face was grave and tragic. "I'm sorry," he stuttered. "I didn't mean to insult. The part about money was just a misunderstanding. . . ."

Slowly, Hans calmed down. Seven years was a long apprenticeship in altruism and daring. The logic of that life incurred always one last throw of the dice, one last tug of Hitler's mustache. Lisa and Hans looked at each other. They knew, by the rules they had established for themselves, that to ignore this opportunity that might save lives or deprive them of their own, would be to lose the game. "If someone had to take the risk, we couldn't say, 'Let others do it,'" they thought. "We must be mad." And it *was* a kind of madness, a saintly madness called heroism that draws you back again like the embrace of a difficult but passionate lover. "Just one last time," said Lisa, and a smile broke across Varian Fry's somber face.

———————

AFTER THE DEBACLE of Bohn's boat, Fry had called Bingham at once. The vice-consul hadn't wanted to know the details of Fry's activities in case he was compromised, but promised he would support Fry in whatever way he could. Bingham invited Bohn and Fry over for dinner, and they arrived at sundown, as Bingham was hauling himself from the fishpond after his swim, Feuchtwanger sitting motionless on the sundeck.

Feuchtwanger took the news well, or at least with his usual fatalism. He had escaped arrest in Germany only because he had been in Washington when Hitler assumed power; he had escaped from the concentration camp because he walked along the road when Myles Standish was waiting there: now, destiny would deal him whatever cards were left in the pack. In fact, he cheered up considerably when he remembered the cellar full of fine wines he had been forced to leave behind at Sanary when he was transported to Les Milles detention camp. Marta was back at Sanary now, and she could send some of the best ones along to Marseille. Later, over coffee and brandy, Fry made the suggestion that it might be worth attempting to leave France without an exit visa. Feuchtwanger had been issued with an "affidavit in lieu of passport" by the U.S. consulate, which would get him through Spain and Portugal with the relevant transit visas—up till now still obtainable. The name on the affidavit was Feuchtwanger's old alias, James Wetcheek; Marta could travel under her own name as she was not on the Gestapo's list.

Feuchtwanger thought it over and then agreed to go, on the condition that Fry went with him. Fry agreed instantly. Things seemed to be falling into place: he no longer wanted to send refugees over the mountains above Cerbère unchaperoned; he needed to go to Lisbon anyway, in order to write a long report back to the Emergency Rescue Committee in New York— something he could not, from France, do in the detail he wanted; he had to find out how the search in America for his replacement was faring; he could try and find out about the refugees who had been arrested, and exactly why; he could talk to those in Lisbon who had made it; and he could also drop in to the British embassy in Madrid on his way. He had some business there. Then it occurred to Fry that if the Feuchtwangers were going with him, he should perhaps increase his cargo to include the others who had been booked on the misbegotten boat. Heinrich Mann was weighing heavily on his mind: the Gestapo would be most interested in him, Fry was sure, although the Werfels would not be far behind.

The following day Fry saw Heinrich Mann at the Hotel Normandie and explained his plan. Mann gladly assented and in addition requested that his nephew, Golo, come along, too. The Werfels were also keen. Franz was now on his second attempt at obtaining a French exit visa. Again, he had heard nothing from Vichy. In the meantime he had been dissuaded from going the "demobilization route," passing himself off as a soldier, and escaping to Casablanca. Fry pointed out that he was too fat to fool anybody, and might end up in a concentration camp, or worse. After that, the inventive Werfel, taking advantage of his high profile as a "Catholic" writer, secured through the efforts of Secretary of State Cordell Hull several invitations to lecture in the United States, along with letters of introduction from leading Catholics in Spain to ease his passage through that country. This was all to the good, and Fry worried only that the Werfels, who had made the trade of taxi wheels for legs many years before, would find it impossible to climb over the Pyrenees. He told them the chances were good that there would be no problems and they could travel straight across on the train, although he crossed his fingers as he did so.

Fry set about securing the necessary transit visas, and fixed the date of departure for Thursday, September 12. On the day before that there were two more disappointments. The first was tinged with regret, for Franz von Hildebrand, having overseen the departures of the Austrians, was ready to set out for America himself with his charming Irish wife and their young child. This was something to which Fry would have to accustom himself: trusted coworkers leaving in the midst of ongoing work, which seemed always heavier by the day. It was not simply a member of staff departing, either; in the intense atmosphere of underground work, such people quickly became friends, and felt almost like family. Each departure would be a wrench, and some unbearably so. Each was like a death for him, and he died a little too when they left. But they all had to escape themselves: almost nobody Fry worked with was entirely safe, and all knew things could only grow worse as time went on. Franzi had his visas in order and had to take his chance, and Fry would meet up with him in Lisbon the following week, if all went well.

The other disappointment was tinged with yet more disaster. The news flashed around the Marseille grapevine that Spain, whose frontier policies had been uncoordinated, erratic, but usually amenable to regulation by bribery, had finally closed its borders to *apatrides*—those unfortunates who were without nationalities and passports. This meant the Manns and Feuchtwangers, who had been stripped of Reich citizenship by Hitler. It only affected Lion Feuchtwanger, though, because the Manns had later been given Czech nationality. Although he had his American "affidavit in lieu of passport," Feuchtwanger did not have a passport proper. Bill Freier was working on a *carte d'identité* which might at least keep him safe for a while longer, and

Fry told Feuchtwanger that although he could not safely be included any longer on tomorrow's trip, he should not give up. Fry would check out conditions at the border, and maybe take him out soon enough. But Fry knew, of course, that even if Feuchtwanger made it across the mountains, without a passport all he could look forward to was a Spanish prison. Would it be better than a French concentration camp, now the rumor was that Franco was cooperating with the Gestapo? He recalled Luis Companys, the Catalan trade union leader who was picked up in Belgium and returned by the Germans to Spain. Franco's Seguridad strangled him very slowly with piano wire. Could Feuchtwanger expect the same, and could Fry risk sending him to such a death? Revolving such unanswerable questions in his mind kept Fry awake that night despite the exhaustion.

UNDER THE ALIAS of Monsieur Dupont, the Italian politician Emilio Lussu was living just outside of town. His career, since he fled Mussolini, had involved publishing an émigré newspaper in Paris called *Justice and Liberty,* named for the group he belonged to, and which opposed the Fascists. Now, at Marseille, Lussu was involved in the same sort of work as Fry: the illegal exporting of refugees rather than providing legitimate aid. Fry had a cover, but Lussu's operation was fully underground, as it had to be. He was attempting to get away Spanish Republicans and Italian freedom fighters, and his opinion was that for these men the overland route through Spain was impossible.

Fry had instinctively warmed to Lussu, who, though no longer young, was daring and resourceful—a combination Fry admired and needed to associate himself with. They decided to cooperate. The Italian was a Houdini character, an expert on the precise planning of escapes. His own, from one of Mussolini's prisons on the island of Lipari—the Italian San Quentin—had succeeded after several failed attempts, and Lussu had gained great, and harsh, experience in the process. Now he applied himself to the problem of helping the enemies of Franco and Mussolini escape from the heavily blockaded port of Marseille. Bohn's failure did not surprise him, and he looked on it as a haphazard and amateur arrangement. The police might not know everything, but they were not entirely stupid.

To take a boat out of Marseille and away to safety, Lussu had concluded, was impossible. The only way to do it was to have a boat come in from somewhere else, and anchor off the coast nearby, at a point that the refugees could be ferried to by dinghy. His research had been meticulous: Lussu had somehow purchased nautical charts of the whole area and had pored over them for months. Through a contact in the French navy, he had managed to prepare exact topographies of minefields and decide upon a route and an anchorage that would be safe and near yet out of sight, if such a boat could be made to come. It couldn't be an Italian boat, or a French boat. It had to be a Spanish or Portuguese one, and it needed to be sent by the British. They had many troops left over from the recent defeat of France who had not been evacuated from Dunkirk in the north. These soldiers were surreptitiously billeted throughout Vichy France (many were in Marseille), and they needed to get back home. Lussu saw a common cause between his Italian and Spanish fighters, and the British soldiers stranded in France. "Perhaps," he said to Fry, stroking his gray goatee as was his habit, "you could meet the British Ambassador in Madrid and explain to him my proposition." If the British would help the Italians and Spanish off the mainland, Lussu and Fry would ensure that the British troops also got away.

He gave Fry the map of the area he had prepared, with the point just east of Marseille, Cap Croisette, marked as a pickup spot. He had also devised a migraine-inducing but fairly secure code based on a passage of Thomas Carlyle's writing, by which messages to and from the British in Madrid could be conveyed. Each letter of each word in the passage was numbered in sequence. The code began with the number seven, so that starting from one, though logical, would defeat a code-breaker. Lussu's method also meant a particular letter could have three or more numbers applied to it, which would further confuse anybody attempting to crack the code. To decipher a message, one needed to have the original chunk of Carlyle's prose—chosen for its wide range of vocabulary, and therefore its encryption possibilities. When a coded message was received—bursts of apparently random numbers—one scanned through one's copy of the passage reassigning each one to its corresponding letter, until the message was complete. No code was uncrackable, of course, but this one was encased in a hard shell, and if the passage on which it was based was regularly changed, it was probably good enough.

Fry already knew about the British; some were in an "open" prison, and some were housed in secret locations around the city. He planned in time to send them with the Fittkos over the mountains above Banyuls. He told Lussu he would try out the idea on the British when—if—he got to Madrid. Again he had the feeling that he was sinking into Marseille: it was embracing him with its schemes and deals, and Fry experienced once more the feeling that he was being transformed from the man he had been a mere month ago. In helping the British to escape, he was becoming dangerously enmeshed in matters of real warfare. If he was caught doing this, not only the French would be interested in him. He would be a spy, and could be executed as a spy.

———————

DAWN HAD NOT YET BEGUN to leak through the clear night sky when he ascended the broad and ghostly stairway of the Gare St. Charles and saw looming above him the great black slab of the station. Inside the building, he checked his Patek wristwatch: it was ten minutes to five. In a far corner was a small cluster of people, and as he approached, Fry made out the figures of Ball, Heinrich and Nelly Mann, and Franz and Alma Werfel. Nelly waved to him.

Fry had two questions for his assembled travelers. The first was who on earth did the lofty ziggurat of luggage stacked against the wall belong to. He had told everybody to bring only essential belongings. It looked like the necessary equipment for a hundred-strong Sherpa expedition. Alma Werfel protested that it was all essential, and that lodged within the tiers of suitcases were holograph music scores by her dead husband, Gustav Mahler, and the original manuscript of Bruckner's Third Symphony, not to mention her dear Franzl's latest work in progress. Fry regarded the mountain of luggage skeptically, but moved on to his second question: Where was Golo Mann? There was no answer, but Leon Ball volunteered to go and look for him.

By the time Fry had returned from buying seven one-way tickets to Cerbère, Golo had arrived. The group, led by Fry and followed by a porter pushing a cart loaded high with the Werfels' luggage, walked along the dark platform until they reached the train's first-class section. At precisely half past five o'clock, the locomotive pulled out of the station, into the panorama of Provence, still under its blanket of darkness. The train rattled through the outskirts of Marseille with its jumble of old factories and depots, the ragged skirts of an ancient city. It picked up speed as the group emerged onto the wide flatlands of the Camargue—a featureless landscape from a speeding train, but one that held the travelers rapt with childlike awe. They were no longer in Marseille. They were really leaving, at last.

When the train stopped at Nîmes two gendarmes climbed aboard and the group held its collective breath. But the policemen walked past the carriage pausing only to nod "good morning" to Fry and his companions. Clearly, if you were in first class, you were not likely to be a criminal; certainly not a penniless refugee. Steaming southward now, the sun sloped higher into the sky, and the day began its long, slow burn. Soon they sped past the vineyards of Languedoc; long rows of trained vines, like spokes, went wheeling by. Almost every image that met their eyes conveyed the idea of motion, of travel, of *away*.

By ten in the morning they had reached the small port city of Sète, and caught their first glimpse of the sea, millions of glittering diamonds conjured by the Mediterranean sun. Boats lined the harbor, and the group looked on, enviously.

On the way to Narbonne, the heat assaulting the closed carriage began to take its toll, and by the time they arrived at Perpignan just after midday, everybody was glad to be able to climb down into the open and draw deep lungfuls of the southern air. There was a three-hour wait for the connection to Cerbère and the border. Fry, wary of leaving the station with Mehring's arrest still vivid in his mind, insisted that everybody stay where they were. He sent Ball off to buy sandwiches and wine. A proper meal would have to wait until the evening.

The Cerbère train was slower, smaller, and even hotter than the earlier one, although the discomfort was somehow less noticeable. The jagged rim of the Pyrenees, now clearly in sight, had the effect of freshening the air with hope and expectation. Fry himself hoped that nobody would notice how deeply they had traveled into concentration camp country. He had seen a sign not long before to St. Cyprien. Near that lay Rivesaltes, where so many children were interned, and forced to scavenge their nourishment from garbage pails; and Le Barcarès, Bram, Agde, Septfonds, Brens-Gallac. He and Beamish were already beginning to prepare reports on the conditions of these terrible cesspools, and were collecting eyewitness accounts as well as inmates' pathetic tales.

One French army officer had written to Fry: "After my demobilization, I returned to the place of my birth. I live near camp Gurs. I am forced to look at this ghastly place every day. As a Frenchman I implore you to do everything possible in order to save these unfortunate people from the ghastly death which inevitably must overtake them, and to save France from the ignominy that thousands and thousands of innocent people perish miserably in this awful camp—people who have struggled, and even bled for France." Fry turned his head toward the sea to flush the images from his mind. But on that side he found himself thinking of the camp at Argelès, which must have been Vichy's idea of a sick practical joke. It was a concentration camp all right—nothing more than a filthy collection of huts ringed with barbed wire—but it was actually on the beach. The poor inmates could at least look at the ocean even if they were not allowed to swim in it. Or was that a worse torment? The entrepreneurial commandant kept his prisoners occupied making dolls: Mickey Mouses, Little Red Riding Hoods, Snow Whites and the Seven Dwarfs.

The train passed down a little canyon that had been carved from the rock, then nosed up high enough for a tantalizing glimpse of sea and vineyard, before plunging again, this time through a dense canopy of foliage. As it drew clear of these trees on either side, the lights snapped on in the compartment, and the train entered a tunnel.

At the other end was the little seaside town of Collioure, which was scattered over the hillside down to the water's edge. Soon enough they were steaming through another tunnel, then briefly emerging at Port Vendres before disappearing once more into the underworld inside the mountain, for a long while now. When finally the train emerged, Fry and his companions found themselves at the crest of a hill. The train wheezed to a halt by a two-story white building, on the side of which was painted one word: BANYULS. It looked to Fry like all the other picturesque, sleepy little towns on the *Côte Vermeille,* the unutterably beautiful Vermilion Coast: a small cluster of white houses with red tiled roofs in the lee of a church, spilling agelessly and endlessly into the sea. It looked a simple world, and he longed for it right now.

Fry looked up to the mountains far above him. The Fittkos were installed in a house in the village; at that very moment they could be up there, in the mountains, exploring ways through to freedom. He tried to follow a route through with his eyes, but was soon lost in the depressions and peaks. The rugged lower slopes had been carved into terraces on which grew the inevitable vines; the distant, higher ones were softened by the effect of perspective and the rinsing of color in the distance. He couldn't imagine what it would be like to have to walk through there, at night. Pursued.

The train pulled itself back into life, and began to roll deliberately the final few kilometers to Cerbère. Everybody instinctively craned their neck to glimpse the view hidden beyond the final bend of the track winding through the coastal hills. They were soon rewarded with an eagle's-eye view of the town, from the huge viaduct above it that not only carried the railway track but held the station as well.

Their journey had taken the whole day, nearly twelve hours, most of it sitting down in the cramped and stuffy compartment. When Fry opened the door and helped his charges down onto the platform it was almost five in the afternoon, but it seemed later, for the slanting rays of the sinking sun were filtered out by the dirty glass roof of the station. An eerie twilight hung in the air about them. They all looked at the rails that headed away to the west, two hundred yards in length before they disappeared into the last tunnel, the one that emerged in a foreign country. Far above the tunnel's entrance, high up in the mountain, Fry could make out the white shape of the French frontier post. He hoped to God they would not meet its inhabitants on the mountainside.

THE PLAN WAS to catch the connection straight through to Port-Bou, so that they would arrive in Spain that very evening. But after surrendering their tickets and entering the main station building from the platform, it was obvious this was impossible. The police were there in force, and panic spread like a stain through the party as they saw passengers lined up for an inspection of papers. Fry was the only one *en règle;* the others could plausibly be arrested. But Ball took charge of the situation, gathering their passports and disappearing into the office where the police commissioner was sitting.

He came out again rather later looking glum; the officer in charge had strict orders not to allow anybody without an exit visa aboard the Port-Bou train. There would be no Spain for them tonight. However, Ball had persuaded the policeman to keep the passports and think it over, so they were cleared to leave the station and walk into town, where they could eat and rest up at a hotel overnight. In the morning Ball would try again: it was truly a lottery with the regulations, one day impossible rigidity, the next day no problem. They stashed most of the luggage safely at the station and left under a cloud of gloom.

As they walked down the hill into Cerbère, Fry dropped back with Ball, and he looked at the motley collection he was chaperoning. There was an elderly, stooped German trudging heavily alongside a curvaceous younger blond woman. Then came a short, plump man with bottle-bottom glasses, hurrying to keep up with the purposeful stride of an imperious woman at his side. Behind them came the slim, dark-haired, intense young academic, the son of a Nobel Prize winner. Fry himself, smartly dressed with a wilting carnation in his buttonhole, was pacing beside a lard-salesman from Montana who was at this very moment assaulting Fry's ear with a succession of fruity oaths. It was a moment of lucidity, one in which Fry found himself asking, "How did I come to be here?"

Fry realized he should have known the journey would not be straightforward. Personally, he was anxious about the nautical charts he had pasted behind the lining of his suitcase. The reality of what would happen if he was discovered with such documents suddenly surfaced in his imagination. He remembered, though, that there were certain very simple things that each man had to do at certain points in his life, like Beamish had said. Fry simply had to work at keeping calm. Beamish had to work at being French. The refugees, though, this odd and disparate group of actually quite brave and hardy people before him, had to work at staying alive. That was very much harder.

Any lingering hopes of going through by train to Port-Bou were dashed the next morning. Ball tried and failed to change the mind of the police officer, and emerged from the bureau spitting with fury. They now had several options. The first was to stay in Cerbère and try again tomorrow, and perhaps the next day, and perhaps the one after that. But Ball had been advised not to wait around for something was in the air, the policeman had told him, that made it unsafe to stay. The next option was for Fry to go alone to Perpignan and attempt to secure exit visas for all his charges. But it was now Friday, and by the time Fry arrived at Perpignan they would already have missed the afternoon train through the tunnel to Port-Bou. In addition, he probably would not be able to get visas before Monday morning, if at all. That would leave them marooned in Cerbère again, all weekend. It was not, of course, advisable to return to Marseille. The situation would inevitably be worse if they tried the whole operation again at a later date. That left the third and only option: go over the hill. It was exactly what Fry had hoped they would not have to do. For there was an old and infirm man in the party—Heinrich Mann— and another—Franz Werfel—with a dangerous cardiac condition. The day was already hot, and the hill looked most steep and intimidatingly high. Yet there was no alternative, so Fry and Ball walked to the group, sitting at a table in the station café, to give them the bad news.

The unfortunate passengers talked things over, until Werfel's voice, filled with horror, rang out above the hubbub. He had just remembered that it was, on top of everything, Friday the thirteenth—not the perfect augury for this sort of ill-advised adventure. He decided that it would be better to wait, but Alma swiftly silenced him, hissing "Das ist Unsinn, Franz!" ("That's insane!"). Nelly Mann was also beginning to falter. She muttered rapidly in German to her husband: Fry looked like a pleasant young man, she said, but he could be leading them into a trap.

Fry, who remembered his German quite well, and had been given ample opportunity to brush up on it recently, glared at her. "Im Gegenteil, Frau Mann. Ich versuche Sie aus der Falle herauszuführen." On the contrary, he said in his best German, he wanted to lead them *out* of a trap. "Mrs. Mann blushed crimson at this," Fry reported, "and we heard no more from her."

Everybody realized there was nothing to do but attempt the mountainside, even though they were not dressed for it, especially Alma Werfel with her billowing white dress, like a great flag of surrender, visible for miles. Fry found a *tabac* and bought about fifteen packs of Gitanes and Gauloises for the Spanish guards, who couldn't speak English or German but were fluent in tobacco, and distributed among his protégés a whole dictionary's worth of cigarettes. Leon Ball would lead the party up the mountain and leave them only when the *douanier* post of Port-Bou was in clear sight. Fry meanwhile, who had his exit visa, would board the train with all the luggage, and meet them on the far, the blessed, side.

Fry walked with them down to the cemetery—at last seeing for himself the place he had described for so many others. The trip downhill took about forty-five minutes, and when they finally reached the eastern wall of the cemetery, and contemplated the rugged terrain above, Fry knew there was not much more to say. Heinrich Mann had taken off his hat, and with horror Fry saw the initials "H. M." stitched in the hatband. Mann was traveling under the name of Heinrich Ludwig, and such carelessness could give away everything—as if clambering over a mountain would not, of course. But Fry took out his pocketknife and sawed through the material until he had detached the incriminating letters. Mann was appalled. He had been brought to this, acting like a common criminal. Arguably the most famous writer in Europe was now reduced to effacing the last shred of his identity on a windy mountainside. There really was nothing left to say. Fry wished them luck, and began his walk back uphill toward the viaduct.

When he reached the station, it occurred to Fry to inquire about what he had taken for granted: that, as he had been told back in Marseille, the Spanish had closed the border to stateless persons. The policeman he asked looked puzzled. Wherever had Monsieur heard such a thing? So it was just another false rumor. Expressions of relief and dismay fought for possession of Fry's features. He could have brought along Feuchtwanger after all, instead of leaving him billeted with Harry Bingham. It remained to be seen whether the false information would turn out to mean Feuchtwanger had been lucky or not.

ALMA WERFEL'S AUTOBIOGRAPHY is stupendously unreliable, but one passage at least is accurate. "It was sheer, slippery terrain that we crawled up," she remembered of the climb over the mountain that hot September day in 1940. "Bounded by precipices. Mountain goats could hardly have kept their footing on the glassy, shimmering slate. If you skidded, there was nothing but thistles to hold onto." It was indeed a treacherous climb, and Leon Ball decided to lead them to the summit in two groups, first the Werfels, then the Manns, with Ball, Golo, and Nelly Mann practically carrying Heinrich the entire way. When finally they were all gathered on the crest, attempting to stand upright in the treacherous gusts of wind, the dreaded *gardes mobiles* appeared as if from nowhere. These paramilitary units had been sent to the border to reinforce the sometimes lackadaisical frontier police. In other words, they were an embodiment of Vichy's German-inspired hostility toward fleeing refugees. Everybody had the same thought at once: now it was a concentration camp for sure.

AT CERBÈRE STATION, Fry checked in all seventeen pieces of luggage, relieved that the *douanier* barely glanced at them. Almost as bad as explaining nautical charts would be accounting for the bales of women's clothes packed in the suitcases. The train ride between the French and Spanish sides was barely twenty minutes long, almost all of it through the tunnel blasted out of the living rock of the Pyrenees. At Port-Bou Fry was waved through customs again with nary a glance at the luggage, and after that he hired a porter to take all of it to the hotel where he had stayed back in August, a lifetime distant, on his way into France. There was no sign of his traveling companions, though, and when Fry described them in unmistakable detail to a frontier guard, the man swore that nobody like that had come through today. Fry quickly grew worried and agitated. The guard suggested he try the highway sentries farther up the hill.

"It was a long, hot climb," wrote Fry. When he found the sentries, they acted haughty and indifferent. Over the centuries the Spanish had seen everything and experienced all manner of human tragedy. Now there was *nada*, nothing, especially since the Civil War broke the country's spirit. Spain was weary of turning its gaze outward, even for a moment. Slowly the guard turned his gaze to take in Fry. "Wait here," said the guard with a cryptic brevity, leaving Fry puffing on a cigarette at a table in the hut, not knowing whether he was under arrest or not.

ALL EYES WERE on the rifles of the *gardes mobiles*. "Shot while resisting arrest," the report would say. The moment of truth had come for the Werfels and the Manns, on the run for so long, and now trapped at the last moment.

"Are you looking for Spain?" asked one of the guards.

"Yes," came a voice, probably Alma's.

"Well, follow the footpath here to the left. If you follow the one to the right, it will take you back to the French border post."

The guards saluted the group of ragged travelers, and left. All they could do was look at one another. Fate had dealt them one last ace.

The danger was not quite over, though. When the party at last had clambered down the hillside and gone inside the Spanish *douanier* hut to collect their *entrada* stamps, the guard looked long and hard at Golo's "affidavit in lieu of passport," which stated he was traveling to Princeton University to see his father.

"So you are the son of Thomas Mann?" asked the guard.

Golo was too fatigued, and too angry by now at the humiliations of concealment, to deny it any longer. If it meant his doom to admit it, then well and good. He would die as himself rather than live cowering under an alias.

"Yes," he answered. "Does it displease you?"

"On the contrary," replied the guard. "I am honored to make the acquaintance of the son of so great a man."

The sentries eventually returned to where Fry sat sweating and smoking in the little wooden hut by the highway barrier. They told him his friends were down at the customs house, which they had just passed through. "I don't think I've ever been so relieved in my life as I was by those few words," said Fry. He gratefully handed the sentries all the packs of cigarettes he possessed, and rushed back down the hill to Port-Bou.

They had made it.

PART 4

FRIENDS

CHAPTER 14

URSULA

Rare though true love may be, true friendship is rarer still.
—La Rochefoucauld

I N THE SUMMER of 1940 it looked as if the British were doomed: the
European continent was locked against them, their fragile seaborne empire was under threat and overextended, and their armed forces had suffered a decisive and crippling defeat. Nearly all the motorized equipment and
gunnery of the British army had been spiked and left behind, or simply destroyed in action, in the fields and roads of France during the rout of June.
The Royal Air Force had been more than decimated on the ground by enemy
airplanes on May 10 and 11, and was now woefully understrength. Its few remaining craft were no match for Goering's Luftwaffe, and its inexperienced
pilots were steeling themselves for the September onslaught on British airfields and cities that would become known as the Battle of Britain. Only the
Royal Navy could provide a tenuous lifeline, by attempting to keep clear vital
shipping lanes. All in all it was not a promising situation. What was left of the
civilized world looked on in sadness at the imminent demise of a once great
nation. The United States was determined to keep out of the fight, whether to
save Britain or to defeat Fascism.

The odd thing about the British was that they seemed not to recognize this
woeful litany of disadvantages. Arrogance and imperialism of spirit had long
been quintessential if not very endearing British traits. The true scope of
British world power had shrunk over recent decades, the stiff upper lip, the
defining characteristic of the military class, had become a subject of gentle
humor and often outright mockery. Yet in the face of everything, the British
still believed that there was no way they could lose the war. It was as if the
worst had already happened; they were now confined to their small island,

with their backs to the wall, and yet something in the British character relished the forthcoming combat. It is a cliché that the British always cheer on the underdog; now, at last, they *were* the underdog, with a fighting leader in Winston Churchill. He was a man ignored and derided for his warnings about Hitler throughout the thirties. Now he was out for his revenge, and the subjects of the kingdom he served seemed to be saying, "Jolly good show." It was deluded and admirable at the same time.

As Varian Fry entered the British Embassy at Madrid, he was about to come face to face with this wartime spirit.

THE MANNS AND WERFELS were safely on their way to Lisbon, after a minor fright in Port-Bou. As they were celebrating their arrival with an alcoholic evening meal, a man walked over to the table and whispered in Fry's ear. He asked in English if he could have a word with Fry outside. There he explained that he recognized Heinrich Mann, and that the chances were the Spaniard sitting in the corner soon would as well, for he was the local head of Franco's secret police. "He's not a very pleasant chap, really," said the British consul to Fry. The party broke up immediately, and everyone made their way upstairs to bed.

They reached Barcelona the next day, Saturday, and managed to secure two seats on the only flight leaving for Lisbon. These Fry allocated to Heinrich and Nelly Mann, who were still in real danger despite their American affidavits and the fact that Fry had managed to burn their incriminating Czech passports on the train between Cerbère and Port-Bou, lying on the toilet floor so as not to breathe the acrid smoke. The Manns took off on the morning of Monday, September 16. Following that, Fry dropped into the American consulate—and found a much more pleasant atmosphere than at its sister establishment in Marseille. The fate of the refugees who had been arrested after they had crossed into Spain preyed on Fry's mind. He needed to know exactly why they, and no others, had been stopped. The vice-consul kindly promised to look into the matter.

By Tuesday Fry, Golo, and the Werfels were in Madrid, and there Fry was able to put Franz and Alma on another Lisbon-bound airplane. Golo spent the afternoon walking around the Prado, and caught the Portugal train that same night.

COLONEL WILLIAM WYNDHAM TORRE TORR—"Bunny" to his friends—was the military attaché at the British embassy in Madrid. Previously he had been in Lisbon, and afterward in Washington, with responsibility also for Mexico and South America. So Torr knew Americans well, and he would have had plenty of dealings with the State Department, and probably with Sumner Welles himself, who had been a Latin American specialist.

Torr sat back down and Fry began to explain the business that had brought him there. Suddenly, Torr disappeared from sight. Fry leant forward and discovered him on the floor under his desk, wrestling with the telephone wire. Soon he held the plug end aloft, triumphantly.

"You can never be too careful," he whispered. "They can use these things as listening instruments even when the receiver is down, you know."

Fry made a mental note about that for the office on the rue Grignan. Then he explained in detail about Lussu's plan for the British to send a boat to pick up the British, Italians, and Spanish from Cap Croisette. Torr was delighted with the idea, but he told Fry that there was no chance of lending a Royal Navy ship for the purpose. The Admiralty had a strict rule of never detaching a unit from the fleet. Torr himself was trying to strike a bargain with the Spanish to let the British soldiers who made it over the mountains into Spain go on to Gibraltar instead of being imprisoned by Franco. If that happened, said Torr, there'd be no need for any boats. If it didn't, they would have to think of something else. Torr's attitude was extremely optimistic, almost blithely unaware that Britain was losing the war.

Captain Darling, the British vice-consul at Lisbon, whom Fry would meet in a few days' time, knew better than Torr the real situation with the Royal Navy. He told Fry that Torr was simply wrong in his assumption that a navy boat was unavailable for the refugee escapes. "Torr could quite well have said Naval Units could not be detached," he later told Fry, "either for security reasons or because he was such a fundamentally silly man (though kind and pleasant), that the Embassy never told him anything for the sake of security. In actual fact not only *were* Naval Units detached, but there was quite a phoney little fleet available for these purposes. One submarine, at least, one large trawler and several large fishing boats—all 'converted.'" Torr's wife, a practical woman, took the same approach with her husband. "All our servants are 'reds,'" she told Darling of their situation in Madrid, "otherwise we could not get any food from the market. But for God's sake don't tell Bunny."

Unaware of the true situation with the Royal Navy, Torr asked Fry to return in about a week. By then the British would have a clearer idea of what was happening. But he said he liked the idea of getting out the troops—liked it very much indeed. They shook hands, and as Fry left the office, Torr disappeared beneath the desk again to plug back in the phone, which began to ring immediately.

Fry's next destination was the local headquarters of Franco's dread Seguridad. He still wanted to discover the reason for the arrests of the refugees who had been sent over the mountains in the first week of September. Perhaps it was because the Spanish security forces had a list, given to them by the Gestapo. But his protégés, Fry reminded himself, had been traveling on false identification papers. Unless a Gestapo man had been present at the border to identify each of the refugees personally (which even Fry felt was a far-fetched idea), how had they failed to gain entrance to the country? And why hadn't everybody been arrested? It wasn't that their forged documents were unsafe, because so many of the others had successfully reached Lisbon using similar examples of Bill Freier's artwork. It was a mystery. He felt sure it could only have been due to some stupidity on the part of the refugees themselves.

All Fry succeeded in extracting from the Seguridad was a half promise to look into the matter, and after that, there was nothing more for him to do in Madrid. Having had quite enough of trains for the time being, he checked out of his hotel and went directly to the airport. He planned to stay there until there was a seat on a plane for Lisbon, and did not have to wait long. Two hours later, Fry was in the air, and had reached Lisbon before nightfall.

ONLY A LITTLE MORE than a month had passed since Fry had stopped over in Portugal on his way to Marseille, yet in that short period of time Lisbon had changed dramatically. This time, the *douaniers* at the airport were less polite, more surly and suspicious. Suddenly it was easy to remember that Portugal was also a dictatorship. Fry noticed that the newsstands now displayed fewer American and British newspapers, and more journals from the Reich and Vichy France. He also noticed that on the streets, in cafés, and in hotel lobbies, there were Germans wandering about in groups of two or three, all trying hard to look as if they were tourists.

Lisbon, too, had its rumor factories. One of the most recent stories referred to these "tourists," who were thought to be the advance guard of the fifteen Wehrmacht divisions Fry had heard were massed on the Spanish border. Almost everybody believed that Hitler was about to occupy Spain, and maybe Portugal too. It was a reasonable guess, although not quite the truth of the situation. British intelligence intercepts of German top-secret communications between Hitler and Franco, released by the Foreign Office in London at the end of 1997, revealed that Hitler's idea had not been to invade Spain but to seize Gibraltar from the British. "Spain's participation in the war," wrote Hitler, "must begin with the expulsion of the British Fleet from Gibraltar.

Once Gibraltar is in Spanish possession the Western Mediterranean will cease to be a sphere of operations for the British." Strategically, such a move could have won the war for Germany, for without Gibraltar the British would have had no access to the Mediterranean, and could not have continued to supply Crete, Malta, or—more importantly—its forces in North Africa.

If the Germans controlled Africa, Britain would have no easy way to reach Asia and the Far East; its empire would have been sliced in two at Suez, to be then devoured by the Japanese on one side and the Germans on the other. Gibraltar was the fulcrum of continued British resistance. Franco admitted to the Führer that Spain had been planning to seize Gibraltar anyway—he had commissioned military studies of the rock's defenses and vulnerability, and had been disappointed when his generals informed him that air attack alone could not destroy the well-entrenched defenses of the fortress. A chagrined Hitler decided instead to send his fifteen divisions, complete with enormous railway-mounted eighty-centimeter guns, through Spain to its southeastern coast, in order to pulverize Gibraltar from a mainland position. Perhaps that had been the reason for Himmler's presence in Madrid—to attempt to persuade Franco to allow passage for the panzers all the way down the east side of the Iberian Peninsula.

Although Hitler threatened Franco with invasion if he refused to cooperate, the Spanish dictator would not agree until "Suez had fallen." A wise tyrant, he believed in consolidating the territory he had won, unlike the expansive and reckless Hitler. Franco had watched the defeat of France and, like the rest of the world, had expected to see the capitulation of Britain soon afterward. But Britain showed no intention of surrendering, and had even hit back at Germany with air raids that, while costly, boosted British morale. Now, Franco was less than completely convinced about the future course of the conflict. He refused to commit himself entirely to the Nazi cause until Hitler had ejected the British from Africa, and Hitler could not risk opening another front in the West, against Spain, because he was already planning his invasion of Russia in the East, and at the same time continuing his efforts to subdue the British. For his part, Hitler refused to give Spain French North Africa—Franco's demand in return for active participation in the Axis—as his share of the spoils following the defeat of France. Meanwhile, Churchill had promised Franco that the British would lay siege to the Canary Islands if Gibraltar was attacked. The three-handed struggle would end as a "Mexican stand-off," although when Fry landed in Madrid, Franco was writing a letter to Hitler agreeing with his intentions: "The first action of our belligerency must be the occupation of Gibraltar." In the circumstances, the refugee telegraph was surprisingly accurate.

Another rumor—this one entirely true—was that the Gestapo had begun to operate in Lisbon, kidnapping refugees off the streets and returning them to Germany. So far at least half a dozen anti-Nazis known by the Germans to be in Lisbon had disappeared in this fashion. Fortunately none was from Fry's list. But Fry thought of the postcards sent from here, which chatted happily about the escape routes, and he shuddered. It only took one of his clients to be discovered in Lisbon by the Gestapo and the entire operation could collapse.

Fry went straight from the airport to the Hotel Metropole, where Dr. Charles Joy of the Unitarian Service Committee had established his offices. Franz von Hildebrand was working there, and a happy reunion ensued. Dr. Joy told Fry the Werfels were esconced in a palatial hotel out in Estoril, the exclusive resort not far from the capital used by the international set. The Manns were in town, staying at less impressive lodgings, and Fry dined with them that evening.

The next day he set about his tasks, foremost of which was to gather intelligence concerning the experiences of the refugees who had made it to Lisbon. It was vital that Fry keep up to date with conditions at the border with France, and with Spanish policy and attitudes in the interior. Only in this way could he remain reasonably sure he was not simply sending his clients straight to prison, or worse.

The news from the refugees who had made it was good, but not entirely reassuring. The stories he heard ranged from the horrifying to the comical. Some refugees had been stopped and searched at Port-Bou; others sent their luggage through as Fry had done, and collected it later on the Spanish side of the border with absolutely no problems. Some travelers had breezed past the Spanish frontier only to be inexplicably detained for questioning at the Portuguese border. Although all the refugees complained about the common experience of fleas in the third-class Spanish railway carriages, their encounters with Spanish officialdom varied wildly. Some had come through with minimal checks of their papers; others found the scrutiny so fierce that they were forced to pay bribes in order to reclaim their passports. One German client had his Polish passport returned only after he had given the Spanish guard his word that it was a forgery!

It was a terrible headache for Fry to try and regularize all this conflicting information into future instructions for further escapees. At least all of them had made it over the mountains above Cerbère safely, even if several had nearly been trapped by the *gardes mobiles*. One actually had been caught and turned back, but tried again a few hours later and made it. Clearly the whole

Varian Fry and his mother, Lilian Mackey Fry, 1908
(COURTESY OF ANNETTE FRY)

Varian Fry at Coney Island, 1912
(COURTESY OF ANNETTE FRY)

Varian Fry, age 12 or 13
(COURTESY OF ANNETTE FRY)

Varian Fry, circa 1920s
(COURTESY OF ANNETTE FRY)

Varian Fry in Berlin, 1935
(COURTESY OF ANNETTE FRY)

Eileen Fry, circa 1948. Photograph by Varian Fry
(UNITED STATES HOLOCAUST MEMORIAL MUSEUM, GIFT OF ANNETTE FRY)

*Members of Fry's staff, including Daniel Bénédite, hans Sahl, and Marcel Verzeano,
meet secretly in the office at night to review "client" files
and plan rescue operations, Marseilles, 1940.*
(VARIAN FRY PAPERS, RARE BOOK AND MANUSCRIPT LIBRARY, COLUMBIA UNIVERSITY)

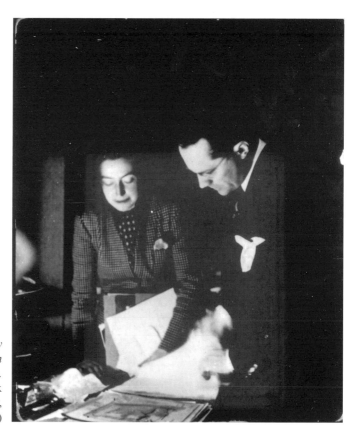

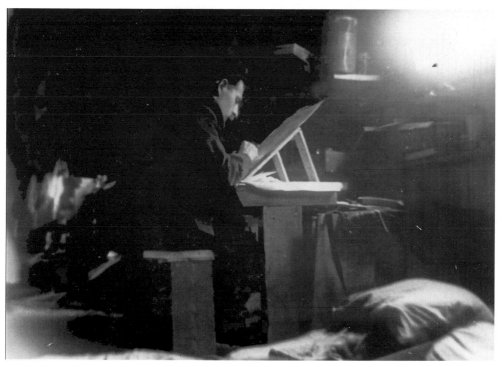

Bill Freier (Willi Spira), artist and forger for Fry's secret operation, in a French internment camp, 1940 or '41

THESE ARE SOME OF THE MEN AND WOMEN WHO MATCHED WITS WITH THE GESTAPO AND SET UP THE UNDERGROUND FROM FRANCE.

BEAMISH—so-called for his impish eyes, alternating pout and broad grin.

VARIAN FRY—the young American leader of the underground. (The artist said that his chin vied with his nose for leadership.)

DANIEL BENEDITE—he had decided opinions on wine, women and politics which he expressed on every likely occasion.

MEHRING—one of the best of the modern poets, but so small that he was generally called "Baby."

JEAN GEMAHLING—a flaxen-haired, blue-eyed youth from Strasbourg.

MIRIAM DAVENPORT—the interviewer. She was always either laughing or coughing.

Cartoons of Varian Fry and his staff
by Bill Freier for the original Surrender on Demand
(COURTESY OF ANNETTE FRY)

This photo of novelist Lion Feuchtwanger in the French internment camp Saint Nicolas, near Nimes, in 1940 alerted Eleanor Roosevelt to his danger. (COURTESY OF ANNETTE FRY)

Charlie Fawcett
(COURTESY OF CHARLIE FAWCETT)

Marcel Verzeano, Marseilles, 1940
(COURTESY OF MARCEL VERZEANO)

Marc Chagall, a reluctant refugee, was at work on this painting when Fry arrived to explain escape plans.
(VARIAN FRY PAPERS, RARE BOOK AND MANUSCRIPT LIBRARY, COLUMBIA UNIVERSITY)

Varian Fry
walking in Marseilles, 1941

Members of Fry's staff (left to right): *Charles Wolff, Theodora Bénédite, Daniel Bénédite, Lotte Feibel,*
Ludwig Copperman (Louis Coppée), Marcel Verzeano, Jean Gemähling, Marseilles, 1941.
Photograph by Varian Fry

Jean Gemähling and Consuelo de Saint-Exupéry in a Marseilles restaurant, 1940 or '41
(VARIAN FRY PAPERS, RARE BOOK AND MANUSCRIPT LIBRARY, COLUMBIA UNIVERSITY)

Albert "Beamish" Hirschman, right, shows a refugee a map of the escape route.
(COURTESY OF ANNETTE FRY)

Varian Fry and Consuelo de Saint-Exupéry in the branches of a tree at Villa Air-Bel,
outside Marseilles, 1940 or '41

André and Jacqueline Breton, with their daughter Aube, eating outdoors at the Villa Air-Bel, outside Marseilles, 1940 or '41 (VARIAN FRY PAPERS, RARE BOOK AND MANUSCRIPT LIBRARY, COLUMBIA UNIVERSITY)

Varian Fry in Marseilles, 1941
(VARIAN FRY PAPERS, RARE BOOK AND
MANUSCRIPT LIBRARY, COLUMBIA UNIVERSITY)

Jacqueline Breton at the dinner table of Villa Air-Bel outside Marseilles, 1940 or '41. Photo by Varian Fry
(VARIAN FRY PAPERS, RARE BOOK AND MANUSCRIPT LIBRARY, COLUMBIA UNIVERSITY)

From left, Jacqueline Breton, André Masson, and André Breton confer with Fry before their escape to Spain, in the office of the Centre Américain de Secours (American Relief Center) on the boulevard Garibaldi, Marseilles, April 1941. Photograph by Ylla
(PHOTO ARCHIVES, MUSEUM OF MODERN ART, NEW YORK)

Varian Fry's colleagues await his expulsion from France at the train station at Cerbère, August 1941.
(VARIAN FRY PAPERS, RARE BOOK AND MANUSCRIPT LIBRARY, COLUMBIA UNIVERSITY)

Annette and Varian Fry on their wedding day, November 11, 1950

ABOVE: *Varian Fry, 1951. Photograph by Annette Fry* (COURTESY OF ANNETTE FRY)
BELOW: *Varian Fry with Tom and Sylvia, 1959* (COURTESY OF ANNETTE FRY)

Varian Fry teaching Greek, 1963 or '64
(COURTESY OF ANNETTE FRY)

Varian Fry on acceptance of the Légion d'Honneur, France 1967. Left to right: Edouard Morot-Sir (French cultural ambassador), James Fry, Varian Fry, Sylvia Fry, Annette Fry, Thomas Fry
(COURTESY OF ANNETTE FRY)

endeavor was a lottery, one in which the odds were still excellent, but for how long? Fry wondered.

Then he heard a story that chilled him to his marrow. A couple who had gone over the mountains by the Cerbère route on Saturday, September 14, just a day after the Manns and Werfels, reported that they had seen uniformed German officers on the road that went past the cemetery. The couple had only got through by heading into the mountains further west. They spent a cold night in the open at an altitude with the *tramontane* wind blowing, before coming to the Spanish frontier by the "back door"—almost following the Fittkos' path from Banyuls.

Had the route been blown? Fry's next thought fell even more heavily. He had telegraphed to send the Feuchtwangers over the mountains at Cerbère *after* the German soldiers had been sighted. Had he sent them directly into a trap? Fry hurried back to the Metropole to find that nobody had heard anything about Feuchtwanger, and to be handed a cable by Franzi that Fry tore open at once.

There was a brief cryptic message:

BABY PASSED CRISIS BETTER NOW BUT OTHER CHILDREN QUARANTINED DOING OUR BEST LENA

Fry guessed that "Baby" was Mehring—but what was the crisis? And the other children, probably refugees, what "illness" were they suffering from? Did quarantine mean concentration camp? Had the police swooped? Thankfully Lena was discreet, and wouldn't write anything the censor might understand. Unfortunately, her discretion also made the message virtually indecipherable for its intended reader. All Fry knew was that this cable implied bad tidings concerning Feuchtwanger, and that his own return to Marseille was imperative. First, though, he had to get back to Colonel Torr at the Madrid embassy.

Fry worked fast over that weekend in Lisbon, interviewing more refugees and finishing his detailed situation report for the Emergency Rescue Committee in New York. He inquired of it why replies to his cables were taking so long, and were so erratic in their responses. He told (rather than asked) Ingrid Warburg and Mildred Adams at least to number the telegrams, like he did, or they were worse than useless. This sort of sloppiness and delay deeply annoyed Fry. It was also seriously beginning to hamper the need for speed in transferring money using the Kourillo method, and in securing "emergency" visas for those refugees who needed to leave France extremely quickly. That unpleasant task dispensed with, Fry went out and bought a few dozen cakes of soap. An aspect of the French rationing that was beginning to bite badly even at this early stage was the dearth of sugar, fats, and above all detergents. It was not just personal hygiene that suffered. "Shirts, socks, handkerchiefs and underwear grew frayed and full of holes," said Fry, "and the process was hastened by the fact that the laundress, having no real soap, followed the directions given in the newspapers and in *Marie Claire,* soaking them in a solution of wood ashes overnight, and then rubbing them on stones to get them clean." Lena had strewn his luggage with little notes, each bearing the word "soap" in all the languages she knew; hence "savon," "Seife," "sapone," "jabon," and words in Polish and Russian he assumed *meant* soap, which fluttered floorward every time he pulled out a clean shirt or pair of socks.

Unlike Heinrich Mann, who had nearly panicked, Fry remained composed when he noticed once more the portrait of Hitler hanging in the Lufthansa office early on Monday morning. His intention was to see Torr as soon as he got to Madrid, and after dropping his luggage at a hotel, he did just that.

This time, the elderly British ambassador, Sir Samuel Hoare, sat in on the meeting. He, too, affirmed that it was impossible for the Royal Navy to send one of its ships to collect the soldiers and the Spanish and Italian refugees—although why Hoare said this, when he presumably knew of the clandestine flotilla, remains a matter of speculation. Probably the British did not wish to provoke open warfare with the French, who were on the verge of breaking off all communications with the British at the time. What Hoare did suggest, though, was that Fry attempt to send British troops over the mountains into Spain, as he had been doing with the refugees on his list. Apparently Torr had succeeded in his negotiations to have the troops repatriated by the Spanish authorities.

Fry demurred. He told the ambassador he was bound by his first duty: to honor his agreement with Lussu and to concentrate on getting away the Italians and Spanish Republicans. It was a canny negotiating move, for Fry deftly made it clear he was unwilling simply to be a line manager for the British underground railway. There had to be some give and take. Hoare gave way, and offered Fry the considerable sum of ten thousand dollars if he would undertake to attempt the mountain route. His compromise was that the British would endeavor to find boats to pick up both British troops and Lussu's fugitives, and the only condition was that Fry should never place British and Spanish, or Italians, on the same boat together. If a boat, laden with such a mix of furtive allies, was discovered, it could cause an embarrassing international incident.

Fry agreed. He was now a British agent. He had already overstepped his orders from the committee in New York once before, by assenting to Beamish's proposal to open the original list to many more refugees. This was justifiable, as it had been an adjustment to the reality of a situation in France that nobody back in New York could have foreseen when Fry's job was created. Now, though, it was arguable that he was abrogating his responsibilities in a far more drastic—and deadly—manner. In taking the "King's shilling," Fry was inviting much more attention from the Gestapo than even his previous role had warranted. It could be argued that his decision was foolish, or reckless, or even heroic. Fry only knew that those Resistance fighters he had come to call his friends would have approved. Beamish above all would approve, and that meant a lot to him.

Before he left, Colonel Torr attempted to press on Fry the ten thousand dollars in the form of banknotes—a sum that must have occupied at least the volume of a briefcase, and a very risky package to try and get past customs at the French border. Fry had managed it with three thousand dollars strapped to his legs when he first arrived, but he was a leg short for this amount. Instead he told Torr to wire the money to New York, so it could be drawn on, via Kourillo's extremely favorable exchange rate, as needed.

TUESDAY AFTERNOON found Fry back in Barcelona, on the last leg of his Spanish journey. Before he had left for the airport at Madrid, Fry had returned to the offices of the Seguridad to see if the police had decided to tell him anything about the imprisoned refugees, but they claimed to know nothing. That was unlikely, for at the American consulate in Barcelona, where he hastened as soon as his plane touched down, Fry was given all the information he wanted. Sure enough, the refugees, including a German couple called Ernst and Rosi Scheuer, had ignored their instructions and bypassed the Spanish border post and their vital *entrada* stamps. They had all been charged with clandestine entry and smuggling. There was nothing more sinister to the matter than that, and it meant the prisoners would probably be sent back to France, where they would be interned like so many others. "Serves them right" was an uncharitable but justified thought. And it was, paradoxically, the best news Fry had heard in days.

It was followed by devastating news. A vice-consul at the consulate asked Fry if he had seen the September 19 issue of the *New York Times*. You'd better read this, he told Fry, and handed him a ready-folded copy with an article marked out:

FEUCHTWANGER IN BERLIN

———

**STILL HELD BY POLICE—BEHEADING
IN PARIS IS DENIED**

———

BERLIN, Sept. 18—Lion Feuchtwanger, German writer who
fled from the Reich in 1933, is in the hands of Berlin police,
it was reported tonight.

A well-informed source denied that the writer was beheaded
in Paris as was rumored abroad.

Fry could read no further. He put the newspaper down on the desk and
walked out.

CHAPTER 15

THE FALL

W HEN VARIAN FRY arrived back at Marseille, on the morning of
Thursday, September 26, 1940, summer seemed to have disappeared. The steel gray sky and premature stirrings of the *mistral*—
the icy Provençal wind that whips down from the mountains to cut right
through one's clothes and chill the bones—certainly made it feel unseason-
able. And it was soon apparent that a new season of frigidity and opposition
awaited him, too. "For some reason which we couldn't understand," said Fry
shortly afterward, "the Gestapo had given us more than six weeks to get the
refugees out. We had never been able to explain the delay, but we had been
grateful for it, and we had profited by it. Now we knew that our days of grace
were over."

He ate breakfast with Lena and Beamish, who had eagerly awaited his return, and they presented him with some information that was much more
palatable than the ersatz coffee—pompously called *café national*—stale
bread, and tasteless grapeskin mash that had to do duty as *confitures*. Nobody
in Marseille had seen the *Times* article concerning Feuchtwanger's arrest and
like Mark Twain's, the announcement of the novelist's death had been thankfully exaggerated. A few hours later Leon Ball returned from another of his
clandestine border trips to explain in detail how he had successfully conducted Feuchtwanger over the mountains several days before. Lena had
despatched the Feuchtwangers to the frontier, laden with packs of Camels for
the *douaniers,* as soon as she had received Fry's telegram. They were accompanied by a man Fry had met in Lisbon when he first reached Europe—the
Reverend Waitstill Sharp of the Unitarian Service Committee in Marseille. He

went through on the train with the luggage, as Fry had done, and Ball led first Lion, then Marta over the mountains. At Barcelona, they decided to take the train to Lisbon instead of an airplane: only Lufthansa was flying, and Feuchtwanger was too well-known to risk being spotted on a German airline.

In the end, the train proved dangerous as well. As camouflage during the trip, Feuchtwanger carried Sharp's briefcase with a large Red Cross symbol emblazoned on it. Once he was in the two-stall bathroom with the case at his feet when the door opened and a Gestapo officer walked in and unbuttoned his fly. He saw Feuchtwanger's briefcase, and began asking him, in Prussian-accented English, about America. Feuchtwanger replied, in Bavarian-accented English, and managed to bluff his way through the brief conversation. At the Portuguese border a cry of "Mr. Feuchtwanger!" went up from an American journalist while he was standing in the customs queue. Somehow she had learned he was a passenger on the train that had just pulled in. People began to look for the celebrity in their midst, and Sharp pulled the young woman aside and told her to shut up. "I just wanted a scoop," she said, but kept silent after that. The rest of the journey was mercifully uneventful.

THESE TIDINGS HELPED Fry's delicate digestion to cope with the gruesome rations the Splendide served up. He also asked Lena what the devil her telegram was supposed to mean. Again the news was relatively welcome. There had been a few moments of high drama—this was what the cable had tried and failed to communicate—when, on the orders of Monsieur Fleury, *Chef de la Sûreté*, the police arrived at the hotel to arrest Mehring, who was still in his bed pretending to be sick. The command had gone out to arrest four men, in fact: along with Mehring, the handcuffs were out for the complacent Rudolfs, Breitscheid and Hilferding, who were still sitting all day in their café (though now with vials of poison in their waistcoat pockets), and a German journalist called Arthur Wolff—whom, sadly, Fry would later come to know all too well. That was what "quarantine" referred to. They were not to be sent to a concentration camp, but rather placed under house arrest in the nearby town of Arles, where presumably they could be kept quiet and out of the way. Also, of course, it meant the Gestapo could collect them at its leisure. Breitscheid and Hilferding were Frank Bohn's responsibility, and so far Wolff was nobody's; but "Baby" Mehring belonged to the Centre Américain, and Lena and Miriam had fought like mother tigers to stop the police from taking him away.

Lena had positioned herself between the "bedridden" Mehring and the grasping *Sûreté* agents while a message was got to Miriam. She soon arrived at the Splendide to find Lena distressed and shaking like a leaf, with the police on the point of pulling back the eiderdown and physically lifting the terrified poet out of bed. Downstairs, more gendarmes were interrogating the hotel manager. Miriam had to think fast, and the first thing she thought of was to telephone trusty Harry Bingham. Then she confronted the police in Mehring's bedroom with a torrent of abuse and exhortation, which consisted of belaboring the point that Mehring was an accomplished artist, foremost among the practitioners of modern German literature, and that they should be ashamed to be arresting somebody—a sick man!—who had never broken the law, and that France would be plunged into ignominy by their act. The policemen looked hesitantly at each other and shrugged.

In the midst of Miriam's inspired harangue, Bingham walked through the door—a *coup de théâtre* that set up Miriam's punch line: "And there behind you, gentlemen, is living proof of my government's concern for the welfare of Mr. Mehring!" There ensued a long typically French discussion—first between the gendarmes on the scene, then between them and their superiors at the *Evêché*. Bingham's lofty presence swayed the matter, and the police eventually announced, with all the dignity they could muster, that if Mehring could produce a new doctor's certificate of his illness that so threatened his health then they would leave him be. So "Baby" remained in room 207, more skittish than ever.

This entertaining tale also restored to Fry some of his depleted spirits, and he was further buoyed by a cable that afternoon, which announced that Mr. and Mrs. Wetcheek—the Feuchtwangers—had arrived safely in Lisbon. Now he could begin with a relatively clear head to address the other disasters that had complicated the situation while he had been away. The renewed interest of the French police was the least of Fry's worries, although it remained an important one: the agents who came to take away Mehring had told the poet that they were acting on orders from his "compatriots," which was as good as saying they were now working for the Gestapo. Prior to this incident they had all suspected it but lacked hard evidence; now they had some, and there was soon to be more.

Fry soon met an Austrian friend of the Werfels, a Catholic writer called "Big" Klaus Dohrn, by arrangement at the Gare St. Charles. Dohrn had been a close collaborator of the Austrian president, Schuschnigg, and had escaped from Austria the night the German army walked in by swimming across a river into Czechoslovakia. He was waiting for his connection and staring gloomily into a cup of ersatz coffee, dressed in a uniform of the *prestataires*—

the forced labor gangs Vichy established to make use of the wretched refugees. Fry persuaded Dohrn to desert then and there, and showed him the safe way out of the station. Eventually, Fry would manage to send him on to Lisbon. It was Dohrn who told Fry and his colleagues about the renewed activity of the Gestapo agents hiding in the Kundt Commission, and who were traveling round the concentration camps of France, "selecting" those prisoners they wanted and transporting them back to Germany. In the light of the information trickling in, Fry had the telephones at the rue Grignan office changed so they could be unplugged between calls, just like the one in Colonel Torr's office, and he instituted regular "bug sweeps." Other than that there was nothing Fry could do except to carry on regardless, but with care.

A bigger problem was the sudden turn toward outright hostility that the American consular officials had taken. Fry had expected active cooperation from the American Foreign Service, but had been quickly disabused on the day of his arrival at Marseille. Following that, he at least relied on passive support, and a modicum of civility and protection to which, as an American citizen, he should have been entitled. On the contrary, it now appeared he was seen as a thorn in the side of United States foreign policy, and was to be given every encouragement to pack up and leave. Hugh Fullerton, the consul, was a relatively amenable first line of contact, but he was like the cowardly general store owner in a western town terrorized by outlaws. "Fullerton understood Fry's job and was sympathetic to it," said Howard L. Brooks, who was in Marseille on behalf of the Unitarian Service Committee. "He was fully alive to the suffering all around him among both the French and the refugees. Whenever he could help, he did. But Mr. Fullerton was timid. Having been a long time in the consular service, he understood the enormous importance of remaining on good terms with the government to which he was accredited. Like the majority of the American consuls in France, he didn't understand that in these times the really important thing was not to be on too good terms with the new French government, any more than with Hitler's government." Fullerton was also a man keen to act on orders from above. These of course came from Consul-General Hurley, who was acutely distrustful of refugees and anybody who had anything to do with them.

As soon as Fry returned from Spain, Fullerton showed him a cable he had received for him from Washington, sent via the embassy at Vichy and signed by Secretary of State Cordell Hull himself:

MUST REQUEST YOUR RETURN IMMEDIATELY COMMA NOT ONLY IN VIEW OF OUR UNDERSTANDING BUT ALSO OF LOCAL DEVELOP-MENTS WITH WHICH YOU ARE FAMILIAR

It was a stab in the back for Fry, and he was dismayed to learn the message had already been passed on to the prefect of police. It probably accounted for a recent raid on the offices of the Centre Américain: the French now knew that Fry was not protected by the United States government, and acted accordingly. "So the State Department had let me down," Fry later concluded. "It had permitted me to crawl out onto the end of a very long limb, and had then cut the limb off. There could be no mistake about that. It had been perfectly well understood from the start that I was going to try and evade the laws of France. My passport had been given me for that purpose and no other. What did the department mean by disowning me now?"

The answer lay in the stark realities of international diplomacy. A cable had gone out to all the consuls in France from Washington that warned them directly against having anything to do with Fry:

THIS GOVERNMENT DOES NOT REPEAT NOT COUNTENANCE ANY ACTIVITIES BY AMERICAN CITIZENS DESIRING TO EVADE THE LAWS OF THE GOVERNMENTS WITH WHICH THIS COUNTRY MAINTAINS FRIENDLY RELATIONS

Roosevelt had appointed Admiral Leahy as Ambassador to Vichy solely for his ability to talk boats with the French admirals, and so hopefully keep the fleet out of German hands. This was what was meant by "friendly relations," and missions such as Fry's had to be subordinated to that greater project, no matter how shortsighted it would prove to be. Leahy was next to useless for anything else in France, and it had disastrous consequences. "The truth is, of course, that Leahy is one of Roosevelt's worst appointments," wrote Fry at the time. "Having no experience of diplomacy, and being by nature a timid little man, he depends upon his secretaries for guidance in everything. And his secretaries, as Fullerton himself has told me, are all young men of consular and vice-consular rank. Thus, in effect, our diplomacy in France is being made by consuls and vice-consuls, most of them in their early thirties. It is too bad, for the post, one would think, might be an important one today. But even the French have noticed how feebly it is being filled, and many of them have been discouraged by the discovery."

Clearly Fry had been denounced to the police—that must have been what "evading laws" meant in the cable sent by Cordell Hull. The police had visited Fullerton, and Fullerton, instead of denying it and talking to Fry before taking action, had panicked. Hurley, delighted with developments, contacted Washington, and Washington, desperate to stay on the right side of Vichy, had decided to sacrifice Fry.

Fry had to act speedily to save the situation, and he speedily dispatched a telegram to the ambassador at Vichy, denying the crimes he had been found guilty of on hearsay, and asking for a chance to present his case.

MR FULLERTON HAS JUST COMMUNICATED ME CONTENTS OF YOUR RECENT TELEGRAM STOP YOUR INFORMATION BASED ON GROUND-LESS RUMORS STOP SHALL GO TO VICHY EXPLAIN TRUE SITUATION SOON AS POSSIBLE STOP MEANWHILE REQUEST YOU RESERVE JUDGMENT AND ASK OTHERS CONCERNED DO LIKEWISE STOP WOULD ALSO APPRECIATE YOUR INSTRUCTING DIPLOMATIC AND CONSULAR OFFICIALS NOT TO SPEAK ABOUT CASE TO ANYONE

It failed to do any good. In fact, the embassy and the Marseille consulate refused to have anything more to do with the matter. Fry was told a report had already been made, and that he was wasting his breath in attempting to add his testimony. Worse was to come. Back in America, the State Department had been in touch with Frank Kingdon, who, as chairman of the Emergency Rescue Committee, was ultimately responsible for Fry's conduct. Faced with the reality of lawbreaking (even though it was unproven, and if true, commendable), the committee lost its nerve. Soon after the devastating cable from Secretary of State Hull, Fry received another from his colleagues on Forty-second Street. Perhaps out of shame, they persuaded Eileen to send it:

MILDRED FRANK PAUL ALL BELIEVE YOU MUST RETURN IMMEDI-ATELY STOP SITUATION SERIOUS YOUR PEOPLE ENDANGERED STOP SUCCESSOR WILL LEAVE EARLIEST POSSIBLE DATE STOP CABLE DE-CISION

Fry wrote back to her when things had cooled down a little, with one eye on the censor, brazenly denying every allegation and explaining the "true" situation. "It appears," he lied, "that the prefecture had got the absurd idea that some members of my staff had been conducting persons illegally over the border. Actually no member of my staff had been near the border or has been since. . . . The only trouble we have is with certain members of the American Foreign Service (clerks, doormen, and secretaries), who evidently busy themselves with slandering and libelling our organization and the Americans active in it. . . ." Privately, Fry confided that he was "amazed by the documentary evidence I found of treacherous treatment I received from the American Embassy in Vichy."

The best he could do was to play for time. Hurley called Fry in and demanded he leave France at once. Fry refused. Then he assured the prefect and Fullerton that he was anyway awaiting a replacement, and that he could not possibly leave before that person arrived. Now that he had been formally recalled by the committee in New York, that time could not be far away. Fry was deeply angry at developments, and at the faintheartedness of those who were supposed to be on his side. They wouldn't get rid of him that easily, he decided. Typically, this new antagonism succeeded only in making him more determined to carry on.

Others gave way. The bullying Fry had resisted proved too much for Frank Bohn, and he returned to the United States at the end of the first week of October. Donald Lowrie quite rightly had to place his duties to the YMCA above his loyalty to Fry, and regretted that he could no longer have anything to do with him, officially at least.

AT JUST THIS TIME, the war looked as if it was also taking a turn for the worse. Goering's Luftwaffe had begun to bomb Britain day and night, and on September 24 the French at Dakar on the African coast repelled an Anglo-Free French force led by de Gaulle himself, which was most discouraging news. That same night, the French Air Force dropped six hundred tons of bombs on Gibraltar. France and Britain were now effectively at war with each other. On September 27, a mere three days later, Germany announced the signing of a tripartite pact with Italy and Japan. This, along with her continued treaty of friendship with Russia, and with no sign of America coming in on the side of Britain, looked black indeed.

Coming on top of all these dire international circumstances were the new Vichy laws, which began to be announced on what seemed like a daily basis, each one making life a little harder for the refugees, and especially for all Jews. The first *statut des juifs*—Jewish Law—was passed on October 3, ordering a census of all non-French Jews. The day after, prefects throughout the unoccupied zone were authorized to intern foreign Jews in camps or place them in *résidences forcées* (under house arrest). This applied even to those whose papers were in order, and was singularly racist. The situation was not helped by the Bishop of Marseille publicly condemning the Jews ("Already we see the face of a more beautiful France, healed of her sores which were often the work of foreigners . . .").

The effect of these terrible measures—followed by many more bans and harassments over the next weeks and months, far in advance of anything taking place in the German zone—was to spread renewed terror through the refugee population. It added to the considerable pressure that Fry and his staff were already under, especially when police swoops—the dreaded *rafles*—began to take place with even greater frequency. The pressure was showing on everyone, and Fry knew now that they could count on protection from nobody.

The situation was even unnerving the insouciant Charlie Fawcett. He found himself sleepless and increasingly paranoid, and feared that he was alone in his misery. Covered with shame and humiliation at what he thought were cowardly feelings, he asked Fry to meet him for a cup of coffee (discussions could only take place safely in crowded bars). "You know," said Charlie, "I'm scared to hell all the time." Fry looked him straight in the eye. "So am I," he replied evenly.

In the midst of this turmoil, hardly anyone noticed an ordinance banning the sale of maps. Indeed, when compared to the human misery being viciously compounded by Vichy, such a move seemed capricious, a mere bureaucratic by-blow designed to make life a little more difficult for everybody. Fry knew better, and saw it as a subtle move designed to thwart further emigrations. He was confirmed in his suspicion when Vichy-approved maps quietly went on sale shortly afterward. On these new maps, many small towns and villages, especially near the Pyrenees, had simply vanished. For any foreigner without a guide, the border area would now be an impenetrable maze.

Given the latest conditions, ever more refugees were turning up at the Centre Américain. The anti-Jewish riots on the streets of Marseille on the evening of October 3 did nothing to help the situation. Fry and his staff began to think of themselves as "doctors during an earthquake," fighting a losing battle against an unrelenting tide of victims that Vichy was regularly enlarging at the stroke of a pen. Like a captain on the burning deck, Fry rallied those around him, working round the clock, doling out money, advice, and encouragement. He was always impeccably dressed, with a fresh handkerchief displayed in his breast pocket ("One to show and one to blow," as he always said), and a carnation in his lapel. It gave the refugees hope to encounter a benign paragon of respectability, and even style, when they thought the world was ending; but Fry was desperate, too.

Now that Vladimir Vochoč's passports were common enough to risk arousing the suspicion of the authorities, Fry was forced to turn to the oily Frederic Drach. Beamish had made enquiries about him, and discovered that in fact the man was not all bad. He told Fry that in Germany Drach had been a sincere Social Democrat who had let his lust for money get the better of him. A sense of guilt resulted in sometimes giving out a passport for free. He had made a gift of one to a refugee named Wilhelm Herzog, which pleased Fry, because Herzog was one of the worst "pests" and had taken the next-door room at the Splendide. He would accost Fry every morning on his way out, and again every evening when he returned. Drach also gave a couple of his Danish passports to Masloff and Ruth Fischer, two German political refugees in considerable danger in France, and they went safely to Cuba on them. Beamish guessed Drach's actions arose out of "a combination of remorse and nostalgia." So they took a chance on him, and it worked. Several refugees managed to get away using his Dutch and Danish passports. Bill Freier, meanwhile, continued to toil away on his exquisite forgeries in the narrow garret he shared with Mina.

The enemy was closing in. More serious than the anti-Semitic gangs on the streets of Marseille were two smaller, but infinitely more dangerous ones, now planning Europe's future. On Friday, October 4, Hitler and Mussolini met at the Brenner Pass; at the same time, half a continent away in Madrid, Himmler was telling Franco about the new arrangements between Germany and Spain. It was obvious to Fry that time was running out. There was no leisure for him to undertake his usual aim at perfection. The escape routes would have to do as they were, a reasonably well functioning *pis aller,* and Fry well knew they might not exist tomorrow. The Fittko route had been operational for the past two weeks, at first apparently from Port Vendres, and now that they had found a lodging there, from Banyuls. Because the Gestapo had been sighted near the cemetery at Cerbère, Fry began to send large numbers of his clients down to Banyuls. So far the Fittkos were handling them without, it seemed, any difficulty.

TWO OR THREE TIMES A WEEK, Hans or Lisa would lead a small group of refugees up through the steep vineyards of the lower slopes and over the mountains, following the route to Spain carefully described to them (and on more than one occasion demonstrated) by Vincent Azéma, the warmhearted and brave Socialist mayor of Banyuls. The Fittkos' apartment was too small to hide refugees, but there was a friendly hotel in Banyuls, and they were told to stay in their rooms. The owner's daughter brought them their meals on a tray.

They would begin early, at four or five o'clock in the morning, and walk along the path with the workers starting out for their day's toil among the vines. The refugees would be clad in workers' clothes—dungarees and tatty old suits, with espadrilles on their feet. In that way, they were less likely to attract attention from the border guards who stood in the bushes and scrutinized the morning "commuters." In truth, the guards were not malicious, and would do everything they could to turn a blind eye to what was going on—an atmosphere of tolerance for foreigners and enemies of Vichy that was quietly and unobtrusively replicated, in small villages and more out-of-the-way places, throughout France. The refugees had only to travel light, leaving what bags they had behind them and carrying only a *musette*—knapsack—like the genuine workers.

A stroke of good fortune meant that their luggage could still be transported to Spain in another manner. Monsieur Azéma was friendly with the mayor of Cerbère, Leon Ball's friend Cruzet, who owned a freight company. This man's business partner happened to be the mayor of Port-Bou on the Spanish side. Azéma arranged it with these men, who were both sympathetic, that the luggage of the fleeing people could be loaded on a train on the French side of the border, and then picked up on the Spanish side, eliminating the needs to carry any burden over the mountains, and easing the duty of the guards to inquire after suspiciously large packages being taken on "picnics" (a usual and acceptable explanation for the upward journeys).

Many of the refugees were elderly and infirm, and seven or more hours of steep climbing at altitude was simply beyond them. Another piece of luck took care of this difficulty, for one night while returning from a successful trip, Hans Fittko met a smuggler who claimed to be a Greek and worked for the French railways. The man was proud of his locomotive, which ferried passengers the length of the tunnel connecting France and Spain through the Pyrenees. For a consideration ("Il faut manger, quand même!"—*We all have to eat!*), he agreed to make some "bogus runs," whenever the mountain route was too difficult for a party in the Fittkos' care. "The Greek" would allow the refugees into the cab of his locomotive, and would then trundle from Cerbère almost to the far end of the tunnel. Then he would let his passengers down, and reverse back to the French side. They then had to walk only a further few hundred yards to the Spanish border post. As a result Beamish called the Fittkos "the light at the beginning of the tunnel."

Everything was moving like clockwork, and the Fittkos were escorting, in one way or another, at least half a dozen people a week out of France. One refugee, Reine Dorian, reported that when she passed through, the hotel at Banyuls was practically heaving with refugees and fugitive British soldiers. She and her husband, Heinrich Mueller, were surprised when suddenly at one o'clock in the morning there was a knock on the door. They were terrified: "Was it the police?!" Fry later recalled asking them. "No, a young English officer who said he had a boat ready to round the point in. Did they want to come along? They said no, they'd go by foot."

Lisa reported that Hans no longer tossed and turned in his sleep, making long, unconscious speeches. All the Fittkos asked of Fry was an occasional pack of cigarettes, so they would not have to smoke the dried tree leaves rolled in newspaper to which they had been forced to accustom themselves.

Back at Marseille, Fry had contacted the youthful officer in charge of evacuating the remaining British soldiers. His name was Fitch, of the Northumberland Fusiliers, and his men, about three hundred of them, were interned at Fort St. Jean, one of the two towers that guarded the entrance to the Vieux Port. It was a relatively simple matter to send these soldiers in pairs and threes down to the Fittkos at Banyuls, because their imprisonment was in name only. During the day, they were free to amuse themselves in the city, safe in the knowledge that they had free lodgings at night. Each morning there was a desultory roll call made by the commandant of the prison, but he never checked names and only took a head count. Because of this, Fitch was able to replace the missing soldiers with civilians from the British Seamen's Institute nearby, and the French were none the wiser—or didn't care.

The British soldiers did present Lisa Fittko with one headache. The French of the area were like Catalans, short, stocky, and dark. By contrast, the British were tall, slim, and fair, so they stood out awkwardly among the vineyard workers even in the dark before dawn. Furthermore, they spoke little French, and what they did was of a hopeless schoolboy kind. Confusingly, said Lisa, they all seemed to be called Tom and Bob and Charlie. On the other hand they were always strong, and resolutely cheerful, and never asked unnecessary questions. To avoid the border patrols, Hans would set out with them at three-thirty in the morning, and ascend through the trees to Puig Del Mas, the hamlet further up the mountainside that was the ancient original that had spawned Banyuls itself. They called this method the "Britannia Special." The British were never scared, and being healthy as pigs they made good time over the peaks. The British went to the Spanish border control and surrendered as escaped prisoners of war under the Geneva Conventions.

"It's always a pleasure with them," Hans said, as he unloaded the firewood he collected on his way back, and which formed his practical alibi. Throughout October and November, as the situation in France worsened, and well into the next year, the Fittkos tirelessly and fearlessly kept up their often freezing-cold excursions, ferrying many soldiers and refugees to safety. "Not a single one of them was ever arrested," marveled Fry, "or even questioned by the police."

IT HAD BECOME almost a routine for Fry to be summoned to the American Consulate at 6 rue St. Ferréol, to be harangued by Hurley, so on Monday,

October 7, Fry did not take it as out of the ordinary when he was again beckoned. This time, though, there was a truly serious development, and one that came from a disappointing and unexpected quarter.

Feuchtwanger was in the news again. He had traveled aboard the American Export liner *Excalibur,* and docked at New Jersey the previous Friday. It was a high-profile, celebrity arrival, with battalions of pressmen eager to welcome the famous writer to the safe shores of the United States. They wanted to ask how Feuchtwanger had managed his escape, and he did not disappoint them. Bingham, who was angrily pacing up and down, handed Fry a copy of the late edition of Friday's *New York Times.* His heart sank as he scanned the front page headline:

FLIGHT DESCRIBED BY FEUCHTWANGER

—

American 'Kidnapped' Him,
Gave Him Women's Clothes
to Escape Nazis

—

DRAMATIC STORY BARED

It was indeed bared. Except for leaving out a name here and there, Feuchtwanger had stepped off the boat two days earlier, blinded by flashlights and sheer relief, and had revealed to the world exactly what Varian Fry was up to in France. Everything he had been so strenuously denying, to the American embassy and to the French authorities, was spelled out in black and white. "The author spoke repeatedly of unidentified American friends," ran the article. These had turned up "to aid him at crucial moments in his flight." Feuchtwanger courageously revealed how he had been led by a man (Leon Ball) "over the Pyrenees, and they climbed together for four hours, entering Spain." Entranced by such derring-do, the reporters savored every word the novelist spoke, going so far as to expose the "vast rescue machine that has worked quietly and efficiently for Mr. Feuchtwanger and many others in similar circumstances."

Feuchtwanger's "unidentified American friends" were stunned, speechless, livid. There was no explanation for what Feuchtwanger had done, except perhaps an unplumbable naïveté or an unforgivable and opportunistic ego. A few indiscreet sentences, uttered thousands of miles away, had ruined Fry's camouflage. Fry was in shock. "Isn't it unbelievable?" asked Lisa Fittko of similar stupidities among the German refugees. "Such people—known for their eminent intellects—are found shambling around throughout history with blinders on. Sometimes it seems that the higher the mind, the bigger the blinders."

Having had no qualms about quoting Feuchtwanger's lip-flapping interview, the American journalists quickly discovered there was mileage in criticizing Feuchtwanger for his recklessness. *Time* magazine talked to Fry's colleagues in New York and reported that, "Far from charmed was the Emergency Rescue Committee. They thought Anton [*sic*] Feuchtwanger might as well be talking to the Gestapo. They wondered why he had talked at all, believed that, whatever his motives, he had gravely jeopardized the Committee's undercover rescue work in France."

George Weller, writing in the *New York Post,* was particularly acerbic, for he had been in Europe and knew what conditions afflicted the refugees. In an article sometime later, headlined "REFUGEE TALES WRECK UNDERGROUND RAILWAY," he wrote how the famous escapees "who entrained upon the 'underground' earlier have soaped the rails by talking freely of their experiences on their arrival in New York. . . . Several prominent creative artists now safely settled in America, including a well-known German novelist [Feuchtwanger], were so elated over the circumstances of their escapes that they dramatized mildly adventurous details, in a manner now reacting painfully on their colleagues still marooned in France."

The one good effect that Feuchtwanger's disastrous interview had was that it made those who came after him a little wary of giving too much away. When the Manns and Werfels arrived on the *Nea Hellas* the following week, they were guarded in what they said to the battalions of journalists who mobbed them on the quayside. Werfel snuffled and tried to be evasive, answering that he couldn't talk because he still had colleagues attempting to get out of France.

It was not enough. There appeared a small article in the *New York Sun* a few days later that went almost unnoticed. It was an Associated Press dispatch that had come via London, and it announced some grave news. "SMUGGLING RING REPORTED IN SPAIN," it said. "The German radio reported today that the Madrid security police had uncovered a secret organization which has been smuggling politicians, Jews and men of military age from France to England via Spain, Portugal and Gibraltar. All British Consulates in Spain are involved in the machinations of the organization, the broadcast declared."

Almost immediately the Spanish border was closed.

MANY PEOPLE IN MARSEILLE naturally blamed this latest and perhaps most grave disaster on Lion Feuchtwanger. There had been evidence of his selfishness while he was interned in Les Milles; now he had proven that he was calamitously self-centered. Fry, although shaken by events, and growing cynical of all about him, including the refugees (one of whom stole a beautiful fountain pen he had bought on Broadway), was less inclined to condemn the novelist. Spain knew very well that refugees had been pouring over the border, and for some time had appeared unperturbed by it. Always, the question to ask was, "Why now?" What had changed was that Himmler had entered into discussions with General Franco. Spain's new hostility was most probably the result of a bureaucratic spasm inside a government attempting to remain neutral while resisting great pressure from the Nazis to join the belligerent Axis nations. Support for this argument was that the very next day the border reopened; then it closed, opened again, and closed once more. The frontier became a swinging door, allowing through some refugees, and slamming shut arbitrarily on others. As the birthplace of the Inquisition, Spain's latest instrument of torture easily outperformed those of Vichy.

There were tragedies. Late one night, Lisa Fittko answered a knock on her door, and found standing before her the courtly figure of Walter Benjamin. This man, one of the most insightful, original, and eccentric intellectuals of the twentieth century, had arrived to be led like the other refugees over the mountains. He was only forty-eight, but he looked older, and he was in frail health. Lisa asked him if he thought the mountain climb worth the risk. Not to go, he replied, represented the real risk. Far more important to Benjamin than his own life was his latest manuscript, which he had dragged all the way to the border with him in a large briefcase. Lisa naturally told him to leave it behind, but he insisted on keeping it with him the whole way. He would not even send it through using Cruzet's transportation service.

Benjamin always took the hardest course: he said it strengthened him. Hans Fittko had been in Vernuche concentration camp with him, recalled Lisa, and one day the philosopher told him that he was no longer going to smoke cigarettes. Hans thought Benjamin otherworldly, and advised him, given the trying conditions, not to quit just then. "I can bear the conditions in this camp," replied Benjamin, "only if I'm compelled to concentrate my mental strength on one single effort. Giving up smoking costs me this effort, and thus will be my deliverance." And so it had been. He took the briefcase.

Now, as he climbed higher into the mountains, Benjamin walked steadily for exactly ten minutes, then rested. He kept up the rhythm all day long, calm and collected, and only lengthened his pauses as his strength ebbed away. With Spain finally in sight, and just before Lisa turned back, they came across a swampy pool. Benjamin knelt down to drink from it, but Lisa told him not to, as he would probably poison himself. Again, Benjamin outlined his logic to her: if he did not drink, he would not have the strength to carry on. If he died of typhoid fever *after* he crossed into Spain, he would have been successful, because his manuscript would be safe. "You must pardon me, please, *gnädige Frau,*" he said, as he bent forward and put his lips to the scum. Lisa bade him farewell and good luck.

That night, in a hotel at Port-Bou, Benjamin swallowed the fifteen morphine tablets he had brought with him, and was found dead by shocked Spanish police the following morning. In the evening, when he had reached the customs house, Benjamin had been told the border was closed and that he would have to return to France. He was permitted, because of his weakened condition, to stay overnight in the town before being expelled. Charlie Fawcett believed that Benjamin's death was his own fault, and that if he had followed Fry's instructions—to return to France if he was *refoulé* (rejected), and simply try again later—he would eventually have struck lucky and made it. But the essential point for Benjamin remained the safety of his manuscript. Had he recrossed to France, he might have been kidnapped by the Kundt Commission—but to Benjamin that did not matter, and it was not the reason for his suicide. If he returned with his manuscript, though, it too could be seized, and *that* would constitute his real defeat and obliteration. He could not risk it.

The truth is that Benjamin probably killed himself to save his manuscript. He must have assumed that his death would be noted and that someone would come for his belongings, take away his briefcase, and see to it somehow that his masterwork was published. He had made a single fatal error of logic. Unlike Benjamin, who preferred a Socratic demise, other people understandably cared more for their own skins than for literature and philosophy. Nobody took his posthumous hint, and the manuscript has never been found. In the death register at Port-Bou, Benjamin's black leather briefcase was noted, and within it *unos papeles mas de contenido desconicido*—"Papers of unknown content." They were probably used for kindling by the mortician's wife one night during the unprecedently cold winter of 1940.

The very morning that Benjamin's body was discovered, the young Hungarian journalist Hans Habe was safely crossing the border into Spain, although he was one of the last to manage it. Now the Portuguese decided they had had their fill of refugees. They declared that their consuls in France had to obtain explicit permission from Lisbon for every single transit visa that was issued. This in itself would have introduced torturously long delays to an already slow process. What made the new measure even more callous was that the Portuguese insisted on seeing documentary proof of a fully paid passage on board a ship leaving from Lisbon on a specific date before it would authorize a visa. At several hundred dollars, such tickets were beyond the pockets of most refugees, so there grew up in Marseille a flourishing trade in fake ones. Right away, the Thomas Cook travel agency began offering them for two hundred francs (about five dollars) from its office on the Canebière.

It was a worthy effort, defeated by Madrid quickly falling into line with Lisbon. To be granted a Spanish transit visa, a refugee now needed to show the Portuguese visa and boat ticket (real or fake). It was almost completely frustrating, because while the Portuguese visa was valid for only two weeks, the period that the Spanish took to process one of their own visas often meant that by the time one collected all the necessary stamps, at least one of them was out of date and the entire rigmarole had to be repeated—and by now, of course, the ship shown on the ticket would have sailed.

For good measure, Spain also announced it would no longer recognize the American "affidavit in lieu of passport," which was often the only form of identification a refugee possessed, and was needed to book transatlantic passage on board a ship. It was also the document given to those who had been deprived of their Reich citizenship by Hitler, and was therefore a particularly nasty slap in the face to the enemies of Fascism. The new regulations were truly a "paper wall," far more effective than mountains and *gardes mobiles*.

Fry tried hard not to show how dispirited he felt. The hope of too many people was pegged to his own resilience. But he wrote to Mildred Adams in New York of his despair at the situation:

> What all this means in terms of individual human distress is illustrated in the case of David Schneider, his wife and two children. They had valid Polish passports issued in Paris four to five years ago. After weeks of waiting, they finally obtained their American visitors' visas; they then got their Portuguese and Spanish transit visas and because they were born in the part of Poland occupied by Russia, they obtained the French "sortie" visas, they went down to Cerbère and through the tunnel to Port-Bou. There they were "réfoules" by the Spanish four times. They tried again at Bourg-Madame and were also "réfoules." This after weeks of effort getting all the necessary visas. They are still here in a state bordering on despair. Another one of our clients Benjamin Walter [*sic*] committed suicide a few days ago, after going through the same procedure as Schneider. This makes the third suicide on our list, the other two being Hasenclever and Weiss.

Fry detected the hand of the Gestapo in these new developments. His own theory was that their targets were hard to find in France unless they were already in concentration camps—and Fry was working hard to keep the refugees at large and in hiding. If, though, Spain passed on transit visa applications to the Germans, the Gestapo could tell them which ones to authorize and have a good idea when a certain fugitive was making a dash for freedom. An agent could wait at the border and simply make an arrest when the hapless refugee appeared at the Spanish customs house sometime within a week. "It would be just the sort of trick the Gestapo delighted in," said Fry. Thus, paradoxically, to be turned away from the border was good news: it meant your name was not on the Nazi hit list.

With foreign transit visas too dangerous even to apply for, the route over the Pyrenees was closed except to the British soldiers, who could surrender on the Spanish side and be interned as escaping prisoners of war. Or to those refugees who could be conducted all the way to Lisbon by trusted underground cells working in Spain. Fry immediately began to make contact with groups such as these. He was learning to counterpunch.

CHAPTER 16

HAPPY BIRTHDAY, VARIAN

F RY FOUND IT DIFFICULT to believe he had been in France for less
than two months. In that time he had established an organization that
spanned three countries with its illegal activities; sent well over one
hundred endangered refugees to safety; set up an intercontinental money-
transfer system that bypassed the restrictions of two governments; forged
productive links with several "factories" providing him with fake documents;
selected and employed expert and experienced staff; familiarized himself
with the Marseille underworld; and been subject to official obstruction from
his own government, and police harassment from the French. He had worked
harder, suffered more disappointments, and met with more successes than
ever in his life, and all on less sleep and nutrition than he would have thought
possible. Varian Fry was living at the limit of intensity. He needed a break, but
instead he became even busier.

Frank Bohn's departure around October 5 meant that all his previous
clients became Fry's responsibility. This added the "politicals" to his lists of
artists and intellectuals, and placed the intransigent Breitscheid and Hilferding, now under *résidence forcée* at Arles, within Fry's duty of care. With all
those extra clients, he plainly needed to recruit yet more staff. So far there
were Beamish, Lena, Miriam, Charlie, Oppy, and some highly qualified
refugees that worked for the Centre Américain for varying periods before
they left for more hospitable climes. Fry found that their knowledge of the
German and Austrian emigration—like Franz von Hildebrand's—was invaluable. He added refugees like Hans Sahl to his *comité de criblage*—the "sifting" committee, to determine which were suitable cases for assistance.

It was not a perfect solution: the turnover of temporary staff destroyed any real continuity, and Fry was necessarily purblind to the infighting and prejudices endemic to such a pressurized and factionalized population. Also, with the Vichy authorities growing ever more fascistic, his mostly Jewish staff was progressively endangered. Lena was attempting to get her United States visa sorted out so that she could leave to marry her American fiancé, Melvyn Fagen. Beamish, who had established a reputation in academic circles for his work on Fascist economies, had been contacted by John B. Condliffe, an academic at the University of California at Berkeley, who had managed to get him a Rockefeller Foundation fellowship. This secured Beamish his United States visa, and although he was not planning to leave yet, Fry knew he would not stay indefinitely, especially because the Gestapo was bound one day to catch up with him. Yet Beamish and Lena leaving him was something Fry could hardly bear to contemplate.

Even Miriam was destined to depart before too long. She was still engaged to her Yugoslavian, and was desperately attempting to persuade the consulate to validate her American passport for travel within Europe. As Miriam joked at the time, she was the only person in Europe trying to stay *out* of America. But she had some friends who she believed could be just the people Fry was looking for.

During the *pagaille* of June when almost the entire country was on the move, Miriam had met in Toulouse a young American WASP named Mary Jayne Gold, an heiress of considerable wealth. Mary Jayne was a late version of what was called a "flapper" in the twenties—a good-time girl, who lived in a large apartment in one of the better *arrondissements* of Paris. She was outgoing, a little dotty, blond, and beautiful in a chipmunkish way, and had her own low-wing monoplane (a Vega Gull, the sports car of the skies) which she flew around Europe, following the snow in winter, and the sun in summer. When war was declared she donated her plane to the French air force, and it was probably one of the fastest craft they possessed.

When the women arrived at Marseille they struck up a friendship first with some British soldiers, then two Americans and a young Frenchman called Raymond Couraud, who claimed to be a Foreign Legionnaire. It was true, but he had now deserted and returned to his previous gangster occupations, and Mary Jayne was soon involved in a passionate affair with him. They christened him "Killer," with innocent accuracy. Fry, distrusting money as a motive for inclusion in his line of work (he preferred principle), had repeatedly dodged Miriam's hints that he should meet Mary Jayne with a view to taking her on the staff. As money grew tighter during the fall, due to the difficulties of cabling New York as openly as before, the argument that Mary Jayne could inject some cash into the rescue operation became more persuasive. Practical Beamish, "that demon of ingenuity with the puckish smile," as Mary Jayne described him, eventually arranged an "accidental" meeting of them all on the Canebière, and Fry agreed to go along with them for a drink at Basso's in the evening. He began to find things for Mary Jayne to do, although he remained suspicious, and unimpressed with her talents, calling her a "brainless little rich girl." He also correctly predicted that her boyfriend meant big trouble.

More useful than Mary Jayne were some friends of hers from Paris. She had been intimate with the Bénédites, a respectable Alsatian family, for several years. The eldest son was called Daniel or "Danny." He was like a brother to Mary Jayne, and teased her terribly. Danny was married to an attractive and very straight-backed English girl called Théodora ("Théo") Prinz, who had worked in Paris for IBM. They had made their way south during the chaotic summer, bringing with them their three-year-old son, Pierre. The Bénédite family owned two beautiful villas in the south of France, and they guessed that life in the "free" zone would be preferable to Paris. Fortuitously, Danny had worked for the prefecture of police in the capital and gained much experience of dealing with foreign refugees, especially Germans. He had developed a reputation among them for kindness and understanding. His willingness to renew residence permits and help fugitives from Hitler in any way he could distinguished him from most of the officials the refugees had been forced to deal with. Danny was like a gift from God to Fry.

He was tall, slight, with short, dark slicked-back hair, and a narrow mustache below a straight nose surmounted by heavy black spectacles. His appearance was very formal and so was his manner; like Théo, he was upright, and an absolute stickler for detail and procedure. This meant he was somewhat humorless at times, but magnificently and tirelessly efficient. He possessed the self-righteousness of the well-off young bourgeois who has received the revelation of the Marxist gospel, but if he could appear slightly arrogant, he was also brave and daring. Like Beamish he had fought in the war. Danny had in fact been on the beach at Dunkirk when the British and some French soldiers were miraculously evacuated earlier in the year. Luckily for Fry, even though he was evacuated to Britain, Danny had decided to return to France.

The Bénédites were to prove the consolation prize for allowing Mary Jayne into the circle (although over time she would work hard to show Fry that she too could be conscientious and helpful: this was the effect Fry had on all those around him). Miriam and Mary Jayne also managed to find work at the Centre Américain for a boy they had "adopted" on their way south. The thirteen-year-old Justus Rosenberg—"Gussie"—quickly became the eager and hardworking office boy at the rue Grignan. As a foreign Jew he was in direct danger from the French authorities, but everybody gathered around to protect him, and Gussie would soon grow far beyond their expectations.

Fry was again having to think very fast. With the terrible new visa restrictions, he realized that the job he had been sent to do could not be completed in a few more weeks. He began to plan, in his own words, "for a long haul." For reasons of safety and survival, Fry decided to begin the divorce of the official aid operations at the rue Grignan offices from the peripatetic undercover work that all his present staff were involved in. As one of the "old-timers" left, he or she would be replaced by somebody fresh who would have no knowledge at all of what Fry was really up to. That was the basis on which Danny and Théo were originally employed, as were the next two recruits, Jean Gemahling and Marcel Verzeano. The weakness in this idea quickly became obvious: the underground roles of the departing staff could not all be undertaken by Fry alone, and some of the new people inevitably—and eagerly— slid into more illicit work. As time wore on, emigration became an almost completely illegal matter for the most endangered refugees. Everybody knew this, but those who worked purely in the office maintained a very good pretense of ignorance concerning the activities of Fry's inner circle.

That inner circle gathered at Fry's room in the Hotel Splendide on the evening of October 15. It was Fry's thirty-third birthday, and this was the first excuse they had been able to concoct for a small celebration in all the tumultuous time since Fry had arrived at Marseille. The weather had turned cold, and there was a coal shortage, of course, so everybody was freezing, and Fry's hotel had hot water only on weekends. The food situation was growing worse, and the ration books were almost meaningless because there was no food around anyway. The underground railway had almost been frozen over by the new international cooperation between the enemies of democracy (Fry included the State Department in this), and they were running out of money. But there was still liquor, and everyone except Beamish grew happily drunk.

This intimate group sat around speculating about the future. Fry feared a long war, five or ten years, but he also believed that Britain's continued resistance would encourage the stirrings of resistance in France to grow into something more substantial. Beamish believed that when the universities reopened (they had been closed during the "emergency"), the traditionally volatile French student population would add to the momentum. In fact their spirits had been lifted by the first signs of public defiance of the German occupation, which had taken place on the streets of Marseille just six days earlier.

On October 9, 1934, Jean-Louis Barthou had been assassinated in Marseille together with Alexander I, the King of Yugoslavia. Fry had admired Barthou for being the first European politician to warn the world openly about Hitler's intentions—which was probably the reason for his death. The men were murdered on the steps of the Marseille *bourse* (stock exchange) on the Canebière, and the previous Wednesday morning, the sixth anniversary of the shooting, several bouquets of flowers had appeared on the spot. The event, had it stopped there, would have been no more than a minor curiosity. Yet it seemed to stir not only people's memories, but also their will. Throughout the rest of the morning more bunches of blooms were added spontaneously, until by the afternoon there was a huge mound, stretching all along the sidewalk in front of the *bourse.*

Soon enough, the police arrived and began to remove the flowers. But after a while it became clear they were fighting a losing battle: faster than they could remove them, new bouquets appeared. Eventually the police were forced to place a cordon and guard around the area. At that point, the large crowd that gathered moved to the square across the street, facing the police with flowers and hats in their hands. In almost a dress rehearsal for the scene in *Casablanca,* where French voices drown out German ones at Rick's Café, they stood and sang the *Marseillaise:* "Citizens, to arms!" rang out across downtown Marseille.

Fry decided that it was too soon to give up, and besides, he was beginning to fall in love with France. One fine Sunday in mid-October he called Miriam at her hotel and suggested they take a trip to Arles. She met him at the Splendide and they walked to the Gare St. Charles, where Miriam spotted a young man she introduced as Stéphane Hessel. He was the son of the writer Franz Hessel, a client of Fry's and the German translator of Jules Romains and Proust, who was staying with his wife Helen at Sanary-sur-Mer. Fry felt an instant rapport with Stéphane, and he and Miriam tried to persuade the young man to join them. Stéphane had to meet his wife at Aix, so he declined, but Fry and Miriam set out for the country of van Gogh and Cezanne, and Fry was stunned to find how each painter had captured different but equally accurate impressions of the landscape: "The brilliant light, the patches of sun filtered through leaves, the trim fertile fields, the peasants' bright blue carts, the arched bridges, the polychrome fishing boats drawn up on the banks of the Rhône, those tortured columns of black flame we lamely call cypress trees. . . ."

Despite the war, the sensation developed in Fry that he had been put down in paradise. Just beyond the city, Provence contained the beautiful churches and haunting, ruined abbeys he had been taught about at Harvard, a landscape that seemed to fit his own interior emotional world, and a quality of light that lifted his spirits above anything Vichy or the Gestapo could contrive to destroy them. The very next Sunday he set out again, alone this time, for St. Gilles. Again he met Stéphane at the Gare St. Charles, and this time persuaded him to come along. It was the beginning of a very important friendship for Fry. Cycling along country lanes with a kindred soul, eating and drinking together in out-of-the-way places, and exploring ruins together was a sort of Utopia for Fry.

Before his demobilization from the French army, Stéphane had fought bravely against the Germans. He impressed Fry—as he had himself been impressed—with the fanaticism of the Nazis. One time Stéphane had been commanding a machine-gun nest on the brow of a hill, and at its bottom truck after truck backed up and disgorged extremely young German soldiers, wearing lederhosen and carrying submachine guns. These boys had advanced up the hill, walking in step and singing the "Horst Wessel" song. There was nothing Stéphane could do to stop them except to keep up the rattle of his overheating gun until every single one was dead. Then another truckload would begin to advance, and the process of butchery would be repeated. The slaughter continued until his crew ran out of ammunition, and had to beat a retreat. "They were so young you hated to kill them," he said. It was a sobering experience to know what single-mindedness France was facing. That night Fry and Stéphane took a room at the Hotel du Nord after cycling back to Arles, and Fry returned the following morning. The peacefulness of the countryside and the conversations with Stéphane renewed Fry's strength and resolve for the struggle that awaited him at Marseille.

BEFORE FRY LEFT NEW YORK, Paul Hagen had given him a list of his most trusted and worthy colleagues at the *Neu Beginnen* organization of exiled German Social Democrats. Of these, there were four whom Hagen had especially pleaded with Fry to try to track down. By now Fry knew where these men—Hans Tittel, Franz Boegler, Siegfried Pfeffer, and Fritz Lamm— all were: interned at a nearby concentration camp. In constant fear of arrest and deportation, Fry nonetheless resolved that somehow he would honor the promise he had made to his friend, and rescue the four ardent democrats before they fell into Hitler's hands. The German prejudice against them was underscored by the fact that Vichy had thrown them in Vernet, one of the worst camps—a place where criminals and undesirables, so called, were sent to rot. These included novelists like Arthur Koestler, who wrote of it in *Scum of the Earth:* "In Liberal-Centigrade, Vernet was the zero-point of infamy; measured in Dachau-Fahrenheit it was still thirty-two degrees above zero." It was much harder to escape from a "criminal" camp like Vernet, where there were extra fields of barbed wire and armed guards ordered to shoot on sight. Likewise, it was much more difficult to arrange releases through legal and diplomatic channels, as Fry had succeeded in doing in other, less contentious cases. It was true, as Lion Feuchtwanger said in one of his more helpful interviews with the American press, that France had turned her unofficial motto inside out, and now proudly proclaimed, "The enemies of our enemies are our enemies."

Fry suddenly realized he had a secret weapon: Mary Jayne Gold. Young, glamorous, and seductive, she might be able to succeed through the use of feminine charm where other more conventional approaches had failed. Miriam broached the subject with her, and keen to prove her worth, Mary Jayne agreed to lay down her body for the democratic principle. The simple plan was that she would meet the commandant of the camp—an attractive American woman should be able to make it past the secretary—and attempt to arrange some nocturnal quid pro quo.

A few days later, Hagen's friends arrived at Marseille by train, accompanied by two guards, having received permission to collect the emergency United States visas Fry had managed to organize. In her account of the episode, Mary Jayne claimed that she never had to compromise her honor to accomplish this impressive feat. She simply met the commandant in his office, hinted at what was an offer, and arranged to meet him at a local hotel restaurant in the evening. Night fell, and the primped and powdered Mary Jayne arrived at the rendezvous, nervous but determined. She ordered a drink at the table and waited. An hour after the appointed time the commandant had still not shown up, so Mary Jayne had another drink and began to feel self-conscious. By midnight, still unfed and with several drinks inside her, she figured that the commandant had developed cold feet, so she walked, somewhat un-steadily, back to her hotel.

The next day Mary Jayne returned to Vernet and her would-be paramour's office, where she was received with apologies and considerable embarrass-ment. Shortly before he was due to meet her, Gestapo officers had come to the camp and requested the pleasure of his company that evening so that they could all look over the list of inmates at Vernet to decide which ones Ger-many was interested in collecting under the "surrender on demand" clause of the armistice agreement. This had taken all evening and he had been unable to keep their date. The gallant Frenchman assured Mary Jayne that there had been no question of where he would rather have been.

The fortunate consequences of their failed rendezvous were, first, that he felt himself in her debt; and, second, that the proprietorial attitude of the

Nazis had reawakened his sense of national pride and inclined him to sabotage their plans for extradition. He could not release the men permanently, but he would grant them a furlough to visit the American consulate at Marseille and pursue their visa applications.

Her account has the neatness and symmetry of a good short story, but others—Charlie Fawcett for one—are more skeptical about Mary Jayne's wide-eyed account of miraculous good fortune. Whether she made the supreme sacrifice or not, the point was that she had been prepared to do so for the good of the rescue operation.

Thanks to Harry Bingham, the four men picked up their valuable paperwork the same day they arrived. They were supposed to return to the camp soon after, but Fry had other ideas. The plan had been to send the prisoners over the frontier with the Fittkos and then on to Lisbon, but in the meantime the Spanish had closed the border, so Fry sent Beamish down to the Vieux Port to see what he could find in the way of boats for hire. A yacht called the *Bouline* was Beamish's best hope. A trip on it was already planned by some Gaullists, sailing with Belgian and Polish army officers for Gibraltar. It was agreed that for a considerable price the skipper would add Hagen's friends to the passenger list, even though it would leave the small vessel quite low in the water. The camp guards could be persuaded to forget about their charges if they were escorted to a brothel and left with sufficient funds for wine and women. By the time they sobered up the next morning, the prisoners would be long gone.

It was a leaky and not particularly seaworthy strategy, for the police would not have to look far to find the true author of the escape. Fry must have thought he was to be expelled from France any day now, and assumed that he could afford to take the blame, hopefully leaving the Centre Américain intact. Either that or the whole escapade was an example of naïveté in action. In fact, Fry was called into the prefecture shortly before the *Bouline* sailed, where he met a sympathetic police inspector named Dubois, a man who would extend to Fry considerable assistance and eventually suffer the curtailment of his career for doing so. Dubois knew exactly what Fry was doing, and told him so with a smile that indicated he approved of smuggling humans out of the country. He also allowed Fry to see the dossier that the police were building on him. It contained the usual collection of misspelled anonymous denunciations, half of them probably written by the police themselves to secure search warrants.

But there were other, more interesting documents too. "One was a report to the Prefect, from the Centre d'Informations d'Etudes," Fry noted at the time. "It reads something like this: 'Because he insists on occupying himself with persons who are undesirable not only from the point of view of France but also from the point of view of the Reich and the United States, the activities of Varian Fry might prove embarrassing to the French Government in the present circumstances. On the other hand, Mr. Fry is too well-known in the United States, and has too many influential friends, to be made the subject of an expulsion order. Above all he should not be made a martyr of. The desirable solution would be for him to leave France of his own accord." Fry knew he was an object of official attention but he had not realized the consulate was helping the French police to build their case against him. "Curious they should have thought that I was helping people who are 'undesirable' from the point of view of the United States," he observed wryly. "If they knew how unknown I am in the States, they might not have hesitated to expel me."

Dubois was a storehouse of useful information; and he knew all about the *Bouline.* He warned Fry the yacht had been hired and sold for the present purposes numerous times, but had never actually left port, and was not likely to. In other words it was yet another gangster scam. Fry, trusting Beamish's intelligence and shrewdness, decided not to take Dubois at his word in this case: the police do not know everything, he recalled Beamish saying. After double-checking everything, they decided to go ahead with the voyage, and late one night Beamish turned up at the Splendide to say that the *Bouline* had sailed with Tittel, Boegler, Pfeffer and Lamm all aboard. With a mixture of relief and regret, Fry resigned himself to the consequences.

THE LAST MONTHS of 1940 were a deeply frustrating time for Fry and his little band of conspirators. With the frontier closed and Lisbon a lifetime of visas away, there was little to be done in the way of illegal emigrations except what could be accomplished through the narrowest sea lane, for which the *Bouline* was the as yet unproven test case. That left only legal emigration, which was dependent on the Emergency Rescue Committee in New York harrying and hurrying the State Department to process emergency visas—an uphill task to say the least—and one with which Fry, under so many conflicting pressures in France, was not inclined to sympathize.

The sheer volume and pace of work had also contributed to a certain neglect in his relations with Eileen. He wrote infrequently, and more and more his letters were full of business matters. He was also growing increasingly hostile to Mildred Adams, Ingrid Warburg, and the others at the Forty-second Street offices of the ERC. Paul Westheim, for example, the art critic and historian, was fast losing his sight to glaucoma because of the lack of medical attention. Where was his visa? The famous German tenor Ernst Busch, and

Professor Stein, the eminent Byzantologist, were still awaiting their visas, too. Fry reeled off a list of other distinguished names for whom the New York committee, in Fry's eyes, was doing nothing.

> And the *maddening* thing is that I get neither cooperation nor under-standing from those *boobs* in New York. . . . Certainly they will be in-terned if I leave, as those blithering idiots in New York ordered me to do a month ago. . . . Are those imbeciles in New York interested in their for the most part very stupid and uninteresting "friends"? Or are they really interested in doing something to rescue what is left of European Culture before it is too late?
>
> If only it were a real committee, instead of a bunch of Peters. . . .

With Fry watched so closely by the authorities, part of the problem was that he could no longer cable New York even with guarded instructions to de-posit dollars in a certain account, or to concentrate on a particularly urgent case of a refugee who may have been in hiding, as many were. Instead, a new method of transmitting illicit messages across the Atlantic had to be worked out. Once again, Beamish came up with an idea: the Tubogram.

Each time a client left, legally or illegally, for Lisbon, he would carry in his luggage a number of toothpaste tubes. Inside these, wrapped in a condom in-serted through the crimped end of the tube, was a message containing in-structions and reports. Onion-skin paper was used, and each line of writing was snipped into a single length; each length was glued end-to-end, and then the tightly rolled coil of paper, waterproof in its rubber wrapper, was slipped into the toothpaste tube. Once the client arrived at his destination, the con-tents could be extracted and safely passed on to New York. Fry had to rely on the refugee carrying the messages not to lose his nerve en route and simply discard the tubes. Likewise, he had to hope that an ungrateful client would not casually throw them in a wastebasket once he was safely in Lisbon, which unfortunately some of them did, or merely forget about them altogether, which also happened (a horrified client might realize several months later in California or Mexico or Panama that he was still in possession of several "ur-gent" messages). It was a slower and less reliable method of communication than sending a telegram, but it was an ingenious and relatively safe one, and under the circumstances the best that could be devised.

Not only had funds from New York slowed down, but the committee there was pleading with Fry to cut his costs, and hinting that he had hired too many people. This was like waving a red rag at a bull. "If you really want us to re-duce the staff," he thundered to Mildred Adams,

. . . you must tell us what category of people we are to deny our services to. Are we to refuse in future to bother with painters? If so we can drop one worker. Are we to ignore people in camps? If so we can let another go. Shall we in future ignore any person who is not in Marseille, or who cannot tell us what he wants to tell us in a letter subject to censorship? If so we can reduce the staff by perhaps two. Please don't tell us to reduce the staff to one or two, without also specifying what kind of work, if any, you want us to confine ourselves to in the future. . . .

It was left to the unfortunate Eileen to try to smooth things over:

MODERATE YOUR TELEGRAMS MILDRED ANNOYED STOP HAROLD MADE IT TWENTY THOUSAND OCTOBER STOP ADVISE YOU AWAIT FRIEND [the replacement] IF CONVENIENT

Eileen was clearly suffering from the separation, made worse because she could only share in the momentous changes taking place in Fry's life in piecemeal and vicarious fashion. He could not tell her a tenth of what was really happening, of course, and it left her feeling bereft. In November a note of urgency and conflict entered into the correspondence between them; mostly, to begin with, on her side:

I have no hope that anything interests you now except your own activities and surroundings. Of *course* I *know* they are from any *ultimate* point of view more significant than what goes on here in your friends' personal lives; but is the *ultimate* point of view the only one between husband and wife? . . . Of course I feel you are best able to decide whether you will come back, or stay for the duration, but if you decide on the latter, even in a modified form, you *must* write me a personal letter, about your plans (and mine!). . . . *How are you?*

In return she received another cable, that dealt again with the unsatisfactory situation in New York:

PLEASE MAKE THEM REALIZE WE HAVE UNDERTAKEN IMMENSE TASK SAVING CULTURE EUROPE AND THAT LARGE SUMS AND CLOSEST TEAMWORK ARE REQUIRED PROPOSE REMAIN FRANCE UNTIL COMPETENT SUCCESSOR ARRIVES UTTERLY UNTHINKABLE LEAVE BEFORE WHY DONT THEY SEND YOU MEOW = FRY

In defiance of Mildred Adams, he continued to expand the staff of the Centre Américain. Lena left with Frank Bohn near the beginning of October, and Fry hired a new secretary called Anna Gruss, "a queer little gnome . . . with a good heart, a sharp tongue, an immense capacity for work, and the virtue of genuine innocence of our undercover work." Then Lena came back, *refoulé* at the frontier due to the latest Spanish regulations, which barred any Pole at all from entering the country. Lena could hardly have explained that she was really Russian. Fry kept both women on the staff, using Lena for the undercover work until she could try to leave France again.

Then there was Jean Gemahling. Like Danny and his family, Jean was from Alsace, a territory of long-disputed ownership between France and Germany. Frenchmen like Jean from the regional capital, Strasbourg, tended to be especially antagonistic toward their neighbor, and as a result more than commonly averse to the German presence in France. Young Jean brought out Fry's paternal instincts. He was blond-haired and blue-eyed, with a longish "Norman" nose he seemed to peer around. He spoke extremely good English, having been educated at a British public school, where he had been sent by his professor father. Jean had qualified as a chemical engineer, but science seemed not to interest him. He preferred politics and poetry, and was very shy, flushing pink whenever he was asked a question. Danny was wary of Jean—he seems to have been wary of almost everybody—and thought him naïve. Fry disagreed, or at least saw potential in this young and eager student of underground work, to which he moved on quickly (to Danny's chagrin) after first being employed as an interviewer in the rue Grignan office.

This was also the case with Marcel Verzeano, a newly qualified Romanian doctor originally hired to deal with the onrush of hysterical refugees. Verzeano quickly took to what he saw as the glamor of illegal work, and began calling himself "Monsieur Maurice." Charlie Fawcett says that Maurice's sangfroid in escorting nervous refugees was a master class in deception, invaluable in drawing the Gestapo and police away from the scent of a fugitive. But Danny was unrelentingly scathing about what he called "cloak-and-dagger" play-acting, seeing in it a manifestation of the *mythomane,* and the temptation to take uncalculated risks. Maurice became Fry's chief liaison officer with the Fittkos at Banyuls. Later he would be the coordinator between Fry's operation and the Spanish and French underground cells running other clandestine routes over the Pyrenees (starting from Port Vendres) and all the way to Lisbon. To begin with that would be another endeavor which would call forth Danny's implacable scorn, although later he would be grateful for it.

The expansion of the rue Grignan staff did not stop with Jean and Maurice. Fry was concerned that his organization should appear free of partisan prejudice. This was a matter of prudence, for Socialist organizations had been banned by the Vichy government, and if the prefecture thought the Centre Américain was one such, they could close it down. So if most of those Fry and his colleagues helped and hired were of the political left, he felt that he should also ensure the right was conspicuously represented. Franz von Hildebrand had been very useful in that capacity, but he was gone. The arrival of Marcel Chaminade, an oleaginous right-wing fop, was greeted with unanimous disbelief and outright horror by both Danny and Beamish. Chaminade, like Franzi, was another Catholic conservative who, Fry said, opposed equally the Fascism and anti-Semitism of the Vichy regime and the egalitarian principles of the defunct Republic. "Some of our New York friends would have a fit if they knew," wrote Fry to Eileen, "as Monsieur Chaminade is a monarchist and has written a book on Franco, whom he claims to be on the best of terms with."

To say Chaminade was unprepossessing in appearance would be to flatter him beyond reason. His large ears were the most attractive feature of his corpulent body, which swayed with overstated obsequiousness. "When I first met him he bowed so low in shaking my hand I thought for one horrible instant he was going to kiss it," said Fry. Short, bald and pompous, Chaminade nonetheless moved in the right circles. He was the son of the late composer Moriz Moszkowski and the nephew of the German publisher Alexander Moszkowski, a close friend of Einstein. After the First World War, he began a diplomatic career as a *consul de France* in Egypt. Later at Paris, he became the "Secrétaire Général au Service de la Presse Etrangère Aux Affaires Etrangères" at the Quai d'Orsay—just the kind of elongated title that would have pleased him. His usefulness to Fry lay in these credentials rather than in his personal qualities.

In the cloying atmosphere of Vichy where name and connections meant so much more than merit or talent, Chaminade could seem sleek as a dolphin with his faux-aristocratic airs. In short order Fry appointed him the centre's unofficial ambassador to Vichy and all its officers. It says something about Fry's executive ability (and his mischievousness) that he was willing to override the objections of two trusted lieutenants in favor of somebody he did not like but recognized as both useful and necessary.

FRY WAS WONDERING WHY the police had not come to arrest him. It had been several days since the *Bouline* set sail, and no word had been received from the four escapees. He was inclined to assume they had reached Gibraltar; but if that was so, their absence would have been noted at Vernet once the shamefaced guards returned. The alarm would have been raised, and that would have led to questioning if not handcuffs for Fry himself. Instead, nothing at all had happened.

The riddle was answered by Leon Ball, who swerved into Marseille one day while following his irregular orbit through city and frontier. He claimed to have seen all four men—Tittel, Boegler, Pfeffer, and Lamm—in chains at the railway station when he arrived at Marseille a few minutes earlier. Fry couldn't believe it at first, although their arrest would explain why there had been no word from them, and why there had been no police at the rue Grignan. He contacted Maître Murzi, who agreed to investigate what had happened, and Fry soon had the full story.

It was genuine bad luck rather than corruption or incompetence that had put an end to the escape attempt. The evening of the second day out from Marseille the little yacht was still making good headway when the skies thickened and a raging storm grew up about it. She soon lost her sails and probably the rudder, because she turned side on to the waves, which swamped her with water. After a while the overloaded pump broke, and everybody had to bail out with whatever vessel was at hand. Apparently it had been one of those nights—helplessly adrift in a fatal, indifferent sea—when a sailor realizes either death will come or it will not, and thinks no more of it because he has too much to do. The yacht was lucky not to capsize, and in the morning calm the other passengers were so exhausted and seasick that they ignored the desperate pleas of Fry's clients to continue south. The captain turned the boat round and began making way back to Marseille. The French coast guard soon spotted them and escorted the *Bouline* to a small port. There, the four friends of Paul Hagen were arrested and sent to Aix-en-Provence to be put on trial for illegally leaving the country. Ball had seen them at the station as they were awaiting their train connection.

It was another disaster, and Fry wearily set about rounding up lawyers to defend the men. As a consolation, at least he knew the fiasco was not their fault but that of the army officers who had insisted on turning back. The failure of the *Bouline* had not proved that escape by sea from Marseille was impossible: if anything, it demonstrated the opposite and showed once again that the police did not know everything. Fry would carry on, pushing the boulder back up the hill once more.

An idea had come to him that would further protect the Centre Américain. Fry went back to his desk and began to write letters to some of the most famous and distinguished people in France. He figured that with a raft of impressive names appended to the letterhead of his organization the authorities would be less inclined, or at least less able, to harass him out of existence.

Only the week before, when he returned to Marseille from a brief trip, he discovered the police were ready to search the premises for false documents. Chaminade had proved his worth by accompanying Fry to the Prefecture and making a florid speech that so impressed the police that they turned the search into a formality rather than a wrecking ball.

So Fry wrote to André Gide, Henri Matisse, Jean Giraudoux, Blaise Cendrars, Pablo Casals, and Aristide Maillol, among others, explaining his work and asking them to join a "Committee of Patronage." With that patina of respectability, he could buy time. He had also been in touch with an ex-captain in a French armored regiment, who was in hiding farther up the coast. The man's name was André Malraux, who would become after the war a member of de Gaulle's cabinet. He was already one of France's favorite novelists. Malraux at this time was attempting to organize the French Resistance, and desperately needed to communicate with General de Gaulle in London. Fry told him that he could get letters to Britain by way of his escaping refugees and soldiers. If Fry was on the ropes, at least he was keeping his guard up and getting his wind back. He refused to go down and take the count.

They all wanted him to go home—the French government, the police, the State Department, and his friends in New York. But Fry refused to budge. The more difficult circumstances became, the more stubborn he felt about staying. Admittedly, he felt terribly scared and isolated, but at the same time he found himself exhibiting a sort of nothing-to-lose daring that thrilled him. He was acting very unlike himself, and he was getting to like it. He was also developing a set of friendships—more than that, dependent intimacies—of a kind from which he had always held himself aloof. To an extent this had included Eileen, whom Fry knew he was not missing as he should.

The dangerous, secret alliances he had established in Marseille, the frightened people who relied on him and to whom he had made reckless promises—these were more rewarding than the domestic routines and emotional ruts of marriage, or the predictability of civilian life in New York. Charlie's friend Bill Holland, the nephew of the Stülpnagel clan, had supplied Fry with the ultimate reason for staying on. Holland had been talking with a German officer friend in Paris, and amazingly Fry's name had come up. The Germans knew all about him, it transpired, but the officer said they were not concerned about his activities: "We're confident he won't succeed."

So the Germans thought they were smarter than Fry. Stronger, no problem. Better informed, fine. More ruthlessly determined, okay. But not smarter. Nobody had ever proven he was *smarter* than Varian Fry. The gauntlet had been cast down.

CHAPTER 17

THAT SINKING

FEELING

S TANDING IN HIS TATTERED Ambulance Corps greatcoat, Charlie
Fawcett blew on his fingers and stamped his feet to keep the circulation
going. The *mistral* was tearing down from the mountains and the cold
was bone chilling. Next to him in the dark stood Walter Mehring, muttering
quietly to himself. Nearby were Klaus Dohrn and Georg Bernhard, whom Fry
had tracked down and sheltered. Crouched around them, in the lee of the
lighthouse that stood on the *Anse des Catalans* to the east of the Vieux Port,
were about seventy British soldiers, with Emilio Lussu's Spanish and Italians
mixed in. It was midnight on the last Sunday of October, and they were waiting for a boat. A big one.

It had been Leon Ball's idea, following a warning to Fry from Captain Darling that Torr's deal with the Spanish had lapsed. It was no longer safe to send
British soldiers over the mountains into Spain because they were now being
thrown into camps and kept there. The best thing was to try and get them
away from Marseille by sea. Ball's dirty mouth had won him the friendship
and confidence of the denizens around the Vieux Port, or so he believed, and
after making inquiries for about a week he found a trawler that could take
nearly a hundred people. It was authorized to leave the harbor at any time to
go fishing, and the captain was eager to supplement his income even if it
meant fishing far out from Marseille—in the waters around Gibraltar, for example. His price was frighteningly high, which seemed somehow to endorse
the authenticity of the offer, and the *type* who put him in touch with the skipper claimed to be a ferocious Gaullist. Fry, as was becoming his habit, re-

mained skeptical, and Lussu refused point-blank to have anything to do with what he thought was a transparently obvious confidence trick.

Young Fitch of the Northumberland Fusiliers checked it out, and decided the proposal was genuine enough. The leader of the Italian Republicans, Randolfo Pacciardi, whom Danny condemned as a hilarious "idealist," agreed that this was a fine chance to export a good number of their charges to freedom. Sir Samuel Hoare's instruction never to mix Italians and Spanish with British soldiers was forgotten: a chance like this could not be passed up. Fry rehearsed his anxieties to Ball, but the American's confidence, bolstered by the unrelenting success of his numerous trips across the Pyrenean frontier, had by now made him an expert with a "take it or leave it" attitude.

Fry pointed out that for the *chalutier* to sail from the harbor to the pickup point, she would have to pass under six low bridges, and all of them would have to be raised to allow her passage. How exactly would this be managed? Ball dismissed this with a wave of his hand and a word about bribes. In his mind, the police and the Gestapo had ceased to exist: he was now a part of the true Marseillais, and he knew it was the gangsters who really ran things.

That, thought Fry, was the problem. He knew this opportunity was either a complete con or a wonderful opportunity, but which? In a way, the very improbability of the plan vouched for it. He agreed to go along with the scheme, and changed three thousand dollars into francs. But he was also careful, and ensured the arrangement was to pay half up front and half on delivery. Fitch kept the rest of the money, and divided it among his troops. No matter how tough the gangsters, they couldn't hope to intimidate nearly half a company of seasoned soldiers. Actually, Fry had wanted to cut each big five-thousand-franc note in half as an extra precaution, and pay the installments in that fashion, so that not even the downpayment could be stolen. Ball, though, refused to allow it, saying the boat's owner would not agree.

Then, on the night he was to set out, the skipper naturally wanted to renegotiate. All the money was required up front or the owner would not release the boat from its mooring. Heated discussions took place at Snappy's, a small bar on the Vieux Port. They were so close to success, and by now so pathetically trusting, that eventually Pacciardi and Ball persuaded Fitch to gather the second payment from his men and hand it over. The skipper left to pay for the boat, and they all went out to the lighthouse to await their deliverance.

They waited and waited. Finally, at around two in the morning, Beamish arrived. He told Charlie that there was no boat and never had been. The skipper had skipped and got away with all the money. Slowly, everyone walked back to town. For Mehring it was a further twist of the knife, another sign that destiny was against him. He continued to mutter nonstop to himself all the way back to the Hotel Splendide, composing in his head what was to be one of his finest poems, "The Phantom Ship of Marseille."

"Hope cracks and crumbles," it began.

Taking refuge in poetry did not appeal to the disappointed and enraged soldiers, who were tough northerners and Scots. They invaded the Vieux Port, hunting for members of the treacherous gangster clan that had duped them. Several were found whom they dragged back to Fort St. Jean. There, the soldiers vented their frustration on the terrified crooks, who were soon no more than living bruises. But these lowly operatives could not supply any answers concerning the vanished captain of the phantom ship, and eventually one of them managed to drop a scribbled note pleading for help through a window. It was picked up by a passing gendarme, and soon both gangsters and soldiers were all in court.

The incident snapped Leon Ball out of his boastful reverie; in fact, it utterly unmanned him. Several times over the next few weeks he would suddenly appear, distraught and raving, at the offices on rue Grignan. He pleaded with Fry for forgiveness, promised that he would leave nobody out of pocket even if he had to sell his lard factory. He advanced several desperate theories about what went wrong, and on the last occasion ran from the building, unable to control his emotions. The irony was that nobody was very angry at him. Ball had undertaken such sterling work for Fry that his esteem could withstand what was not, after all, their first disaster—and would by no means be the last. But soon afterward Leon Ball disappeared. Nobody ever saw or heard from him again. Whether his pride and shame led him to suicide has never been discovered; but he vanished completely from sight.

Fry was growing very tired. "The Sunday after the failure of Ball's great escape I went to Nîmes," he wrote. "All afternoon I sat in the lovely eighteenth-century Jardin de la Fontaine, listening to the water running through the colonnades of the central basin, watching the yellow leaves drift slowly down from the plane trees in the thin, late-autumn sun, and feeling for all the world like the last act of *Cyrano de Bergerac*."

LITTLE BY LITTLE, life in Marseille was growing harder and more depressing. Yet the accomplishments could not be overlooked, and Fry was now godfather to several thousand unfortunate souls. They needed him more than ever, for on October 24 Marshal Pétain met with Hitler at Montoire, and the meeting formalized a crossing of the public-relations Rubicon for the Vichy administration. Until then, many French people desperately wanted to believe the fiction that their government was doing only what was essential to safeguard the honor of France. After Pétain's subsequent broadcast to the nation on October 30, in which he declared "I enter into the way of collaboration" it was obvious that a choice had been made to serve their German overlords. In short, Fascism was to be actively established in France, and the time would soon approach when the people would have to choose sides. Another layer of conflict would soon be added to the awful conditions of the occupation, and the refugees would be trodden even deeper underfoot.

Just as significantly, the rightward momentum of the Vichy government made Fry realize that he would soon have to think about helping even more people. Until now he had been concerned with the German (or more properly "Reich") emigration, because by the terms of the armistice Vichy was forced to hand over Reich citizens on demand. But if Vichy was turning Fascist, that meant French citizens themselves were in danger from their own government, just as Germans had been since 1933. If Pétain was really to collaborate with Hitler, he would hand over whichever French people Germany asked for—namely Jews, artists, and intellectuals, as usual.

Not long after Fry had written to André Gide and Henri Matisse, to ask them if they would add their names to the "Committee of Patrons" of the Centre Américain, he wrote to them again. This time it was to inquire whether they would like his help in leaving France. He also wrote to many other famous people he thought were now in danger, including the sculptor Jacques Lipchitz and the painters Marc Chagall and André Masson. Lipchitz and Chagall were Jewish and Masson had a Jewish wife. He was cordially rebuffed. All except Masson wrote back thanking him for his concern but refusing to leave. Masson himself was reluctant to leave until he heard on the radio details of Vichy's new race laws, at which he spontaneously vomited, and then began to rethink his position. Fry's mind turned to Breitscheid and Hilferding, still under arrest at Arles, and at the mercy of the Gestapo. They all thought fame had conferred on them immunity, that they were too important to be persecuted. They were wrong.

It was another disappointment, and what added to Fry's depression was how different things were from the "early days", the buccaneering days of August and September when he was running his outfit on the hoof from the Splendide and sending so many people over the border into Spain. Now he was reduced to the respectability of a director in an office. He did not regret the change, but felt the deflation of spirit that afflicts the amateur who turns professional, or the freelancer who takes a salaried job. And he was endlessly busy, despite crackdowns by Vichy that meant more and more refugees were being interned.

On the day of the "phantom ship," Fry on Beamish's advice had taken the train to Tarascon, to have the alibi of being out of town—Mafia style—if the police discovered the plot. He met Stéphane Hessel there and spent the rest of the weekend with him instead. During the journey he had written to Eileen that he was receiving up to a dozen phone calls an hour, and twenty-three letters a day. The Splendide was becoming impossible to live in because everybody knew where to find him. One morning, Arthur Wolff's wife had walked into his room unannounced while Fry was in a state of undress. That seems to have been the last straw. When the police had undertaken their latest *rafle,* Fry confided to Eileen, "I was actually glad to have a few of the most insistent and most pestiferous 'clients' carried shrieking off."

The compensations of this sort of life were few, but the Sunday of the phantom ship episode gave Fry a timely if brief vacation. He cycled with Stéphane from Tarascon to Les Baux. Bauxite, the red crumbly ore that produces aluminum, was first found in that area, and was named after the town whose narrow southern approach between chasmic black-stained cliffs was known as the Val d'Enfer. It was supposedly that place that inspired Dante's landscape in *The Inferno,* and as they cycled through the abysmal landscape, Fry understood why. On the way they visited the primitive Romanesque chapel at St. Gabriel, and saw its shell-like Gallo-Roman altar carved out of the hillside. At Les Baux they wandered through the tumbledown castle of the almost abandoned town, then carried on to spend the night at St. Remy. "Stéphane slept soundly enough," said Fry, "but I had nightmares." Despite the distance and good company, he could not rid his mind of the refugees' fate.

Fry was late back at Marseille on the Monday, having visited Les Antiques and seen the asylum where van Gogh spent his last unhappy years. He allowed too little time to cycle to the station to catch his return train, and this reflected some hesitation about rejoining the war after such an idyllic interlude. Fry was anxious to hear about the outcome of the escape the night before, but at the same time he was nervous about resuming the thankless pace of his city life. The police might well have been preparing to arrest him, but more disturbing were the responsibilities that definitely awaited his return.

Alas, the weekends with Stéphane were too infrequent. Fry found himself drinking more than usual, which he probably needed under the intense pressure, but Vichy was even scheming to thwart him in this by instituting its *jours sans alcool* when no liquor could be served at all. This was effective four days of the week. Ironic *patrons* pinned up notices in their bars announcing the official edict along with a depiction of a beached fish expiring on the strand. Food rationing was severe, but more severe was the fact that there was no food for which to exchange ration coupons anyway. There were now official days without meat, too, which was a sort of joke, for nobody had seen meat for a long time. Nobody except the enemy, that is. Fry had hungrily observed the Italian army officers of the armistice commission, the best-fed people in Marseille, and tracked them to La Dantesque, on the rue du Lycée, the restaurant where they ate their meals. Afterward, he ate there too. But he was being worn down by too much work and a diet lacking vitamins, protein, and fats.

Despite the closeness to his colleagues, Fry remained essentially a solitary figure at the head of his organization. He was feeling lonely and neglected during this period, and told Eileen about it, in his characteristic way of composing considerate half-truths and lukewarm endearments. "Here everything is strange," he wrote, "including the language, and I have no distractions, accustomed or otherwise and a great many acquaintances but no friends. It is a strange feeling being so far away from home so long. I have been before but then it was different for there wasn't anything to make me want to go back. . . . Also the nights have been getting colder and colder and I have been wanting more and more your companionship in bed. I have tried *maisons closes* a few times but they are nasty and I don't want them anymore." Fry had indeed visited brothels with Beamish, and admitted elsewhere that he liked it rather better than he confided to Eileen (although the fact that he told his fretting spouse at all, and so casually, reveals a lot about the nature of their marriage). But Fry was an intensely private man deprived of his privacy, which war destroys quite effectively, and this was more of a strain on him than either hunger or separation from Eileen.

He wanted out. Not out of Marseille, not out of the lives of the refugees for whom he had assumed responsibility—no matter how trying they could be— but out of the life he had created for himself. Out of the busy loneliness of his routine. Out of the Splendide. *Out.*

IT WAS MIRIAM who solved the problem. She and Mary Jayne had taken the trolley one afternoon and ridden due east from the city center to the semirural district of La Pomme. They were walking along the Avenue Jean Lombard through the ravishing autumn scenery when they came across a sign saying "A LOUER". It was planted in the ground at the beginning of a long drive, and at the far end they could see an imposing house three stories high, surrounded by gardens, woodland, and water. There was also a fabulous view across the valley to the distant, shimmering sea. The building appeared closed up and unoccupied, and Miriam suddenly had the thought that fate had dropped this place and its beautiful surroundings right in their laps. The sign said it was called "Villa Air-Bel." She and Mary Jayne hastened back to town, eager to tell Fry of their discovery.

Fry liked it very much indeed: it stimulated his Epicurean glands and set forth images of aristocratic grandeur. In fact the Villa Air-Bel was a big, bourgeois family residence on the nineteenth-century model, but everything Fry might have wished for.

The broad gravel terrace out front was lined with mature plane trees, and beyond lay a formal garden filled with geraniums, zinnias, and marigolds, and a lily pond with goldfish bubbling away in it. In the villa itself there were eighteen rooms spread over its three floors. The ground floor had a kitchen with a coal stove twenty feet long. It also had the only bathroom, containing a grand old zinc tub and faucets in the shape of swans' heads, but no toilet. There were many bedrooms, each in slightly impersonal manner equipped with large mahogany beds, embellished marble fireplaces, and marble-topped washstands. There was even, on the second floor, the room Fry had always imagined should belong to him: a library. By chance, this one was papered with monochrome wallpaper depicting scenes from Greco-Roman mythology. The first one he identified was Aeneas's flight from Troy—Fry agreed with T. S. Eliot that Aeneas was the original refugee—and like Miriam, he, too, was overcome with a feeling of destiny.

Fry calculated the enormous savings he could make on hotel rooms if he could fill the place with staff and friends. He imagined the impossibility of his more annoying clients risking the trip out there to pester him. He pictured scenes of elegant living and lazy picnics in the grounds. He looked around the faded vastness of the place, contemplated the turgid landscape paintings that hung on the walls, and thought it over. In the midst of the war, with all the crowds and panic, the villa's dubious elegance and serenity was almost surreal.

He signed the lease the very day after he had first seen the villa, and at thirteen hundred francs a month it proved scarcely more expensive than his room at the Splendide.

There followed a term of halcyon days, time almost out of time, and more extraordinary than Fry had expected when he first contemplated his new domain. Beamish declined Fry's offer to take up residence at the villa. He disapproved of Fry's rustic withdrawal, partly on the grounds that it put the boss out of touch with the office, especially as there was no telephone. Of course, that was precisely Fry's aim, and Beamish's, truth to tell, was more likely that he preferred the action in the city. Instead of a siesta, Beamish would inspect *le choix* at Madame Coste's or some other place, and he was probably unprepared to exchange the convenience of that for more bucolic delights.

But the Bénédites moved in immediately with their young son, and so did Miriam Davenport and Jean Gemahling. Mary Jayne Gold took a room, but also kept one in town for her trysts with Killer, who was starkly unwelcome at the Villa Air-Bel. In his volatile, chip-on-the-shoulder manner, Killer despised the people around Fry anyway. Except, that is, for Victor Serge, the Russian novelist who was a client of Fry's and another early resident at Air-Bel. Killer had great respect for that old fighter. Serge brought with him his girlfriend, the dark and austere Laurette Séjourné, and his twenty-year-old son, Vladi. Fry liked to have somebody around to argue with, and a red-hot young Marxist like Vladi was perfect. "Come now, how can an intelligent young man like you swallow all that garbage!" was a typical Fry rejoinder.

Rather like Paul Hagen, Victor Serge had traveled the revolutionary road from violence to tolerance, from Communism to something like Democratic Socialism. As a teenager exiled in Paris he had joined the Reds for the 1917 October Revolution in his native country. He was a Leninist, then when things turned sour a Trotskyist, but he balked at Stalin. A close friend of Trotsky, Serge was likewise a well-known enemy of the Soviet dictatorship (Stalin had exiled Serge to Siberia for three years), and he feared the NKVD as much as he did the Gestapo. With his bristly silver hair and his collarless Russian jacket, Serge already looked like an old man of the century, seemingly carved from wood.

Another client of Fry's who moved in straightaway was André Breton, the poet commonly referred to as the Pope of Surrealism—and the soubriquet was imperial as well as religious. Breton was a charismatic man, a true high priest, both leading and inspiring the Surrealist movement, which had its spiritual home in France. He was also demanding and dictatorial where "his" Surrealism was concerned. And as a pope, Breton could both baptize and excommunicate. For example, he had once quarrelled with Max Ernst, the great German Surrealist and another of Fry's clients, and banished him from the movement. At the Villa Air-Bel, something of a temporary rapprochement was effected between the two men.

Breton brought with him his blond and equally Surrealist wife, the stiletto-tongued and deadly sexy Jacqueline Lamba. He had met her, suitably enough, when she had been an aquatic dancer in a giant fish tank in a Paris club near Les Halles. Their daughter, Aube, was another youngster happy to roam the acres. With a housekeeper, Madame Nouguet, and several maids, the company at the Villa was an impressive size. Its numbers were further swelled when word got around that Breton was staying there. He proved a magnet for nearly all the Surrealists and Cubists in France, who by this time seemed to have either congregated in Marseille itself, or dispersed themselves among outlying towns and villages. Very soon, they all began to forgather *chez* Fry.

The rest of that autumn, magically softened and lightened by an Indian summer, and through the bitter winter into spring, a riotous and creative assembly took place at the Villa Air-Bel. It included André Masson, who had been loaned a hunting lodge on her estate by Countess Lily Pastré, and who made the nearly hourlong train ride from Montredon to La Pomme with regularity. Had it not been for the lingering animosity between Masson, Breton, and himself, Max Ernst would have moved in as well. As it was, he visited often, traveling from his studio at nearby St. Martin d'Ardèche, after Paul Eluard had managed to secure his release from the St. Nicolas concentration camp at Christmas. He brought with him "a great roll of his pictures, which he tacked up in the drawing room, so we had a show which people came all the way from Marseille to see," said Fry. Benjamin Péret would come and read his obscene and scatalogical poems, to the approval of the crowd, which included the black Cuban Cubist, Wifredo Lam, one of Picasso's very rare pupils. The Spanish Surrealist Oscar Domínguez would turn up like the rest every Sunday afternoon, together with the Romanian painters Jacques Hérold and one-eyed Victor Brauner—Peggy Guggenheim's current beau, soon to be replaced by Max Ernst. The novelist Kay Boyle—whom Fry described as "like her books: intense, emotional and finely wrought"—came too, and so did the Comtesse de Saint-Exupéry, wife of Antoine, the famous French novelist and aviator. After she had evacuated the paintings from her museum at Grenoble in December, Peggy Guggenheim arrived as well, and provided some much-needed funds for Fry that eased everybody's existence a little.

With Breton as master of ceremonies, the crowd would delight in playing the sort of games Surrealism was famous for, such as "Exquisite Corpses," where each player added a section of a drawing to a piece of paper and folded it over as it was passed around. The next person had no idea what was already drawn, and added only his own inspiration. The idea was to produce a surprising and disturbing image that arose from a sort of collective subconscious. The same thing could be done with word pictures, and each was designed to disrupt the conventional flow of perception and assumption to reveal a new and more honest—and also creative—version of reality. It was a good antidote to the one promulgated by Vichy.

There were also art auctions, and painting competitions, and all manner of sophisticated rowdiness, laughter, and arguments. Nobel Prize winner Otto Meyerhof had escaped with his wife from France in early October, but his eighteen-year-old son, Walter, was still there, and he once visited the Villa Air-Bel and witnessed the proceedings. Being young, and having lived a sheltered life so far, he was overawed by the glamorous people at the dinner table, flirting with their lovers and each others', joking and generally being brilliant. Walter, now emeritus professor of physics at Stanford University, says he is always asked what it was like to be there: the truth is he was intimidated and fled to his room, where he closed the door and hid himself away.

The meals themselves were an experiment in visual Surrealism. The dining room was grand and so were the place settings, and the wine was plentiful and delicious. But the food itself was sparse. Today it might be called *nouvelle cuisine*, but in 1940 it was just an artichoke or a rutabaga sitting alone in the middle of a plate, boiled because there was no oil, and without sauce or savour for lack of sugar or starch. And this was the regular diet, day in, day out. Breton enlivened the sparse tableaux by letting his pet praying mantises wander about the table. He was entranced by the females, which killed and ate their mates after copulation.

One of the most beautiful creations of the Air-Bel days was a collective effort, a pack of redesigned Tarot cards. Breton decided to replace the four traditional suits with new ones. Instead of the club, the diamond, and so on, he substituted his own symbols. The flame stood for love, a bloody wheel for revolution, a key for knowledge, and a black star for the dream. He replaced the King and Queen with "genius" and "siren," and the Jack with the magus. The artists all contributed their own designs for individual cards (which still exist, in a private collection in Paris). "This talisman deck," wrote the art historian Martica Sawin, "memorializes that tense and uncertain interval during which the Surrealist artists, poised in a void, redid the . . . symbols of the ultimate powers of fate."

The atmosphere at the Villa Air-Bel, despite tension in the world beyond, proved a fillip for Fry, who managed further to overcome his natural reserve and allow himself to be carried along by the mayhem and even be inducted into the true spirit of the whole "mad group," as he called it. There exists a photograph of Fry fooling around up a tree, while the Comtesse de Saint-Exupéry bounces on an outlying limb. To have seen Fry up a tree only a few months earlier would have been as unlikely as finding an elephant wedged in a submarine. He was certainly coming out of his shell, and the Villa Air-Bel—renamed "Chateau Espère-Visa" by Serge—was truly a magic castle for Fry, balancing his need for remoteness with a developing desire for play and companionship that he had really never enjoyed during his lonely childhood and oversophisticated adolescence. Now, engaged in underground activities that could earn him the death sentence, Varian Fry was actually discovering a freedom of the spirit, a certain lightness of being.

ONE MORNING early in December, the idyll at the Villa Bel-Air was rudely shattered by the ugly forces lurking without. The weekend had been a somber one for Fry, because Miriam had left for Yugoslavia at the very end of November. The American Consulate at Geneva had finally succeeded in securing her an Italian transit visa, which meant she could travel to Ljubljana to meet her fiancé, Rolf Treo. That had always been her plan, and Fry was prepared for it, but that didn't stop her farewell feeling like a loss. Beamish had also left Marseille temporarily, after he heard that Marshal Pétain would be passing through the next Tuesday on his way to inspect the fleet at Toulon. He told Fry he knew from experience what to expect when a dictator came to town.

Now Fry was to find out for himself. It was a cold, gray day, and he had arranged to work at the villa. He found himself waiting for Lena, who finally turned up at ten o'clock, apologizing for being arrested on her way there. She explained that because of Pétain's visit, a lot of the refugees were being rounded up in a huge *rafle*. Just then, a maid knocked on the door of the library and nervously announced that the police were downstairs. This time there were no courtesies, and no allowances made for an American. A burly bully of an inspector, flanked by three equally imposing plainclothes detectives, shouted that he was going to search the premises. The warrant he produced was merely a mimeograph stating that he was authorized to enter premises suspected of harboring Communist activities. The policeman overrode Fry's hectic objections ("Tell it to the judge," he said), and sent his men out over the house.

They soon had quite a haul. Breton had sketched a picture of the *Maréchal* as a cockerel, with the slogan "Le terrible crétin de Pétain" written beneath it. The poet couldn't argue his way out of that one, and soon a detective also found Breton's service revolver (as a doctor, Breton had served in the Medical Corps). Then they turned up Serge's pearl-handled pistol he kept close to shoot himself and thus swindle the Gestapo or the NKVD if it looked like he was finally trapped. With firearms and sedition there was plenty of evidence to detain the entire household. Just then, as if on cue, Jean and Danny returned for lunch and were arrested as well. Fry managed to argue that the children and their mothers be allowed to remain, but everybody else was herded into a *panier à salade* and taken to the Evêché.

Before they left, Fry managed to make an excuse to fetch a handkerchief from his room, and during the few seconds' grace he had in there, he threw a false passport onto the top of his wardrobe, and rode into Marseille praying there were no other incriminating papers left lying around. He was always careful, but nobody was perfect. Lena managed to dispose of her pocketbook, and at the police headquarters she flushed away another seditious document of Breton's. Then they waited, along with many others similarly apprehended, to see what was to be done with them.

The fact was, the police rounded up nearly seven thousand people in Marseille on Monday, December 2, 1940. They were taking no chances with Pétain's safety, and the logic of detention was arbitrary and indiscriminate. All sorts of people who were *en règle* were detained, including a Paris banker and foreign businessmen, Marseille surgeons, and hapless cases whose papers passed an inspection one moment, only to fail another a minute later on another street. There was an atmosphere of exasperation, anger, and naked fear in the crowded hall, and Fry was self-conscious because he recognized many of his clients. It would not help their spirits to see their savior in the same helpless situation as they were.

At this point Fry was unaware of several things. Eight years earlier, during the visit of the Prince of Wales to Marseille, a bomb had been placed on the railway line that went past the Villa Air-Bel. It exploded harmlessly and the saboteurs were never caught, but there was of course an investigation that recorded details of the villa and its tenants, who had changed several times by the time Fry and his friends moved in. Now, just before Pétain's visit (he was to travel by the very same train line) Jacquie Lamba-Breton's sister had arrived, in fact late on Sunday night, swathed in a headscarf and carrying a suspicious-looking suitcase—almost everything was worthy of suspicion in Vichy France. Fry's later theory, when he heard about the villa's history, was that the porter made a few francs by reporting Huguette Lamba's arrival, with her suspected "bomb" suitcase, to the police. They in turn pulled out the old file and, against all natural logic (but in tune with that of a police state), deduced that the same anarchists who planted the earlier device were still resident at the villa (where, according to all the evidence, they had never lived in the first place). The new report doubtless stated that the ruthless bombers were found on Monday morning in possession of two loaded side arms and a lethal cartoon.

The other thing Fry didn't know at the time was that André Breton possessed a police record that was as long as his arm. In his younger days, Breton had been the enfant terrible of Dadaism, a fiercely disruptive, belligerent, and wickedly inventive anti-art movement that believed in practicing what it preached, which was basically *épater le bourgeois*. "Once," said Fry, "he [Breton] and a friend went to the theater and began eating dinner, which they had brought with them, opening cans, cutting bread, uncorking bottles and talking as though they were at the table. Nobody dared interfere, apparently." One of Breton's favorite pastimes was heckling and talking back to actors from his theater seat. When an actor asked a question, Breton would supply an answer before the other actor could respond, and tricks like this invariably stopped whatever play was in progress. Breton despised actors who couldn't ignore him—those, in other words, who did not fully believe in their art, and were just the usual bourgeois puppets and stooges.

Things did not always go so well for him. He and his anarchistic friends once turned up uninvited at a fancy banquet, bringing with them their own copious supplies of soup and spaghetti. These they soon began to slurp up noisily and conspicuously, to the outrage of the respectable invitees present. When the speeches began, they interrupted every sentence, and eventually the grandees at the head table decided to call the management and have Breton's gang ejected. Ready for such an eventuality, all the Dadaists and Surrealists rushed to the windows and flung them open, crying "Fire! Fire!" at the top of their voices into the night air. As Breton was being manhandled away, the fire brigade turned up and began to hack down the doors amid general pandemonium. "For all these manifestations of exuberance André was arrested some twenty-five times in Paris. A fact I hadn't known before the police came," Fry noted ruefully.

At eleven o'clock on Monday night, the *Brigade des Rafles*—the large room where Fry, Lena, and the others had been kept since early evening—began to empty. Everybody was carted off to the commercial docks on the west side of town, where large ships awaited them. Fry tried once again to confront a laconic gendarme with his sheer *Americanness,* but again he failed to impress. As he walked up the gangplank between Lena and Mary Jayne Gold, he could just make out through the gloom the name of the ship painted in white on the dark hull. It was the SS *Sinaïa,* the same ship on which he had sailed from New York to Europe in 1928.

There were third-class cabins for the women to crowd into, but only burlap bags full of straw for the men in the hold. Of them all, only Victor Serge, the veteran of a hundred roundups, had thought ahead. He frankly disbelieved the promise, made by the police inspector at Villa Air-Bel, that they would not be kept for long. He knew they could be kept for months if the whim of the state dictated, and there was nothing any of them could do about it. Wisely, but hastily, he had grabbed a novel on his way to the police van.

Now he brought it out of his pocket and swore quietly to himself: it was one he had written himself. That night they all slept under open hatches, beneath the starry sky.

The next day Fry tried fruitlessly to persuade the guards to let him contact the American consulate, and when he failed, he began to read the novel Serge had kindly given him, which was about life in prison. He read it with rapt attention. Food was provided, but it was terrible, and on Tuesday afternoon everybody was ordered below and the hatches were slammed shut and bolted. This was deeply disturbing. Fry had heard of forced labor being sent to work on the grandiose scheme for a Trans-Saharan railway. Many refugees who had volunteered for the French Foreign Legion as a way to fight on behalf of France (and stay out of the concentration camp) were duped into becoming slave labor at "workers' camps" in the desert, where they were now dying like flies. On board the *Sinaïa,* word spread among the frightened passengers that this was where they too were headed—an anxiety increased by the many whistles heard blowing shrilly from the quayside. Fry thought of himself breaking rocks under a burning sun, unable to let anybody know of his whereabouts.

Later, though, after the ship had remained still for several hours, the hatches were again opened and the inmates of the makeshift prison allowed back on deck. Marshal Pétain had gone past in a motorboat that afternoon, and security decreed the prisoners be battened in cabins and the hold. It was a relief, but even though the head of state had gone on to Toulon they were not to be released, for he would be passing back through Marseille the next day. It looked as though Fry and his friends were in for quite an extended stay. In the evening they wrote a message for the American consul, wrapped a bank note around it, and dropped it over the side of the boat onto the dock, where a small boy picked it up. To their amazement, he returned some time later with a package of sandwiches, and Hugh Fullerton's calling card: the message had made it to the Consulate, and this gave them hope. That night, as the wine went round, the passengers of the *bateau ivre* sat singing songs to while away the time:

> *Les femmes de France sont intrigantes*
> > *Elles font l'amour pour de l'argent*
> *Tandis que nous, pauvres pupus,*
> > *Nous faisons l'amour pour riens du tout,*
> *Tandis que nous, pauvres pupus,*
> > *Nous faisons l'amour pour riens du tout.*

(The women of France scheme on:
  They make love for money alone
Whereas all of us poor beggars,
  Make love for nothing at all
Whereas all of us poor beggars,
  Make love for nothing at all.)

Lena piped up with her own variant:

Tandis que les petites anglaises,
  Elles font l'amour pour rien du tout.

(Whereas the little English girls
  Make love for nothing at all.)

It was almost a busman's holiday for Fry, whose days were full of accounts of life in prison camps, and he was overjoyed to see Harry Bingham on Wednesday afternoon, after Mary Jayne had managed to send a message to the captain and got them invited up to his cabin for a drink of beer. Harry walked in and the captain suddenly remembered he had some cognac after all. Bingham explained he was doing all he could, but in the bureaucratic chaos surrounding the Marshal's visit, the Prefecture had been almost uncontactable, and all officials were out in their best uniforms bowing and scraping to the great leader. It was to be another night on board the creaking ship.

Everybody was finally processed and released, scruffy and dirty, onto the quayside the next afternoon. Fry realized it was Thursday—he had lost nearly the whole working week, but at least he knew firsthand now what his clients were going through all the time. "To me," he wrote, "accustomed to the principles of Anglo-Saxon and Roman law, this was one of the most surprising and shocking experiences of my life. To be searched without a search-warrant, arrested without a warrant of arrest, held incommunicado, and then released without ever having a charge brought against you—surely this is enough to make you wonder where you are."

That was not all Fry would wonder about. The consulate cabled New York when it heard of Fry's plight, in such urgent fashion that another emergency was precipitated. Instead of protesting that American citizens should be protected against such gross illegality on the part of Vichy, Consul-General Hurley (or one of his factotums) dictated a straight lie for the eyes of the State Department, who passed it onto the Emergency Rescue Committee:

FRY AND MISS GOLD WERE TAKEN INTO CUSTODY PRIMARILY BE-
CAUSE THEY WERE ARRESTED IN SUSPICIOUS CIRCUMSTANCES
AND IN SUSPECT SURROUNDINGS STOP THEY ARE IN COMPANY OF
A SUSPECT PERSON (ADEREK LEYYU) AND CERTAIN OTHER INDI-
VIDUALS WANTED BY THE POLICE STOP

Years later, Fry said he was still trying to find out who on earth Aderek
Leyyu and the rest of the "individuals wanted by the police" were. Worst of
all, the incident precipitated another argument with the New York committee, who panicked (probably out of the best motives of concern for Fry's
safety) and ordered him home. "As it is," Fry complained to Mildred Adams
in a furious letter, "we lack support from the Embassy, get only luke-warm
support from the Consulate, and are horrified when we get into slight trouble
(as on the occasion of the Marshal's visit) to have you telegram *en clair* telling
me to return at once. *You should do exactly the opposite* in such circumstances:
cable the Embassy and the Consulate in terms of the utmost indignation; demanding my immediate release, and apologies from the authorities. . . ."

A FORTNIGHT EARLIER, Fry had suffered another "family bereavement"
when Charlie Fawcett left for Lisbon. His departure was prompted partly by
his desire to make it to England, where he planned to join the Royal Air Force.
It also resulted in part from the fact that his Polish admirer Lili, who continued to pursue him even after Charlie had reunited her with her husband, was
growing ever more demanding and troublesome. Most of all, Charlie knew
the police were aware of his continuing work for the French Resistance. At the
Centre Américain, everybody who left for the border was presented with a
petit cadeau, and Charlie was weighed down with them. He had secret messages wedged into the third valve of his trumpet, which he tightened with a
wrench. He quickly learned to play some tunes fingering only the other two
valves, in case the border guards were suspicious. He also took several heads
he had sculpted. They were hollow, and Fry filled them up with illegal maps
and lists that Charlie was to hand over to Bunny Torr at the British embassy
when he got to Madrid. Sealed over with plaster, who would believe they were
an artistic death sentence for whoever was found with them? When the terribly nervous Charlie left for the frontier he was carrying enough secret information to compromise a good proportion of the underground work taking
place in unoccupied France at the time.

Luckily he made it over the border, but only after being closely questioned
by a whole group of French police who seemed to know an astonishing

amount about the Centre Américain de Secours. Charlie said he recognized among them one man who had twice applied for a job at the office. In anticipation of just such a situation as this, in which his nervousness might betray him, Charlie had put his artistic talents to further good use by drawing several pornographic pictures (a prostitute lounging on the railway platform gave him the idea), which he stowed at various places in his luggage. As the French police searched through his belongings, they were diverted from their original mission to find illicit documents by a very different kind of illicit document. They began to laugh and pass around Charlie's little masterpieces, and eventually, absorbed in them, casually waved him through. It wasn't until he reached his hotel in Barcelona that he was actually arrested, by Spanish secret police who followed him there from the American consulate. They conducted him back over the border by train into France and handed him over to the Gestapo at Biarritz. Charlie Fawcett, twenty-one years old, still had all his incriminating maps and lists with him.

CHAPTER 18

THE TURNING YEAR

FRY WAS IN THE TOWN of Vichy. The Spanish and the Portuguese had decided at the beginning of November to relax their border controls. Again, refugees as well as British soldiers could cross the mountains using the Fittko route from Banyuls, putting the Centre Américain back in business. Fry's trip to the spa town headquarters of the Pétain government was prompted by the realization that escape over the Pyrenees—not to mention the legal emigration of those with American visas and French *visas de sortie*—was being hampered by the fact that many of Fry's clients were still languishing in concentration camps. The situation for these people—and tens of thousands of other innocent foreigners shackled in frankly disgraceful conditions—was growing no better. "The women in the camps have no sanitary pads or any kind of substitute for them, and nobody, man, woman, or child, has any toilet paper unless he is sick enough to be in hospital," wrote Fry in his journal. He and his staff were already distributing humanitarian aid to many hundreds of internees, but it was a mere drop in the ocean. Pressure needed to be brought to bear on the Vichy administration, and Danny Bénédite had been delegated to tour the camps and bring back a detailed account of the true conditions along with testimonials from inmates. With his natural precision, he was the perfect man for the job, and the reports Danny produced at the time, which have remained unpublished for sixty years, make for harrowing reading.

There were 17,000 people, for instance, including 2,000 women and children, on the beach at Argelès near Perpignan. At nearby Le Barcarès, Danny discovered facilities that could expand its population to 60,000—a truly

enormous concentration camp. At Bram near Carcassonne, at Agde outside Montpelier, at Septfonds, Brens-Gallac, Récébédou, Clairfonds, and
Montaudran, all clustered around Toulouse, there were another 20,000 internees, many of them families. Camp Gurs, between Pau and Oloron,
held 15,000, including 5,000 Jewish women and children. Then there was
Castelat, Rieucros, Le Vernet, Carrigues, St. Hyppolyte-du-Fort, and Mas
Boulbon, all out at Nîmes, then the one at Montelimar. Around Marseille, besides the aptly named Les Milles, were St. Marthe, Carpiagne, and Bompard.
It seemed like the whole of the unoccupied zone was one great, heartless
prison.

"In these statistics," Danny dryly added in his conclusion, "are not included the military camps nor the *prestataire* [forced labor] camps (Montauban, St. Antoine, Langlade, Rivesaltes, La Viscose, Miramas etc). There are
about 25–35,000 *prestataires* and foreign workers under military control. The
number of civilian internees is actually of about 60,000. But one has to suspect that very soon it will be more than 100,000." There were 120 concentration camps in Vichy France.

And people were dying. Danny gave as an example the death toll for a
single day at Gurs, where there were 300 mortalities a month. Four old people
had died of untreated heart diseases, and a further seven of the aged from
other unspecified causes (there was naturally no coroner around). One forty-
three-year-old man died of malnutrition, and a sixteen-year-old girl of dia-
betes. There were no drugs or medicines at all. A two-year-old child expired
from enteritis, and another child from polyencephalitis. One woman had suc-
cumbed to pneumonia. That made sixteen people dead on a randomly chosen day, and it was still only November. "The wooden barracks have neither
windows, nor light, nor floor," wrote Danny. "Heavy rains enter through the
roofs. Neither stoves, nor fire wood." With the really cold weather about to set
in (and it was really cold weather in the extraordinarily harsh winter of 1940–
41), the situation would inevitably decay from chronic to acute. "There is no
leave for the camps [*sic*] except for funerals."

Lena was furiously typing all this information up on her small portable
machine, while sitting on the bed in the tiny hotel room Fry had managed to
find in Vichy. The small, ugly, provincial town where Pétain's government had
adjourned to carry on its shameful maladministrations was hovering at just
above zero on the moral-centigrade scale, as Koestler would have put it. Fry's
plan when he arrived with Lena and Marcel Chaminade was to persuade the
authorities, in the face of the overwhelming evidence Danny had collected, to
show a little mercy, and at least to release the sick and the young from the
camps. The oily Chaminade was in his element, but he was managing to effect

introductions to many if not all of the members of Pétain's cabinet. "He was really valuable in Vichy," Fry wrote to Eileen, "as he knows so many people there."

Fry saw Henri du Moulin de Labarthète, Pétain's *directeur de Cabinet.* He also met René Gillouin, Pétain's speechwriter, but a man marginally sympathetic to the Jews. Gillouin—by no means a "yes man"—would later present Pétain with a report he himself had composed, and which tore to shreds the legal bases of the anti-Jewish laws. He told Pétain racism was a Christian heresy (in 1943 he would be forced to flee the country for Switzerland). Fry presented his case to the cabinet ministers Sébilleau and Chaussard; he lobbied Caziot, "The fine, bewhiskered Minister of Agriculture"; found himself disgusted with Gaston Bergery, "the suave and somewhat rodent-faced apologist" for the *Statut des Juifs.* He argued with the Ambassadors St. Quentin and Chambertin. He pleaded with Comte Suzy and many others.

Up and down the corridors of hotels he went, where the ad hoc government had its offices, the nameplates scraps of paper tacked up on the doors of the bedrooms. Again and again he presented the politicians and bureaucrats with the direct and undeniable evidence of injustice that Danny had scrupulously assembled.

Fry had discovered that Germany was deporting insane, aged, and crippled "non-Aryans" to French camps, and that people had died in transit. "The sane are very afraid of the insane people," wrote one inmate. Danny had described the meager rations—far less than was needed for long-term survival—which were reaching the prisoners in only piecemeal fashion. A twenty-year-old girl in her deposition described how "dysenterie [*sic*] has broken out because of insufficient food. . . . My body has been covered with eczema. . . . There are scores of insects, cats and dogs which disturb us in the night. . . . It is to terrible to feel like parias [*sic*], being buried alive. . . ." A high-school teacher, also trapped in a camp, testified that "the rats and mice are quite terrible and they have got so used to us that they run about quite fearlessly and even climb the tables at mealtimes and nibble at our food." Touchingly, a carpenter wrote about the lack of furniture:

We have no tables, no chairs, no beds in our barracks, and some straw only covers the naked earth. This straw is never changed and decays and swarms with insects. During the rains in the fall the ground, which is all the floor the barracks have, becomes soggy and wet, and for weeks we didn't get dry. We only have a thin blanket for cover at night, but most of the time we are unable to sleep. . . .

One refugee told of the horrifying story of flash flood that swamped the camp at St. Cyprien one night. He had survived, but he reported seeing several bodies of inmates floating in the water the next day. After the autumn rains had begun, as the carpenter had complained, everybody remained more or less permanently wet. Danny found evidence that Germany was breaking the armistice agreement: Gauleiter Bürkel had rounded up Jews in Germany and unceremoniously dumped them in France. A Jewish girl interned at Gurs attested how, on October 22, at seven o'clock in the morning, the police came for her and her family in Germany. "We had to get out of bed. He announced: 'You have to be ready in ten minutes!' They brought us to the town hall, later to Heidelberg, from there to the railway station. We were in the train for three days and three nights. We were very exhausted when we arrived. We are sleeping on straw. I have with me nothing but the cloth on my back. The French are very nice but they have only limited means."

There were tragedies. Danny told the story of Dr. Hans Schindler:

> . . . seriously ill, weighs only 40 kgs (the normal weight of a fifteen-year-old boy). The poor man has had to suffer particular hardship. His wife, a doctor, living in Brussels, learned that her husband had become ill, and succeeded, in spite of great difficulties, to come from Brussels to Perpignan with their little daughter of twelve years. They were sent to me, after their arrival from the five days trip, without any names or identification papers. I paid their hotel and their living during one week. When she first tried to pay a visit to her husband in the camp, she was threatened with arrest because she had no travel permit. The second visit was still more difficult, and the third time she was not allowed to enter the camp. She stayed in front of the gate for several hours; finally, exhausted, she fell, fainted. Transported to the hospital, she died the same evening.

He said that the distraught (Jewish) husband and daughter were now both in the camp: it was Gurs. "No description can possibly exaggerate the horrors of the concentration camps," concluded Fry. "I think Edgar Allan Poe could not make them worse than they are."

After almost two weeks of incessant lobbying and patient attendance on mostly arrogant and uninterested officials ("What is wrong with our concentration camps?" demanded a "pasty faced young fascist" when Fry dared to suggest that it was not natural for children to be imprisoned behind barbed wire), Fry concluded that he was "being given the runaround everywhere."

The charge included the staff of the American embassy who, he said, were neither helpful nor polite. He composed a long letter to H. F. Matthews, the Chargé d'Affaires at Vichy, defending himself against the willful misunderstanding the Foreign Service had cultivated since the flurry of telegrams in September, when the Marseille Prefecture had informed Consul Fullerton it was *inquiète* concerning his activities.

Fry had acted swiftly to smooth over that matter with the French authorities, and he had largely succeeded. Not so with his own government. In his frustration with the Americans, Fry's attempt to explain the truth of the situation drew from him intemperate words. "I cannot be satisfied with a purely negative attitude on the part of our Foreign Service," he wrote. "It is not enough for them to refrain from indiscreet and slanderous statements." Fry was starting to suspect that in some way he had been singled out for victimization by the State Department and its representatives. "We have the consent and the approval of the French authorities, but I gather we have neither the consent nor the approval of the American Foreign Service. If you know any reason whatever why this should be denied us, I should be very glad to hear it," Fry added, in barely concealed anger, before asking formally for an interview.

His request was refused. The embassy had accused Fry of evading French laws, without seeing any evidence, or even considering whether, if true, the laws he was evading broke every code of natural justice—laws that could be happily observed only if America was prepared to sacrifice its moral authority. Fry left Vichy with the knowledge that it was so: America was prepared to do anything to keep Vichy happy.

FRY HAD ONLY BEEN BACK in Marseille from Vichy a few days before he and his friends were arrested and imprisoned on the SS *Sinaïa*. When finally he got back to the rue Grignan office, Fry was relieved to discover it was still functioning: only those at the Villa Air-Bel had attracted the attention of the police during the marshal's visit. But he learned that in total, over the three-day "emergency," twenty thousand people had been arrested and held on boats, in sports stadiums, and in barracks. When Pétain made his progress through the streets of Marseille, the police had locked the doors of all the cafés and restaurants, trapping the customers inside.

With Danny still under arrest, Lena was deputized to visit the sympathetic Captain Dubois, to see what could be done about freeing him. Dubois was angry that the police had arrested anybody from the Air-Bel ("Que ces gars là sont bêtes!" he said—What a bunch of jerks those guys are!), and he pulled on his jacket right away and set off for the docks. In a matter of minutes Danny was free. Dubois also gave Lena a warning: Fry should tell Charlie Fawcett to leave town. The police were about to arrest him for "pro-British" activities. Lena played dumb, but Dubois was unimpressed. "We know all about him," he said.

At just this time, Charlie Fawcett was in the Gestapo headquarters at Biarritz in the occupied zone of France, waiting for his interrogation to begin. If the French police knew what he had been doing for the Resistance, then it was almost certain that the Gestapo would, too. For Charlie this meant not a prison term, but rather most certainly that he would be executed.

He had been sitting for hours in a corridor, wondering if this was part of the treatment designed to break a suspect down before the interrogation began. He had been watching people come and go, when at last a high-ranking German officer stepped through a door at the far end of the hallway and walked past him, closely followed by somebody who was clearly a French informer. The body language was everything. The Frenchman was hurrying to keep up with the Nazi's long stride, while his master was ignoring him. "The Germans were so arrogant," said Charlie, "that they couldn't even bring themselves to look at the people who were collaborating with them." In a flash he saw his chance, and leaped up to open the exit door for the officer, who naturally ignored him. Then Charlie tagged on behind, not so close that he attracted the Nazi's attention, but close enough that it looked as if he was being led by him. Juggling his suitcase, sculptures and trumpet, he simply followed him across the courtyard, out of the gate and onto the street.

The officer climbed into a limousine; Charlie looked left and right, then set off toward the station, where he crept aboard a train. As it began to pull out of the station, he walked the length of the carriages to the rear end, and jumped off the slowly moving vehicle. Then he crossed the tracks and boarded another train, which left once darkness had descended. The next day he was in Madrid, handing over his secret material to Bunny Torr. Charlie is perhaps the only man to have simply got up and walked out of a Gestapo prison. "It was easy," he maintains.

A few days later Charlie reached Lisbon, where at last he received his reward for all the daring and selflessness he had shown in France. He was, as he said, "cooling his heels" while awaiting a ship that could take him to England. Still wearing his Ambulance Corps greatcoat (Lena thought the reason he was arrested was that he had not dyed it a civilian color as he promised her he would do), Charlie wandered the streets of the capital. One afternoon he came across a poster advertising a performance by the opera singer Lillian Fawcett the next evening at the Théatre Trinidad. Thinking that she might be one of his many distant cousins, Charlie turned up for the show, and was instantly enamored of the beautiful young woman with the heavenly voice he saw on stage. Somehow he thought he recognized her, but he couldn't recall from where. After the performance he went backstage, and letting out a scream, Lillian Fawcett flung her arms about him.

She was Charlie's wife, or rather one of his many wives. In the concentration camps, the girls had all cut their hair off, and made themselves look as ugly and dirty as possible so that the guards would be less inclined to rape them. It was no wonder Charlie had difficulty placing her. But here in Lisbon, restored to her natural beauty, the Hungarian singer found no difficulty in recognizing the American who had saved her life. That night, as Charlie and Lillian sped toward Oporto, they consummated their "marriage" for the first and only time, in the observation car of an express train.

Charlie made it to England, where, as a natural athlete and high-school football star, he was perfect pilot material and was welcomed by the Royal Air Force. Soon he was flying fighter airplanes. During one high-altitude sortie, Charlie found himself short of oxygen, and as he took deep breaths, he began to cough. Back on the ground he saw spots of blood inside his mask. It spelled the return of the tuberculosis that had shadowed his life, but not the end of his war.

FOLLOWING THE RELEASE OF FRY and his associates, there was evidence that police surveillance of the Centre Américain had been stepped up. The evidence was reliable, since it came from Captain Dubois, who assured Fry he was being followed around the clock by plainclothesmen. Fry had obviously made quite an impression at Vichy: the orders came directly from the *Sûreté Nationale*. Fry was not the only one to suffer the attentions of the police. Mary Jayne Gold also wrote of her experience when, at the same time Fry was being followed, she was accosted and taken to the Evêché. They interrogated her in order to discover how she managed to live, and when Mary Jayne innocently admitted what was the truth—that she had money of her own—the police mistakenly assumed she meant she was a high-class prostitute. They put a surveillance team on her, which observed a stream of men visiting her hotel room, where she was ill in bed with a cold but still busy interviewing refugees. This confirmed their suspicion that she was a hooker, and Mary Jayne was subsequently left alone.

It was not all a French farce. In mid-December—suitably enough, in fact, on Friday the thirteenth—the police once again came to the rue Grignan office. This time they were looking for "the one who calls himself Hermant."

Beamish was out of town, and Fry had the presence of mind to tell the officers that Monsieur Hermant had resigned several weeks ago and that he had no idea of his present whereabouts. Fry was assured that there were serious charges against this Hermant, and he promised to let them know if he ever saw the "dirty de Gaullist." At least they still thought he was French; it probably meant the Gestapo was not after Beamish yet. Probably.

Beamish was down at Banyuls that day, to see the Fittkos and hand over the latest batch of names for the refugees who would soon be making their way down to the little coastal resort. The system used was to give Hans and Lisa a torn strip of paper with a code number on it. A refugee, when he arrived, would give them the other half of the same strip, with the matching code number. This was neither a sophisticated nor foolproof method, as Lisa pointed out, since possession of the paper was no guarantee of identity. But it was better than nothing. Lisa Fittko was looking distinctly pale and feverish. The lack of vitamins was affecting everybody, but Beamish thought he had seen the signs of something more serious. Lisa thought she had caught a cold from washing her hair in cold water; then, as her skin turned yellow, she thought she might be suffering from jaundice.

It was turning into an eventful weekend. The same day that the cops came for Beamish, Pétain staged a cabinet putsch with the aim of halting the ambitious maneuverings of his Minister of Justice and Vice-Premier Pierre Laval, who was beginning to do his own deals with the Germans, and whom Fry called a "bitter *parvenu,* scheming grafter and convinced fascist, who engineered the Vichy counter-revolution and presided over its disintegration into naked, brutal police action against his fellow countrymen, in the interests of the Germans." Pétain had the right-wing fanatic Laval arrested (not because he was right-wing but because he was a rival), prompting the German ambassador at Paris, Otto Abetz, to send two truckloads of machine-gun-wielding Wehrmacht troops to Vichy. The ambassador's good friend Laval was soon released and Pétain now knew exactly where he stood in the new order: "I have a rope around my neck and it can be tightened at will," said the old man, according to a reporter Fry spoke to. On Sunday, the ashes of Napoleon's son, the Duc de Reichstadt, were reinterred at Les Invalides in Paris, and Pétain gave lasting offense to the Führer by not attending (he was afraid of traveling into the occupied zone in case he was kidnapped).

When he walked into Fry's office at the Centre Américain on Monday morning, Beamish noticed that a newspaper account of this macabre torch-light ceremony was the only thing on the otherwise bare desk. Fry gave him the news that he was now a wanted man. For a few moments Beamish stared out of the window as if he had not heard, then he turned to Fry and smiled. They shook hands, then Beamish left. It was as simple as that; nothing needed to be said, and there was nothing to say. He returned straightaway to the frontier, not even stopping at his hotel to collect his belongings.

Fry wrote to Eileen the following day that he had never felt so lonely and bereft in his life. It didn't help that little Bill Freier had been surprised by the police and arrested in the midst of his forgery work, or that the Lithuanian Honorary Consul had also been taken away. These two prime sources of fake documents had dried up at the same time that Fry's most trusted lieutenant had been forced to flee. There wasn't time to mourn, though: Beamish needed to be replaced quickly, and Fry had the idea that perhaps it was time to promote Maurice—already acting as a courier between Marseille and Banyuls—and young Jean Gremahling to the illegal side of the work at the Centre Américain de Secours.

Fry called Jean up to his office and explained what was really going on, and what the deal with the British was. Jean had been conscientious but unenthusiastic about his bureaucratic duties. Now, suddenly, the expression on his face changed. "I wasn't prepared for the strength of reaction I got to my revelation," Fry later recalled. "Jean's face lighted up as though I had just told him he had inherited a million dollars, and he looked at me as though I were a combination of General de Gaulle and his best girlfriend."

WHEN BEAMISH REACHED BANYULS he found Lisa Fittko gravely ill. She was hemorrhaging badly and had a high fever. Hans could only try to remain calm. A doctor from nearby Port Vendres had given Lisa camphor injections but told him she needed to get to the hospital at Perpignan straightaway. Hans had miraculously managed not only to hire an automobile but also to find some gasoline. Not being *en règle,* though, he could not risk driving her there. Beamish told him not to worry. They laid Lisa on the rear seat and, ignoring the danger he was in himself, Beamish set off on the road north.

Lisa remembered lying barely conscious in the automobile for a long time outside the hospital. Meanwhile, Beamish was inside attempting to persuade the staff to accept the woman without proper papers and no financial guarantor. He eventually succeeded by handing over the money for a month's treatment in advance—nearly all the cash he had brought with him for his escape across Spain. When a doctor eventually examined Lisa three days later, he told her she had scurvy. It was in fact hepatitis.

Back at Marseille, Fry was dealing with his sense of disappointment over many matters, not least the seemingly abortive mission to influence both the

French government and the American embassy at Vichy. Yet, when the newspapers containing the account of Laval's arrest appeared, people rushed to buy them. The population's apathy concerning current events was overcome. They stood in groups on the streets all over Marseille, engaging in heated conversations on the latest rumor thrown up by the governmental crisis: the Germans were coming to occupy the rest of France and would be at Marseille anytime now. It was the prospect of being released from their humiliating limbo that was both terrifying and exciting for the French of the unoccupied zone. Whatever happened, conditions could now only grow worse for the refugees.

Yet Fry was forced to remember that Vichy was not so monolithically pro-Nazi as he assumed in his more hopeless moments. He wrote to Eileen that

the most interesting thing about Vichy is the intellectual atmosphere. It seems perfectly evident now . . . that everyone was sure, in June, that the war would be over in a few weeks, and that there was nothing left—no choice but to try to work out a *modus vivendi* with the victorious powers. Now that five months have passed, and the war goes on . . . many officials—including some of the very highest—are beginning to think again. The result is a split into two groups, the group of those who believe that Germany and Italy will win in the end, and the group of those who think they will lose. Obviously the control of the press and the radio is in the hands of the former group. . . . But the second group is not without its power, too, and it undoubtedly has the backing of the overwhelming majority of the French people. This is no news to anybody, even the Germans. Monsieur Bargery [*sic*] told me that at the conclusion of his interview with Laval, Marshal Goering said, "Come, come, Monsieur Laval, you know that 95 percent of the French people are against you."

Something was happening, it was true. On the walls there had begun to appear large painted "V"s—well-known by now to be Winston Churchill's symbol for victory. The police had them quickly painted over, but new ones appeared faster than the old were obliterated. Some daring young souls had even started to make public display of their disloyalty to the Vichy regime, albeit in a cryptic fashion. Suddenly, on the streets of Marseille, there were men to be seen walking around with two fishing rods slung crosswise over their backs. The Germans would not understand the gesture, and the authorities would find it difficult and humiliating to try to prosecute a visual pun. For in French, two fishing rods translates as "deux gaules."

It is possible Laval's ejection from the cabinet had been a sign of a stiffening in Pétain's attitude to the Germans. It was indeed an almost encouraging development, and so too was the appointment in December of André Jean-Faure as the new inspector general of concentration camps. Jean-Faure was apparently sympathetic to the sufferings of the refugees and not overtly anti-Semitic. He believed in Pétain's *Révolution Nationale,* and was eloquently craven about France's mistaken experiment in democracy, but he was shocked by what he saw in the camps. He told Pétain they were an "object of severe criticism in the foreign press . . . that is dangerous because justified."

Was it sheer coincidence that Jean-Faure's appointment followed directly from Fry confronting Vichy with the evidence of Danny's report? It is not clear that the new inspectorship was anything more than a public relations exercise on Vichy's part, and Jean-Faure was destined to become a frustrated man as his own damning reports and emergency recommendations were ignored. Nevertheless, Vichy had somehow been embarrassed into making a gesture, and the likelihood is that Fry's efforts were the determining factor, the first coherent outcry against what would soon develop into full-fledged holocaust.

The freezing December days hardly cooled the atmosphere of feverish rumor, and soon an unofficial date of January 1 was set in the minds of the Marsellais for the arrival of German troops. Fry could not afford to ignore the possibility that this was true, and he set off once more to try to convince some famous French personalities of the danger they were in. After writing again to Lipchitz at Toulouse, Fry visited André Gide personally at his house in Cabris, a village near Grasse in the mountains above Cannes. This was easier said than done. By late 1940 there was almost no gasoline to be found, and automobiles—those that still ran along the eerily quiet and empty streets—were propelled on the gases given off by a wood-burning stove attached either to front, rear, or top of the vehicle, or towed behind in a small trailer. *Gazogène,* as this system was called, proved unreliable and slow—the bus Fry took to Cabris stopped half a dozen times while the fire was restoked—but it smelled wonderful. And there was the advantage that *Gazogène* acted as a warning: if the smell of real gasoline was ever in the air, it meant the police were nearby; only *their* autos were allocated any of the precious and dwindling supply of fuel.

"I have been braver in my writings than in my life," wrote Gide at this time, but it was a distinction that was to lose any meaning after his second refusal to allow Fry to help him. The grand old man of French literature, perhaps the only writer he met that Fry was truly in awe of, was subtly and ingeniously resisting the attempts being made by Vichy and Nazi stooges to co-opt him into endorsing the new order. Gide was customarily hard on himself, and on the conduct of his life, and there is a certain amount of evidence that although he did not believe he was in real physical danger, neither was he by this time very much afraid to die. His pronouncements, double entendres and subtle ironies were an early spiritual focus of the resistance to the Germans and their thought police within the collaborationist sections of the French press and government. Gide was certain that he could best help France by staying where he was, and running rings around the enemy using carefully chosen words to communicate secret messages of solidarity to the underground. This he was to do in a series of articles in the newspaper *Le Figaro,* which was subject to strict censorship, but which Gide masterfully evaded to get his anti-Vichy message across. (Varian Fry wrote an essay on these that must stand as the most incisive and sensitive reading of Gide's tactics.)

Fry had a pleasant meeting with the seventy-year-old writer, who was depressed and suffering from what he called nephritis but that looked to Fry like a common cold. Gide was happy, like Aristide Maillol and Marc Chagall, to be on the *Comité de Patronage* of the Centre Américain, but he "flatly refused" to leave France, said Fry. He merely managed to extract from Gide a promise that he would call if he ran into trouble with the authorities. After Fry left, Gide wrote a one-line entry in his famous journal: "All human acts involve more chance than decision." He had decided to let fate take its course.

Fry fared no better in his attempt to persuade Henri Matisse to depart—either before the Germans arrived, or before the French police acted any more like Germans. His studio at Nice was most agreeable, after all, and filled with the artist's birds and his collection of African masks. "If all the talented people left France," Matisse told Fry, "the country would be much poorer. I began an artist's life very poor, and am not afraid to be poor again. I will lock myself up in Nice with my 200 birds and paint." Fry liked Matisse, but was frank in his estimation of the man: "With all his genius, he was the successful bourgeois at heart, happy in the comfort he had surrounded himself with." Fry was afraid that Matisse would starve to death before the end of the war, even if the Germans left him alone. As it was, Matisse survived, but he allowed his birds to die instead of releasing them when the food finally gave out.

THE DAY AFTER BEAMISH had seen Lisa safely into a hospital bed, he set out in a small group across the mountains and into Spain under the guidance of Hans Fittko. Beamish was astonished to see that one of his fellow travelers was Ernst Mai, an old family friend from Berlin. There was also a small, frail old man whom they had to carry part of the way. Hans still counted the trip as one of the quickest and most pleasurable he had undertaken. But Fry's own last trip of the year, taken again with Stéphane Hessel, was a little more interesting.

The two friends caught a train from the Gare St. Charles to Vichy on New Year's Eve, a Tuesday. The first thing Fry did when he arrived at the sleepy spa town was to go and see his friends at the American press bureau. He found them heartily depressed. The big news was that an old associate of Hitler's, an industrialist called Fritz Thyssen, had been arrested with his wife, Amelia (who was a good friend of Mary Jayne Gold), by French police at his Cannes hotel and handed over to the Nazis at the town of Moulins on the demarcation line. It would have been an international scandal, except that under the vigorous new censorship conditions in the fortnight since Pierre Laval's arrest, no reporter had been allowed to file the story. Fry knew of the incident because he had gone straight to Cannes after leaving André Gide, where as planned he met Valeriu Marcu. The Romanian historian told him the news, and Fry had confronted the manager of Thyssen's hotel to confirm the story. It was not that Fry cared anything for a Nazi financier, but he did not like the precedent that was being set. It made him think uneasily of Breitscheid, Hilferding, and Arthur Wolff, all still under house arrest and on the Gestapo's wanted list.

Fry also knew, like the frustrated newsmen, of the arrest and disappearance of Largo Caballero, the ex–prime minister of Republican Spain, who had been living in exile in Paris. Nobody in France knew what had happened to him and whether he too had been handed over to the Germans. But the rest of the world had not even heard of his detention. Mel Most, the Associated Press's second man at Vichy, wanted to get a transfer.

"You get better stories here, but you can't get them out," he complained. "I'd rather be in Berlin. I wouldn't get such good stuff there but at least I could get out what I got."

Fry told them he had something that might cheer them up. Chaminade had been hard at work, and given Fry what he claimed revealed in detail all the arrangements made between Vichy and the Nazis for a planned wholesale extradition of exiles back to Germany and Spain. If true, it was a blueprint for mass murder. The journalists whistled. They told Fry to be very careful. Even if the report had been woven out of whole cloth—not unlikely, considering Chaminade was the source—it was an extremely dangerous document to carry around. Fry told them he was taking it to the American embassy, to see if the Chargé d'Affaires would agree to take it out of the country by diplomatic pouch. Archambault, the New York Times staffer at Vichy, was skeptical.

The embassy was closed for the New Year holiday, but the doorman promised to give Chaminade's report to a secretary the next day. Fry scribbled a note to accompany the document, and the doorman gave him an envelope marked "The Foreign Service of the United States," into which he slipped all the papers. He addressed the envelope to Dr. Frank Kingdon, at the Emergency Rescue Committee offices on East Forty-second Street. On a calling card, Fry left a message for the secretary asking him not, under any circumstances, to mail the document back to him at Marseille if it could not be sent to America by diplomatic pouch. Fry underlined "under no circumstances" three times. If the French censor came across it, Fry could be in serious trouble.

Then he left Vichy with Stéphane still accompanying him as a bodyguard. They talked things over on the train and decided to try—where the journalists had failed—to alert the world to Caballero's arrest. With some time to kill at Lyon awaiting their connection, they left the Gare de Perrache and hopped on a trolley car heading for the Place Bellecour in the middle of the city, where they went to the central post office. From there they cabled to Eileen's sister (for purposes of camouflage) a cryptic message elaborating Caballero's plight:

FIELDING ESPECIALLY WORRIED ABOUT HIS EARNEST FRIENDS STOP MAJESTIC MAN HAD SUDDEN STROKE TWO WEEKS AGO LAST MONDAY AND HAS BEEN UNABLE SPEAK WORDS SINCE STOP GRAND FELLOW BUT STAFF DOCTORS REFUSE COMMENT AND DAUGHTERS FEAR WORST STOP ASK YOU INFORM UNCLE ALVAREZ ED JAMES HUGH AND CREIGH STOP IMPOSSIBLE BREAK NEWS BY CABLE BUT FEEL EVERYBODY SHOULD KNOW

Incredibly, someone (probably Eileen herself) understood what it referred to, for on January 4, 1941, the news of Largo Caballero's disgraceful betrayal by the French was flashed around the world on the front pages of British and American newspapers. Fry learned of the success of his transmission from a four-line AP report in a Swiss newspaper a few days later. It was a small but heartening victory to round off what had been a long, hard year.

PART 5

ENEMIES

CHAPTER 19

THE FRIEND

In scuffling they change Rapiers.
—STAGE DIRECTION, HAMLET, V

WHEN FRY WENT to the office on December 26, he heard that another of his protégés, a young photographer from Paris, George Reisner, had committed suicide while he was at Nice with Henri Matisse. Reisner, Fry noted, "had been waiting for his American visa since July and the strain had proved too much for him. A few days after the funeral we got a note from the Consulate that the visa had been authorized at last." The incident seemed emblematic of the behavior of the American Foreign Service, and the consequences of that behavior. But Fry still hoped his report would somehow reach the free world.

Soon afterward, he received a package by mail from the American embassy. With mounting horror and disbelief, he opened it to discover Chaminade's incriminating report. Insult was added to injury by the accompanying letter from a secretary: "Serious trouble will ensue if the Embassy finds that you in future make use of official envelopes for your correspondence." Worse still, the package had been opened by the French censor. However, the returned letter was the least of his worries. Fry was now fighting battles on many fronts. The first bombshell had exploded just before Christmas, when he had received an anonymous message—it sounded almost like an order—to meet its author in the bar of the Splendide. At the appointed time, Fry left the Centre Américain and hurried to his old hotel, where he recognized with sinking heart the face of Jay Allen. He was sitting drinking good Scotch with a rather elderly lady who was introduced as Margaret Palmer.

In 1940, Allen was something of a name to conjure with. Fry called him "Jay Allen, the American journalist," as if there were only one, and the expression was not wholly ironic. The thirties had seen, in the slipstream of Hemingway's continually rising star, a breed of mannish writer emerge who shared the tough-talking, war-chasing, hunting, fishing, and bull-fighting pastimes of the great pack leader. The Hemingway imitators and hangers-on succeeded in varying but always lesser degrees, and Allen might be classed as one of the *better* minor Hemingways. In fact he and his wife, Ruth, were part of the inner orbit of the crowd around "Papa" (Ruth was a good friend of Pauline Pfeiffer, the second Mrs. Hemingway). Like Hemingway, Allen had been a newspaper correspondent in the Spanish Civil War, from which he still derived considerable prestige. He had arrived in France via Casablanca because he feared, or perhaps just liked to believe, that it was unsafe for him to travel through Spain.

While in North Africa, Allen had managed to get an interview with the Pétainist French military commander, General Maxime Weygand. Now he fancied having a shot at interviewing the marshal himself, and was thus en route to Vichy. This information was delivered by way of greeting, in the hearty, booming tones of a fully paid-up member of the Hemingway entourage. The impression he gave was that this war belonged to Jay Allen. Miss Palmer, clearly an amanuensis, sat gazing up at him with watery-eyed admiration.

Fry, as much a temperamental opposite to Allen as one could possibly imagine, sat aghast as he was informed, en passant, that Allen was also Fry's replacement sent from New York by the Emergency Rescue Committee. Fry had recently been exchanging bad-tempered cables with the "pals" in New York on the subject of sending over a "friend" to supplant him. Fry had failed to discover who they had in mind, and he had steadfastly refused to return until after a period of consultation and training with whoever arrived in France. His was a sensitive and complicated operation, he had pleaded; he couldn't just disappear. Nevertheless, cables signed by Frank Kingdon had been arriving with regularity, telling Fry to prepare to leave.

Allen said he didn't see himself actually *visiting* the office, of course, or even meeting the staff. That was what Miss Palmer was here for. She would be Allen's go-between, and could relay his orders to the Centre Américain while he was off tracking down journalistic scoops and generally winning the war. He believed his credentials would spare him the unwelcome attention that Fry had encountered from the police.

Fry hardly knew where to begin to untangle the affronts to his competence from the frightening misapprehensions about the nature of the underground work and what it actually involved. He was shocked and almost speechless at the manifest absurdity of what was taking place. "I assume you are making preparations to leave," said Allen. "You will consider me *in charge* as on January 1." Fry could only concede.

Back at the office, though, he convened a council of war. Gathering around his closest associates, Fry told them that if they wanted him to stay on, they had to mobilize every ounce of support they could find, and make as much noise as possible. Everybody in the office was worried: they knew a disaster would ensue if Fry suddenly vanished. A cable war with New York quickly developed, with Lena firing the first salvo:

THIS MESSAGE SENT REQUEST CLIENTS STAFF PLEASE CONTACT INGRID EXPLAIN FRYS LEAVING THIS POINT DISASTROUS WORK WELFARE VERY LIVES HUNDREDS ALL IMPLORE EMERESCUE NOT INSIST HIS LEAVING JUST NOW

A reply stated that Allen was replacing Fry because of "Washington and local pressure," and the fact that staff expenditures in Marseille had been "OVERLARGE CONSIDERING EMIGRATION RESULTS." Melvyn Fagen (soon to be Colonel Fagen), Lena's betrothed and now a worker at the Forty-second Street offices, sympathetically cabled that Ingrid Warburg in his opinion had made a "FUNDAMENTALLY INCORRECT DECISION." So there were some in New York who were still on Fry's side. It was a sign of hope.

"The Friend is dictatorial and stupid," Fry wrote to Eileen as soon as he had taken Allen's measure. "He is incapable of listening to anyone (proverbially) and he is utterly uninformed about what we are doing and apparently quite uninterested in learning. He just keeps bullying me into going, without ever stopping to consider the consequences." Meanwhile, Lena was tigerishly defending Fry. She cabled Fagen again, telling him that Ingrid's claims were "baseless." "EXPENDITURES NOT OVERLARGE CONSIDERING AMOUNT WORK," she said—which was by now something of an understatement. Fry and his employees had enabled more than three hundred escapes and emigrations by now, and with the French deciding suddenly to relax their moratorium on exit visas at the start of the new year, the export business looked like it would once again soon be in full swing. Even during the dark days of November and December when the border was sealed tight as a drum, scores of people had successfully managed to cross into Spain using the Fittko route. The truth was, the committee in New York had the bargain of the century, but was about to throw it all away because of what looked like an internal power play.

In the meantime, the underground locomotive could not be allowed to decelerate. Fritz Thyssen's "official kidnapping," as Fry described it, alerted him to the urgency of getting out of France as many clients as possible as fast as he could. With Chaminade's report of plans for Franco-German mass extraditions, it looked like the ax was about to fall on them all. The paradox of exit visas suddenly becoming available for no apparent reason near the end of January could perhaps be explained by the fact that the Gestapo had finished going through its lists. Maybe everybody it sought was cooped up in camps ready for collection, in *residences forcées,* or on some list held at the border. Perhaps they just wanted the rest of the Jews to get lost. Whatever it was, Fry knew the best thing was to move fast. And many endangered clients—like the *Bouline* four, or Breitscheid, Hilferding, and Arthur Wolff—were still interned or under house arrest. They needed to be sprung before they could be spirited away to Germany.

NOBODY KNOWS WHY Fry suddenly moved out of the Villa Air-Bel that December. It could have been that after the police raid and the arrests, he could not risk the association of a house with a criminal record, so to speak. André Breton was manifestly a bad boy, and Victor Serge a dangerous person to have around—in fact, Fry had ordered him to leave the villa straight after their brief imprisonment on the SS *Sinaïa.* Fry's residence for the next few months at the Hotel Beauvau on the Vieux Port might also have been determined by his need for a private life. The villa originally served that purpose, but it was so much a commune by now that the cerebral and solitary Fry may have felt the need simply to get away. Plus, it was a perishingly cold season and there was hardly any heating for the many fireplaces in the large house out at La Pomme, where the rain came pouring through the skylights. Fry might have relished the slender comforts still on offer at a commercial establishment—and the gangster Sabiani ran the hotel restaurant, where for a price one could eat real food. Roasted chestnuts were on sale on the streets of Marseille that winter, and dates and figs abounded, but the staples had disappeared onto the black market, and Sabiani's was one of its rare outlets.

Fry's move could also have been prompted by the need for a different sort of privacy, an intimate one he did not feel he could share with the people he knew. Or he could have wanted proximity to the new offices at a hectic time: business was now so brisk that the Centre Américain de Secours had been forced to relocate to larger premises, at 18 Boulevard Garibaldi. Now there were three large rooms for seeing clients in addition to Fry's own offices, and work was initially obstructed not by leather goods, but by the bulbous hair dryers of the beauty parlor the place had so recently been.

Whatever the reason for leaving Villa Air-Bel, Fry and Clovis—a large and unruly black poodle he had recently acquired and failed hopelessly to house-train—moved into the grandly appointed hotel. The first night there, Clovis emptied his bowels all over the floor of the bathroom, and Fry was in terror of what the *bonne* would do. When she came in the next morning he cringed. But she took one look and said, "C'est un peu mou. Est-ce qu-il est malade?" He was happy at the Beauvau after that. In fact, despite everything, Fry was simply happy.

"The truth is that I like this job better than any I have ever had in my life," Fry wrote to Eileen. "One of the other American relief workers here has called me 'the ideal type of social worker, intelligent, humane, and highly social.'" Eileen must have blinked at that last description. But Fry explained how he felt he was "using all my capacities . . . for the first time in my life. That is probably why I like it so much, why I flourish so under it, why I am so well and happy, sleep so soundly, eat so hugely, etc. . . ." The pace and pressure of Fry's existence had also succeeded in unbolting his aggression, which was probably necessary for his survival. But the combativeness Fry needed in France could not simply be turned off, and some of it spilled over into his communications with New York—especially now the walking insult named Jay Allen was at large. "The pals always do the wrong thing, as far as I can see: viewed from here, they seem like a bunch of blithering, slobbering idiots."

At Vichy, Allen had failed to see Pétain, whose own ministers were lucky if they spoke to the senile old man during his daily hour of lucidity. Instead, he was roving around the unoccupied zone, meeting with Fry's contacts and making a quite dangerously visible show of himself. Allen was particularly friendly with Randolfo Pacciardi, the genius of the phantom boat debacle, and he was increasingly angry at Fry for still being in France. Fry noticed that Allen had withdrawn 152,000 francs from the business without saying what it was for, and this in turn angered *him,* because in Fry's opinion Allen was not yet the new director, and the war with the committee in New York was continuing.

Poor Eileen was again in the unhappy position of mediator, and was herself losing patience with Fry's apparently belligerent attitude. "You really are making a great mistake in being so full of complaints in your letter to the ERC. They are as good as they can be, which everyone knows is pretty poor. The job you have undertaken is enormous, but you *could* have shut your eyes and come home, and you can hardly blame them because you didn't."

That, thought Fry, was to miss the point entirely. He wasn't blaming them at all for his not returning home; he was blaming them for their incompetence in sending Jay Allen and for their continuing slowness in dealing with the detailed visa requests he was sending to New York, as unto a black hole.

"People here think you have done pretty well despite your insults to your fellow workers," wrote Eileen, which only further incensed him. People's lives were in danger in France, and Fry had no time to care about whom he had insulted, or what they thought of him. Such was his growing despair that he had deliberately begun to establish a certain financial independence for the Centre Américain over the past couple of months. Mary Jayne Gold had donated 500,000 francs when she first became involved back in October, and another 200,000 at the end of the year. Peggy Guggenheim had given 500,000 francs at the beginning of December, and at least another 500,000 had been contributed by other donors. Even Oppy had pitched in with 200,000 francs. In addition, there were the proceeds from the currency exchanges arranged through Kourillo. It was true that Fry was by no means free of the need for New York money (Harold Oram had raised $100,000 between the beginning of July and December 31, 1940). But he felt proprietorial about the little empire he had built up, and he was certainly unprepared to surrender it without a fight to a baboon like Allen. Fry's attitude was hardening.

In late January, Mirkine Guetzevich, one of Fry's clients who had been a law professor in Paris, was ready to leave the country. He had $8,000 in gold coins to unload, and Fry agreed to credit him with $15,000 paper in New York in exchange. Given that the unofficial franc-dollar rate in France was by now three times the Vichy value, it was a good deal for both parties. The gold was handed over, and suddenly the atmosphere of strained cooperation between Fry and Allen was shattered. For over a month, Allen had barely tolerated Fry's continuing presence; he certainly would not suffer executive fiscal decisions to be made by him. On January 20, he finally laid his cards on the table. "I must request you *formally* to do nothing without discussing it with me, otherwise I shall take *effective* steps to make you realize what your present position with the ERC actually is," Allen wrote in a furious memo. "I will moreover speak to Mirkine Guetzevitch and explain matters. Surely you do not want to provoke a situation, do you?'

That was exactly what Fry wanted. His friend Harold Oram innocently clarified the mood of confrontation with a letter that arrived several days later. It seemed to stress the difference between how Fry, on the ground in France, and how his "pals" in New York saw the refugees. "If Albert Einstein could be brought to America today," Oram confided, "we could raise one million within a short time by exhibiting him throughout the country. [Pablo] Casals is probably worth one hundred thousand. Picasso fifty thousand. Your trio [Werfel, Mann, and Feuchtwanger] brought in thirty-five thousand. Since their arrival we have had nothing good to offer the public and they are pretty shopworn by this time. See if you can dig up something big."

It was a measure of how Fry had changed since he had arrived at Marseille back in August that now a monetary value, placed on certain "names," seemed irrelevant and distasteful. He was judging people on a different basis by now, and wanted to save everybody he could, famous or not. Fry also had the resources and expertise that meant he could afford to defy New York if need be. His correspondence with Eileen at this time reflects his simmering passions. "I have devoted six months of my life to creating an organization which is known all over free France as the one hope of the refugees." he said.

> As for Jay, he has not had the time—or, apparently, interest—to listen to what I have learned in six months of work here. He has not come once to the office, and almost all of the time he has not even been in Marseille. Yet on the occasions of his rare and fleeting visits—during which he does not often have the time to see me—he takes a dictatorial manner which I consider wholly unjustified and insulting.

"COMMITTEE FULL CONFIDENCE IN YOU. AVOIDANCE CLASH WELCOME. LOVE: OTTO ALBERT," cabled Beamish, now arrived in New York, in an attempt to calm the situation. "Of course at this end the villain is Mildred [Adams] . . ." wrote Eileen, sensible to Fry's reasoning and still playing the peacemaker. "She has sent unauthorized cables, and certainly sides with Jay. She is a dishonest woman, and not well meaning as far as I can see. but you simply MUST have confidence in the intelligence—I mean it—and the cooperation and willing support of your friends on 42 St." Needless to say, at this point Fry had nothing of the sort. His colleagues at other aid agencies were weighing in with their support, and Dr. Charles Joy of the Unitarians cabled on his behalf to New York:

> ALL I KNOW OR HEAR OF ALLEN FORCES ME TO SAME CONCLU-
> SION. . . . BELIEVE FRY'S LEAVING DISASTER FIRST MAGNITUDE
> DO NOT BELIEVE FURTHER COOPERATION UNITARIANS EMERES-
> CUE POSSIBLE UNDER ALLEN HIS PLAN FANTASTIC STRONGLY
> URGE YOU TO BACK FRY.

"If the committee backs Allen, I will continue to cooperate with you to the full extent of my power," Joy told Fry. Captain Donald Darling, Fry's British diplomat friend at Lisbon, contributed his own testimony: "For the sake of the British soldiers in France it is of crucial importance that Fry should remain." Such support simply could not be ignored.

Fry in turn reminded Eileen that he had by now lost the editorial job at the

Foreign Policy Association, not that he particularly cared. "Certainly the job I'm doing here is far more interesting and, I think, far more important than the FPA one," he said. "In fact I now realize (at last! you will say) how really piddling that job was." Now, said Fry, he was free to remain in France indefinitely, and that also strengthened his position.

Realizing that they had acted insensitively, and impressed by Fry's shrewd politicking, the committee attempted to draw back a little from their previous commanding position. Ingrid Warburg sent a cable on January 30 that sounded like an offer of a cease-fire:

CABLES SIGNED KINGDON UNAUTHORISED HAVE FULL CONFI-
DENCE IN YOU WILL DO EVERYTHING POSSIBLE TO REACH AMICA-
BLE SOLUTION HAVE PATIENCE KEEP THIS CONFIDENTIAL

It was too late. Fry's anger had overtaken him, and he wrote a letter to Forty-second Street that altered the terms of the conflict altogether. "There is another aspect of this question, too," he revealed. "This office is not your office: it is an independent committee consisting of various American citizens residing in France. It has received funds from many sources, including some very substantial ones." The Centre Américain is mine, Fry effectively declared. He dared them to cut him off and take the consequences in terms of catastrophic bad publicity back home. He believed that no criticism of his work could stand up under scrutiny, and that therefore he had the whip hand.

In short, I cannot adequately express my dismay at the bullying, pig-headed, bull-in-the-china-shop attitude of your "friend." . . . I am not accustomed to being addressed as a servant by anybody, and least of all by Mr. Allen. Read this letter again, and make up your own minds.

With a two- or three-week delay in the mails between Europe and America, Fry would have no option but to wait for the committee's decision. Until then, Jay Allen was still whirling around Marseille convinced that he was in charge of the operation and setting up his own plans for evacuating refugees.

FRY HAD OTHER problems to consider besides Jay Allen. Unoccupied France had not been invaded by the Germans at the beginning of 1941, as the people of Marseille had predicted and feared. Vichy and Gestapo hostility to Jews and anti-Nazis was entrenching itself, though, and the best option for the refugees remained somehow to get them away from the mainland. Although exit visas were once again, inexplicably, being granted, not every applicant was given one. Fry said the process was still shrouded in mystery, and he could only assume that those to whom visas were denied were in more than average danger. Still, a lot could be done. Of the three main categories of refugee, the one with transit visas for Spain and Portugal was the luckiest. Even without an exit visa, such refugees could take the Fittko route over the Pyrenees into Spain, and many continued to do so.

Those who had exit visas but could not travel through Spain might still get away. France's small colonial presence in the Caribbean meant that by early February, regular sailings of commercial ships would be taking people to Martinique. Because Martinique was a French "department" (region), it still counted as France, and travel there was possible. New York, Cuba, and Latin America could then all be reached from the land platform Martinique afforded. True, French colonies were still Vichy-controlled, with all that implied, but it was far less likely that meaningful Gestapo influence extended so distantly, and the effort to bring a refugee back once he or she had landed in the Caribbean would have been immense, and the logistics impractical. So in February Fry began to buy sea passages for those for whom he managed to secure exit visas to leave continental France, on the basis that the money would be repaid to the ERC in New York so that it could then be recycled to the next wave of travelers. Unfortunately, such repayments proved rare indeed.

That left the third category of refugees, those whose exit visas had been refused, and who could not travel through Spain either. For them, another avenue of escape had to be invented.

The British had been pouring over the Pyrenees, usually fetching up in Spanish internment camps since Bunny Torr's agreement with Franco had been superseded by Himmler's. Meanwhile, Frederic Fitch had left by the Fittko route and so by now had his temporary replacement (this was Captain Treacy, who was shot down and killed a few days after rejoining his squadron in England). The new commander of the British troops at Marseille was a pilot officer called Murchie, whom Fry renamed Murphy in *Surrender on Demand*. He decided that the soldiers should no longer go through to Spain, and that North Africa or the Middle Eastern coast was a better idea. Murchie, who had made his way south after a forced landing in occupied France (an increasing occurrence with Britain's air force now raiding the continent) struck Fry as another *mythomane*, a cloak-and-dagger specialist of theatrical overcaution, which alternated with reckless overconfidence. But Fry agreed to go along with Murchie's plan to smuggle people by boat to places like Syria,

Gibraltar, Rabat, Casablanca, and Dakar, so long as soldiers and not refugees were used as guinea pigs. The worst that could happen to them was imprisonment. The refugees, without the protection of the Geneva Conventions, could be shot.

Charles Vinciléoni, the gangster who ran the restaurant Dorade, was the facilitator of this new operation. As a black market shipping magnate he could procure crew cards for soldiers on merchant vessels bound for the various destinations, and his prices were reasonable—between thirty and seventy dollars per passage. Soon, troops were being successfully ferried over the Mediterranean. Some jumped overboard from those ships that sailed past Gibraltar and swam ashore. Others, once a ship reached Oran, were usually interned again by Vichy, but this was counted an improvement over their internment in France, from where they would eventually have been sent to Germany. Because nothing ever seemed to go wrong at either end of the voyages, Fry began to send "medium risk" refugees along as well. These were the ones who could not afford to apply for, or had been refused, the exit visa (*visa de sortie*), or who did not have transit visas for Spain and Portugal. He calculated that, unlike the soldiers, his people would not end up in prison.

The refugees, whom Fry had supplied with false identity cards and who generally spoke French, managed on arrival at Oran, or Dakar, to blend into a less hostile environment than they had endured in Vichy France. The movie *Casablanca* (in which almost every minor character is Jewish, although it is never mentioned), is the best illustration of what the conditions in these cities were actually like. It was hardly a sanctuary, but the refugees were far better off than they had been in Marseille, which was crawling with undercover Germans by this point.

Emilio Lussu, the serious Italian, and Pacciardi, the unserious one, were also sending their own people to Oran because the Italian Republicans could on no account attempt to go through Spain. Lussu, in his careful and deliberate way, was slowly establishing a reliable underground railroad overland from there to Casablanca. He planned eventually to figure a way to carry his Italians onward from Casablanca to Lisbon and then to Britain, or, rearmed, back into Italy to join the freedom fighters. Fry was paying for the sea passage of these anti-Fascists and that was the extent of the arrangement. Lussu promised that once all his men had reached Casablanca, he would open the railroad to Fry's refugees. Until then, Lussu's obligation had to be to members of his "Justice and Liberty" group, and Fry fully understood. This left his own people stranded at Oran, but as long as they stayed where they were, they would be all right.

ON THE LAST DAY of January, Fry and Stéphane Hessel traveled a little way east along the coast to Toulon. It had been a draining month for Fry, the last week perhaps the most draining of all, and he badly needed a few days' rest. The two men booked into the Hotel Continental Métropole on the Boulevard de Strasbourg, and over the weekend, sitting with Stéphane drinking white Burgundy at the Café-Restaurant Jane Madeleine, Fry tried to process and order in his mind the sequence of events that had recently taken place.

Although he disliked their arrogance and pomposity, Fry had felt duty-bound to help Rudolf Breitscheid and Rudolf Hilferding leave France. The ex–Social Democrat leader of the Reichstag and his right-hand man had eventually been persuaded to flee their *résidence forcée* illegally, and to travel from Arles to Marseille in a gangster auto that Fry had hired, together with a beefy chauffeur, at great expense. Then, as he sat at the Dorade awaiting their arrival late on the agreed night, a very angry driver walked in and announced that the two politicians had refused to come. He said he had driven all the way to the Hotel Forum at Arles to collect them, and they had sent him away as if he were an impertinent salesman. Charlie Fawcett's estimation of the bothersome Germans—"a couple of sons of bitches"—was then echoed somewhat more forcefully by the driver.

Fry had planned to send the two Rudolfs into hiding in a safe room he had negotiated within the gangsters' warren of the Vieux Port, until he could put them on one of Vinciléoni's cargo boats to North Africa. But in the time that elapsed between then and their aborted pickup, Breitscheid and Hilferding had been told by the *sous-préfet* at Arles that they were entitled to exit visas, and would soon receive them. This explained the newfound confidence. Fry, though, felt very uneasy about this latest development: if Breitscheid and Hilferding were already under house arrest because Hitler wanted to lay hands on them, it was illogical to assume Vichy would let them go, no matter what they had been told. But Fry's advice to continue with the illegal escape was ignored. "They thought of themselves as great statesmen," Fry wrote acidly, "and were unaccustomed to taking orders from anybody, and not very favorably disposed to accept even polite suggestions, at least when they came from me."

Then, in the early part of the preceding week, Oppy told Fry he had managed to book passage for himself and his family on a steamer called the *Winnipeg*. This was the first Fry had heard about the Martinique route, which began officially on January 24, 1941, when the penultimate remaining member of Fry's old "first team" set sail. His skepticism about the two Rudolfs' exit visas was allayed on Monday morning, January 27, when both of them visited the offices on Boulevard Garibaldi and flourished beneath Fry's nose their own, fully stamped papers, which they had just picked up from the prefecture. He was baffled at the sudden change of heart by Vichy, but gladly admitted defeat and wished them bon voyage. In fact the next boat for Martinique was leaving about ten days later, on February 4, and their old secretary, Bedrich Heine, now working for Fry, went to book the tickets for them. That was when the trouble started.

Every single cabin on the ship had already been sold, and not even a third-class place was left. The steamer had been converted to accommodate bunks in the hold, and there were still some of those free, but it was beneath Breitscheid's dignity to travel thus, never mind that of his wife, and he refused to sail until something better came along. Fry's jaw dropped in disbelief. He frantically attempted to persuade Breitscheid to take the chance and get away while he could, but again his advice was spurned. The politician returned to Arles still convinced that Hitler would never dare touch him. Then, for the first time in his career, Hilferding decided to "disobey" his domineering master, and bought a steerage ticket for himself. Bedrich Heine left a request for extra places at the booking office in the hope that Breitscheid would change his mind. The next day, though, he was informed by Monsieur Berthomieu, the director of the shipping line, that the steamer was full.

At least one of the troublesome duo would be getting away, thought Fry— that was, until Friday, when he heard the exit visas of both Breitscheid and Hilferding had been summarily withdrawn. Then Lena told him she was leaving for Lisbon in a few days' time. That evening an exhausted and down-hearted Fry called Stéphane Hessel and asked him if he felt like spending a weekend on the Côte d'Azur, getting good and drunk.

OFFICERS OF THE Italian Armistice Commission had moved into the Splendide, terrifying Walter Mehring and forcing him to look for accommodation elsewhere. This was a problem in itself, because his provisional permission to live at Marseille and not in a concentration camp specified he stay at that particular hotel. Once again Baby was in a tangle, and after Fry got back to Marseille from Toulon it occurred to him that not only was there was a ticket for the Tuesday sailing to Martinique, but there was no longer any Rudolf Hilferding to fill the bunk. It was time for Mehring to make his bid for freedom.

Next morning the small, scruffy poet nervously shuffled in line toward the customs point at the Marseille docks. Beyond was the shimmering mirage of a steamship bound for salvation; in the foreground was an officer of the *Sûreté Nationale du Port,* minutely scrutinizing the papers of each prospective passenger. When Mehring's turn came the officer turned to a shelf behind him, and from the "M" section pulled out one of a series of cards. It bore the following instruction:

Walter Mehring
Interdit de sortir de France
Décision de la Kundt Commission

He was forbidden to leave France on the orders of the Gestapo. They had trapped him at last. The French official disappeared into a back room, and left Mehring sweating profusely. "He called the Prefecture," said Mehring, "and ten minutes later he gave back to me my papers and said, smiling, 'C'est peut-être un autre Walter Mehring. Partez!'" *It must be another Walter Mehring. Go on!* He went. After all his misfortunes, Baby was at last handed just the piece of luck he needed. A month later, he arrived in Florida. A month after that, Mehring was in Hollywood, writing for the movies.

Breitscheid and Hilferding were arrested by French police at their hotel on the following Saturday evening. Breitscheid's wife wrote to Fry that he said to one of the officers, when they arrived later at Vichy, "Why do you torture us this way if you only want to extradite us in the end?" "You have a very low opinion of France, sir," replied the detective, who declared on "parole d'honneur" (on his word of honor) that it was not a question of handing the two politicians over to Hitler at all. But they were kept incommunicado, denied the right to see a lawyer, and sure enough delivered to the Germans at the demarcation line early on Monday, February 10. When Mrs. Breitscheid tearfully pleaded with the American embassy to do something, it was pointed out to her that Article Nineteen allowed for such extraditions. The embassy refused to issue a protest or raise the matter with the State Department. Indeed, neither the Chargé d'Affaires nor the ambassador would even agree to receive her.

Fry discovered what had happened when he arrived at the office that Monday morning, and he straight away called his friend Archambault at the *New York Times* bureau to give him the story. Minutes later, an old acquaintance walked in. It was Alfred Apfel, the lawyer whom Fry had first met five years earlier at the Pension Stern in Berlin. At that time, Apfel was defending the accused in the Reichstag fire show trial. Now, he was yet another law-abiding refugee from the Nazis, living proof of Germany's essential illegitimacy. They talked over the weekend's depressing events and Fry warned Apfel to be careful himself. The reserves of denial that kept so many refugees intact seemed to desert him. Suddenly, as Fry put it, "a shadow passed over his face," and Apfel slipped from his chair, clutching at his chest. Fry leaped up and managed to catch him, and held the lawyer as he died. Apfel had a weak heart but he was by no means a weak man. Even so, just the realization of his true situation was enough, coming in a flash, to snuff him out.

Fry said this was the most shocking thing that had happened to him in all his time in France so far. It showed vividly how close to the edge were all the refugees, and it reminded him that he could not give up.

The next day Hilferding was dead, too. The Germans had found the poison he carried, but he managed nevertheless to hang himself in his prison cell shortly after arriving at Paris for a stopover on the way back to Germany. Breitscheid was sent to Buchenwald concentration camp, where he survived until August 1944. The Nazis claimed that he was the victim of an American air raid. For once, they were telling the truth.

Fry was left to wonder, rhetorically, "Is there no bottom to the baseness of Vichy?"

CHAPTER 20

FULL STEAM AHEAD

O NE BRIGHT MONDAY MORNING in the middle of March, Fry arrived at the Boulevard Garibaldi offices to hear a glorious piece of news: Jay Allen had been arrested. It signaled the de facto end of the running battle that had begun back in December, and which Fry would soon learn he had won by a technical knockout.

Allen had finally run out of patience in the middle of February, and had turned up at the Centre Américain (it was his first visit) screaming, shouting, and slamming doors. Fry's account of the episode recalls the farcical scene. "He said he would like to break my neck," Fry wrote to Eileen.

> He promised to do his utmost against me as soon as he got back to New York. . . . All during our conversation he boasted how important he was and how successful (". . . I'm a bit of a success . . .") and promised to have me fired out on my ear the minute he got back. He said he had never hated anyone so much in his life, that I was slippery and dishonest, that I was a "careerist" (what is a "careerist"?), that I was "washed up," that he would "show me". . . . It was really a regular tornado he let loose in my office. . . . Miss Palmer says he is a genius, but I am inclined to think now he is slightly nuts.

He stormed out, and then sent a note demanding that Fry meet him at his hotel. There, Allen thrust at him a garbled account of their irreconcilable differences. It amounted to nothing more than a character assassination, and Fry naturally refused to sign the document. After more shouting and threats,

Fry retired. "I don't like him very much, frankly," he concluded. "But far madder than he is the choice of him as delegate. My god, my god." Soon afterward, Allen announced he was going to Vichy for forty-eight hours, and that was the last Fry heard of him for a fortnight.

Although Allen was out of the frame, at least for a while, Fry remained under intense pressure to return home. But he knew that the tide of refugees, and the fantastic opportunity opened up by the regular sailings to Martinique, decreed he must stay. His broadside to the ERC in New York had clarified his alienation, "because it made *quite clear for the first time,*" wrote Eileen, "that you consider yourself a representative of various outfits, not even primarily apparently of the ERC. This has made a good deal of difference in the attitude of people here who are on your side, and as for your opponents . . ." Well, that was just too bad. There were still a number of refugees to worry about who had no chance of leaving on the blessed steamers. Arthur Wolff, for example, had been at the Hotel Forum at Arles when Breitscheid and Hilferding were arrested, and he had turned up soon after at Marseille begging Fry to hide him. Fortunately, the room in the Vieux Port was still available, and Fry had put him there, secure in a tiny space behind piles of boxes, until something further could be done. The Bernhards were living in a *maison de passe*—like a certain sort of motel—where the *patron* simply assumed they were enjoying an illicit middle-aged affair. But they could not stay there indefinitely. There were others Fry suspected of being on the Gestapo's list, as well, but so far he was in the dark. In the meantime, he had various agents, including the French writer Giono, searching out properties for rent in the countryside around Marseille. These, like the farm he rented at Rocher d'Ongle, near Manosque, and a cottage at Revest-des-Broust, were out-of-the-way places Fry planned to use as safe houses and long-term residences for those people whose exit from France was particularly problematic, or even impossible.

It was a curious mental space in which to exist: on the one hand Fry was fully occupied with arranging emigrations, resisting the police, and fighting the State Department and consulates; on the other, he was preparing "postmortem" arrangements for when he would no longer be around. But he would be around as long as possible, and continued to fight his rearguard action against New York through Eileen. "How do they expect their work to be continued if I leave?" he asked her.

Obviously they don't expect it to continue. Does that mean they think it's finished, or that they have lost interest in it, or what? I've never been able to understand. As for "switching between requests to be relieved and allowed to come home and frantic refusals (literally 'frantic'?) to come" there's no inconsistency whatever in that. I asked to be relieved; they replied "Come home without being." I replied "That's not what I asked." Perfectly clear and consistent, as I see it.

Lena's departure had hit Fry badly ("I again feel depressed and lonely . . ." he told Eileen), but he soon hired the vibrant Lucie Heymann as a replacement. He liked her as an office manager, although he still felt that a "severely repressed spinster" would have been more suitable. Meanwhile, Ludwig Copperman, another young German employee who had wisely renamed himself Louis Coppée, was falling heavily for Lucie's daughter. Erich Lewinsky was one of the highly qualified refugees who joined the staff before fleeing to safety in America, and he quickly took responsibility for many of the "cases." Fry also hired Austrian-born Paul Schmierer, and his Russian wife, Vala. He even hired Charles Wolff, the Paris journalist and Konrad Heiden's friend, whom Miriam Davenport had run into at Toulouse on her way south during the *pagaille* of the previous summer. Wolff, together with the Alsatian Jacques Weisslitz, would be in charge of looking after the many intellectuals who had fled from the Strasbourg region after the German invasion. The plan was eventually to turn the Villa Air-Bel into a reception center for them.

Although Fry was glad that Jay Allen was no longer around, he had no idea of the reason for the arrest. Thus, his relief was mixed with dread. "Suppose they torture him?" he wondered, not without a certain relish. "Will he be able to keep his mouth shut about us and our work? Or will he break down and talk when the matches are pushed up under his fingernails and the fire bites into his flesh?" And Jay Allen's was not the only arrest. On Friday, March 14, Fry had seen Bill Freier on the Canebière: astonishingly, the tiny cartoonist had been released from Le Vernet. Unlike the old New York Fry, the new French version had flung his arms around Freier and Mina and kissed them right there on the street. The next day, though, Freier was rearrested and Mina came to the office, visibly pregnant, and inconsolable. Then Fry learned that on Sunday Vladimir Vochoč, the Czech consul who supplied so many passports and helped so many refugees to escape, had also been detained and placed in *résidence forcée* at the village of Lubersac, suspiciously close to the demarcation line. Next he heard from Lena Fischmann, who reported she had been stopped and strip-searched at the border: the guards had known all about her. "They are getting the range," said Fry.

Lena also told the story of a woman who had been turned away from the Portuguese border the evening after, because her transit visa was due to run out at midnight. The woman was sent back into Spain, from where she would inevitably be deported to France. She had utterly broken down and turned almost insane on the spot. "Oh France," lamented Fry, who despite everything was falling in love with it, "what have you become, that people should go out of their minds at the thought of returning to you?"

Coming on top of these casualties, perhaps the worst loss of all was Fry's closest friend Stéphane Hessel, who smuggled himself to Casablanca, from where he hoped to travel to England to join de Gaulle. "I realize once again how terribly alone I am here," Fry wrote in his journal that night, and it was true. Everybody he had originally combined with after his arrival in France had now disappeared. On the one hand it was a happy circumstance, and a testament to success and continuity that he remained himself with a new staff—and Danny and Théo were becoming his new family. But on the other hand he was left dangerously exposed, just as the forces ranged against him were closing in. The American Foreign Service, except for Harry Bingham, had by now entirely distanced itself from Fry, and Vichy's Fascist slant was sharpened by the promotion at Marseille of the police chief—a vicious aristocratic anti-Semite with the long and cumbersome name of Maurice Anne Marie de Rodellec du Porzic—to the post of *Intendant* of the Bouches du Rhône region. This gave him terrifying powers. Du Porzic and his right-hand man, Robert-Stéphane Auzanneau, hated Fry, and in league with the American consulate they would attempt over the next few months to do everything in their power to eject him from France. For Fry, yet another battle was looming.

He was not the only one who felt alone. Back in New York, Eileen was alternating between resentment that her husband had seemingly abandoned her, and guilt at that resentment whenever she reminded herself of the value of what he was doing. Moreover, her emotions were complicated by the fact that she was stoutly defending him at the ERC offices, while at the same she felt undermined by his petulant complaints and seeming ingratitude. Plus she was angry at his apparent lack of concern for her. Or lack of love. "I cabled you in November," Eileen wrote testily in late February,

> to ask "for my private information" when you might be returning, and you replied as soon as a successor is found. Now I realize the picture has changed, in that, if you can stay, you will. You are surely right in that, because the work you are doing is undoubtedly very valuable to many fine people, and very agreeable to you. . . . However, when you get this letter I should *very much appreciate* it if you would send me a cable giving me your present idea of your plans. . . . Much love, if you're interested—Eileen.

At other times, her tough resolve broke down, and she almost pleaded with Fry for an intimate response. "Do you ever think about me, as I do of you, in any personal way? I mean, do you wonder whom I have dinner with, what clothes I'm wearing, and whether I'm happy? Or do you simply have too much pressing business on hand all the time? I imagine the latter. I suppose it seems funny, but I should feel more that you missed me if you had some close friend instead of me, than if you have none, just your work, as I suppose is the case, though I didn't believe that until lately. . . ." The harsh reality was that Fry now had another life altogether—and true enough, it filled all his time with the workload that it entailed. But it was also a fact that his personality was changing, a rare thing in an adult, but possible under extreme conditions. To Eileen, Fry seemed distant and briskly businesslike, and she was in a terrible position from which to defend herself emotionally. Fry once again suggested that the committee send her to France, but this was simply a blind: he knew it would be impossible for her to come, and if she did, it would be as his replacement, which solved nothing.

IN SPITE OF everything Fry's organization was, incredibly, still expanding: he was employing around twenty people by the mid-spring of 1941, and thanks to the regular sailings from Marseille to Martinique, the departures of the refugees were fast turning into a torrent. Each farewell to a friend was a source of both sadness and celebration. For example, Fry had no sooner moved back into the Villa Air-Bel, once the weather improved, than André Breton left with his wife, Jacqueline, and their daughter aboard the *Capitaine Paul Lemerle*. With Breton's disappearance from the Villa Air-Bel, the magic drained away from it, too, like air escaping from a balloon. The remaining Surrealists turned up a few times afterward, but the atmosphere was heavy and somber, and everybody felt uncomfortable. Soon, they did not come at all.

The Bretons were following the many others who had begun to embark as early as February 18, when about fifteen clients (including the film critic and notorious pest Siegfried Kracauer) left on the first scheduled sailing. On the same steamer as Breton there were Victor and Vladi Serge, Oscar Goldberg (a famous Hebraic scholar), Hans Tittel and Siegfried Pfeffer—two of the *Bouline* victims who had been miraculously released at Fry's request from Le Vernet—the novelist Anna Seghers, and even the anthropologist Claude Lévi-Strauss (who had managed on his own to order his papers and buy a ticket). They in turn were followed by another twelve clients, including André Masson and his wife, the German anti-Nazi Emil Kirschmann, Johannes Caspari, and the art scholar John Rewald on the *Carimare* a week later. Some sailings on these boats, and others like the *Winnipeg* and *Wyoming,* carried up to forty clients of Fry's at a time. At last he was doing what he wanted, simply sending people away to safety with the minimum of fuss—although that minimum should not be underestimated.

For every client who sailed, there was the invisible history of many man-hours of help from Fry and his staff, who had to bully and cajole both the American consulate and the French authorities into granting the visas and papers to which the refugees were entitled. Fry's labors also included lengthy liaisons with the ERC in New York (on whom he depended not only to badger the State Department, but also to secure affidavits from relatives and prominent citizens in America guaranteeing that the prospective immigrants would be financially secure). In Washington as in Vichy France there was a massive go-slow and a callous obstructionism on the part of Breckinridge Long's administration. There is absolutely no doubt that had it not been for the Centre Américain, many of the people who got away *legally* would have never received visas and thus would have been doomed to perish in the Holocaust that began in earnest the following year, when the Vichy government eagerly cooperated in loading foreign and then French Jews into cattle cars bound for Auschwitz.

A case in point is that of Richard Berczeller, his wife, Maria, and son, Peter. He was not a famous man, just an ordinary doctor, forbidden to practice and slowly starving in an assigned residence in a small French village. Only the kindness of his French neighbors had so far kept him out of a concentration camp. Eventually, the American consulate contacted him to say that his emergency visas had been approved and that he could come to Marseille to pick them up. Dr. Berczeller undertook the dangerous journey (there were no longer safe conducts being issued for refugees), and on arrival attempted to collect the visas. "When I reached Marseille," he recalled in a *New Yorker* article in 1964, "the American consulate was closing for the day, with a long line still waiting in front of the door. The next morning, I made a point of being amongst the first in line. I produced the telegram and the clerk, speaking in French after trying me in English, said 'Yes, you and your family will receive visas, but according to regulations, only after you are able to show us tickets for a ship sailing from France.'" One problem was, of course, buying a ticket without a visa, or buying a ticket at all with no money—a common position for refugees to find themselves in. "Where could I find such a ship?" asked Dr. Berczeller "I'm sorry," said the clerk, who knew very well. "I really can't say. I'd like to help you, but . . . Good luck."

This was one of the ways the consulates carried out State Department directives to give visas to everybody except those who wanted one. Luckily, Dr. Berczeller was soon told of the Centre Américain by another refugee. He and his family made it to America, and he was eternally grateful to Varian Fry for the efforts made on his behalf to get what he was entitled to, in the teeth of noncooperation from the American Foreign Service.

But obstructionism was a relatively benign form of opposition. As far back as November, Fry had been suspicious of the true attitudes of consular staff. While he had been at Vichy that time, a friend from the Quaker organization, Celine Roth de Neufville, had retailed a disturbing story concerning a particularly virulent case of anti-Semitism at the embassy. She was having a conversation with one of the secretaries.

"I hope you're not helping Jews to get to the United States," he said.

"What would you do with them?" she asked.

He hunched his shoulders in the position of a man holding a sub-machine gun.

"Ptt ptt ptt ptt ptt," he said.

Fry also recalled hearing that when Avra Warren, the chief of the State Department Visa Division, had toured Europe in the summer of 1940, he had told the American consul at Lisbon to make sure that not a "single goddam Jew" got to America. Many more instances of pro-Fascist malevolence would soon convince Fry that there was actually an enemy within his own government. "One might say that the State Department has become America's open scandal," he told Danny. "Everyone talks about, but nobody does anything about, this extraordinary situation. And yet wars have been lost by Trojan horses within the gates. . . ." Fry always seemed to forget that America was not yet at war, and that its policy (though not Roosevelt's) was to stay out of the conflict.

AT THE BEGINNING of March it looked like Jean Gemahling and Maurice had found a solution to the problem of spiriting the Arthur Wolffs and Bernhards out of France. A local gangster promised a diplomatic car that could take them directly to Lisbon without pause. Fry was overjoyed at this, and gave his blessing to the scheme. "It seems almost too good to be true," wrote Fry in his journal. Then, on Saturday, March 8, he left with Harry Bingham in the big red Chevrolet to visit Marc Chagall at Gordes. Persuading the Russian painter to part with France for the imagined wasteland of America was proving a difficult task, and so far Chagall had parried Fry's epistolary attempts to describe the joys of emigration. It was a delightful, bucolic weekend escape from the tribulations of Marseille life. Fry found Chagall to be "a nice child, vain and simple," with an overriding need to be assured there really were cows in America. But the real revelation was the landscape, reawakening after its unaccustomed freeze, and "beautiful beyond belief." "The almond trees are in bloom," wrote Fry, "a delicate pink against the soft gray-green and sage-green and dark cypress-green of the Provençal landscape. . . . In this, of all places, it is hard to believe that men, given the beautiful world to live in, can sully and destroy it by war." At least he came away with a promise from Chagall that the artist would begin to arrange his affairs for a transatlantic crossing.

Back in Marseille mixed news awaited him. Vichy had just announced the formation of a bureau to deal with the "Jewish Question," as the Vichy government was starting to call it. The Commissariat Général aux Questions Juives (CGQJ) was headed by a man called Xavier Vallat, an anti-Semitic French parliamentarian deputy. His new bureau would be in charge of expropriating and then disposing of Jewish assets, instigating the *numerus clausus* decrees limiting Jews in professions and Jewish children in schools, overseeing the census of France's native Jewish population, and ultimately collaborating with Himmler in genocide.

To Fry, the American Foreign Service was apparently the other claw of this racist pincer movement, and back at the office he resumed his skirmishes with the various consuls in unoccupied France. Lately, Fry had been harassing Clark Husted, the vice-consul at Lyon, whom he accused of slowness and prejudice. Husted had squirmed on the sharp end of Fry's rhetoric, first attempting to justify not giving visas to Jewish children on the grounds that, as their parents were liable to be interned, they would inevitably become a public charge in America (". . . the parents would have no way of extending their aid . . . because of the race"). "I very much hope," Fry pointedly replied, "that your letter does not mean that you are discriminating against persons of the Jewish faith on the grounds that, at some undetermined time in the future, they may be more liable to internment than persons of other faiths?"

Husted was forced to retract his argument and plead that he was simply short-staffed, to which Fry had responded by informing the vice-consul that he was sorry to hear it, and had therefore asked his influential American friends to make representations at Washington in order to rush the Lyon consulate more staff immediately. Caught out in his lie, Husted panicked and sent an *exprès* letter to Fry ("They have never been anything like so prompt before," he chuckled): "I hope that you have not as yet gotten in touch with your friends in the United States in regard to the personnel question at Lyon," wheedled Husted. "I am apprehensive that the reaction at home would be un-

favorable to any mingling in a matter which is of course one of purely depart-
mental concern." Fry was exultant: "What a *pity* I have already gotten in
touch," he wrote in his journal that evening.

He had also been pestering Vice-Consul Felix Cole at Algiers over the matter of quotas: Marseille had received instructions to issue a certain number of
visas, but Algiers had done nothing. Fry wanted to know why not, because it
meant clients of his in North Africa were at an illogical disadvantage. Cole
also replied with a transparent evasion: the orders had just arrived that very
day. But that was fifty-five days after Marseille, Fry replied. Why the discrepancy? He knew Cole was lying. "And a delay of even one day can mean the difference between life and death to a refugee."

It was a zero-sum game. His small victories over lies and hypocrisy were
ultimately self-defeating, for with every visa he managed to wring out of the
Foreign Service, Fry increased their resistance to helping him at all. He knew,
though, that each visa was one that would otherwise never have come.

Then came the awful news that Maurice's gangster car was a terrible hoax.
All the preparations for moving the fugitives to the hotel at Les Baux, which
Fry and Stéphane Hessel had discovered back in late October, had been for
nothing. From that high altitude, and with no automobile, the Wolffs and
Bernhards could only have escaped by walking through the Pyrenees for
nearly a whole day and night to Andorra, at a height of nearly seventeen hundred meters, through winter snows and freezing temperatures. Wolff, who
was old, used crutches and wore callipers, obviously could not even attempt
the climb.

Danny was congenitally skeptical of Maurice and Jean's dealings with
shady characters. In fact, at this juncture he lost his temper and denounced
them, although Fry confided that he knew the anger was truly directed at
himself. Danny was both right and wrong. It was, as he claimed, an example
of unforgivable naïveté to deal with crooks one hardly knew, and into whose
grasping hands were delivered the very lives of the people you were supposed
to protect and bring to safety. "We did not choose our agents wisely," said
Danny in his biannual report in late 1941. "Some of them were reliable but
others grossly misrepresented the situation. They did not know sufficiently
well how to maneuver independent of the Committee," he went on. "If Jean
and Maurice, with their conspiratorial airs, have any other business between
them more serious than sending refugees into the camp of Miranda, then I
feel sorry for all of us." It was a damning indictment, but Fry was correct to
defend Jean and Maurice. With problem cases like the Wolffs and Bernhards,
and Berthold Jacob, a longtime German anti-Nazi, there was simply no other
course of action but to find an illegal way to help them travel across the Iber-

ian Peninsula. As Fry said, one had to take chances; to remain in France was even more dangerous than planning unlikely escapes. As it was, they were as careful as they could be.

Nevertheless, Maurice was angered by Danny's accusations and tendered his resignation. "I said," he recalled, "that, like all of us, I was risking my life handling the refugees, that I had done my best under very difficult circumstances and, if he was not satisfied, he could assign the job to someone else." Fry persuaded him to stay.

Maurice and Fry then began to think of other solutions, but Wolff himself was unimpressed at their efforts to save his life. Maurice described the tense atmosphere in the aftermath of the gangsters' latest confidence trick:

> Wolff's anger was terrific. He called us crooks and highway robbers, and with floods of tears threatened to report us to the police. (As we had obtained false identity cards for him and would have been in real danger had he done so, we must admit that we were somewhat troubled.) Finally, after a good deal of effort, we managed to calm him down. We sketched other plans, without success, while Wolff continued to call down on us a storm of insults and threats, during his constant moves from one place to another, talking to anyone who would listen about his adventures and the way he had been tricked by Fry and his accomplices. He talked so well in fact that one day the police picked up his trail again, and we had to come to his rescue *in extremis* by fabricating a new identity for him. . . .

Jean Gemahling, who characteristically took his work extremely seriously, collapsed and suffered a minor nervous breakdown in the wake of the failure of the diplomatic automobile. He took to his bed, and Fry carefully had to nurture Jean's wounded self-respect and bring him back to health. Maurice was more resilient. He soon discovered a Spanish anti-Fascist named Silvio Trentin who had lived in Toulouse for many years. Trentin passed Maurice on to a man known only as "Garcia" (Fry calls him Carlos, but this was the name of a guide), and who operated an underground route that by means of trusted contacts along the way, could conduct illegal travelers straight through to Lisbon in safety. Danny sighed at hearing this new caper floated by Maurice on the troubled waters of the latest disaster. He was suspicious that Garcia was demanding so much money. But Fry held firm: they had to try everything.

Soon, Berthold Jacob had been taken across the mountains, and the Bernhards had crossed into Spain, too, under the escort of Garcia's men. The border post still had to be avoided, for the new rules meant that Madrid had to be contacted to confirm each immigrant's serial number and name. But in the country itself, the transit visas and stamps would supposedly pass muster with no problem. Garcia had promised some strong guides to carry Arthur Wolff across, but the attempt had to be abandoned, and soon Maurice brought the moaning lawyer back to the Banyuls starting point, where he was billeted with the poor Fittkos.

Things seemed to be moving along well, and Fry's agents in Marseille were also providing him with important information. In fact, he was effectively spying on the Gestapo itself. For a long time, the biggest drawback to the illegal emigrations had been not knowing exactly who the Nazis were searching for. Intelligent guesses and deductions could be made, but never anything like a reliable list compiled. Then, in mid-March, Fry hit paydirt, thanks to Emil Kirschmann, who was just getting ready to leave for Martinique. Fry had given him money to bribe an official at the prefecture to copy the mythical list—which had been circulated to the French police—whenever his boss was out.

Now at last he had it, and the next days were taken up with scrutinizing the hundreds of names it contained. One of them was Heinrich Mueller's, who was working at the Centre Américain, and he left immediately to meet the Fittkos at Banyuls. Many names they had never heard of, although others were familiar. Best of all, although it was the most current list available, it contained the names of many enemies of Hitler who were long gone. Even Otto Strasser was on it. This early supporter and later critic of Hitler's had already been in Lisbon when Fry arrived from the United States in August 1940. It was encouraging to know that they were still one or two steps ahead of the Gestapo. "Now," said Fry, "at least to some extent we know where we are at." He was even beginning to receive intelligence about particular Nazi agents. One, called Host, was the regular supervisory officer at Marseille (Fry already knew about Kramer, the Gestapo agent at Madrid), and he had recently been joined by two more: Hans Biert and Gustav Rietmann. Fry knew where they lived, and now he could watch them watching him.

IT WAS PLEASANT in Marseille now that the warm sun was returning, and Fry basked in it as much as possible. After all, it was about the only way to get vitamin D into the body, given the acute shortage of food, which was growing ever worse. By now his weight had dropped from 174 to 154 pounds, and he was haggard and drawn ("No wonder my cheeks are hollow!"). Surprisingly husky for a sensitive intellectual, in New York Fry used to work out at the

YMCA with ritual application, and in Marseille there happened to be a gymnasium, described by its owner, "Kid" Francis, a former boxing champion of France, as "the most beautiful and the best equipped in the country." "There are hot showers all the time," marveled Fry. "I don't know how he gets away with it." It was at this point that he began to go there three times a week with Danny. Fry could ill afford to burn up precious calories, but he knew that under the mental strain of his work it was impossible to carry on without some physical exertion to restore his overall balance.

This new activity was blended with weekend breaks, taken with Danny and Théo Bénédite. "I am really awfully tired," wrote Fry, "and would welcome a rest like nothing else in the world, not excepting butter." At the end of March they traveled to Antibes, which was all the better for being out of season and in wartime, and meant the usual bunch of flappers, gamblers, and power-boaters were absent. For all Danny's harshness and self-righteousness at the office, he was far and away Fry's favorite of all those on the staff. It was probably because the two men were so similar: Fry was indulgent because he recognized something of himself in the young Frenchman who was both stern and a perfectionist, and he found in Danny an equal when it came to arguing over politics, an activity to which they were both dedicated. Fry also quietly approved of Danny's antagonism toward women, which was complicated by his paradoxical softness toward Théo, of whom Fry was likewise extremely fond. Above everything, he found to his surprise he could truly relax with these people.

And he needed to relax, for when he returned to Marseille he was confronted with several disturbing events and developments. First, Chaminade informed Fry that the Gestapo were looking for Lussu and Pacciardi, and although Danny routinely brushed aside all Chaminade's intelligence on the basis that he suspected him of being a police agent, Fry was sufficiently worried to pass the warning on to his Italian friends. Again, the question was "Why now?" Lussu's underground route from Oran to Casablanca was up and running, and this meant that soon Fry would be able to send through his people hiding at Oran. If the railroad was working, then the Gestapo could not know about it, so why the sudden interest in Lussu?

Another unsettling piece of news was Vichy's recent decision to stop any Spanish leaving France, thus abrogating the August 1940 agreement France had signed with Mexico to let the Republican refugees emigrate there. Some had even been ordered off the latest steamer to Martinique. In fact, it now transpired, all the Spanish—7,000 so far, out of an eventual 100,000—were being smartly rounded up and sent to North Africa to work as slave labor on the Trans-Saharan railroad, emigration visas notwithstanding. There had been riots among the Spanish inmates in the concentration camp on the beach at Argelès when this became general knowledge. Fry learned the French had been forced to send in infantry to restore control, and a bloodbath inevitably ensued.

The day after the riot Fry learned that his invaluable and sympathetic contact in the Prefecture, the gruff but honest Captain Dubois, had been posted to Rabat in Morocco. That was the equivalent of being busted back to traffic duty, and Fry well knew that it was because Dubois had helped the refugees and was pro-British (or at least pro–de Gaulle). Dubois's humiliating demotion was thus an early and ominous sign of the direction of de Rodellec du Porzic's new regime. It meant no more advance warnings of police raids and *rafles,* and Fry would probably have to begin bailing people out of prison once more, by paying bribes to Barellet's chauffeur brother. But before he left, Dubois had at least managed to reassure Fry about the circumstances of Jay Allen's mysterious arrest: it had nothing to do with Fry's organization, he said. The journalist had crossed the demarcation line illegally and made his way to Paris, where he had consorted openly with several persons under close observation by the Germans. When Allen left to travel back south, he was followed by the Gestapo and simply picked up as he attempted illegally to cross back over into Vichy France. Allen would be in jail for a good little while, said Dubois. Immediately Fry received a letter from Eileen confirming what had happened. "The papers here report that Allen is to be held in the cooler for approximately 60 days," she wrote. "Perhaps it will be good for him."

By this point Eileen was also worrying about what was good for her husband. Spring was the season of love, and she had her worries about Fry's life in Marseille. "Will you tell me one thing which has been preying on my mind lately," she wrote:

> quite wrongly as I am almost sure? But you could reassure me, or tell me the truth, if you will not mind my asking. The whole thing was crystallized by my happening to read and be absolutely appalled at Mann's *Death in Venice.* I expect you remember it. That of course started my mind working and doubtless distorting. But will you let me know how you feel about this particular tendency under the rather peculiar circumstances in which you find yourself. I have looked hopefully for some signs that you had a nice kind girl to look after you, but I realize that you won't say so in any case. Please don't be annoyed at me for this anxiety, it is only a sign of daftness. By now you probably haven't the faintest idea what I am driving at. . . .

Far from being annoyed by her worries (which had a sound basis in a distant past with which Eileen was familiar), Fry replied in an open and unoffended fashion. "I would like to have you back in my bed very much," he wrote, "for, despite all your suspicions, I always sleep alone and DON'T like it. You shouldn't read so many wicked novels. Rubbish. Even if I had the inclination, I haven't the time! And the inclination is long since dead. My name is neither Aschenbach nor von Aschenbach, and Marseille is not Venice, especially today."

Whatever Fry's sexual inclinations were by this point in his life, it's clear that his overall preference was for close male friendships, although that was probably all they were. If there was anything else, male or female, it was on the level of casual encounters limited to visits to brothels. What Eileen feared most was an enduring romantic attachment to a man (she seemed not to worry about women), and in assuring her that he had none, Fry was probably telling the truth. In fact, he had experienced among refugees in Marseille the difficulties presented by *affaires du coeur* when applying for United States visas. "It is almost impossible to make Europeans understand the American attitude toward 'moral turpitude,'" he noted. The consuls had apparently reacted with horror at the idea of émigrés asking for visas for their "secretaries." "Even more difficult is the problem of boyfriends," Fry wrote in his journal.

> There is, for instance, the case of a noted French literary critic, who, because he was born in France, could get an immigration visa without any delay as soon as his affidavits arrived. But he will not leave France without a certain Mr. Goldstein, aged 21, who had the misfortune to be born in Turkey. The Turkish quota is closed for twelve years or thereabouts, and I scarcely think that Mr. Goldstein can qualify for a special visitor's visa.
>
> There is also the Czech actor, Z——. He has a boyfriend too. I could probably get a visa for Z——, but how can I possibly ask for one for his boyfriend? And yet I am sure the actor won't leave without him.
>
> Ah, love!

FRY'S LIGHTHEARTED ATTITUDE over visa applications was forced to end on April 9, when de Rodellec du Porzic again gave vivid notice of his fascistic reign over Marseille law and order. That day there were huge *rafles* in town, in which both foreign and French Jews were targeted. Fry was alerted to developments when Chagall's wife called up, crying that her husband had been arrested at the Hotel Moderne, where he had been staying since Fry persuaded the artist to leave Gordes and come to Marseille to await a ship. Something inside Fry snapped at this point. He picked up the telephone and asked to be put through to the Evêché.

Using his most icily controlled tone of voice, Fry told the policeman on the other end of the line in no uncertain terms that Chagall was one of the most famous artists in the world, and that should news of his arrest leak out, France would be humiliated and the man himself severely reprimanded. The policeman promised to investigate, and when Fry put down the telephone, Danny put his arm around Fry's shoulder and squeezed him, saying with pride, "That's the way to talk to them, boss!" Half an hour later, the artist's wife rang again to say that Chagall had just returned to his hotel. The staff were duly impressed. "Varian acknowledged the compliments with a grin," Mary Jayne Gold later wrote. "Then the smile fell from his face and he assumed his usual expressionless mask. He took off his horn-rimmed glasses and wiped them, muttering to himself, 'No, we should be able to save them all. Why just the world's greatest painter?' Then he said out loud, 'Bring me that file on Dobos.'" The poker face indicated Fry's customary composure at the office and around town. It expressed a part of him, the part that had to be strong for the frightened and hopeless refugees whose lives he was trying to save. He had always been a good actor; he could keep it up. But it was in his private moments that, along with the fear, his humor and naturally mischievous irony returned. That night, he allowed himself a wry comment: "Chagall came into the office this afternoon to thank me for getting him out of the clink. All the reluctance he used to feel to leave France has disappeared. Now he is rarin' to go."

Peggy Guggenheim, who had evacuated her museum at Grenoble by now and was back at Marseille, had also been arrested in the *rafle,* along with another American, Herbert Katski of the Joint Distribution Committee. Peggy had been questioned about her "race," and replied simply, "I'm American." But that hadn't satisfied the police, who interrogated her for several hours. An American passport was no longer a guarantee of immunity, that was certain, and Fry reminded himself that he no longer possessed one. It had expired at the end of January, and the consulate refused to revalidate it for anything except immediate travel back to America. Not only would it not protect him, but it now seemed that the Foreign Service wished to place Fry in direct danger. It refused even to provide him with the necessary letter of recommendation for the Swiss consul so he could obtain a vital visa for that country. All the other Americans had one, so that in case of emergency (that is, if panzers appeared in the streets of Marseille overnight), they could flee to safety. The letter was a mere courtesy, and Fry alone had been refused one.

With the State Department, the French police and the Gestapo closing in on him, and with the ERC in New York still determined he should return, Fry began to think he was moving toward the endgame. All that could keep him going in France from now on was luck and cunning.

CHAPTER 21

BETRAYALS

JAY ALLEN SHOULD HAVE counted himself lucky he was still in a
Paris prison when Fry returned from a weekend away with the Bénédites
at Aiguèze. For on Fry's desk lay a sheaf of documents outlining the catastrophic failure of Pacciardi's attempt to establish a shuttle to transport Italians, Spanish, and Fry's clients from the beach at Oran north to Gibraltar. The
incident had occurred nearly three weeks previously, on March 25, but it had
taken this long for an account to be pieced together because so many of those
involved were now in jail in North Africa. The entire episode was testament to
exemplary amateurism and fatal loose talk. It was also a plan that Fry had
been quite unaware of, at least insofar as it concerned his own protégés. But
Jay had known all about it, for he had secretly masterminded and financed
the whole fiasco: *that* must have been what his unauthorized drawings on
Centre Américain funds had been about. Everything fell infuriatingly into
place as Fry read through depositions outlining the disastrous escapade.

Pacciardi had led a large group of refugees down to the beach to meet a
boat that would take them away. But when the group arrived, they found not
one but several vessels, and none of them friendly. There were in fact two
Vichy sub-chasers and the coast guard anchored offshore, and from behind
the dunes suddenly appeared the *gendarmerie,* the *douane,* the *Sûreté Nationale,* and the *Deuxième Bureau.* They had walked straight into a trap. Luckily it was dark, so everybody scattered, but this did not stop many being
arrested on the scene and others being rounded up afterward. Everybody who
managed to escape was now in hiding. It was an utter shambles. Eight people
had so far been caught, mostly friends of Jay Allen. But included among them

were two very endangered clients of Fry's: Walter Oettinghaus and Hans Kakies. Two others, Maas and Molins, were at large but at risk. Erich Lewinsky, who was in charge of Kakies's emigration file, hadn't even known he had left metropolitan France. That must have been why the Gestapo were looking for Lussu, thought Fry, the blood no doubt draining from his face: they must have discovered the underground railroad to Casablanca from one of the prisoners.

Fry's one crumb of comfort amid this chaos tasted of vindication: Allen had been a fool. "Naturally I was kinda pleased," wrote Fry to Eileen. "It was too perfect an end for a boasting, blustering fool not to give observers the moral satisfaction of seeing someone reap his just rewards." At last Fry could demonstrate to the committee in New York that he had been correct about "the friend" all along—and he took great delight in doing so:

> Last January I sent Frank [Kingdon] a cable saying among other things that if the friend's policy ended in disaster they shouldn't say I hadn't warned them. I had no idea then that the disaster would be to the friend. But I was convinced there would be a disaster of one sort or another. It is some satisfaction to have been right. Unfortunately the friend is not the only victim: he has thrust a number of other persons into almost exactly the same situation, and it is now up to me to get them out. . . . I feel sorry for him not so much because of the discomforts he must be suffering as for the ludicrousness of his career here: it was loudmouthed, spectacular, reckless and brief, and it ended suddenly and foolishly. He must be bursting with hatred for me right now and so, I suppose, are his backers at home. But the fact remains that I was right and he was terribly, incredibly and stupendously wrong. His own final foolish venture was typical of everything he did. . . . It is an almost unbelievable story.

An enraged Emilio Lussu turned up at Boulevard Garibaldi a week later, but it wasn't the unearthing of his underground railroad he was unhappy about. It had remained miraculously intact. Rather, it was the quality of the "genuine" transit visas that had been supplied through Maurice's Spanish contact, Garcia. Lussu was attempting to travel to Lisbon in order to complete the arrangements for the last leg of his railroad, from Casablanca. To this end, Fry had bought visas for him, and they had been put into Lussu's very good Lithuanian passport. Now that he had it back, Lussu smacked down the passport on Fry's desk, and explained the inferior quality of what were, even to an amateur's eyes, the obvious fakes. "He pointed to mistakes in the spelling of some of the Portuguese words and the trembling line of the signature of the Spanish consul, which we could see had been traced with a pencil and then haltingly inked in." It was yet another shock in a series of demoralizing setbacks. "Danny, thank God, was away at the time," wrote Fry.

It was not just Lussu's chances of getting to Lisbon that had apparently been ruined: he was still relatively safe in Marseille. But other refugees like the Bernhards, Wolffs, Jacobs, and a brave young German anti-Nazi lawyer called Werner Wille, had all been sent across the border, either with Garcia's men, or from Banyuls with the Fittkos. And all of them had the incriminating forgeries stamped in their passports.

Sure enough, it was not long before Fry heard that George Bernhard and his wife were detained at Madrid, unable to renew their (bad) Portuguese visas, and at the mercy of the Spanish authorities, who were now backed up by Gestapo agents. Then came the terrible news that the Berthold Jacobs— traveling on papers that identified them as Mr. and Mrs. Rollins—had been arrested at Madrid, where they had allowed their transit visas to expire while wandering around the Prado for nearly a week. Frantically, Maurice attempted to contact the Fittkos from a café across the street from the Centre Américain, and he eventually succeeded. He discovered that Wille had already gone over the mountains, but that Arthur Wolff and his wife were still at Banyuls. "Save us from this awful man" was the essence of Lisa's message to Fry. Maurice and Paul Schmierer set off straight away to bring Wolff back to his hiding place at Marseille.

At Banyuls there was a hot quarrel, with Hans sharply criticizing Paul and Maurice. "How can one work with adventurers who gamble with the lives of refugees?" he shouted. Lisa attempted to calm the situation, but she was angry, too. Meanwhile, Fry and Lussu decided to travel to Toulouse and meet with another Spanish refugee who called himself an anti-Fascist, and whose organization might potentially replace Garcia's. As a travel agent, Garcia looked as if he would soon be out of business. And not only that: "If the Spanish ever find out who the Rollins really are, I'm afraid we'll never see them again," Fry lamented. "And if there is a far-reaching investigation and the Gestapo learns who got them the passports and visas and sent them into Spain, our game will be up." And there were still many other refugees to get out.

Their interview with the new candidate—whom Fry found oily and untrustworthy—resulted only in an offer of a diplomatic automobile. It was the same gangster scam that had been worked on them before, and Fry walked out. He really had no option except to continue the existing arrangement, and Lussu made the point that although there had been arrests, at least Garcia's associates seemed to have solved the problem of crossing the mountains. Really, he said, the route only needed perfecting.

After the interview, Fry took a little time out to escort the enraptured Lussu around the huge Byzantine church of St. Sernin. By a delightful coincidence they ran into Jacques Lipchitz, who was living at Toulouse and due to travel to Marseille in a few days' time, from where he would prepare for his journey to Lisbon. Fry pronounced him "one of the warmest, the most grateful and the most unassuming of my many protégés."

A week later, the news of the Jacobs's release came through. Garcia tried to claim the credit, but Fry said it had been the hard work of Dr. Charles Joy at the Unitarian office, whom he had begged for help, that had secured their freedom. Then Fry heard that Werner Wille had reached Lisbon, and that the Bernhards had received their Portuguese transit visas and were leaving Madrid. With these problems solved, it looked as though there was hope for Garcia's route. Which was just as well, because on Sunday, May 11, the Fittkos came to tell Fry that their work was finished. Hans said that the Spanish were now arresting everybody without a French exit visa. What was even worse, detectives were inspecting travelers' papers on through trains to Portugal, and were in possession of the Gestapo lists. Now, said Fry, "Carlos [Garcia] is the only thing we have left."

IT WAS PLAIN Fry's enemies were plugging the holes to freedom, but not everything was doom and gloom. The Martinique-bound steamships were still leaving regularly, after all. On May 6, the *Winnipeg* departed with sixty clients aboard, including the wives of Breitscheid and Hilferding, the Paris photographers Ylla and Lipnitski, Wilhelm Herzog (another of Fry's "pests" for whom Drach had provided one of his passports), the orchestra leader Eduard Fendler, and Baron zu Franckenstein, one of Kay Boyle's friends. The next day, the Chagalls left for Lisbon to catch a Portuguese line boat, the SS *Pinto Basto,* bound for New York. They followed Max Ernst and Peggy Guggenheim, who had gone on the first of the month. Ms. Guggenheim had booked seventeen seats on the Yankee Clipper for her friends and paintings. By now, her affair with Ernst was well under way, and poor Victor Brauner was out in the cold—literally so. Fry's best attempts to help him emigrate failed in the end, but one-eyed Brauner survived the war as a shepherd in the vast French wilderness, where the Nazis never found him. The *Mont Viso* left on May 10, carrying another seven clients, including the pianist Erich Itor-Kahn. Less than a week later the *Wyoming* cast off with another fifty of Fry's charges; Jacques Lipchitz left for Lisbon with his wife and child a day later.

These were great successes, quite independent from the illegal escapes that were still being made with regularity. Fry had sent three more men across with Garcia, and although two had been arrested at Madrid, he knew that it had been largely their own fault (they had spent over a week there, swanning around and accosting women). The Garcia route itself seemed tenuously intact and improving all the time, and Fry had even managed to find a brave lawyer in Algeria willing to fight for the release of Oettinghaus and Kakies. Big Klaus Dohrn was set to cross the Pyrenees, and Lussu had already taken his chances, saying "*Enfin,* within a week I shall either be in Lisbon, or back on Lipari!"

On top of all this, Fry reported that the Centre Américain had never been so busy, and that well over a thousand people had passed through the offices in the first two weeks of May. The black spot was Harry Bingham's sad news that he had been ordered to Lisbon, and from there was likely to be sent back to the United States. Both he and Fry knew why this was. Bingham had been Fry's only ally at the consulate, and he had finally been made to suffer for it. Now there was not a single French or American official on whom Fry could rely for information or support. It was now a race against time to get the refugees out before the noose around the neck of his organization was pulled tight.

Then, as if his suspicions had been overheard, strange things began to take place. Not the least of these was Fry's discovery, due to the clicking sound of a cracked dictaphone machine when he answered the telephone, that the office was indeed bugged. As if to clarify this, the day after Bingham's departure an incident occurred while Fry was working late at the Boulevard Garibaldi offices. Chaminade had warned him that the Fascists of the local Vichy youth group were planning to smash up the Centre. As Fry locked up and began to descend to the ground floor, about an hour before midnight, he heard noises and saw go past him up the stairs several figures wearing baggy green trousers and the blue berets of the *Jeunesse.* He hid in the lobby as, from the upper floor, came the sounds of rattling locks and loud cursing: the young Fascists only failed to break in because Fry had just strengthened all the bolts on the doors. He stood invisible in the shadows as the visitors left, and the next morning reported the incident to du Porzic's lieutenant, Auzanneau, "a filthy little Fascist and anti-Semite himself." Fry thought he had probably organized the raid, and now that Auzanneau knew that Fry knew what was planned, he would have to call off the *Jeunesse.* But Fry still hired an intimidating Spanish night watchman to be on the safe side.

The next incident was more mysterious. Fry had been exchanging with Kourillo, in amounts of $500 at a time, portions of the $8,000 in gold that

Professor Guetzevich had left the Centre Américain back in early February (a further $1,200 came from Arthur Wolff). There remained a tidy sum. "I like to go to the safe at night and take out the little bags and empty them on the table and run the coins through my fingers," wrote Fry. "They are amazingly heavy." Directly after the attempted raid on the offices the gold was transferred, and Fry buried it in the pine woods behind the Villa Air-Bel. This was a time at which the exchange rate was falling from its March high point of 175 francs to the dollar, so Fry was looking to unload the more than $5,000 dollars in gold he still had left.

Kourillo, as a trusted agent of eight months, was informed of this general intention. Then a few days later the police arrived yet again at the villa, and this time it was not false papers they were looking for but Fry's secret fortune. They did not find it, of course, "but how did they know we had gold?" he wondered.

He was reminded of what had happened to Captain Murchie, shortly before he left to be replaced by the new British commander, Garroway. When Lena set off for Lisbon, she carried with her a request for funds to deliver out of France all the remaining British soldiers. "Tell Ursula we can take care of her children beautifully if we have enough money—say $50,000. With that we can take care of *all* of them." Dutifully, Lena saw Sir Samuel Hoare at the British embassy in Madrid, and passed on the message. Nothing further was heard from that quarter, and eventually Murchie decided to raise the funds himself by converting a load of dollars he had hidden in the room he shared with his pretty young Corsican girlfriend. He informed Kourillo of his intention, only to find the day after that his lodgings had been burgled by gangsters while his lover was held at gunpoint. All the money, worth 600,000 francs, was taken. "Murchie is sure the girl is straight," Fry wrote at the time. "I'm not so sure myself." The girl worked for Vinciléoni, counting the change at the Dorade. Murchie was not always discreet, so it was difficult to say who would and would not have known about the money.

Now, with the police on the trail of Fry's gold, he decided to unload all of it, and asked Danny to fix up a date to make the exchange. "On May 18," said Danny, "I told Kourillo of our intentions and he said he would try to find a buyer. On the 20th he advised me that he had found a taker for the $2,000 at the interesting rate of 270. I then delivered the bag in question to his hotel, as he was to make the exchange that evening and the next day. At the time he told me that $2,000 more could be exchanged, one half for francs at the rate of 168 and one half for paper dollars at the rate of Frs 125 to the dollar. Kourillo told me that he wanted the money that afternoon so he could settle with us for both deals at the same time."

Fry agreed to this, and Danny set off for Kourillo's hotel with the gold in his briefcase. When he arrived, the Russian was standing outside. He shook Danny's hand and told him there was trouble and to make himself scarce. Danny started down the street, but had not gone more than a few paces when he was approached by three customs and excise officers. They arrested him but let Danny go for the night after he had made a statement at the *douane* in which he claimed the gold came from Max Ernst as a parting gift, and that the exchange had nothing to do with Fry, who had already refused the illegal currency. In sum, he took all the blame on himself. That evening Danny paced up and down swearing Kourillo had betrayed them. Fry could not quite believe it.

The next day, when Danny returned to the *douane* for arraignment, he was taken away to Chave prison. The lawyer said Danny could get five years for what he had attempted to do, and Fry was distraught: "I have made a criminal and ruined the career of a young man who had everything to hope for before I came along," he agonized. "And I can hardly bring myself to look Théo in the face. She looks so reproachful."

Kourillo still owed francs to the value of $2,000 for the first bag of gold, and Fry sent Jean Gemahling to collect it the next day. Kourillo told Jean the police had searched the room and confiscated all of it. But Kourillo had not been arrested. He had not even been searched, realized Fry. "Now I know who robbed Murchie," he said. "Now I know who betrayed Danny." Under French law an informer was allowed to keep half of any monies recovered by the authorities, so Kourillo had half of the money seized from Danny, and all of the other sum: $3,000 in gold for a day's dirty work. There was only one thing to do. Fry went to see Charles Vinciléoni at the Dorade, and took out a murder contract on Kourillo, who subsequently fled for his life. Fry learned later from Gaston Defferre that Kourillo had bought a villa on the Côte d'Azur, where he was breeding racehorses. "Rather a rapid rise for a former clerk in the American Express Company, isn't it?" he wrote to Beamish. "A typically Gestapo rise, in fact!"

Astonishingly, Harry Bingham's replacement at the consulate, a callow and snobbish young man who despised refugees and quickly made clear his intention to withhold every visa possible, agreed to plead for Danny with the *douane*. Even more astonishingly it worked, and on May 31, Danny, "dirty and unshaven and very thin and pale" was released on probation. Fry was overcome. "I know I am a sentimental fool," he confessed, "but when he came into the room I couldn't help throwing my arms around him and hugging him and holding him tight. And I couldn't help crying."

From now on Danny was severely disabled insofar as his work at the Centre Américain was concerned, for he was a focus of police attention, the weak link in the chain that held Fry fast to French soil. This was confirmed by a summons to Auzanneau's office, where he was told of the serious consequences of Danny's crime for his organization. Fry didn't blink, and stressed that Danny was acting on his own initiative and without his knowledge. Still, he could see Auzanneau's eye teeth glinting. There would be worse to come, no doubt about that. Before anything else, though, Fry and Danny had to talk, because while he was in prison another catastrophe had occurred: the Martinique route had been closed down.

This time, it was not the French or the Germans who had done the damage, but the British. They captured the *Winnipeg* on the high seas just before she reached Martinique, and took her to Trinidad as a war trophy. The poor passengers had all been interned by the British, who were "hinting that they are Gestapo agents," noted Fry. "But I know at least ninety who are not: those sent by us." For its part, Vichy immediately ordered the *Wyoming* and *Mont Viso* to put in at Casablanca and stay there. There were to be no more sailings, and all the unfortunate passengers stranded in Morocco had been placed in French concentration camps there. The fear was that they too would be press-ganged for slave labor on the Trans-Saharan railway. At the same time Portugal, now stacked to the gunwales with refugees, decided to stop issuing transit visas altogether. Those refugees left in France were stranded, and Vichy, which had just passed its second *Statut des Juifs,* had begun to round up Jews in earnest, throwing them into concentration camps without appeal. According to the new law, for someone to be classified Jewish in Pétain's France it was sufficient to have three grandparents who were Jewish. In Hitler's Germany it was two. In other words Vichy was looking almost as hard as the Nazis for people to persecute.

"THE LAST TEN YEARS WERE THE LIVELIEST THANKS AND LOVE," cabled Fry to Eileen on their anniversary, to which she replied, "MY DARLING . . . YOUR CABLE WAS BEYOND MY WILDEST DREAMS I SHALL NEVER FORGET." It was an exchange that briefly overcame the tensions that continued to develop between Fry and Eileen through the summer of 1941. To begin with, the difficulties with the ERC in New York remained, although Fry's hand was stronger after Allen's arrest (he was eventually exchanged in August for a Nazi held in America, and left his French prison thirty pounds lighter). Eileen had taken the fallout from the ongoing saga, though, and Mildred Adams's claque at Forty-second Street blamed her for undermining the committee in the matter ("Evidently there is some feeling there that you have won out owing to the machinations of your wife," she wrote to Fry). Eileen believed Fry had not helped matters: "If you had only written calmly, and often, and naturally," she chided him, "I believe they would have retained confidence in you." But Hans Sahl's arrival in New York, where he was now working at the ERC, underlined the strength of Fry's earlier criticisms, and somewhat calmed Eileen's frustration with her husband. "Hans, who talked to me a long time this afternoon is very depressed, partly from the usual reaction that strikes them all as soon as they get here, and partly because he had been through the files and discovered case after case on which you had worked and which has bogged down here. I hate to tell you this but you probably knew it anyway." "Hans has been through the files," replied Fry, "and found case after case that had died there—you're telling me! I cabled myself hoarse about that, until finally gave up in despair. I hope Hans has not only discovered but resurrected."

Many of the émigrés had begun to settle into their new lives in America by now, and quite a few were leaving a poor impression on their hosts and helpers. This was another source of strain between Eileen and Fry. He had forged friendships with them under trying circumstances, and looked at them from a different perspective than the New Yorkers, who saw only what years of fear mingled with sudden relief will do. Fry's enthusiastic letters about his friends piqued and provoked Eileen to reply that it "shows that you are under a misconception as to the number *or* the nature of the 'clients and colleagues' who arrive here. The *only* one who has been at all friendly was Hirschmann, and him I was mildly inclined to suspect because he represented himself as a great pal of yours, yet brought no message or note of introduction. After a while he was friendly enough, and came once to Irving Place (the *only* one who has ever set foot inside it, except for some of the October imports). . . . He was on the whole a pleasure rather than a bother, but certainly not *superior* to the ERC, as you implied in your last letter—Europeans just *aren't*, you know."

Some refugees, especially the more famous ones, proved very trying indeed. Many, like Alfred Döblin, Alfred Polgar, Hans Lustig, Wilhelm Speyer, Paul Elbogen, and, last but by no means least, Walter "Baby" Mehring by now had "courtesy" contracts in Hollywood, bestowed by Jack Warner, Louis B. Mayer, and other big studio bosses and producers. Some were humble and grateful, despite the terrible shocks endured from the cultural uprooting and the language barrier—to say nothing of the serflike status of the screenwriter in Los Angeles, which must have been humiliating to artists widely respected in their own countries. Others were turning out to be greedy and egotistical, and were developing a reputation for conspicuous extravagance. For example, Mehring was tooling up and down Sunset Boulevard in his shiny new

Packard roadster, which provided the excuse, despite his well-paid studio contract, for not repaying any of the money lent him by the Centre Américain de Secours in Marseille. In this matter it was not only Eileen who was disgusted. "If I were in New York," Danny told Fry (not realizing the poet was on the West Coast) "I would certainly have punctured the tires of Mehring's automobile every night, throw stones through the windows, and put sugar in the gasoline until he had paid back the 31,000 francs that we advanced him."

Fry later acknowledged such behavior could not simply be explained away, and lamented to Danny that, "you are quite, quite right in saying that people like Mehring compromise all of the refugees. The German refugees who got jobs in the movie industries in Hollywood have behaved far worse than any others. They are drawing very large salaries and are spending their money as soon as they get it. The result is that the rich movie magnates are fed up with refugees and will give nothing more to refugee relief organizations." Fry told Eileen that when Feuchtwanger and Werfel lived in their villas at Sanary-sur-Mer, they paid only 600 francs per month. "No wonder they are all so tight about money when they get to the US," he wrote in an attempt at explanation. "They must be terrified at what they have to pay for things there."

Eileen was unimpressed. "Lena [Fischmann] tried to speak with Franz Werfel on the phone," she reported, "saying she had a special message from you, but he refused to come to the phone, though admittedly in the house. Same attitude of course when she tried to contact Baby [Walter Mehring] though why anyone would bother with that dope, I don't know." "Yes," replied Fry, "many of the imports are pretty terrible. But they make Art, some of them; and you don't have to bother with the people much, you can just read their books, or look at their pictures." His point was that just because these people had been persecuted, it was not fair to expect them to be any greater, morally speaking, than other human beings. Harsh treatment and terror can harm the personality as well as improve it. "What did you think of the surrealists?" he asked. "Masson is rather blah, in my opinion, and his wife is a terror. Breton I like very much; he is *quite* intelligent, and a *very* good actor. Chagall is too Russian and cute and self-centered to be wholly satisfactory. Lipchitz is the best of the lot: polite, intelligent, and enormously grateful. Chagall and Lipchitz both gave me drawings; but Masson of course gave me nothing. Ernst (the most agreeable of the pure surrealists) gave me a small oil."

Fry was hoping that once the artists were collected together in New York, they would be able to help raise funds. "Max Ernst left for Lisbon last night promising to do big things when he gets to New York for the committee," wrote Fry in early May. "He and André Breton could put on a surrealist evening, with Breton reading Benjamin Péret's poems (he is *épatant* at it) and someone auctioning a picture of Max's for a fabulous price. There will also be Masson, but he's mad at us because we refused to steal his transatlantic passage money and give it to him for living expenses when he reaches New York. Chagall is too girlish to do anything—Mrs. Guggenheim says he's a shit. (Jewish ladies are *so* outspoken!) I guess she's right."

In the end, Fry proved himself very tolerant of human frailty where the refugees were concerned. "However irritating the individuals may be," he wrote, "one must continue to try to help them for reasons of principle, and one must also remember that all of them have suffered at least as much as one has oneself, and many, a great deal more. . . . Perhaps it is because I accept them for what they are, with all their weaknesses, all their unpleasant qualities, and like them for it none the less, that I am never disappointed in them—what never? Well, *hardly* ever!"

Since Lena Fischmann had been in New York she too had been working for the ERC, but her obvious partiality to Fry had alienated the Mildred Adams flank of the committee, and she was made to feel unwelcome at Forty-second Street. But Lena was fast friends with Harold Oram, and when they made a trip to Hollywood at the end of April 1941, in an attempt to drum up more funds for the work in France, Eileen was forced a little more to sympathize with her husband's complaints about the uselessness of the New York office. "It is rather amusing that since he has been out there Harold has adopted completely the tone of your letters at their most bitter," she admitted to Fry. "He writes airmail to everybody at the office every day, alternately cursing, begging, cajoling, and threatening them. . . . He writes that he now for the first time appreciates what you have been enduring all winter, and has invented a new verb, as you will see from this line in one of his letters: 'I want to know why I have not received an answer from Ingrid regarding my repeated requests for speakers for a Hollywood dinner. You see how I am frying out here?'"

"I am sorry they let Harold down," Fry wrote back. "They also sometimes let our clients down very badly." He cited one whose affidavits "they apparently received early in October, whose birthdate and place I telegraphed in February, and for whom they told me in early May that they had no affidavits, could not get any, and needed to know her place and date of birth. Meanwhile, through direct cabling, I had received very fine affidavits for her direct from Donald Ogden Stewart (who they told me refused to give them), and she will now get her visa, thanks not one jot to them. . . ." His conclusion about the New York office was a simple one: "I must say that from here, their office looks like a rat's nest of confusion and inefficiency."

Another strand of the growing tension between Fry and Eileen was the on-going argument about sending a replacement for him. The latest suggestion was Harold Oram himself, who was certainly capable, but also Jewish. Again and again, Fry would write why one person or another was unsuitable. In Oram's case, he "wouldn't do because official antisemitism is very strong here and getting stronger every day." Eileen understood the problem intellectually, but not having experienced the vicious repression of Vichy, she remained un-sympathetic to Fry's reasoning. "We are already in bad odor because we help so many Jews and have a number of Jewish employees," he pleaded. "I insist upon having them to cope with the clients—they are the only people who can stand the strain. No Christian I know could bear up under it for more than a few weeks. . . . I have even been suspected of being a Jew myself (tell Henry [Bennett—a close friend]: he will split with laughing, it's so funny). If Harold were in my place he would find the hoeing much more difficult than even I do, for Jews—even American citizens—are now treated with supreme con-tempt officially."

"This all makes me think," replied Eileen, "that you will perhaps no longer feel you need to return, especially as they have found no successor, though still looking half-heartedly and spasmodically for one." It was true there was always a perfectly good reason for staying in France, but by now Eileen's anx-ieties about her husband's real affections were taking deep root.

IN MARSEILLE, du Porzic's collaboration with the Gestapo was becoming nastier and more purposeful. Celine Roth de Neufville warned Fry of agents provocateurs. One had recently visited the Quaker office posing as a French soldier who wanted to get to England to link up with de Gaulle. He persisted in the assumption that they would help him escape even after being told most firmly that the Quakers had nothing to do with such matters. In the end, the receptionist grew suspicious and asked to see his identity papers. The man handed them to her. "Bitte," he said politely, inadvertently letting slip his Ger-man identity.

Soon after, it was the turn of the Centre Américain to be tested. This time a pimple-faced French teenager came to the office asking for "Captain Smith" of the Royal Air Force. He claimed to have plans of the German airfields of occupied France, stolen from Paris. Fry threw him out, and then watched from the window as the boy crossed the street and joined two obvious plain-clothes detectives. There was a Gallic shrugging of shoulders, and they walked away. "But suppose they had sent someone less green at the job," Fry wrote in his journal. "I am getting increasingly nervous."

The pressures were great and small. Mary Jayne Gold was still seeing Killer, but he was proving to be more and more troublesome. Still a deserter from the Foreign Legion, and thus a magnet of police attention, Fry had banned him from the Villa Air-Bel, which suited both men. Now, though, he had joined with a local gangster called Mathieu, and the two men had murdered a half-caste who owed them money. For a joke, Killer told Mary Jayne he had buried the corpse in the grounds of the villa, although he had of course thrown the body, Marseille-style, into the harbor. There was brief but general panic, followed by a particularly nasty burglary of Mary Jayne's room. In view of the ongoing chaos caused by her boyfriend, Fry understandably asked her to leave the Villa Air-Bel.

Killer had stolen all Mary Jayne's jewelry, which he quickly sold; then he expected her to get Fry to help him leave the country because he now fancied himself in London with de Gaulle. "Varian refused politely but instantly," she later wrote. "I don't blame him. I only wish he had been more reluctant." As Fry described her, Mary Jayne probably was exactly the spoiled rich girl, and it was true (as she feared but denied) that the others saw her as being Killer's besotted sex-slave. She convinced herself she was merely tending to a lost young boy (at twenty-one, Killer was eight years her junior, although she also claimed he lied about his age). Still, Varian's necessary harshness was hard for Mary Jayne to bear. Fifty years later she remained sad when recalling a visit to the villa after her banishment: "Jean [Gemahling] and Charles [Wolff] greeted me as usual. . . . Of Varian and Danny Bénédite I only saw their backs."

This stony hardness was partly a temperamental response to the knife-edge conditions on which everyone tried to balance, and partly it was simple professional practicality. The underground work not only had to be kept utterly secret for its own sake, but also to protect those in the organization who were uninvolved—and Fry still attempted to make sure he compromised as few people as possible in the execution of the illegal aspects of his work. This may have been a polite fiction, because it is certain all his employees knew what was really going on. He supposed that at least they had to be shielded from the details, for by now he was openly risking the death sentence. Just before Murchie left in March (to be imprisoned in Spain and for some reason left to rot there by the British embassy in Madrid), Fry had told him that he could have no more to do with helping British flyers and soldiers to escape. The Germans announced that anybody found doing so would be shot, and Fry's first duty was to his refugees.

Nevertheless, he still courted the firing squad through other sorts of activity. In truth, he was by this point actively involved in setting up Resistance cells—which he kept a secret even from Danny. Fry had imperceptibly drifted into an entirely new world. Sensing a serious change in him, Eileen made sweet and desperate overtures to elicit from Fry something more than a friendly or businesslike response. "I begin to suspect," she wrote, "that you really have developed into a pretty tough proposition, who can survive a good many storms and buffets. I am quite proud of you for having stayed on as you have, in the face of disappointment and discouragement, and I hope you'll come out of all this with something that will stand you in good stead all your days." "Yes," he replied, all business, "I have developed into a very tough proposition. You have to be to stick it out here. . . . You won't even recognize your husband again after this experience; stern, grim-faced, even hard. Oh yes, a very tough proposition, I assure you. . . . One does not go home any longer because one is not welcome: one stays put until put out—or locked up. Too bad the embassy is so sissy about it."

This was not what Eileen needed to hear. She wanted Fry to assure her he was the same man despite everything, and that he loved her as much as ever. But as she had come to realize, Eileen had gradually become—by virtue of time, distance and circumstance—a little irrelevant to Fry's new life. By the end of May she could wait no longer to reveal her fears. "Had a lot of talk with Henry [Bennett] this weekend about you," she wrote, in a letter that would change everything between them.

I realize that many of your qualities are dim in my mind already. You must have forgotten what I am like almost completely, what a break. I think a year's separation is enough if we are to take up life together again . . . if you stay beyond August I think we'd better call it a day for both our sakes. I feel we'd be trying to bridge too wide a gulf, and might as well not try. In this life of separation I am constantly looking for dead ends down which to run and though I can immerse myself easily enough in such activities, they are unproductive and violently out of proportion to their results for me. A year is long enough. I have not said anything like this before, but I feel that I do myself great harm by living longer so vicariously, and that if you are not back by August, I had better face facts . . . I cannot write personal details in a letter which is read by an indefinite number of censors, but they are not important anyway. The conclusion is that I think we ought to want to see each other after a year, and if we don't then we might as well postpone it indefinitely. I am sure that I will always be glad to see you when you do come back, and you have many ways of appealing to me and charming me which will remain in every case. . . . If you don't want to come back enough to come at the end of a year I am quite ready to accept a large part of the blame. . . . Perhaps I am too old to talk like this, no doubt it is grotesque, but I should like to feel that some real warmth of feeling was still possible for me with you, and if not with you then with someone else. . . . I don't know why I feel so gloomy except that I have written several such letters to you in recent months and then torn them up. Anyway, a year is a long time, and please come home, or else let me know.

The unfolding tragedy of Eileen's loneliness was compounded by the simple logistics of the international airmails that bleak summer. An unpredictable period of at least three weeks between dispatch and arrival meant that many efforts at apology and reconciliation were canceled by an earlier and angrier letter that arrived first—or worse still, later, rehearsing complaints already disowned. "This place is marvellous!" wrote Fry ecstatically of the Provençal summer, just as Eileen was steeped in despair. "If only we could afford something like it in God's country! But in God's country only millionaires and Catholic sisters of charity can live in such big houses, with such beautiful gardens. . . ."

When she received this, chance had made it appear to be a response to Eileen's great emotional outpouring. Since that letter she had posted another, retracting much of what she had proposed: "I have been sorry since then that I wrote to you so, because of course it is selfish of me to do so," she admitted. "It is terribly vicarious to have you do something so important while I go on in the old . . . rut, going to the Brearley school, keeping up your life insurance, etc. etc. But these are fortunes of war, and we can do nothing about these vile days except to try, if one is strong like you, to fix things up a bit, and to make for oneself if there is room left over a happy personal life. What it comes down to is that I have lived too long and too happily really in spite of everything with you to be able to live happily alone, and I have been driven to some rather strange devices in learning that." Although she knew it was due to the vagaries of air and sea transport, it still *felt* as though her husband were ignoring her feelings.

In the meantime, Fry had received neither Eileen's "bombshell" letter, nor its later correction, which was delayed (probably in Portugal). Being romantically unsophisticated, Fry would have been shocked to learn of Eileen's apparent unhappiness and her drastic decisions. As it was, he wrote a long—businesslike, newsy—letter at the end of May, which crossed with Eileen's somewhere over the Atlantic. It probably appeared to her, in her run-down state, as if Fry was having a fine time without her. In reality June and July in

Marseille were terrible, trying months in the teeth of aggressive police harassment and difficulties with helping clients to emigrate. Fry's of May 31 was the last letter to Eileen he wrote in over a month. It didn't help that he ended it, in complete candor, with a description of the latest police tactics: "They are even trying to 'frame' me on a morals charge," he innocently admitted, "sending both girls and boys. I must sound as though I had gone stark nuts, but it is the plain truth. Needless to say, I don't touch the people sent any more than I touch the 'important documents' which people tell me someone told them I could get to the British authorities for them. . . ."

Eileen sat in New York worrying about what she had written ("Have I done something to annoy you?" she asked near the end of June, still having not received his response). Finally, with the tide of her emotions turning once again toward anger and impatience at Fry's apparent silence, she declared war: "As for not hearing from you goes, I only hope that unemployed refugees have not sat down and written to you the same sort of disturbing stories about me that they favor me with about you. Because I can assure they are not true, any more than the pictures they obligingly paint for me of your days and especially nights are true. I could easily go nuts if I paid attention to them."

"Have they continued to get out Headline Books?" came Fry's chronological reply, due purely to the mails. "I wouldn't much enjoy having that job back, because I feel too grim to want to explain things to the kiddies and ladies clubs in words of one and two syllables any more. The only one syllable words I could explain it in now wouldn't do at all in a Headline book." Then, having received Eileen's long, unhappy outpouring, Fry responded solicitously: "I don't think we shall find the separation has been too long," he reassured her. "On the contrary, I think we shall find it has been a good thing for both of us. Neither of us has found any substitute for the other; perhaps for that reason we shall respect one another more in the future than at times we have in the past. . . . Yet I agree that a year is long enough: in another we should probably be compelled by biological necessities to find substitutes, however unsatisfactory."

It was too late. Before Eileen read this, she had already sent an angry and almost abusive letter that crossed with Fry's latest disarming explanation of the rumors that had disturbed her so. "What sort of stories have the refugees been telling you?" he asked. "I find it hard to imagine. Or are you referring to Mme Breton, whom I once attacked rather brutally while under the influence, as the charlady said?" Humor was not what Eileen was interested in by now. Biting sarcasm was more to her taste. "Thanks for the picture of your staff, and those of yourself," she wrote before she had read Fry's latest, which was probably in a mail sack at the Azores. "You look pretty vigorous, I see.

What do you show people when they ask to see a picture of me? . . ." ("I am sorry that I have no picture of you," Fry eventually managed to answer. "Why did you never send me one? I didn't wait to be asked to send you pictures of me. I hope you regret the remark you made under this rubric.")

After her *Death in Venice* fears earlier in the year, Eileen still smarted from what the refugees had told her about Fry's nocturnal behavior. At best, her response to his denial was sniffy. "Your stories about being attemptedly framed on morals charges were interesting," she wrote, "as the stories had already reached me in a garbled form, more disturbing than your explanation, which I was glad to get. However the stories I heard, coupled with five weeks' silence on your part, caused me some distress. . . ." To Fry's harmless praise of the Provençal countryside, Eileen supplied a furious riposte: "Why not stay in France since you like the standard of living so much. A democracy is too good for you." Then veiled accusations of past misdeeds were resurrected: "Someone calls up on the phone about once a month and hangs up when I answer, without a word. Is it your German aviatrix friend, or Ruth Norden?" To round off the barrage, Eileen attempted to provoke him. "How is your Danny?" she wrote icily. "Please don't wait six weeks before writing. Your letters are not calculated to soothe and reassure hurt feelings and suspicions."

In by now typical fashion, Eileen was already regretting her intemperate words at the time Fry was reading them. Thus, when his response to her earlier letter arrived, it hurt her just as deeply as she had hurt him. "Why have you so little confidence in me and in yourself?" Fry asked reasonably. "I know that I don't deserve to be the object of much confidence, but I should think that you would have more confidence in yourself than you seem to have. And, as a matter of fact, I am not nearly so unreliable or so unfaithful as you seem to think me. It is always you, remember, who talk about my remarriage; I never even think of the idea . . . all my plans are based on the assumption that we will continue to live together as we have in the past. The reasons which have kept me here so long are not in any sense of a personal order. They are not that I have found a mistress, or that I like the food, or find living so cheap that I can't bring myself to return to our expensive democracy (by the way, please remember that I am not the only person who reads your letters). . . ."

When he finally received her worst communication, his reply ("What extremely *nasty* digs, my dear, so unworthy of your intelligence") would once again find Eileen receptive and regretful. Nineteen forty-one was a terrible year for both letter-writing and civilization. It was (as Winston Churchill said) the end of the beginning of the war, but it was also the beginning of the end of Fry's marriage.

———————

THE HARD MONTHS of June and July in Marseille had included yet more disappointments and harassments. Danny and Théo, who had wisely looked to leave France after his release from prison, found they were refused exit visas: Danny was of military age, so this was unsurprising. But Fry was hurt by Danny's refusal to be helped out illegally, which was a reflection—Danny made no secret of it—of his regard for the standard of escapes that Fry, along with Jean and Maurice, had engineered with Garcia. Danny made much of the fact that, far from conducting them to freedom, they were simply delivering refugees en masse to Spanish internment camps instead of French ones—by now an inaccurate comment. He and Théo would make their own way across the mountains, Danny told Fry.

Then in mid-June there was another police raid on the office, with a warrant signed by Auzanneau, to search for forged documents. The next day it was the turn of Villa Air-Bel to be nastily and conclusively turned upside down. By this time Fry had at least managed to equal the police's ingenuity, and nothing was found. But it was disturbing. One expected to be badgered—that was par for the course—but the police seemed to know exactly what they were looking for. For example, the second warrant declared the suspicion of an illegal transmitter, a *poste émetteur clandestin.* Did the police have intelligence that Fry had been illicitly broadcasting to London (as indeed he had done, on the Polish General Kleber's radio set)? Or was it just a coincidence?

The truth could not be ignored. Even Consul Fullerton advised Fry that the police knew so much about his activities that there must be a spy on the staff of the Centre Américain. Fry turned the matter over in his mind as to who it might be, but he came up with no answers. Fullerton was not finished. "Why do you have so many Jews on your staff?" he asked. Fry lied that less than half were Jewish. "Well, I think you make a mistake to have even that many," Fullerton replied. The American Foreign Service in France had managed to divest itself of all but one of its Jewish employees, he boasted. It was safer that way, and Fullerton was most concerned with safety. This almost counted as friendly advice, but was so repugnant that Fry ignored it. Otherwise things were even worse at the State Department now. The new visa application form was literally four feet long, and comprised dozens of unfulfillable requirements. The completed paper then had to travel through several Washington departments, each of which had "sudden death" powers of rejection, with no appeal process. Needless to say, the supply of American visas had quickly run almost dry.

There was a good chance that applicants could not even pass the hurdle of being *allowed* to apply for a visa. For example, Fry's employee Louis Coppée had been interviewed by the new vice-consul, who was fond of trick questions, and asked him where he was born. Coppée answered truthfully that he had come to life in Germany. "You have made a false statement before an American Consular official," exclaimed the vice-consul with glee. "I am going to refuse your visa. Furthermore I am going to see that you never get one. You were born in Poland, and you know it." Upper Silesia was made part of Poland after the First World War, *after* Coppée was born. It was German again following the invasion in 1939, but because it was Polish in 1924 when the US Immigration Act was passed, it remained part of Poland as far as the vice-consul was concerned. Coppée was given no chance to explain or defend himself. "Louis was crying when he told me this," said Fry. "The worst of it is that his kids now have to stay here. God knows what will become of them." Coppée was, of course, Jewish.

The same tricks were played by the pro-Fascist young vice-consul at Nice, Francis Withey. He asked a German Jew from the camp of Gurs, "What would you do if you were admitted to the United States and someone asked you to do something against the interests of the Italian or German governments?" The refugee thought for a moment, and then answered, "I would do what was in the interests of the United States." "Visa refused!" snapped Withey. "We don't want anyone in the United States who is going to mix up in politics." "Bewildered and heartbroken, the man went back to Gurs," noted Fry. "He is still there, still wondering why his answer was wrong. His wife and daughter have been refused visas because the man can't get his."

Even gentile Miriam Davenport was having trouble. She and her Yugoslavian husband, Rolf Treo, had stayed with his parents in Ljubljana until the Germans and Italians had invaded in April. Escaping along the one road out of Yugoslavia controlled by the Italians rather than the Germans, they managed to find their way to Switzerland. In Zurich, they had been waiting for Rolf's United States visa. And waiting. "The reason that the Consulate here gave me false information and let me sit around for six weeks believing that I'd taken all the right steps to get a USA visa for my husband," she wrote angrily, "is that they believed me to be the daughter of a 'very simple, very JEWISH family,' to be far 'too smart,' to be paid by 'wealthy Jews' etc etc. The grounds for their belief being that I'd worked for Emerescue, that I was an 'intellectual' and that I didn't wear a hat. . . . PS I forgot to add, so far as my suspected Jewish ancestry is concerned, that the US Consulate and Colony are now suffering from '*Very bad* conscience' because they found out that the Davenports weren't Jews after all! This and *only this* explains why they got into such a heated state the few days before Rolf's scheduled deportation . . . (I must say I'm almost tempted to become a naturalised Jew—I'm so thoroly [*sic*] disgusted.)"

After such heartbreaking frustration, Fry was in no mood to be summoned for an audience before the chief of police, de Rodellec du Porzic, as he was on July 10. There he was threatened again with the grave consequences of Danny's crime, but Fry was unruffled: Danny planned to escape from France in less than a week anyway, and after that the police would be wasting their breath. Du Porzic treated Fry to a stomach-turning speech on the morality of the "New France" ("We believe it is better to arrest a hundred innocent men than to let one criminal escape" he said), and then threatened to place him under house arrest far away from Marseille—"where you can do no harm"— if Fry did not leave the country forthwith.

The worried and panicky Consul Fullerton had already been vouchsafed this information by du Porzic, and had cabled the ERC in New York to recall Fry. He was now informed that this had been done, and it was time for him to go—even though he had heard nothing himself from the office on Forty-second Street. Fry decided to play for time, and said he needed to arrange for a replacement. Could he have a period of grace until, say, mid-August? That proved satisfactory to du Porzic, who frankly admitted that his objection to Fry was that he had given too much help to Jews and anti-Nazis ("parce que vous avez trop protégé des juifs et anti-Nazis"). Fry prepared grimly to hang on, and his reasoning was simple: "I must stay as long as I can, even if it means saving only one more human being."

Messages were received that Vladimir Vochoč had escaped from house arrest and made it to Lisbon, and that Lussu had also arrived there successfully by Maurice's and Garcia's route, which was working well by now. This was good news indeed, not entirely undone by the news of Klaus Dohrn's arrest in Spain. It seems that Big Klaus had walked straight to a Spanish village once he was over the border instead of to the customs post for his *entrada* stamp. He decided to ignore Fry's advice and instead rely on his Catholic friends. He had gone straight to the local priest, who could not stop Dohrn being arrested the next day and taken to the camp at Miranda del Ebro.

It was there that Dohrn discovered the Gestapo was touring Spain with its list, and he narrowly avoided deportation to Germany by inducing a high fever. He managed this by way of a sympathetic émigré doctor who gave him salt injections, followed by injections of milk and typhoid. Dohrn also ate several quinine cigarettes for good measure, and in the end was so dangerously ill that he did not care whether the Gestapo took him away after all. At the same camp, in the prisoner of war section, was Mary Jayne's boyfriend

Killer. In the end Charles Wolff had smuggled him over the border without Fry's knowledge, and he had been arrested. Now Killer began to bombard the Centre Américain in Marseille with fantastically incriminating telegrams, demanding repayment of money he claimed to have lent Klaus Dohrn and other illegal emigrants at the camp. He also spelled out how he wanted Fry to help him escape to England. It was all very interesting material for the censor.

Unsurprisingly, Fry was worn down by this time, but his biggest regret was that he would have to leave behind his beloved Villa Air-Bel. "In a sense it was the beginning of a life-long ambition," he confided to his journal. "A big house with a view and a large garden with infinite possibilities." In a letter he wrote to his mother from Toulon on July 4, Fry gave way to his exhaustion. Toulon was the home of the French navy, and as he looked out over the quiet docks that should have been a hive of activity, a nerve center of the fight against Fascism, there was nothing happening. It was a portrait of the humiliation of a nation hamstrung by an ignoble armistice. All Fry could see stretching away into the future was a war of attrition that would leave Europe in ruins. "Perhaps after all," he wrote, "the best thing is an early German victory." It would be horrendous, of course, but it might be for the best, about a century hence. "Perhaps it would unite Europe, put an end to its silly and destructive wars, mold a single people out of a continent of disparate and hostile elements as nothing has ever been able to do before."

It was a low point. "What I wrote," he decided soon after, was "the product of failure, discouragement and depression. Germany cannot win this war." Fry was so exhausted he hadn't even entertained the thought that, when two weeks before Hitler had broken the golden rule of warfare ("Never Attack Russia"), the Nazi tide might already have reached its high-water mark.

CHAPTER 22

FUGITIVE FRY

F RY WAS DUE to leave France on August 15, but he had no intention of doing so. It was time to circle the wagons and make a last stand. He needed to keep saving people, to keep the office up and running for as long as he could. Every extra week Fry managed to stay in France could mean another two or six or ten people could be brought to safety. The Gestapo was regularly touring the camps, and he heard from Vernet that its latest crop was greeted with this chilling advice: "You don't need to take any baggage with you. You won't need it anymore." Fry had forgotten the risk to himself by now; in fact he confessed that he had lost himself in the adventure. "I like the human relations of it," he said, "the hurly-burly, the sense of urgency, the innumerable complications and problems, perhaps even the danger, which has come to be like a needed drug to me." By now his identity resided in the bonds woven during the course of the year between himself, his friends, and his many dependents. There were still some 472 souls to extract from the looming grasp of the Gestapo, and whatever powers Fry retained he had to mingle with their fates.

There were several tasks to fulfill, the first of which was to root out the traitor within the ranks of the Centre Américain. Danny had always sworn it was Chaminade but Fry discounted this belief because of the intelligence Chaminade had consistently provided. Then Charles Wolff discovered that Chaminade had secretly been writing for the local Fascist newspaper, the Carbone-owned *Midi.* It was only factual reporting, but it was a terrible betrayal of trust and made sense of Danny's prolonged accusations. Chaminade was angry and indignant at being fired, and Fry, who thought Chaminade a "*mythomane* and *bifteckard*" by now, feared revenge: "Sometimes it is safer to keep your spy than get rid of him," he speculated. Straight after this, Fullerton told Fry that the Gestapo was bringing pressure on the French police to arrest him. Early in the year the Germans had laughed at Fry, saying that they knew what he was up to, and that they were confident he would not succeed. But he had succeeded—succeeded spectacularly—and the Nazis were furious. Fry had no time to lose.

He had been reserving some ammunition, and it was time to bring it forth. The letters Fry had been writing over the course of the year to famous and influential people had resulted in an impressive roll call of names. Now he announced officially his *Comité de Patronage*. In addition to Gide, Maillol, Matisse, and other distinguished French people, it included Mrs. John D. Rockefeller, Edsel Ford, son of Henry, and Henry Luce, the publishing tycoon. Fry mailed the list off to du Porzic, hoping that such international public support would afford him a buffer. In reality, it could only provide a flimsy bulwark against the mounting pressure: neither Vichy nor the Gestapo would halt their advance because of a list of names.

Fry must have realized this, for he soon set off to inspect the safe houses he had rented for those refugees who might not finally manage to get away. But he was also planning grander schemes of resettling the more able and rugged in the deep forests of the Var region. There was a terrible fuel shortage in France, and Fry speculated that he might be able to establish charcoal-burning factories that would supply income and security for the refugees. They would remain inconspicuous in the wilderness yet locally useful in the fuel they manufactured, and so safe from denunciation and internment ("There is no hostility on the part of the rural population of France. . . . The rule is rather an attitude of sympathy tinged with amusement."). Also, the plentiful chestnuts of the forest could be made into *crème de marron* to feed internees in concentration camps. Most of all, in the future the primitive woodland locations could become centers of resistance against the Germans—for this was Fry's underlying long-term goal.

When there is no longer any hope of mercy, the only living option is to fight, and Fry was in fact already involved with Jean Gemahling in low-level sabotage of German operations. So far it had simply involved Jean and his idealistic friends breaking into goods yards and steaming off the bills of lading from the sides of railcars. These notices revealed the sack of the French economy by the Nazis, who were exporting back to the Reich the vast majority of its produce. Dutifully, Fry would collate this intelligence and send it to the American embassy in the hope that it would be passed on to the British, who could make use of the information (so much potash destined for explosives factories in Leipzig, for example), and whose interests the American Foreign Service represented in unoccupied France.

The embassy rarely if ever acted, but Fry, undaunted, was still contemplating Jean's request that he begin to fund the purchase of arms and munitions to make the nascent Resistance cell a more formidable outfit. Louis Coppée had met a German refugee who called himself Rameau and claimed he could lay his hands on machine guns. It was an interesting proposition, but the danger was deadly. In the meantime, Fry decided to make another trip to Vichy, and in the last week of July he and Coppée set off to plead the case for exit visas one more time with the "pimping slavies" of Pétain's government.

Railway coaches—or rather their noisy connecting sections—were the only places in France where one could talk freely without fear. Seditious words were carried away on the wind so rapidly that they could not be overheard. It was standing up in one such coach speeding toward Montélimar, that Fry spoke with the angry Frenchmen already planning the downfall of the Fascists. One, a soap manufacturer from Marseille, was already active in a Gaullist group, and he told Fry of a list of traitors his men had taken an oath to assassinate. Du Porzic was not at the top of the list, but he was not far down it either. The battle was on, and Fry was heartened by what he heard. At Montélimar, awaiting a connection to Lyon, he was further galvanized by the terrible news that Marx Dormoy, the French Socialist leader and Léon Blum's Minister of the Interior, had been shot to death in his bed that very morning. It was not the Germans but France's own *Sûreté Nationale* that had done the deed, Fry soon learned. He was on his way to Vichy to try to deal with an unashamedly criminal regime.

FRY PUT OFF actually arriving at Vichy for as long as possible, for it was not something he looked forward to. Instead he stopped off at Cluny to indulge his fondness for walking around old churches. The ruined Benedictine Abbey there had a church (or rather a tower, the remains of an aisle, a chapel and a piece of the great portal) that had once been only a few feet smaller than the largest church in the world, St. Peter's Basilica in the Vatican. His old Harvard teacher had composed a monograph on the Abbey, and Fry spent three happy days pacing it out and studying what was left while reading Professor Conant's work, lent him by the proprietress of his hotel there. He also thought about Eileen and their marriage. Considerably angered by her harsh words, Fry had responded in kind. "I want to say something which I have not said before but which I feel needs saying," he had written. "I think my previous letter says all that needs to be said about my 'plans.' You see from it how very essentially you figure in them. But I do not want to live with a jealous and suspicious wife. . . . I want my wife to have confidence in me; in spite of my numerous faults I think I am worthy of a certain amount—perhaps as much as the next fellow, even." After that, the storm had blown itself out and the balance of the relationship was temporarily restored. Fry went back to being rather diffident and clumsy on the subject of conjugal love, and Eileen resumed her role as the emotionally mature partner.

On his travels around Vichy Fry somewhere picked up a book, *Observations by Mr. Dooley,* an early example of psychobabble. He told Eileen she would find in it a complete explanation of their differences and difficulties. "A man's first, last, and only perennial love, says Mr Dooley, is his job and two weeks after the honeymoon is over it begins to come between him and his wife," Fry quoted enthusiastically. "Whereas a woman is romantic and looks always for outward expression of her husband's continuing affection, a man is highly practical and distinctly unromantic: once married, he takes his wife, and his affection for her, for granted; what he thinks about is his job." Eileen's blistering and utterly justified reply put her husband firmly in his place. "Did you find Mr Dooley's remarks on politics, art, etc as just as his remarks on women and marriage?" she asked,

or perhaps you are better educated in those fields. . . . When I was about fifteen years old I was dreadfully worried by Byron's lines—

Man's love is of his life a thing apart;
'Tis woman's whole existence.

A desire to gain more knowledge on such matters, and to form some sensible conclusion on such points, is a strong incentive for novel reading. By the time one has read all of Turgeniev and Tolstoi and Tchekov (who go quite thoroughly into the matter), the remarks of Mr Dooley seem to throw not much light on the human heart. . . .

In effect, you delight to think of yourself as *l'homme sensual moyen* in your relations with your wife; but do you like to think of yourself as John Doe in politics, or John Q. Public at an art gallery? Admittedly in all those fields, you take the line that the best is none too good for you. Only in the field of personal relations (by which I mean much more than married life) do you fall back on such indolent and uncharacteristic praise of stupidity. And it really is an important field . . . if you can win there, you need never worry again whether your suits fit you or not! I think I still love you, in spite of all you say and do to make me shudder! I shall know definitively when you've been home for a week. How about *you*?'

Fry was suitably chastened ("Your sermon was well written and well deserved. I apologize and surrender"). He was no expert on intimacy, and if he had opened up during the remarkable year he had spent in France it was because, as Saint-Exupéry put it, "There is no growth except in the fulfillment of obligations." Fry had exchanged one set of obligations in America for a more demanding and—there was no escaping the conclusion—more rewarding set in France. It would not be easy to change back again. Beamish had written to Eileen attempting to warn her of just this: "I find it difficult to get rid of the mentality of a soldier on leave, or of somebody triumphant because he is *not* in prison. And I am sure you will find it difficult to re-acclimatize Varian when he is back. This was a great experience for all of us." Beamish was a veteran of conflict, its terrors and exaltations, and knew that to reabsorb himself in civilian life an equivalently dramatic change must be effected from strife to peace. Thus, Eileen soon wrote Fry with the news of Beamish's sudden marriage. ("Whom did Otto marry?" replied Fry. "Something rich, I'll bet. I told him the absence of a certain European institution would force him into it.")

At Vichy nothing happened. Its doors had been closed to Fry, and the few friends he had there, like Réné Gillouin, failed to discover what the Ministry of the Interior had against him. But there must have been something, for Fry—to his utter astonishment was denied permission to stay overnight in the town, "because suspected of *communism*!!!!!!!! Have you ever heard of anything more utterly ridiculous in your life?" he asked Eileen. While he was there he naturally went to see his friends in the Press Bureau. Archambault, when informed of Fry's delicate position with regard to the Gestapo, had a single piece of advice: disappear. Fry took it, deciding not to return to Marseille, even after his August 15 deadline, thus effectively going on the run.

His act being one of passive rather than active illegality, Fry did not exactly have to dart from doorway to doorway with his collar turned up. All he needed to do was to keep a low profile well away from Auzanneau's beat. To this end Fry traveled to Sanary-sur-Mer, and from there to Cannes and Nice, where he saw Matisse again, and staged a photographic session, taking over one hundred shots of the artist. Fry was quite unwell by this time with a sinus infection and various symptoms of malnutrition and exhaustion, and his fugitive existence provided a much needed rest, although he was impatient to return to the office. At Sanary Fry was surprised and dismayed to receive a visit from Danny Bénédite, who was supposed to have been in Lisbon.

Ironically, he and Théo had been arrested at the border with Spain and imprisoned there by the French for ten days. Fry noted wryly that for all Danny's criticism of the escapes that he had arranged, Danny and Théo were the first and only people to have been arrested, never mind jailed, before they had even left France. Danny was sensitive about the incident and full of self-justifications for what was after all quite a disaster, and which Fry knew that, "coming on top of the gold business, is likely to have very serious consequences for him, if not for all of us." It meant at the very least that Danny now had to stay away from the office completely, and also that it was too dangerous for him to attempt another escape from the country. At the same time, he was under examination by the police for two felonies. "If you had taken his [Maurice's] advice, you wouldn't be where you are now," Fry told him. "But some of us are too obstinate for our own good." Danny's future did not look rosy.

The good news was that Kakies and Oettinghaus had been released from prison at Oran, and that an Austrian labor leader called Johannes Schnek had been smuggled into Spain hidden under a load of cabbages. Fry also learned that Frank Kingdon, who had apparently been suffering a minor nervous breakdown, was claiming that he had not agreed to Fry's recall, and never sent any communication to the State Department or Consul Fullerton saying so. Fry didn't know what to think. Kingdon might have been lying, but so might Fullerton, and both could so easily be caught out that to lie seemed stupid. So who cared the least whether Fry discovered the trick? It looked as if the American Foreign Service had struck again.

Staying at the Hotel Majestic in Cannes, Fry resigned himself to his enforced vacation and made the best of it. Fortunately, the hotel had a good stock of Scotch whiskies left over from before the invasion, and Fry worked his way through them all with the dedication of a man unwillingly separated from the thing he loves. He also wrote another of his tepid romantic declarations to Eileen. "If only you knew what a faithful and devoted dog I really am, in spite of my occasional errings," he began. "No, my pet, we have lived too long together, and are both of us too old and too wise to want to start over again trying to learn to live with someone else. At least I am too old and too wise—and too little interested, any more, in 'love' in the romantic, head-over-heels sense. I think I shall never be the sort of man who, fat and fifty, marries a young cutie, to the embarrassment of his friends and the amusement of his enemies. That is one thing you don't have to worry about." By now Eileen was actually more worried that Fry would end up in a concentration camp for the next five or ten years, for relations between Vichy and America were growing increasingly strained, and her husband was most definitely out in the cold.

After a drunken, depressed two weeks during which Fry felt in his own words, "practically ready for a mental hospital," he decided to take a chance and return to Marseille. He had attempted to run the office from Cannes but due to the sheer complexity of the work it was proving impossible. Danny had been with Fry since the weekend and on Tuesday, August 26, they both returned, with Fry rubbing his hands in anticipation of being back on the job. Straightaway, a cable from New York arrived, announcing "SUCCESSOR APPOINTED. MAKING LAST PREPARATIONS TO SEND HIM." Fry decided he would stay at Marseille for a few days, to sort out the confusion into which the office and Villa Air-Bel had descended during his absence: "both very definitely and undeniably need a head, and both fall apart rather rapidly when the head is away. That is why I feel I must stay until X gets here."

In the interim he planned to disappear again, perhaps into the mountains. When his successor—whoever it was—arrived, only then would Fry leave France. "Everyone is convinced," he said, "that if the Committee is left without an American at its head, it will be closed down immediately."

"FRIDAY, AUGUST 29, 11 P.M. I have been arrested. I am writing this on a scrap of paper. . . . They came for me at the office at one o'clock this afternoon. Two young detectives. They had an order, signed by de Rodellec du Porzic. . . . No explanation . . . I have not been allowed to communicate with anybody."

"Remember that you are dealing with an American citizen!" Lucie Heymann cried when the police barged through Fry's office door that lunchtime. With Lena gone, it was left to Lucie to play mother tiger. She went with Fry and the detectives to the Evêché, then ran back to Boulevard Garibaldi and began frantically to make telephone calls. Fry was to be expelled from France. Lucie managed to set up a meeting with Roger Homo, Secretary General of Provence, that very afternoon. She sent Paul and Maurice to Monsieur Fleury, head of the *Sûreté*, to see what could be done with him. She dispatched Louis Coppée and Danny Bénédite to Vichy to try to halt the proceedings. Suddenly, Fry had become Client Number One of the Centre Américain de Secours.

The previous day the Vichy government had been convulsed by the shooting of Pierre Laval and pro-Nazi Marcel Déat at Versailles by a man named Paul Colette, who was part of the circle of would-be *résistants* surrounding Simone de Beauvoir and Jean-Paul Sartre (the idea of Déat as a target had been Sartre's own). The assassin had failed, although Laval's wound to the liver was grave. The real damage was to the composure of Vichy itself, which had already trembled at the killing of a German on the Paris *Métro* a mere week before. Something in France was awakening after the long shock of defeat, and the collaborationist regime suddenly felt itself vulnerable, its mandate openly challenged for perhaps the first time. This meant that for Fry, in France and at large only on a sort of probation, his time was up. Vichy's immediate instinct was to batten down the hatches of power and to make itself feel secure against the coming storm.

It could hardly have been sheer coincidence that Fry's liberty was taken away just then. He had been back at Marseille, openly walking the streets and working at his office for four days. The police had not seemed to care, although they certainly knew where Fry was because they picked him up soon enough when they wanted to. The fact that Fleury had no idea what was happening suggests that the orders to apprehend Fry came direct from Vichy to its local toadie du Porzic.

Fry's staff spent the day making desperate appeals for his release, but they got nowhere. Finally, Lucie managed to secure a brief interview with Auzanneau, but he was cold and unhelpful. He accused Fry of being engaged in secret activities since his disappearance on July 24. He wanted to know what had happened during those "thirty momentous days." Lucie attempted to explain, but made no progress—her account of Fry's perfectly legal movements did not dispel du Porzic's suspicion. The fact was that Fry had of course been involved in secret activities throughout this time; the police had simply decided to revoke his license, as it were. Fry spent the night sleeping on a table at police headquarters ("uncomfortable but not impossible") and when Lucie went back the next morning, she found him, unshaven but smiling broadly, in the company of a burly police inspector named Garandel.

Fry's time in France was over. He was given two hours of freedom in the afternoon to pack his possessions, and was then to be conducted under guard directly to the border with Spain. Lucie cabled Danny and Louis to meet them at Cerbère, and then, in a strange atmosphere of both regret and excitement, everybody made ready for the journey. Fry was taken to Villa Air-Bel to throw his papers and what was left of his threadbare clothes into a trunk. He kissed good-bye the maids, Rose and Maria, and returned to the Evêché at about six o'clock in the evening. From there, Garandel took him to the Gare St. Charles, where Fry walked to the top of the *grand escalier* and took his last look down the Boulevard d'Athènes toward the Canebière. The city shone gold in the late-afternoon sun. In the space of a year, it had become his true home.

Fry's staff insisted on accompanying him on the train, and on Saturday night, after a lively meal at the station restaurant in Marseille, they set off for Narbonne, where they would spend the night. Inspector Garandel stayed close to Fry. Fry in turn struggled to rein in the potentially incontinent Clovis, who had grown very large by now, and was excited by the commotion. Together with Lucie, Jean, Théo, Maurice, Paul, and Jacques Weisslitz, they crowded into a reserved carriage, and began to pass around a bottle of cognac as the train pulled out of the station.

Garandel, with his huge fists and great slab-like policeman's face, soon proved to be quite a discovery. He had been embarrassed at the task he was to perform, and like an executioner had asked Fry's forgiveness. "Nous ne sommes pas des barbares nous Français," he reassured the prisoner: *We French aren't barbarians.* Now, in the darkened railway compartment with the liquor being passed from hand to hand, he began to regale the party with stories of his long career—and his *flair policier*—in the netherworld of the Vieux Port, "Talking," Fry recalled, "in a thick Midi accent, and using his expressive hands to indicate what he was saying—drawing his hand across his throat to indicate a throat-slitting, giving a quick brush-off with his palms to show that he had decided to abandon an investigation that was proving a little too dangerous, reaching out and grasping a piece of air in his strong fingers to mean that he had arrested somebody . . . 'We pinched them!'"

At Cerbère Fry had the last, bitter laugh on Vichy. While still at the Evêché in Marseille he had tried to point out that it was impossible for him to leave the country because he had no valid exit or transit visas. If anybody knew emigration procedure it was Fry, but Auzanneau had airily waved away the problem, saying they could be obtained at the border. When the company, which by now included Danny and Louis Coppée, reached the customs station at Cerbère, the commissaire looked at Fry's visa-free passport and said, "Those fools in Marseille don't know their faces from their arses." Garandel grinned. Fry would not be leaving France just yet after all.

For the next week, Fry and Garandel effectively took a vacation at nearby Perpignan, where the Nazis were overseeing the grape harvest (before stealing all the wine and taking it back to Germany). They ate well at the Café de la Loge, and drank the best wines. Garandel now acted less as a policeman and more as Fry's personal bodyguard. On hearing that he could not yet leave France, Auzanneau had ordered Garandel to put Fry "in the cooler" at Perpignan jail, which in fact had only a single, large dark cell opening on the courtyard. The emaciated men inside clung to the bars of the small barred window and looked out miserably. Fry said the scene looked like a Goya painting. "And it's there they wanted me to put you," the policeman said, and shuddered, after he had found Fry a good hotel room.

"Why not?" asked Fry.

"Why not? You have only done good in France," said Garandel. "You mustn't think it is we French who are putting you out. It is the Germans."

"But somehow I felt I *belonged* in that dark cell," Fry wrote. "A year ago, it would have been different."

During the day Garandel let Fry wander freely while he visited old friends in the area or swam at Canet Plage. At night he stuck like glue to his charge. "The town is full of Germans," explained Garandel to Fry. "You can never tell what they might do to you on one of these dark streets if you walked out alone." For the first time in Fry's entire experience in France, the American consulate enthusiastically cooperated and managed to return his passport, replete with fresh exit and transit visas, in just five days. Client Number One was finally going home.

FRY ALSO HAD the last laugh on the American Foreign Service. By freak chance Ambassador Leahy was on his way into Spain on official business, and took the same train as Fry. They traveled all the way to Barcelona, and the *New York Times* of Sunday, September 7, trumpeted the headline "LEAHY TAKES FRY WITH HIM INTO SPAIN." In fact, Fry made sure to spare the ambassador's blushes by going nowhere near him during the trip, and he stayed well away from the accompanying crowd of reporters. Nevertheless the article appeared, and "apparently caused the Ambassador no end of embarrassment at Vichy," wrote Fry to Eileen,

> . . . for what will the Vichysois think of an American Ambassador who attempts to protect an American citizen suspected of being an anti-Nazi and pro-Jew (as the papers prettily put it)? One of my collaborators has just returned from a trip to Vichy where, she reports, she found the Embassy in a froth of anger against me. . . . I was therefore especially pleased to learn they had assumed that it was I who was responsible for the false report. That is characteristic of their attitude towards me from the beginning. If anything unpleasant happens, if the Embassy is accused of harboring sympathies for the enemies of Nazi oppression, listening sympathetically to the complaints of a Jew, or doing anything to protect the life of an American citizen who has been accused of being an anti-Nazi, it is always that man Fry who is responsible. When I get home I will have the opportunity to clear not only our Embassy, but our entire Foreign Service in France of all such embarrassing charges.

It had been raining when Fry made his last farewells to his staff on the platform at Cerbère station, and clasped Garandel's hand and wished him good luck. When he emerged from the tunnel on the Spanish side, it was still raining. By the evening of that day, Saturday, September 6, Fry was in Barcelona, his head still spinning with the speed of events. And he was deeply depressed, because he felt more like he had been deported from his own country than that he was now returning home. He grew deeply sentimental. "Some day," he wrote to Danny, "I shall be back in France, and then you can show me the parts of France I have not seen, those parts which are barred, now, even to you but which will some day be free again. Then we shall go arm in arm over the hills and into the valleys, singing the songs and drinking the wines, of your beautiful, your incomparable country. Until then, Danny, good-bye. I love France, and I love you: because you are so French, perhaps. Believe me when I say that, for I mean it with all my heart."

"Forgive me, then, if I am sad today," he wrote from his Barcelona hotel to Eileen. "It is not merely the sadness of parting from friends and familiar sights and sounds. It is not merely the malaise that always overcomes me when I have to pack my things and move. It is also, and especially, the terrible let-down that was sooner or later inevitable after such a strenuous and turbulent year. For I have reached the end of the most intense twelve months I have ever lived through, and . . . the experience has changed me profoundly." He left for Lisbon on the following Monday, but instead of returning to New York, he hung on for another six weeks there, working out of the Hotel Métropole with the Unitarians, still attempting to save yet more refugees. His work was the only thing that could lift his spirits, as he wrote to Théo: "Yes there is a great deal to be done, and my gloom of a week ago has disappeared entirely in the face of prospects of new work ahead."

He realized that Eileen was implicated in his reluctance to return to New York, and he attempted to explain to her that she should not expect things to be how they were before he left. "Shall I gradually return to my old self in the familiar surroundings of New York?" he asked rhetorically.

Doubtless I shall lose some of my new qualities; doubtless some of the old, now dormant, will be reawakened by the resumption of a normal, American life. But I do not think I shall ever be quite the person I was when I kissed you good-bye at the airport and went down the gangplank to the waiting Clipper. For the experience of ten, fifteen and even twenty years have been pressed into one. . . . I have learned to live with people, and to work with them. I have developed or discovered within me, powers of resourcefulness, of imagination and of courage which I never before knew I possessed. And I have fought a fight, against enormous odds, of which, in spite of the final defeat, I think I can always be proud. . . . I don't know whether you will like the change or not: I rather suspect you won't. But it is there, and it is there to stay. It is the indelible mark that a year spent in fighting my own little war has left on me. . . .

Here I just want to tell you that you are going to find your husband a changed man—and to put you on your guard against trying to change him back again to what he was before.

Besides working hard in Lisbon, Fry treated his time there as a diver would a decompression chamber on his rise from the depths of the ocean. He was returning from a war, and from hunger, into the civilian life of the twentieth century, and it was a profound shock. To Théo he described how he was "like a child taken for the first time to the circus, goggle-eyed." There were "camera shops *filled* with cameras, all makes, and all the latest models. Typewriters—*new* typewriters—for sale at perfectly ordinary prices. Tailors' shops displaying *English* cloth in their windows. The latest books from England and the United States. *Yesterday's* Times, Daily Mail, and Daily Telegraph . . . Time and Harper's Magazine, the Saturday Evening Post and the New Yorker, all for sale as if it were perfectly natural to be so. A grocer's window boasting boxes and boxes of MacVitie and Price's Petits Buerres, Clotted creams—and Scotch Shortbread. Haig and Haig, Johnny Walker, and Dewar's White Label. Shops where you can just walk in and buy any number of packages of Player's Navy Cut, Goldflake, or Lucky Strike cigarettes, for less than 25c a package. After an hour of that, Clovis and I returned to the hotel and stuck pins in ourselves to make sure we weren't dreaming."

He sounded as if he was recovering from his mood of depression, but in fact Fry was unwell. A year of malnutrition had left him physically weakened, and the chronic lack of vitamins in his system had produced unsettling symptoms: his hands regularly swelled up to twice their normal size, for example. He was also losing his memory, again a sign of vitamin deficiency. Once, when he was discussing the case of a refugee with Dr. Joy, Fry found himself asking who the man was. Joy gave him a very queer look, and told him it was the same person they had discussed the previous day. "Something is happening to my mind," said Fry. "I have never been so frightened in my life." It was finally time for him to go home. A few days later, Fry once again walked along the gangplank and boarded the PanAm Clipper. It was finished.

CHAPTER 23

THE HOMECOMING

FRY WAS BACK in New York by late October 1941. He stood on the sidewalk on East Forty-second Street, outside Grand Central station and across from the ERC offices in the Chanin building, stunned by the roar of the traffic and the noisy voices shouting in what to Fry seemed now like a foreign language—English.

His reunion with Eileen was a disaster. "We had never gotten on terribly well together, always quarrelling and making up again," he admitted, "but after I got back from France it was intolerable." Within a year the marriage was over—or rather, it took a year for them to accept that it was already over when Fry returned. To begin with, a charade of normality covered the rift between them. In large part it was maintained by spending the interest on the marriage's capital stock of affection; also by Fry keeping up the frenetic pace of his efforts on behalf of the remaining refugees in France. He went straight to work at the offices of the Emergency Rescue Committee, where Hans Sahl and Miriam Davenport were attempting to disentangle the mess of stalled emigration files. His presence there was not a success.

It was difficult for Fry to remember that, unlike Boulevard Garibaldi, he was not in charge at Forty-second Street—indeed, a strong body of opposition and resentment was actively working against him, personified by Mildred Adams and lately by Frank Kingdon as well. And it must be said that Fry did not help matters. "The disorder of the ERC office is beyond belief," he wrote to Danny, after he had arrived at the offices denouncing the laziness and inefficiency that had frustrated him all year. The fact was, as Fry himself understood, that everybody "resented my attempts . . . to make people at the committee realize how urgent the situation was, and how much harder they ought to work than they had been working. That of course is something which no one can stand." Fry was right: soon he had hardly any supporters in New York left at all.

At its simplest the problem was that New York lacked a Gestapo or Vichy police against which to unify the staff in the superhuman effort Fry was used to. The New York workers were good people, but they were far away from the crisis and not personally threatened. Their civilian lives still claimed much of their attention, and the committee was a job for them—an important one, but a job all the same. Fry, having almost forsaken his own civilian identity, found it difficult to sympathize with this, and relations quickly and inevitably broke down.

It was also partly Fry's fatal lack of diplomacy, and partly his commend-able naïveté. True to his promise, he had begun to attack the State Depart-ment on his return to America even before he had left La Guardia Airport. In an interview to waiting reporters, he was quoted as saying the State Depart-ment had acted "stupidly," and described one case where because of delays is-suing a visa, a refugee was now in Gestapo hands. Privately, his opinion was much stronger. "Any American official who collaborates with Vichy, and through Vichy with the Gestapo, against an American Citizen," he wrote, "is guilty of something not wholly unlike treason. And yet that is exactly what certain members of the American Foreign Service did in my case." This may have been true, but it was not politic—and certainly not in the interests of the committee, which absolutely had to maintain good relations with the State Department—to declare such sentiments more or less openly.

In November Fry wrote to Théo, "Everybody here finds it extremely diffi-cult to understand how I can have been so popular in Marseille as here I am my usual stiff and self-conscious self. I have tried to explain that the circum-stances had a good deal to do with it, and that besides many people exagger-ate, but it doesn't do as an explanation." In France, for a brief and unique time, the lifelong outsider had become an insider. Now he found himself once again edged beyond the inner circle. Fry's closest relationships at this point were epistolary ones, and he spent much of his time corresponding with his friends in France. Or he saw old friends from Marseille like Consuelo de Saint-Exupéry (who had joined her husband in New York) or André Breton, who was also having problems adjusting to his new life.

Most of the artists had settled in very well. Chagall, whose Metropolitan Opera murals are today an integral part of New York culture, certainly took to the place: there were cows in America after all. Masson was happily paint-ing in rural Connecticut. Ernst was doing well, despite having been arrested as an enemy alien and interned on Ellis Island for a short while upon his arrival. After gaining his liberty he had toured the West, collecting Native American religious objects (kachinas) in an attempt to find a mythic link between the Old World and the New. He and Peggy Guggenheim had briefly tied the knot. "I married him during the war," she said later, "because after Pearl Harbor I decided it was a bad idea to live in sin with an enemy alien." The marriage rapidly self-destructed, though, and Ernst was soon living with the painter Dorothea Tanning, "a remarkably thin and green young woman who looked like one of the less fleshy figures in some of his pictures," said Fry. Lipchitz was well settled, and had taken an apartment not far from Eileen on Washington Square.

Breton, on the other hand, had split up with Jacqueline, who had moved in with the brilliant young Chilean surrealist Roberto Matta, taking Aube with her. Jacqueline was soon to launch a new and highly successful career as a painter herself. Meanwhile Breton was brooding. "He drinks a good deal of red wine and complains that he will never learn English and doesn't want to—always a bad sign, I think," wrote Fry. The penniless Breton had eventually been forced to take a job working at the Voice of America. There he met up again with Claude Lévi-Strauss, with whom he shared the memory of their voyage to America and a brief internment on Martinique.

Meanwhile Fry's continued public pronouncements, and his searing articles in *The Nation,* were doing him no good with the committee. Frank Kingdon, who saw himself as the mouthpiece for the refugee situation, deeply resented Fry's media profile. In November, Kingdon asked Fry to stay away from the Forty-second Street offices for a while. "The Committee felt, and I think rightly, that my activities in France in behalf of refugees had so greatly embarrassed and annoyed the State Department that a guarantee from me was likely to result in automatic refusal of a visa application," he wrote to one refugee. Fry assented to Kingdon's request, and even had the insight to appreciate why he was not being thanked for all he had done. "It is true that Kingdon's attitude has lacked 'gratitude,'" he wrote. "But then I think that if one is to be realistic, one ought not to expect gratitude in this world. As a matter of fact, why should Kingdon feel any gratitude to me? It is rather the refugees who should, and as a matter of fact many of them do, and have given ample evidence of the fact since I got back. As for Kingdon, he, I think, always resented my staying [in France] because it was a kind of insubordination. Furthermore, I think he was jealous of the reputation I had made for myself in certain refugee circles."

It might well have been so, for in the New Year Fry discovered that he had been effectively fired. "Unfortunately," wrote Kingdon in February, "your atti-

tudes since your return to this country have made it inadvisable for us to continue your connection with the Committee. Therefore I must ask you once
again not to speak in the name of the Committee, to accept any commission
in behalf of the Committee, or to make any commitments for the Committee.
Please believe that it is a matter of personal sorrow with me that I have to
make this as explicit as I do." Fry tried desperately to fight his way back in, but
he had been outmaneuvered, as he had been with the Spanish Aid Committee
several years earlier. "Will you be good enough to indicate what 'attitudes' you
have in mind?" he demanded. "The only one you have ever mentioned to me
was my attitude toward the State Department. This, you said, was preventing
clients of the ERC from obtaining visas. It was for that reason that you asked
me to take a month's leave of absence, in an effort to appease the Department. But since you have since publicly adopted the same attitude, I cannot
suppose you refer to that attitude now." What Kingdon really meant, of
course, was that Fry's behavior in general was disruptive and disagreeable.
"Dr. Kingdon does not like me and will not hear of me having anything to do
with the committee," Fry wrote Danny. "That's that."

By this time America itself had joined what was by now a global conflict.
Three days after the Japanese attack on Pearl Harbor, America also found itself an opponent of Germany when Hitler recklessly declared war. It looked
like Fry had gotten out of France just in time. America was not an enemy of
Vichy yet, but all France was as good as German territory by now, and the
South would soon be occupied by the Wehrmacht. The new situation naturally changed the American public's regard for the refugees. With the nation
now at war, little sympathy or cash could be spared for foreigners.

Under Fry's leadership, said Howard L. Brooks, the Centre Américain de
Secours had been a "fighting organization." Remarkably, it continued to fight
on in Marseille even though no American was ever sent to replace Fry. Before
he left, Fry had appointed Jean Gemahling as Executive Secretary pro tem, as
Jean was the only member of staff who was gentile, French, and had no
"criminal" record. Fry had of course kept quiet about Jean's Resistance activities. Danny continued to administer from behind the scenes, but he was
forced to keep a low profile. In the year following Fry's departure, an astonishing volume of covert correspondence was kept up between Fry and Danny,
in the attempt to effect the evacuation of the last few hundred refugees, who
were still trickling through Spain, sailing to North Africa, and being smuggled
over the border into Switzerland. But by now the staff was under terrible
pressure from the Vichy authorities. In late 1941, Lucie Heymann wrote to
Fry in a sort of code: "I am not very gay today. Yesterday a good friend who
wishes me well gave me some advice similar to the advice you received a few

months ago. It seems that I am tired, and that a rest in the country would do me the most good. I suspect that the sage counsel of my doctor will apply to every one of us sooner or later." Yet they stayed and continued the work despite the danger, bound together by an overwhelming loyalty to Fry.

There was no such loyalty toward him in America, and the committee itself seemed to lose its direction and impetus without Fry—who laid the blame at Kingdon's feet. "As far as I can see," he wrote to Danny, "Kingdon is a man with no serious interest in the fate of the refugees. He enjoys the limelight enormously, and likes to make speeches. That, I would say, is about as far as his interest in the work goes. Now he is interested in other things, and he would like to be rid of the refugee work altogether." Unfortunately, due to the very success of Fry's mission, most of the famous names had been rescued by now. The Committee's raison d'être had vanished. In the spring of 1942 it was merged with the International Rescue and Relief Committee. But in Marseille the Centre Américain still operated despite being starved of funds. In America, Fry took up the post of assistant editor at *The New Republic.*

FRY WAS UNPREPARED for the letter he received from Danny early in 1942. "My dear Varian," it began. "This is going to be a painful letter to write, but it must be done." The story Danny had to tell was deeply disturbing. One day late in November, Jean Gemahling had left the office at lunchtime and simply vanished, as they discovered from his girlfriend the next morning. The atmosphere at the office darkened as all their enquiries drew a blank, and the fear was that Jean had been arrested—a theory that subsided only with time, as no police arrived to raid the office or arrest anybody else. Paul Schmierer set out to question all Jean's friends, and eventually uncovered Jean's secret existence as the head of a local Resistance cell.

It transpired that in the course of his Resistance activities Jean had been introduced by Coppée to the supposedly anti-Nazi German exile, Rameau. (Fry knew this very well, but had kept it from Danny, who at that point was contemptuous of "naïve" Gaullists.) Danny wrote that he had found out Rameau was probably a Gestapo agent, or at the least an informer for the *Sûreté*. After that, the rest of the story fell into place. Jean had been inveigled by Coppée into buying a machine gun from Rameau for the purpose of shooting a Vichy official, but had then been denounced to the police and arrested. When interrogated about Jean's disappearance, Coppée, Danny wrote, "behaved like a whipped dog . . . and didn't even dare go and piss first without our permission." He claimed that Fry had set the whole thing up. At a single stroke, it appeared that Fry had undone all his good work and ruined his image with his loyal friends in Marseille. At the time he sat down to write the letter, Danny had just discovered that Jean was in prison—possibly suffering agonies in some Gestapo cellar—charged with gun-running, and his letter blamed Fry not only for this, but also for endangering the Centre Américain de Secours and the liberty of all those who had a connection with it.

Fry was devastated. He wrote to Danny pleading that he had no knowledge of the deal concerning the machine gun. This was, strictly speaking true: he was ignorant of that specific arrangement. "I would like to say once again that I most certainly would never have allowed myself to be guilty of such deceit and treachery as that would have implied," he told Danny. "There was no *autre chose.* You knew absolutely the whole story. I concealed nothing whatever from you—more important than the details of my sexual life." But if Jean was in prison, Fry knew at bottom it *was* his fault. If he was not expressly to blame, he was generally the instigator of Jean's Resistance activity. Now Fry was not only helpless due to his banishment from Forty-second Street, but he was also tortured by the thought that he had delivered Jean into the hands of the enemy. And if Jean talked under torture, the rest of his friends might suffer the same fate.

That spring of 1942 was a time of great personal torment for Fry and it was only after Jean was by some miracle of fate released—emaciated, shaven-headed, his health almost broken—at the beginning of April that Fry's ordeal also ended. The first thing Jean did when he got out was to ask for a pen and paper, so he could write to Fry:

> I am sorry that, in their anxiety, they wrote to you somewhat bitterly about the work we were doing together you and me. In fact, at the time they did not know the exact conditions of my arrestation and they had not understood that it was all due to my own carelessness and lack of prudence. The first days of my imprisonment I was absolutely terrified at the idea of the possible consequences for the Centre, and needless to say I cursed my stupidity. . . . My dear Varian, you are in the bottom of your heart more French than American, and all your French friends need you.

"I want you to know," replied Fry, "that I suffered acute agonies of conscience all the time and experienced a sense of relief, the like of which I can't ever remember having felt before, when I got Danny's word that you had been released." In fact many of the staff had written to him once Jean had been able to explain that Fry was innocent of the charges Danny had leveled at him. Using her code once again, Lucie said "I had the pleasure of learning that Jean was cured. After my first rage I understood that you didn't have much to do with his illness, but the first information about the contagion was so bizarre that you would have understood my indignation." Fry still felt remorse over the whole affair even though he did not regret in principle the encouragement he had given his young protégé. "I did start you on the path," he wrote to Jean, "and I felt in large measure responsible for the consequences of having done so. Or did I? Do I flatter myself? Perhaps like so many others you would have been forced to do what you did in one way or another—even if I hadn't happened along. . . ."

FRY WAS NOW ENTERING a very frustrating period of inactivity. He tried to join the army, and even for some time had a hope of entering the military intelligence service (OSS) for which surely, of almost all Americans, he was uniquely qualified. But the army classified him 4F: they noted Fry's duodenal ulcer and concluded it was "psychogenic" and that he was unsuited to service in a zone of war. The army wanted brave men, not nervous ones. His application to work for the OSS also came to nothing. Fry's troublesome reputation at the State Department preceded him, and the rumor that he was a Communist, brought about by his rescue of so many left-leaning refugees, effectively barred him from helping in any way at all. There is even evidence that at this time Fry was under surveillance by the FBI. But Beamish, a German, did manage to gain a place in the OSS. Maurice, who had arrived in New York in 1942, joined the US Army Medical Corps as a doctor. "It is irritating to have to leave the war entirely to others," Fry wrote to Théo.

His marriage to Eileen continued to founder, and they finally got a Mexican quickie divorce. Fry moved out of the apartment on Irving Place, and for a while lived with the Saint-Exupérys at their house, where he endured a quality of spousal combat that made his marriage to Eileen look like a peaceful idyll. Back in France, the police raided the Centre Américain de Secours for the last time in July 1942. It was closed down, all the files seized, and ten people charged, arraigned, and put on trial. The police had discovered Gaullist documents at the office, together with a microfilm hidden in a toothpick that was itself hidden in a bar of soap. The charges were minor but the sentences severe. Three members of the staff were condemned to hard labor for life, one to ten years' hard labor, and the rest to between two and five years. Danny was not charged; others including Jean had already gone into hiding.

Then, on November 11, 1942, Fry heard this news on his radio:

Here are the latest developments in Hitler's occupation of Vichy France. Marshal Pétain has declared that Hitler's action has broken the terms of the 1940 Armistice. It leaves France free, he said, to defend herself. Unconfirmed reports say that the French fleet which has been kept at Toulon has put out into the Mediterranean. One version declares that they will join British and American naval units now along the African coast. Frontier reports quote Pétain as saying that he will not interfere with any resistance the French people may offer to the German invaders.

Casablanca, the third and last of the big North African ports, has followed Oran and Algiers in hoisting the white flag. Casablanca had asked for and received an armistice.

German troops had poured over the demarcation line into the unoccupied zone, and at last France was free to fight again. But the enemy occupation of Vichy territory threw over it a blanket of darkness. Fry now had another bitter frustration to add to his stock: "Silence, silence," he lamented. "I have tried again and again to reach my friends in France, to have even one direct word from any one of them. I have tried again and again, but I have always failed. Whether I whisper or whether I shout, there is not even an echo to reply; only silence, silence so complete that I can hear my blood singing in my ears."

Occasionally there would be a short cable from Switzerland announcing the escape of one more client. He heard that Franz Boegler had made it there, and that the last member of that *Bouline* four, Fritz Lamm, was in Trinidad. Even troublesome and ungrateful Arthur Wolff had got away. Hans and Lisa Fittko, after many perilous adventures, succeeded in reaching Lisbon, and from there boarded a ship bound for Cuba, where—hostages to their past political activity—they would wait for nearly a decade before their American immigration visas were finally granted. News came that other of Fry's ex-employees, like Walter and Eleanor Bohne, were also now in Switzerland. But from occupied Europe there was never, obviously, anything more than a name and a code word signifying safety. He learned that Berthold Jacob had been kidnapped by the Gestapo off the street in Lisbon as he emerged from the Unitarian Committee's offices at the Hotel Métropole. He heard that little Frederic Drach had been taken for a ride by a couple of Nazi agents and that his bullet-riddled body had later been discovered in his hotel room. He learned that the British were sending back into Spain the Republicans who made it to Lisbon ready to fight for the Allies. All Fry could do was fulminate impotently: "Our job will never be over until Hitler and all his buddies are hanging on lampposts, where they belong."

Fry was cheered by letters of thanks he received from those who had arrived in America, often written in halting English, but all expressing heartfelt gratitude. "I thank you from my deepest heart," Paul Elbogen wrote from California. "If you will die for 115 years, I suppose you will enter immediately a special heaven." Charlotte Feibel, who had worked briefly for the Centre Américain on her way to America, wrote of her time there that "after one year of desperation, sorrow, strain and uselessness it had given me back my first taste of life again. It was worthwhile risking because of your example in your fight for brotherhood among us all endangered people; just you, who came over from the safe shore of America." Erich Lewinsky worked briefly at Forty-second Street, before moving to an upstate town to take a job as a doorman (it was often difficult for refugees to find work compatible with their skills and qualifications). "I am sure you would not mind me talking to you with a complete frankness," he wrote,

> a frankness which I never attained during the time we saw each other so often, daily, in Marseille, and later in New York. There is a reason for that and today I want to tell you the reason: I always felt shy towards you because I really was fond of you. And feeling that there was not or could not be any reciprocity, I became even more shy and awkward being together with you. . . . Let me tell you only this: among the very few things which happened to me during the last ten years and which I regard as a "cadeau du ciel" [gift from heaven] is the fact that I met you.

Fry continued to compose his articles, and once again he found himself cast as a Cassandra, uttering unpalatable truths—for Fry knew what was happening in the east of Europe, and that his prediction, ignored in 1935, was now a reality. In December 1942 his article "The Massacre of the Jews" appeared in *The New Republic*. For anybody who claims that the Allies were unaware of the atrocities committed by the Nazis against the prisoners in concentration camps, Fry's essay exists to give the lie to that claim. Using his wide range of contacts and his intimate knowledge gained firsthand in France and Germany, Fry carefully built up the evidence for his renewed claim that genocide was being carried out. He cited what were—with the gas chambers in construction and the *Einzatsgruppen Kommandos* making their deadly way across the Ukraine, Lithuania, and Latvia—astonishingly precise accounts of the death tolls so far, and of the methods used. Fry claimed that 2 million Jews had already been slaughtered, and that only 2,200 remained in Poland. He described how 8,000 of the Jews of Riga were killed in a single night, and another 16,000 stripped and machine-gunned in a nearby forest just one week later. He even quoted from letters smuggled out of the killing zone:

> "I spoke to Mr Jaeger," one of them goes ["Mr Jaeger" means the Germans.] "He told me that he will invite all relatives of the family Achenu [Hebrew for "our brethren"], with the exception of Miss Eisenzweig [probably means those working in the iron mines], from Warsaw to his mansion 'Kewer' [Hebrew for "tomb"]. Uncle Gerusch [Hebrew for "deportation"] also works in Warsaw; he is a very capable worker. My friend Miso [Hebrew for "death"] now works with him. I am alone here; I feel very lonely. . . . Please pray for me."

With great composure Fry built up a damning and conclusive report that implicitly challenged the silence of his government, and sharpened his earlier accusations against it. Yet there was nothing more he could do except to sit down at the desk of his new apartment on East Forty-ninth St. with Clovis and Clovis's new "wife" at his feet, and begin to write *Surrender on Demand,* his account of his adventures in France.

IN MAY 1941 Heinrich Mann celebrated his seventieth birthday at the house of Polish actress and screenwriter Salka Viertel on Mabery Road, Santa Monica. The party should have taken place in March, but at that time Thomas Mann was due to receive an honorary degree from the University of California at Berkeley, and to follow it with a lecture tour. Thomas was his elder brother's financial guardian in America, so the dependent Heinrich's celebration yielded to Thomas's public acclamation. Finally, on a May evening, the postponed party took place. It was more than just a birthday dinner: it was the semiformal reinauguration of German letters in its new American home.

Every guest was vetted by Nelly Mann, and as she and Alma were conducting a bitter feud, anybody connected with the Werfels was to be "off the menu." Luckily, a truce was engineered by Lion and Marta Feuchtwanger, and on the night nearly fifty people were seated at the tables. Many others volunteered to work in the kitchen in order that they might eavesdrop on the august gathering, which included, in addition to the Manns, Werfels, and Feuchtwangers, Walter Mehring, Alfred Döblin, Alfred Polgar, and Bruno Frank.

After the soup, Thomas Mann arose and took from his pocket a speech in praise of his brother's writing which was so long and detailed that he later of-

fered it to a literary journal as a full-length essay. About an hour later he sat
down, but before the roast beef (done to a turn by now) could be brought in,
Heinrich stood up. A similarly lengthy speech followed, in which he repaid
Thomas with a tour de force of similar compliments on the worthiness and
achievement of his brother's work. Then he praised Nelly for practically carrying him over the mountains above Cerbère. She appeared bashful, but was
really covering her dress. Already drunk, she finally collapsed in uncontrol-
lable laughter, revealing that the bright red garment had been burst open by
her bosom, which everybody saw was encased in a white lace brassiere.

By the time Heinrich sat down, the meat was hopelessly overdone, but the
veterans of Marseille's ungarnished rutabagas and lonely artichokes did not
complain and ate with relish. Salka Viertel remarked to the writer Bruno
Frank what a touching tribute the brothers had paid one another. "Yes," he
said. "They write and read such ceremonial evaluations of each other, every
ten years."

The experience of the exiles in America was varied, to say the least. Werfel's
Song of Bernadette topped the best-seller lists in 1942, following the success in
America of his previous novel *Embezzled Heaven.* It sold 350,000 copies, and
was later a Book of the Month Club choice. Werfel had apparently cracked
the literary code of movie success, as well, for Twentieth-Century-Fox paid
$100,000 for the rights, and Jennifer Jones won an Oscar in the lead role of
the young girl who has visions of the Virgin Mary. Franz and Alma moved
into a lavish Beverly Hills residence. Werfel then followed up his *Bernadette*
success with *Jacobowsky and the Colonel*—an account of a Jew wandering through France during the *pagaille* of 1940 who meets up with an anti-
Semitic Polish officer with whom he escapes to freedom. Danny Kaye made
sure that the film version was a success, after the original theatrical play gar-
nered fantastic reviews on Broadway. Alas, Werfel lived to see neither of these
triumphs, as he fell dead in his study of a coronary in August 1945.

Alma Mahler Werfel—who now officially renamed herself Alma Werfel
Mahler—did not attend the funeral. "I never come to these things," she said.
With nothing to keep her in California, she subsequently moved to New York,
where, as doyen of "The Fourth Reich"—as the heavily Germanic reaches of
Manhattan's Upper West side had been nicknamed after the emigrations of
the Hitler years—she lived until her death in 1964.

Unlike his brother, Heinrich Mann remained a fish out of water in America. Traveling with the Werfels on the way over from Lisbon aboard the *Nea
Hellas,* Alma recalled how despondent Heinrich was about his approaching
new life. "He stayed in his cabin because he was sick." she wrote. "He was feeling angry with the world. When his nephew [Golo] went to see him he was in

bed. He was drawing women with large breasts; sometimes just the latter." A large crowd of journalists and dignitaries, including Thomas Mann, greeted the escapees when the ship docked at Hoboken, New Jersey on October 13, 1940. The arrival made front page news the next day, but the real story and future pattern of Heinrich's American exile appeared coincidentally and ironically, at the foot of the same newspaper page in small print. The best-seller list published on October 14 featured *The Beloved Returns* by Thomas Mann, and alongside it Thomas Wolfe's *You Can't Go Home Again.*

Heinrich never did go home again. The dean of German letters, would-be president of the old Weimar Republic and emperor of the exiles was forced in reduced circumstances to live in a cheap Los Angeles apartment building, writing—for a while—scripts that would end up in the wastepaper baskets of philistine movie moguls. It was almost more than he could bear, but it *was* more than Nelly could bear. Her laughter at the birthday celebration was already tinged with hysteria, and the mentally fragile woman began drinking heavily and swallowing handfuls of pills. Twice Heinrich placed her in a sanatorium, but the treatments she received were expensive failures, and Nelly's behavior continued to grow more erratic and unpredictable. One dinner guest recalled arriving at Heinrich's apartment to have Nelly open the door to him stark naked. Hardly a day passed when she wasn't drunk, or drugged, or both. On more than one occasion the Manns' car had to be pulled from some ditch where she had left it, and this happened once again even after Nelly had had her license revoked for drunken driving.

The night before a scheduled court appearance following her latest wreck, Nelly took an overdose of sleeping pills. When Heinrich discovered her unconscious and breathing heavily the next morning, he rushed her to hospital. There he was turned away because he had no money, and Nelly died before he could find another, cheaper place. That was in 1944, and a year later he heard that his first wife, Maria Kanova, had survived her imprisonment in the concentration camp of Theresienstadt. If someone in her terrible condition could be said to have survived. . . . It took her a further two years to die.

With nothing but his brother's presence to keep him in California, and with nothing but his memories, now painfully tainted, to draw him back to Europe, Heinrich Mann did what any man of his age and in his position would have done: he stayed put. Germany was no longer home, so he lived in Hollywood and began to speak in his native tongue again, with a Lübeck accent—the accent of his childhood. Thomas's wife, Katia, who disliked Heinrich intensely, nevertheless found him a street-level apartment near his brother's estate on San Remo Drive. By now Heinrich had angina and was so short of breath he had been forbidden to climb stairs.

In May of 1949, Soviet East Germany invited Heinrich to become the first president of the newly created German Academy of the Arts in East Berlin. If he returned to live there he could at last collect his royalties and would enjoy the trappings of a high-grade Communist Party *apparatchik,* with a large residence and a chauffeur. The political consequences—in the midst of the Berlin airlift—were uncertain, but how could he resist? He was nothing in America, and Thomas, who had recently been given a hero's welcome in the East German city of Weimar, urged his brother to accept the position. To a friend Heinrich wrote in self-justification: "In fifty years I have not been so completely disregarded as now. If one had no need of dollars, one would laugh. At least let me smile."

The ship that was to transport Heinrich back to Germany left without him. In the early hours of March 12, 1950, he died in his sleep. He finally returned home eleven years later, when his ashes were re-interred in the cemetery of Dorotheenstadt near the graves of Hegel and Brecht.

Thomas Mann fell victim to the attentions of the House Un-American Activities Committee (HUAC) on his return from his East German visit, and the antagonistic pressure on him mounted steadily over the next two years. Finally, in the summer of 1952, Thomas Mann left America for Zurich, his final place of exile.

THE FEUCHTWANGERS ARRIVED in California in January 1941, having stayed on in New York just long enough to feel the real bite of an East Coast winter. Recalling somewhat the Sanary years, their presence in Los Angeles soon provided a focal point for its growing exile community. As in Sanary, Lion Feuchtwanger's days were meticulously organized, and he was just as productive as he had been in Europe: he would write three plays and seven novels in Los Angeles—but the first thing he worked on there was *The Devil in France,* a powerful account of his experiences before and after the defeat in 1940.

With the success of his novel *Simone,* one of the best-sellers of 1944 in America, and his enormously popular story of Goya, *This Is the Hour,* Lion was able to buy a palatial villa overlooking the ocean in Pacific Palisades, where once more he began to build up his wine cellar, and to restock his bookshelves with rare first editions. He lived in this fashion until 1957 when, upon learning that he had cancer, Feuchtwanger actually stepped up his writing schedule. While he had been gravely ill in the French concentration camp of St. Nicolas, the fatalistic Feuchtwanger made a pact with destiny, and swore he would not die until he had finished the fourteen novels he knew he had inside him. Now it was a race against time. The end came just before Christmas, 1958. Marta lived on busier than ever for many years, finally accepting the fact of advancing age on her eightieth birthday by reluctantly giving up her daily swim in the ocean. She made up for it by doing more calisthenics.

When Hertha Pauli landed in America in early 1941, an unscrupulous New York cab driver had taken her last nine dollars after driving her a few miles to a hotel used by foreign refugees. But by the time the Florida train pulled into New York City's Penn Station in late March, she was wised up and acclimatized. As the locomotive jerked to a halt, a diminutive figure wearing a black beret hopped down from a carriage and marched up to her. After a brief embrace he whipped off his hat, glanced furtively around, and asked: "So *now* what do we do?" Walter Mehring had arrived in New York.

He didn't stay there for long, but set off for Hollywood and the purchase of the spanking new Packard Roadster that would prove so unpopular with Danny Bénédite. Mehring worked at MGM for a year writing screenplays alongside Alfred Polgar, and then returned to New York, where he wrote *The Lost Library: The Autobiography of a Culture,* which was widely hailed as a masterpiece upon its publication in 1951. In 1953 he returned to Europe. Hertha Pauli remained in the United States and became a highly successful author of children's books. She died in 1973.

Walter Mehring, who once wrote that exiles are "doomed to end their years in little hotels," found himself fifty years after escaping from Europe living once more in a little hotel in Zurich. Near the end of his peripatetic life, it seemed the natural place to be.

FRY SPENT THE remaining years of the war, from 1942 to 1945, writing *Surrender on Demand,* reliving his time in France but suffering from the vividness of his memories and the tantalizing feeling that his friends were very close around him yet also unknowably distant. He had no idea whether many of them lived or died, and it was becoming almost impossible for Fry to exist in New York, in the midst of a preoccupied and busy city, feeling as isolated as he did. Eventually he retired to a log cabin in the Adirondacks to finish his book. "I have tried—God knows I have tried—to get back into the mood of American life since I left France for the last time. But it doesn't work," he wrote from his mountain fastness, in a foreword to his book that was eventually cut from the published version. Fry found himself haunted by "the ghosts of the living" whose silent presences he felt he must attempt to placate. "Then maybe I can sleep soundly again at night, the way I used to before. Maybe I can become a normal human being again, exorcise the ghosts which haunt me, stop living in another world, come back to the world of America."

After having endured two lonely years of deafening silence and painful separation from his friends in occupied France, Fry's isolation was finally broken at the end of 1944, after the chaos following the Allied invasion of France had started to subside. A cable arrived in time for Christmas, and it was the best present Fry had ever had:

WE ALRIGHT NOW STOP TAKEN IN MAQUIS ESCAPED BEING SHOT THANKS LANDING NOW ADMINISTRATOR DAILY PAPER FRANC TIREUR JEAN [GEMAHLING] MARRIED ANITA [SAUVAGE] STOP PAUL [SCHMIERER] ANNA [GRUSS] GOOD HEALTH JACQUES [WEISSLITZ] DEPORTED GERMANY [CHARLES] WOLFF DIED AFTER TORTURES BY MILITIAMEN STOP WE INTEND RESUME WORK HELP-ING FAMILIES PEOPLE SHOT TORTURED DEPORTED BY GERMANS PLEASE CONTACT COMMITTEE AND REPLY SOONEST. . . .

It was from Danny, who was all business, as usual.

Little by little, Fry was able to discover what his friends had gone through following the occupation of Vichy France by the Nazis. It was a story of courage, determination and tragedy. He had been worrying incessantly since September, when a brief note reached him from Anna Gruss, his gnomish secretary at the Centre Américain. She revealed that Danny had been arrested back in June on the charge of "embauchage illicite de main-d'oeuvre" (ille-gally hiring manual workers), not the most serious of crimes, but dangerous in the context of a panicky regime and an increasingly brutal occupying force. Now, as the mail and cable fitfully returned to normal, the details began to be filled in.

"DANNY AFTER MIRACULOUS RELEASE GESTAPO PRISON NOW MANAGING," Théo cabled Fry in January 1945. Danny's escape had indeed been nothing less than miraculous. Just as he was being led into the courtyard of Beaumette prison in Marseille to face a firing squad, units of the FFI (French Forces of the Interior, the combined Resistance army that arose in large numbers from its shadowy underground existence after the Allied landings) arrived at the prison gates to liberate the inmates, and the guards had lowered their rifles and surrendered. Fry learned that in the years since his return to America, Danny and Théo had been hard at work developing the charcoal-burning fa-cility in the forest of the Var. At least, that was the cover: in reality they had transformed it into one of the largest Resistance garrisons in southern France.

In 1944 the Royal Air Force began parachuting arms caches to Danny's group during the lead-up to the invasion, but one of these drops had missed its target and been discovered by the Vichy police. Danny was arrested on suspicion, although no evidence of illegal activity was found at the fabulously well run charcoal factory. After Danny was imprisoned, Théo herself had taken over as commander of the maquis group, and had been very successful. So successful, in fact, that she was no longer prepared to remain under her husband's wing. "As you certainly have heard," Théo wrote early in 1946, "Danny and I are separated and I, at least, have a chance to 'make good on my own' and no longer live in Danny's shadow and sink my personality in his, which I have stupidly been doing for the last ten years. The relief and ensuing happiness is one of the biggest surprises of my life."

Also came the terrible news that Jacques Weisslitz and his wife had been deported as Jews to Germany. Fry had tried with all his might to secure immigration visas for them back in 1942, before the lines of communication with Europe had gone dead. But the State Department had refused point-blank to consider the couple even though Jacques was a skilled diamond cutter and would easily have been able to support himself and his family. Now Fry discovered they had both perished in a concentration camp. Louis Coppée had also been deported to the East, but somehow he had survived. Stéphane Hessel had parachuted into France and been captured, but he escaped to fight again.

The Centre Américain's young office boy, Justus Rosenberg, had grown up into a fearless Resistance warrior and had actually begun, like Jean, to fight against the Germans and Vichy while Fry was still in Marseille. Fry's young protégés had certainly distinguished themselves in a horrific situation. The Parisian journalist Charles Wolff had been a casualty, though, suffering death at the hands of the French fascist paramilitaries, the Milice. Toward the end of the Nazi tenancy of France these fanatics were allowed semi-official status, and were largely occupied in combating Resistance activity among their own countrymen. It was the typical German tactic of allowing the local population to do its dirty work. Perhaps the German reluctance adequately to arm these fascist bands (a captured British machine gun or revolver might occasionally be donated) contributed to the manner of Charles' death: he was stamped on until his lungs collapsed.

But there were shreds of good news among the bad. Fry thought Bill Freier had died in a German concentration camp, but it was not so. Somehow he survived, although it was a little seventy-five pound skeleton who stumbled through the camp gates and began walking back to France to look for Mina and the son he had never seen. Eventually he found them and François, by now four years old, took his first look at his father. At last, now that he was free, Freier shed his ironical name and went back to his real one, Spira. But it was not so easy to shed the accumulated burden of years of terror and loneliness and scratching for survival. Shortly after they were reunited, Mina lost her mind (she finally died in an asylum in 1953).

"So many things have happened in France and to each one of our little group, since you left, that I have a feeling of not having seen you for at least ten years," wrote Jean Gemahling to Fry in a letter he must have received in January 1945. "The last months of Nazi occupation in France have been so dreadful, so many friends have been tortured, shot or deported, we have lived so exalting moments too, that it seems almost impossible to talk of the past years with a friend who has had different experiences in the meanwhile." Jean's tale was one of sad and disappointed heroism. After his release from prison, he had gone straight back to his Resistance work, and was soon responsible for "recueil et renseignments" (intelligence and information) for the entire Resistance in southwest France—the group called "Fresnay," under General Bertin-Chevance. He also published the underground journals *Petites Ailes, Liberté,* and *Verité.*

Jean told Fry how he had been arrested again at the beginning of 1943 and escaped from Chave prison just a few hours before the Gestapo came to collect him. He left Marseille for Lyon and later went to Paris. He assumed a new identity, dyeing his fair hair black, and shaving off a mustache he had grown. "In the meanwhile," he wrote, "the French Court of Justice has sentenced me to four years imprisonment, and the Gestapo as I learned afterwards, to death." Jean carried on regardless, and headed up an intelligence service for both the Resistance and the Allies. Soon he was sending information by clandestine airmail or radio transmission to London, Algiers, and Geneva. Every ten days he supplied between two and three hundred pages' worth of vital intelligence, plus forty to sixty photographs and maps. In short Jean had been a war hero of the highest order, but now, with the conflict drawing to a close, he was a heartbroken man fearing the worst for his captured comrades. "They were very dear friends to me and men who had displayed a magnificent courage and intelligence in the underground work," wrote Jean. Soon he learned that most had been killed.

> This proportion of three dead men out of four is about the general proportion of the losses among the French Resistance. And generally the best ones have fallen. How could things start well in France with such losses among the Resistance? I am still haunted by my lost friends. I think, too, of the hard law we had to apply not to lose time, energy and money on trying to make our prisoners escape from the Gestapo jails.

All our forces were to be devoted to new work, and not a parcel of it distracted for rescuing emprisoned [sic] friends, at least in most cases, where an evasion [escape] would cost several months' work and great risks. It was very hard. You remember the word: "Let the dead bury the dead." Wouldn't it have been more useful to have saved some of these men who are now so cruelly missing?

Somehow a gulf had opened between Fry and his French friends. The quality of Jean's despair, which was eloquent and inconsolable, could not be matched by Fry's account of his last few years. Fry wrote of his divorce and of his psychoanalysis, which he described with all the enthusiasm of the newly converted. He talked of future marriage prospects ("But not until I have finished my analysis. And maybe not immediately even then") and of how he now enjoyed living alone with his dogs, pictures, and books ("more and more, in fact, as I have progressed in my analysis"). Held up against the hell that Jean had lived through, Fry's cares seemed somehow trivial, and it introduced a note of discordance into the correspondence. Jean was plainly disturbed by his old hero's personal obsession. "What really puzzles me is your psychoanalyse affair," he replied. "I probably have very wrong ideas about it, but I can just imagine that as a boring and rather depressing monomaniac introspection. Something like searching in a heap of rubbish. Does one never get mad or hypochondriac with that psychoanalyse?"

Jean understood Fry better than anybody—better even than Danny, who was louder and more cocksure, and whose fondness for his old boss took the form of argumentativeness. Jean was quieter and unsure of himself, but he had now been tempered in the forge of war, and his words to Fry were probably the most accurate estimation of Fry's existence by the war's end.

"You describe your life as a peaceful and occupied one, rather lonely perhaps," Jean wrote to him. "From the sound of your letter, I gather you do not feel very happy, although you would like to pretend to be. Am I wrong? Still, whether it is due or not to psychoanalytical treatment, you seem to have reached some peace of mind which is the best ersatz known to the impossible dream of happiness."

PART 6

EPILOGUE

EPILOGUE

Admittedly the truth about a man lies first and foremost in what he hides.
ANDRÉ MALRAUX

WHEN VARIAN FRY ARRIVED in Marseille in August 1940 he brought with him a list of two hundred people to be rescued. By the time he was expelled from France a year later he had, incredibly, arranged the escapes of nearly fifteen hundred people (Walter Meyerhof estimates four thousand, including family members). That was not all. The organization he had established in France, and which continued to function under increasingly difficult conditions, almost certainly managed to smuggle several hundred more exiles out of the country to safety after Fry's expulsion. Following the German occupation of the southern zone those who had worked for him, and the refugees who had not escaped from France, banded together to establish practical and militant resistance to Vichy and the Nazis at secret locations, and mutually aided one another during the dark years prior to the Allied liberation.

By any standard, the achievements of Fry and those around him deserve to be written up in the annals of both bravery and humanitarianism. But they must also be noted in the cultural history of the West, for the people Fry rescued and brought to America were destined to change the course of the postwar world. In her book *Illustrious Immigrants,* Laura Fermi, herself an illustrious immigrant and the wife of the great physicist Enrico Fermi, called it simply and accurately "a unique phenomenon in the history of migration."

Before the Second World War, it had been customary for American artists and writers to feel they had to visit and even live for a period in Europe for their "education," as it had been for Hemingway and Scott Fitzgerald and the innumerable Left Bank Yanks in the twenties. Now the tide had turned and

culture had arrived in America, perhaps reluctantly at first, but
ly all the same. America would begin to absorb and adapt the genius
ope that had fetched up on its shores. As a result American artists and
writers would no longer have to look with the same deference to the old continent, in the way a provincial is intimidated by and yearns for the sophistication and cosmopolitanism of the big city. From now on, that could be left to
the tourists.

Also gone was any sense of colonial inferiority, for America had saved Europe in more than one sense. Fry had saved its artists and intelligentsia, and
the U.S. military had saved its land and institutions. Europe had in a way
blown itself out, or up, both morally and intellectually; America was to become the mature democratic culture and home of artistic innovation and experiment. It was Europe that began to look faintly provincial in the postwar
years.

Those artists, poets, philosophers, scientists, musicians, historians, critics,
and novelists who emigrated to the United States would contribute to and
change America's perception of itself in the decades to come. The landing of
Fry's artist protégés in New York is an exemplary tale. Their arrival changed
the avant-garde art scene in America from a slightly narrow, inward-looking
and home-grown modernism into a movement that would redefine painting
and sculpture in the postwar years. So dramatic was the impact of Ernst,
Masson, Lipchitz, and Chagall, among others, that it was said artists who returned home from the war to America had missed the birth of the Abstract
Expressionist revolution. As the art historian Martica Sawin has written, "a
watershed had been reached in American art in terms of its relation to Old
World culture." And with new artistic development came the business, transforming New York into the capital of the modern art world, a position it enjoys to this day. All this played its part in the realignment of western culture
in the second half of the twentieth century, so that America became the
touchstone of art and letters.

WHEN THE SECOND WORLD WAR ended, Varian Fry was thirty-seven
years old, and in a sense his life did not so much resume as begin anew with
the peace. *Surrender on Demand* was published in 1945 to widespread but
modest reviews. It sold reasonably well for a time, but the atmosphere in
America following the Allied victory was not conducive to self-examination.
The public did not want to hear of the duplicity of the State Department, it
wanted to celebrate the triumph of democracy. America wanted to put the
war behind it, to resume normal life and to pursue prosperity. In the effort to

reestablish peacetime order there was not much interest in reading an account of how it had nearly been lost for good. It would be several decades before that would become a consuming area of interest.

Fry had experienced a difficult few years, and as Jean Gemahling had guessed, he was not really happy. A whole population, of course, possessed good and bad memories of wartime. Yet in this respect Fry was dissimilar to the schoolteacher who had experienced combat or the bank manager who might briefly have been an intelligence agent parachuted into enemy territory. To begin with, Fry had not been part of an army, or even (at the time) of a nation at war: he had operated alone. In addition to the obvious enemy, his government was against him, and eventually the people who had sent him to France were against him, too. When he returned to America in late 1941 there were few garlands; instead there was more rejection—first from the Emergency Rescue Committee itself and then from the army.

Fry probably adjusted rather well all things considered, although his marriage to Eileen was a major casualty, and his hypochondria reared up once again (as Jean had predicted) after he had managed to brave real ailments in France. The neurotic past was beckoning him, and it was probably a good instinct that led Fry into psychoanalysis—although it was most unlike him to be so uncritically enthusiastic. It was as if he were trying to bury something of himself, and in the end he claimed he valued the analysis even over what he had experienced in France ("It is the most interesting thing I have ever done in my life, not excepting the work in Marseille").

The comparison with Oskar Schindler is interesting. Fry is sometimes inaccurately referred to as "The American Schindler," for although the results appear similar, they arose from quite different sources. Schindler was a sensualist and an opportunist who stumbled upon a humanitarian duty he could not ignore, although to begin with he probably did try to ignore it. Fry was a sensitive, even prissy individual, an aesthete and an epicure who was driven by idealistic motives to perform a humanitarian duty. Schindler's was the profiteering escapade that went awry once he discovered by chance that life was more important than money. Fry's was a deliberate mission that entailed a change of character (though he drew on resources he already possessed). Despite the differences between them, both men lived for a time at the very limit of their abilities, where they found their personalities at last fulfilled. What Thomas Keneally wrote of Oskar Schindler—"The peace would never exalt him as had the war"—was also true for Fry.

In the end, each man suffered from his discoveries about himself. After the war Schindler found himself deprived of his pure, unsullied pleasure in profit and never made money again, even though he tried. His later financial failure was a debt incurred by his wartime vision of what he could truly be. After the war it was as if Varian Fry found himself deprived of his idealism. His curse was that he had seen how that idealism had been put so successfully into practice. He had been vouchsafed a vision of the flimsiness of words without action, and this complicated his life as a journalist and led him into the broad highway of convention where he could never be entirely happy. This is not the same as saying he was a failure, just as a string of failed businesses did not condemn Schindler as such. Both men remained heroes in the eyes and hearts of those they worked with and saved. Both stories show how heroism can be an awkward burden.

BACK IN 1945 Fry truly believed that his course of psychoanalysis had "cured" him of his ailments, both physical and psychological. This was not, with the benefit of hindsight, quite so. His stomach pain and the duodenal ulcer that was its cause certainly receded, although it would reappear again toward the end of his life. His divorce from Eileen had provoked a candid reappraisal of his emotional and sexual makeup. There is good evidence that Fry was quite at peace with himself for a while at least. Indeed, in late 1945 Fry felt sufficiently confident about himself to contribute his history to Alfred Kinsey. The pioneering sexual researcher thanked Fry for an account that "helped considerably" in the composition of his forthcoming report. Kinsey's work was obviously important to Fry, who kept one of his articles that contained the following conclusion:

> Any hormonal or other explanation of the homosexual must allow for the fact that something between a quarter and a half of all males have demonstrated their capacity to respond to homosexual stimuli; that the picture is one of endless intergradation between every combination of homosexuality and heterosexuality; that it is impossible to distinguish so-called acquired, latent and congenital types; and that there is every gradation between so-called actives and passives in a homosexual relation.

This must have made comforting sense to Fry, who had once been happily married and would soon be again. He was a complex man in every sense, the sexual no less than any other. Ordinarily this would not be worth mentioning except that Fry's sexuality is important in understanding how he became the astonishingly successful "pimpernel" who saved the lives of thousands under threat from the Nazis.

On the surface Fry had looked an unlikely hero. He was temperamental and bookish, a man of words not deeds. And yet the skills that his clandestine work in France would demand made by happy chance a close fit with certain aptitudes Fry already possessed. He had always had a sense of himself as a privileged outsider, for whom normal rules did not apply. From the earliest days, when he would feign illness to escape school, and through the many arguments and resignations in his life, Fry was a man who retained an inflexible idea of what he wanted, and he always felt sure he was right. His sexual ambiguity and his mischievousness fed into this, and bubbled beneath his stern exterior. In that context, the skills Fry had developed to cope with and express his "deviance" from the norm over the years may have stood him in good stead for the illicit and secret activities he took to so naturally and performed so extraordinarily well in France. One great truth that psychoanalysis has bequeathed to us is that our virtues are usually our vices in disguise. Perhaps this is an important clue in seeking the secret of Fry's success.

Fry resigned from his position at *The New Republic* in 1942 following a disagreement over an editorial he wrote condemning Soviet judicial murders. His antagonistic attitude to Communism was hardening. After a bitter quarrel with the magazine in 1945, in which he more or less accused those at *The New Republic* of being "fellow travelers," he asked for his name to be removed from the masthead list of contributing editors, where it had been since he left his staff job. By this time he was editor of the journal *Common Sense,* but he soon left that position as well, as he did his post as executive director of the American Labor Conference on International Affairs, which he had established with Raphael Abramovitch in 1943. Fry joined and left the *New Leader* and took a job as editor at *Tomorrow* magazine, but managed to fall out with the proprietress after a few weeks and before he had brought out his first issue. This succession of resignations was starting to look like serial boat-burning.

It was around this time that Fry applied to a Mr. Joseph S. Cybick, the director of the Cybick School of Designing and Cutting in New York, to inquire how to become a tailor. Fry, the Harvard-trained classical scholar and journalist of international repute, also wrote to the firm of one Thomas H. Uzzell in California to ask for information on a correspondence course on short story writing. Nothing came of these inquiries—they were just symptoms of a man in search of himself. By late 1946 he was associated with the ultraconservative American China Policy Association, headed by Alfred Kohlborg, a friend of Senator McCarthy. The Cold War was beginning and Fry had decided to nail his colors to the mast (though at the same time he was on the Board of Directors of the American Civil Liberties Union).

Emerging refreshed and renewed from his course of psychoanalysis, Fry decided that liberal journalism was no way to make a living—at least in his case. He confided to fellow writer Jean Roumilhac that "my own material security can be assured by my writing if I work very hard and persistently at it, but only at a very low level of income, at least for some time to come, and I am more greedy, or shall I say ambitious, than to be satisfied with that." On the other hand he wrote to an aspirant journalist who asked for some advice: "I sell practically everything I write, which isn't very much because I am lazy." Then, suddenly, perversely, Fry announced he wanted to be a businessman. This was contrary to all the pointers as to what he was and where his friends thought possible happiness lay. It was contrary to all the insights about himself that his analysis had shown him. "As a matter of fact I am a bureaucrat at heart," Fry had told Danny, but this was true only to the extent that he liked to spend his time in his office reading and writing.

Yet with many publications and books under his belt, with his languages and his experience of European politics, it seemed obvious that if Fry no longer wished to practice journalism, he could perfectly well become an academic or a teacher. Aside from possessing the necessary qualifications and connections, the academic style of life would have suited the uncommercial-minded Fry to a tee. He would have had plenty of time for reading and writing. It was a gentleman's occupation. . . . Was that any less "American" than being a businessman? He might as well have decided to be a baseball commentator.

Instead, he decided his destiny lay in the cut and thrust of the world of New York media. He bought out a small television production company called Cinemart, with financial help from his old friend Max Ascoli. But in deciding to escape the man he had been, it's more than likely that Fry was attempting to become someone he was not. "Of course, I can't imagine myself selling anything," Fry had told Danny back in 1942, when he was toying with the idea of becoming a wine merchant (his qualification for that occupation being that he liked wine a lot). But selling was now exactly what he proposed to do—and the brash new world of television was by no means the sedate and rarefied one of the vintner.

Fry, though, was an extremely intelligent man, a quick study, and willfully self-disciplined. He speedily mastered each technical and financial aspect of film production and ran Cinemart successfully between 1946 and 1953. He even became something of an expert in film production. Eventually, Fry declared himself bankrupt, but the true story behind the declaration is that he only did so to extract himself from a business in which he had fallen out with a rich junior partner who wanted to buy him out. Temperament, not incompetence or ill fortune, was the cause of the failure—if failure it was. Fry's own estimation of his foray into the media bear pit—"as a businessman I was a complete disaster"—may have had more to do with his talent for self-dramatization than it did with his lack of talent for making money.

The years in which Fry ran Cinemart were those that saw him find his feet again and enter early middle age. He and Eileen had remained friends; in fact they fared much better as friends than they had as spouses. After the merger of the ERC with the IRRC (later simply the International Rescue Committee, or IRC), Eileen had gone to work at the Emergency Committee of Atomic Scientists, and she stayed there until early 1948, about six months after she was diagnosed as suffering from lung cancer. The news of her disease came as a shock to Fry, but instead of being leveled by it, as many of his friends expected, it seemed to give him new strength, a new sense of himself. He became again the Varian Fry who had once put his arm around quaking refugees and reassured them with the offhanded valediction, "See you soon in New York." This time, though, there was no chance of playing the role of savior. Eileen was dying.

Fry reacted by insisting that she was still his wife. A Mexican divorce did not count, so he reasoned (not for the last time), and he went every day to the hospital to sit with Eileen at her bedside. Now it was Fry's turn to read aloud. The last thing he read to her was a note that arrived on May 4, 1948, from one of her colleagues at the Emergency Committee:

> Dear Eileen
> I feel very sorry that you have had to suffer so badly. You are too unselfish for this world and should have somebody to protect you. I wish with all my heart that you may soon feel well.

The note was signed "A. Einstein."

The year following Eileen's death Fry met Annette Riley, almost twenty years his junior and daughter of the head of the philosophy department at Vassar. They married in November 1950. To him, Annette like Eileen had the kind of lively, unspoiled intellect and curiosity that Fry found irresistible. In all other respects she was the opposite of Eileen, whom Miriam Davenport remembered as "witty, sarcastic and domineering," and who treated Fry as an unruly adolescent. By coincidence, Eileen had taught some of Annette's friends at the Brearley School, and Annette herself had indirectly learned about politics from Fry, whose Headline publications had been employed as textbooks at her school. She remembered those books as excellent, and now she was dazzled by the author himself, who was in addition a real live war hero in her eyes. Fry was flattered by Annette, who was a fresh start for him. A house, a garden, and a brace of bonny children beckoned in his imagination. It was a dream he had shared with Eileen in one of his last letters from France, when things were already falling apart. Then it had been a straw to grasp at; now it could be a reality. Fry believed, as so many similar men of his generation did, that he should above all be married no matter how complicated it might prove. He thought that the secure and respectable embrace of matrimony was the answer to equivocation. As it was, the early years of their marriage, during which he and Annette had three children, were among the happiest of Fry's life.

IN THE SPRING OF 1952, at the height of McCarthyism and the HUAC investigations, the novelist Mary McCarthy wrote to Hannah Arendt thanking her for her hospitality during a recent visit.

> We saw a perfect madman, Varian Fry, at Westport, on our way back, at our friends' house. He was fulminating about the necessity of "protecting our society from dangerous elements" and proposing that the *New Yorker* magazine be investigated by Congress. He himself, ironically, had been investigated for nine months . . . and had the greatest difficulty getting cleared, despite letters from Alfred Kohlborg, Sol Levitas, William Green, John Chamberlain, attesting his anti-communism. Bowden said to him, "All you lacked was a letter from Hitler."

Mary McCarthy was well known for her studied character assassinations, and was in the habit of disappearing in the midst of social gatherings to jot down things people had said, and to make malicious notes about them. In this instance, she had managed to get nearly everything wrong. Fry himself had been (half) joking when he suggested that the *New Yorker* should be investigated, and it was by now characteristic of Fry that his humor sometimes went too far. He seemed to enjoy taking a provocative position and then defending it until nobody could believe what he was saying. Annette said Fry could turn from being "a thoughtful liberal, full of compassion and high ideals . . . into a provocative and unpleasant reactionary." There was obviously mischievousness in this, but probably also anger and frustration. Despite the joking there was an element of aggressiveness there. "Sometimes I'd joke back," Annette recalled, "only to abruptly discover I was tangling with an unpleasant adversary who was infuriated at my not taking him seriously. It was a little frightening." In fact Fry admitted to being baffled by his own behavior.

Mary McCarthy was also wrong in her claim that Fry was being investigated by Congress. HUAC was uninterested in pursuing known liberals like Fry, especially if they were ridiculed by people like Mary McCarthy (who called him a "demi-intellectual") for being right-wing. What had in fact happened was that when Cinemart put in a bid for some military film contracts, Fry had received a reply from a certain Colonel Victor W. Phelps of the Army-Navy-Air Force Personnel Security Board. Phelps refused permission for Fry to undertake work for the army on the grounds that he had been "a Communist Party member since 1937 . . . a close and sympathetic associate of Communist Party members . . . openly and actively engaged in Communist Party activities." Fry's old reputation with the State Department had returned to haunt him yet again, despite the fact that by this time Fry was still with the right-wing American China Policy Association (even though Annette was begging him to give it up). The confusion may have arisen because Fry was also involved in the American Committee for Cultural Freedom (along with W. H. Auden, John Dos Passos, Arthur Koestler, Arthur Schlesinger, Jr., Saul Bellow, and Fry's old friend Reinhold Niebuhr). On one level this organization seemed quite conformist. When the Rosenbergs were executed for espionage and the British philosopher Bertrand Russell called the act "an atrocity," the committee actually issued a press statement disagreeing with him. On another level the Committee for Cultural Freedom meant just that, and it was aggressively independent of any political line. It had criticized Senator McCarthy and his cohorts in another statement, where it said "political opponents have been pictured as enemies of the democratic system."

Fry had set about clearing his name by writing not only to Colonel Phelps but to J. Edgar Hoover himself, claiming Phelps must have been acting on erroneous information collected and supplied by the FBI. Hoover naturally denied this. Although Fry wrote to Phelps, "I am beginning to see the humour of it, and I guess it would give me a hearty belly-laugh if it concerned anyone else but me," the slur was potentially harmful to Fry's business and personal reputation, and there is some evidence that he was indeed perturbed by the matter. It certainly cost him his friendship with a director called George L. George whom he had once hired, when Fry suggested that his own trouble was started by that man's name being mentioned as a Communist during the HUAC hearings. Fry felt himself guilty by association, and wrote to George, demanding that he prove he was not a Communist. George replied bitterly that Fry should be ashamed of himself, and that it was guilt, not innocence, that should have to be proven. George was of course right. Fry must have been feeling under pressure to have acted so gracelessly.

Even with the testimony of Sol Levitas, editor of the *New Leader,* and the literary critic Alfred Kazin, it still took five months, until February 1952, for Fry to clear his name and get the ban lifted. He quit the film business the next year.

Incidentally, Hannah Arendt never wrote a word back to her friend Mary McCarthy in Fry's defense after receiving the mildly slanderous letter, despite Fry having helped her to escape France in 1941.

RESPECTABLE, CONVENTIONAL, UNREMARKABLE—Fry's middle years were settled and basically contented ones. He had put away that part of himself which had responded so notably to cataclysm, and concentrated instead on raising his children and providing for his family. In 1956 he and Annette moved from New York City to Ridgefield, Connecticut, by which time Fry had settled into writing freelance reports, brochures, and documentary film scripts for Fortune 500 companies. Fry made quite good money at this, and at the same time enjoyed ridiculing the doltish mentality of his corporate clients. He kept his hand in at teaching by taking a job as a creative writing instructor at the City College of New York, and gradually became absorbed into more or less full-time work for one of his major employers, Coca-Cola.

But the pull of the Classics led Fry back into further part-time teaching posts around Connecticut in the early sixties, and in addition to Latin and Greek he found himself filling in as a French tutor. At this time Fry was also drawn back by the memory of that original refugee, Aeneas, who had been depicted in his desperate flight from the Greeks after the sack of Troy on the black and white wallpaper in the library of the Villa Air-Bel. Fry began to write a book about the Trojan War.

Voices from the past occasionally reached him, disturbing the tranquil surface of his life. In 1963, after a hiatus of nearly twenty years, he heard from Stéphane Hessel, who now held a position at the French Ministry of Education in Paris. Beamish—no longer Otto Albert Hirschmann but officially Albert O. Hirschman—had enjoyed an illustrious career so far. He had been one of the architects of the Marshall Plan for the rebuilding of Europe, had written two internationally acclaimed books on economics, and had taught at Yale and Columbia universities before moving on to be the Lucius N. Littauer Professor of Political Economy at Harvard. The Institute of Advanced Studies at Princeton was interested in him, and whisperings of his candidacy for a Nobel Prize were beginning.

Maurice—now back to being Marcel Verzeano—was a professor of neuro-biology at the University of California at Irvine; Justus Rosenberg had become a professor of comparative language and literature. Lena Fischmann was working for the United Nations. Jean Gemahling was a nuclear scientist. Bill Spira, signing himself "bil," had become one of France's most popular cartoonists. Charlie Fawcett had starred opposite Sophia Loren in two movies, was a friend of William Holden and Orson Welles, and the lover of Hedy Lamarr. He had fought in the moutains with the Greek army against the Communists, and helped refugees escape from Hungary in 1956, among other acts of heroism. Meanwhile, Fry was getting his Connecticut teaching certificate and giving classes at Greenwich Academy, a girls' preparatory school. "This thing of a wife and three children," Stéphane Hessel reassured him. "It seems to be the right approach."

During this period something continued to gnaw at Fry, perhaps just the usual regrets of a life whose options appear suddenly one day, in middle age, to have been whittled away. Or perhaps Fry felt that his own flight into convention and normality after the end of the war deprived him of some essential expression.

Certainly it was not obscurity that bothered him, according to Annette Fry, but rather "not having enough money to enable him to gratify his sometimes grandiose tastes and his many hobbies." That was certainly part of a larger, unspecified dissatisfaction. Alex Makinsky, the doctor Fry had flown to Lisbon with in 1940, had remained a friend to whom he could turn to unburden himself. By chance Makinsky was now vice president of the Coca-Cola Export Company, and when Fry complained of feeling restless and unfulfilled to the extent that he wished to quit, his friend attempted to help. "Varian, don't feel unhappy simply because things are not *perfect*," Makinsky advised him. "They certainly aren't and I am the first one to admit it. But then where do you find perfection?"

A magazine article on the twenty-fifth anniversary reunion of the old Marseille crew described Fry as "a mild, faintly absent-minded man equally distrustful of revolvers, supercharged cars and exotically spiced foods, who toddles about in a Volkswagen prudently observing the speed limits. . . . For relaxation he curls up with a crossword puzzle in Latin." The article attempted to draw a neat contrast between the war hero Fry had been and the gentle fellow he had become. But this "serenely married father of three children" was inwardly not so calm. Over the years his hypochondria had kept pace with his grouchiness ("There were times when he seemed totally bereft of a sense of humor," Annette Fry later observed) and now his health was really beginning to fail him.

In 1965 he and Annette relocated their family to Manhattan's Upper West Side. That year Fry was sacked by Coca-Cola and was told, after twelve years of solid and commendable labor, that he would never do any work for them again. His crime had been to write a report—at the request of Coca-Cola's Rome representative—on the inferior illumination of its drink dispensers compared to Pepsi's. Fry appended a short essay that analyzed the rise of the Pepsi pretenders to the cola throne as the culmination of Coca-Cola's management negligence over a period of decades. It earned him his marching orders and might have been an example of liberating self-sabotage. At any rate, the next year Fry also fell out with the Reverend Mother Ruth, who was in charge of the Episcopalian Day School on West 113th Street, where he had been teaching Latin and history. An account of his conduct noted "various reports that have been far from satisfactory as to the behavior of the students in your classes." Among other things, Fry had been playing them Tom Lehrer's *Vatican Rag* on the school gramophone. Clearly his old mischievousness had not entirely withered away, and his real reasons for leaving jobs were not far to find, according to Annette Fry. The problem was he "plain didn't like to work for anyone else."

It was around this time that Fry had begun again to work for the organization that had replaced the Emergency Rescue Committee. International Rescue sent him back to Europe, not this time to save refugees, but to track down some of the world's greatest living artists and persuade each to contribute a lithograph on the theme of rescue and flight for an album, "The Flight Portfolio." It was Fry's idea, and would commemorate the escapes from France during the Second World War. The portfolio would be reproduced in a limited edition and sold to raise funds so that the IRC could continue its work.

Secondarily, the project would also serve to give Fry a little of the recognition he deserved for his wartime achievements. Many of the artists to be approached had actually been saved by Fry, and were therefore in his debt, so to speak; and he could be furnished with an introduction to those whom he did not know by those artists he did. Furthermore it meant European travel, and a chance to revisit the places of his former glory. Fry guessed his task would be pleasurable rather than onerous, but he was wrong.

Chagall kindly lent Fry the house at Gordes that he had first visited in 1940 when trying to persuade the artist to flee from France. But beyond that, he seemed reluctant to help with the project, and although he promised Fry a lithograph, it failed to appear. Chagall's daughter Ida blamed her stepmother, Valentine, who dominated Chagall and hated him to do anything for free. André Malraux wrote to Fry that Chagall's hesitance might also have had something to do with keeping his name away from association with the

IRC—which had criticized Soviet Russia, where Chagall was very popular, over its record on human rights.

Chagall was not the only recalcitrant artist. Picasso had promised something "dans le genre de mon *Guernica*," but nothing appeared throughout 1966, and eventually Max Ernst had to reassure Fry and plead with him not to let his anger get the better of him and make a "terrible mistake at the first shock." Ernst's advice and assistance was invaluable, but navigating the lives and rivalries—not to mention old quarrels—among artists almost wholly absorbed in their work, made 1965–66 an extremely stressful time for Fry. For example, he was attempting to persuade André Breton to write the introduction for the portfolio—really, it was the least the poet could do. But in answer to Fry's request Breton claimed that if he did, then others like Ernst might walk away from the project, for the two old enemies had never resolved their differences. When Fry wrote that surely it could not be so, he received only a note from a secretary stating that "Breton says he has given to Varian Fry one of his books with a nice and friendly dedication, but that's all and no more is to be expected." Breton died soon after.

When Chagall's etching finally arrived Fry was delighted—until he noticed that the artist had not signed it. Nor would he sign. Chagall's signature was valuable and his wife could not allow just anybody to profit by it.

It was all very frustrating. For every artist who was keen to help—such as Lipchitz and Wifredo Lam—there was another who had to be tracked down and seduced away from his easel. It was a long list, too, and included Victor Brauner, Oskar Kokoschka, Marino Marini, Giacometti, Graham Sutherland, Otto Dix, Jean Arp, and Dubuffet. Fry even hired a young English artist to try to extract a promised picture from the elusive British sculptor Henry Moore, about whose work Fry was anyway less than enthusiastic. "He's an old dear," Fry advised his young friend, "and, if he doesn't give you tea, will at least show you his Courbet (itself worth the trip). His garden is dotted (dotted? punctured! stabbed! raped! fucked in the arse!) with his own sculptures."

An unexpected bonus of Fry's time on the Continent was his meeting in Paris with André Malraux at the Ministry of Culture. He had not seen the great man for years, and when Fry walked into his office on the rue de Valois, Malraux leaped to his feet and kissed him on both cheeks. Then standing back to look at him, he asked Fry where his ribbon was. "What ribbon?" asked Fry. "Why, the ribbon for your Legion d'Honneur," answered Malraux. "You should wear it with pride for what you accomplished for France in the war." Fry told him he wasn't wearing it because he didn't have the right to wear it, never having been awarded the *Croix de Chevalier* of the Légion d'Honneur. "Quelle Honte!" cried Malraux. *What a disgrace!* From that moment, Malraux began lobbying tirelessly in the French government for Fry to be given the honor he so richly merited.

Fry went back to Gordes, but after the strain of the year he promptly suffered a heart attack, which put him on his back in a Cannes clinic in September, 1966. Or at least Fry claimed it was a heart attack, and described his symptoms to fellow sufferer Max Ernst with the relish of a top-class hypochondriac:

> Did you have pain in your shoulders, radiating down your arm all the way to your fingers, and all along the clavicle to the neck, after your coronaries? These are some of my symptoms now.

Fry was probably in need of a good massage when he wrote to Ernst: a later examination by doctors in New York found no evidence of heart attack. In fact Fry's collapse in France was coincidental with exhaustion and general ill health. This, along with his exposure to the ingratitude of artists—something that could hardly have come as a surprise to a veteran like Fry—may just have tipped him into minor manic depression.

From the hospital he wrote to Annette in terms of almost ludicrous self-pity about how his life had been a failure. "*Tell* the kids," he lamented, "*reality* never hurts. Being *protected* from reality wounds for life. Look at me!" In reality, Fry translated his recent experience into a lack of recognition for himself. This he telescoped into his damning conclusion that his life had been a waste, which his "life-threatening" condition seemed to underline. The floodgates of self pity and panic were opened.

In retrospect events now seem to have come thick and fast. Fry returned to New York in October 1966, still most depressed and convinced his life had been a charade. But his impersonation of someone in the terminal stages of despair was so overdone that a friend who witnessed one of what Annette called his "woe-is-me" performances remarked, "He was so terribly depressed. But sorry for himself in such a self-dramatizing way that it was funny as well as sad." What was not funny was the way Fry began in earnest to take out his frustrations on his family. Not just Annette but, more seriously, his two older children were subjected to the most vindictive behavior. In keeping with his fantasy that—through no fault of his own—his life was misbegotten, he began to accuse Annette of "tricking" him moving back to New York. He claimed the city's "poisonous air" would kill the children he was treating so poisonously himself.

On Wednesday, April 12, 1967, in a ceremony at the French consulate in New York City, and accompanied by his loyal and proud family, Fry was presented with the *Croix de Chevalier* of the Légion d'Honneur by Edouard Morot-Sir, the cultural counselor. Strictly speaking, the award was not for the work Fry had done *in* France, with the refugees, but because of the work he had done *for* France. Specifically Fry was being recognized by the French government for his work with the Resistance. In 1940 and 1941 Malraux had tried to send intelligence to General de Gaulle in London via the American Embassy, and then via the American consulate, but had been refused help in both places. So Malraux had gone to Fry instead, and he had arranged through his British network of escaping airmen and soldiers to smuggle the information out of France.

This recognition changed neither Fry's attitude to his family nor his behavior. By June he could no longer abide his wife merely putting up with him, so he told Annette to "go get a divorce." This she did a couple of months later, flying down to El Paso and getting a Mexican decree in Juarez. In the meantime Fry, who felt that teaching the classics was the only effective medicine for what was ailing him, had decided to take a schoolmaster's job at Joel Barlow High School in Connecticut. He had also begun an affair with a divorced doctor who lived up there and whom (he wrote Anna Gruss) he planned to marry. An affair with a female doctor: it was a hypochondriac's dream. They even planned to write a medical column together "for newspaper syndication," so it was a hypochondriac writer's dream too. But in the end this made him feel no better. By now he was claiming to be suffering from headaches, attacks of dizziness, and tinnitus. He also said he was hearing voices.

His manic attack was broken by a spell in a hospital undergoing tests, all of which proved negative, and Fry called Annette from his bed on Tuesday, August 29, the day after she had returned home from Texas with the divorce. Now, she wrote at the time, her ex-husband was "totally changed from the manic, cold person he had been all summer." Stricken with remorse, he pleaded to be allowed to come home. "Of course," replied Annette, and there was a reunion at the apartment on the Upper West Side. Fry was deep in despair, apologizing for the havoc he had wrought on his family and the damage he had done to his relations with his children. Again, he appeared to have been baffled by his own behavior.

After this reconciliation, Fry readied himself to begin the new teaching job, although it was clear he was not yet back on an even keel. He stayed at the family apartment until Labor Day, and on Tuesday, September 7, he traveled to the house in Easton, Connecticut, which had been lent to him by the sculptor Louise Bourgeois and her husband. But by the weekend Fry was again in mental turmoil, and called Annette from an office he had kept on in Ridgefield since they had moved away. Again she told him to come home, and when he arrived he was sobbing and in a state of emotional collapse. He and Annette spent that Sunday talking over the events of the past year and all the unpleasantness involved. His depression then seemed to have lifted without giving way to mania, and briefly he appeared to be back to his old self. He agreed to stay in Connecticut during the week and return to his family in New York at weekends. It was a practical arrangement that gave Fry the time alone that he (and Annette) wanted and the time with his family that he needed. In good spirits, he traveled back up to Connecticut and taught class as normal on Monday.

IT WAS ANNETTE FRY who insisted on an autopsy in order to scotch any rumors that might begin to circulate due to her husband's recent state of mind. "His health was rotten," concluded Miriam Davenport some years later:

> . . . and his love life had been messed up by his own actions. . . . Varian suffered from frustrated ambitions, true enough. With his very real talents, he should have been a rich gentleman scholar with a good chef, a superb wine cellar, a fine house with a great garden, pedigreed animals, a beautiful wife, handsome children and distinguished friends. He had the expertise to lead "the good life" but not the entrepreneurial go-gettishness and luck to create the necessary fortune. So much said, I think he did pretty well before he began to destroy what he had created for himself. Why? Who knows? Who can know?

Annette had received a phone call from Joel Barlow High School on Wednesday morning, September 13. Fry had not turned up for work that day, and the school wondered if she might know where he was. As soon as the call was over, Annette dialled the Connecticut State Police and asked them to go to the Easton house, where Officer Schwartz found Fry lying propped up in bed with some papers spread across the blankets.

"It appeared to be a work of fiction," said Schwartz, describing the typescript he found next to Fry. But it wasn't. Fry was in the process of republishing a shorter edition of *Surrender on Demand* for high school students. He had farmed the rewriting job out to a friend, and it appears he was checking through some pages of the abridged version of his book when suddenly the pressure he had felt in his head all year finally seemed to be lifting. That must have been when Fry took off his spectacles and closed his eyes.

Who knows whether for a moment he didn't find himself back in Marseille with the Mediterranean sunshine spreading warmly over his body. Perhaps he heard voices and opened his eyes to find himself sitting around a café table on the Canebière drinking wine with Stéphane, and Danny, and Beamish, and Lena. A wonderful feeling of youthful lightness and the day so bright, so blindingly bright. "It's time to go over the mountain," said the voices. . . .

FRY'S OBITUARY in the *Ridgefield Press* stated that death was attributed to a "cerebral vascular accident." There was no suicide, then, but perhaps there had been a dangerous amount of medication. "He was taking uppers and downers," said Annette. "This, together with his customary evening ale and wine, might have contributed to his death." Yet it seems Fry was straightening out when he died. The coroner found that the barbiturate content at death in Fry's body was insignificant: just 2.3mg per 100ml of blood. Likewise there was hardly any alcohol in his system. Whatever killed Fry had long been inside him.

That night, just before he died, Fry had put in a long-distance call to Marcel Verzeano to check some forgotten details about the Marseille days. "At the same time," Verzeano wrote to Fry's son Tom, "he told me that he enjoyed his new position in teaching, that the job would allow him to keep in close touch with his family—which made him very happy—and that he was looking forward to a more stable and more satisfactory life than he had ever had before. His tone was confident and optimistic."

Fry's death was as intriguing and contradictory as had been his life—"a riddle wrapped in a mystery inside an enigma," as he was so fond of saying. "It was endlessly fascinating to try to figure him out," wrote Albert Hirschman of his old friend in the Marseille days. "There was in him a delightful mixture of earnest resolve and of wit, of methodical, almost formal demeanor and of playfulness." Fry was a good actor, good enough to fool the Gestapo, but in his life he was endlessly looking for himself and for the man he truly was. "To fight against play-acting," wrote Malraux, "is to fight against weakness, whereas the obsession with sincerity is the pursuit of secrets." Fry, "obstinately virtuous" in the words of Alfred Kazin, had been privileged to glimpse those secrets about himself in France during the war.

For the rest of his life Fry fought to remember the man he had been, until he found he was almost sixty years old. But by then he hardly recognized the face that looked back at him in the mirror. He had once found his homeland; thereafter he lived an exile.

―――――――

AFTER HIS DEATH Varian Fry was mourned by many people. Jacqueline Lamba-Breton described him as "a magnificent man—he thought only of others, never of the danger he himself was in." "In some way I owe him my life," wrote Jacques Lipchitz to Annette. "I did not want to go away from France. It was his severe and clairvoyant letters which helped me finally to do so. And of what help he was once I decided to go to America! I mourn with you this wonderful man, lost a little in our difficult world and I will cherish his memory to the end of my life."

If immortality means to live on in the hearts of others, today Varian Fry is still on his way to becoming immortal. In 1996, like Oskar Schindler before him, he was pronounced "Righteous Among the Nations" by Israel—the only American ever to be so honored—and a tree was planted in his memory on the Avenue of the Righteous leading to the Yad Vashem Museum in Jerusalem. U.S. Secretary of State Warren Christopher attended, along with Fry's son Jim, who dug the earth for the tree. Christopher used the occasion formally to apologize on behalf of the State Department for the treatment Fry had received during his time in France.

"And about time, too!" Fry would no doubt have replied.

NOTES AND REFERENCES

PART 1: THE LITTLE PRINCE

1. Berolina

Page 3 **The Pension Stern:** See note in *Fry Papers,* Box 6.

Page 3 **Fry always made:** For background on Berlin during the thirties see the opening chapter of Anthony Heilbut, *Exiled in Paradise.*

Page 3 **Another guest:** see *Fry Papers,* Box 6.

Page 4 **All the dubious glamour:** See Milton Mayer, *They Thought They Were Free,* p. 51.

Page 5 **When he reached:** This section is based on a detailed report by Fry of the riot that was published in the *New York Times,* July 17, 1935.

Page 7 **". . . spurts from the knife":** Varian Fry, *The New Republic,* December 21, 1942, p. 816.

Page 7 **The storm troopers laughed:** See Mary Jayne Gold, *Crossroads Marseille, 1940,* p. xv.

Page 8 **Fry had already asked for:** This section is based on another report from Fry in the *New York Times,* July 27, 1935.

Page 9 **As one old Harvard man:** Varian Fry, *The New Republic,* December 21, 1942, pp. 816–17.

Page 9 **The moderates believed:** For evidence of how early on the Madagascar scheme was floated, see Henry Feingold, *The Politics of Rescue,* pp. 57, 119.

Page 9 **Fry pushed Hanfstaengel:** Letter from Fry to Rev. Robert A. Graham in Rome, March 16, 1967 (*Fry Papers,* Box 4).

Page 10 **What made Hanfstaengel:** For a discussion of this subject, see Mayer, *They Thought They Were Free,* Chapter 12.

2. Don't Be a Goop

Page 12 **Varian Mackey Fry:** This section is based on interviews between Donald Carroll and cousin Libby (Elizabeth Richardson Garrabrants) in 1977–78, and between the author and Annette Fry in 1998.

Page 12 **In fact Fry's father:** Letter from Fry to Miss Betty Paysner of the International Rescue Committee, April 22, 1963 (*Fry Papers,* Box 5).

Page 13 **There survive as a kind of family snapshot:** see *Fry Papers,* Box 10.

Page 14 **At school he displayed:** Lincoln Kirstein, *Mosaic—Memoirs,* p. 102.

Page 16 **Nineteen twenty-six was also the year:** Letter from Johannes Skanck Martens to Fry, April 26, 1967 (*Fry Papers,* Box 6).

Page 17 **By the time he reached Harvard:** Lincoln Kirstein, *Mosaic—Memoirs,* p. 101.

Page 17 **In receipt of an allowance:** Annette Fry, interview with the author, 1998; Lincoln Kirstein, *Mosaic—Memoirs,* p. 101.

Page 18 **The plan was:** Lincoln Kirstein, *Mosaic—Memoirs,* pp. 103, 104.

Page 18 **But Fry's confidence:** Margaret Scolari Barr, "Rescuing Artists in WWII," 1980 (personal communication from Annette Fry).

Page 18 **". . . very undisciplined student":** Letter from Fry to Harvard Professor of Classics William Chase Green, September 3, 1942 (*Fry Papers,* Box 6).

Page 19 **Despite the split:** Annette Fry, interview with the author, 1998.

Page 20 **". . . case of emotional maladjustment":** Letter from Fry to A. C. Hanford, Dean of Harvard, September 10, 1945 (*Fry Papers,* Box 4).

Page 20 **In the late afternoon:** Letter from Fry to Eileen June 15, 1932 (*Fry Papers,* Box 6).

Page 21 **". . . so carefully concealed at the time":** Letter from Eileen to Fry, May 25, 1941; letter from Eileen to Fry, September 7, 1941 (*Fry Papers,* Box 3).

Page 21 **Granville Hicks, the critic and writer:** Personal communication from Annette Fry, 1997.

Page 23 **A few weeks earlier:** Klaus P. Fischer, *Nazi Germany: A New History,* p. 409.

3. Sign of the Times

Page 24 **The press was waiting:** *New York Times,* July 27, 1935.

Page 25 **The only man prepared:** Fischer, *Nazi Germany: A New History,* p. 411.

Page 26 **George Orwell wrote:** George Orwell, *The Collected Essays, Journalism and Letters,* Volume 1, p. 565.

Page 27 **Fry's first real adversity:** This is based on Donald Carroll, interview with Harold Oram, mid-seventies.

Page 28 **". . . for all future time":** Fry letter to Daniel Bénédite, May 12, 1942, p. 5 (*Fry Papers,* Box 2).

Page 30 **In July 1937:** For a lucid discussion, see John Pimlott, *The Viking Atlas of World War II,* p. 30.

Page 31 **". . . his bride's enthusiasm":** Heilbut, *Exiled in Paradise,* p. 31.

4. Some Call It War

Page 33 **". . . long and terrible experience":** See *Fry Papers,* Box 11, p. 148.

Page 33 **In 1935, when he first came to New York:** Donald Carroll, interview with Anna Caples-Hagen, mid-seventies.

Page 34 **. . . a teenage terrorist in Paris:** See Victor Serge, *Memoirs of a Revolutionary,* Chapter 1.

Page 35 **In the summer of 1939:** See Fry's notes (*Fry Papers,* Box 8).

Page 36 **. . . a "world revolution":** See Fry's notes (*Fry Papers,* Box 17).

Page 36 **. . . favorite midtown restaurant, Child's:** It was the one on Forty-second Street.

Page 36 **British overconfidence:** See Benjamin Welles, *Sumner Welles, F.D.R.'s Global Strategist,* p. 258.

Page 37 **The storm finally broke:** One of the finest accounts of this period is Telford Taylor, *The Breaking Wave: The Second World War in the Summer of 1940.*

Page 39 **... idealism was useless:** Donald Carroll, interview with Harold Oram.

Page 41 **"... the back of its neighbor":** *New York Times,* June 11, 1940, p. 6.

Page 41 **"... THE CHAMPS-ELYSEE":** *New York Times,* June 15, 1940, p. 1.

Page 41 **... ambassador to Franco's Spain:** For a full discussion of the events at this time, see Ian Ousby, *Occupation: The Ordeal of France, 1940–1944,* Chapter 1.

Page 42 **"... TERMS TO CRUSH FRANCE":** *New York Times,* June 19, 1940, p. 1.

Page 42 **"... AT COMPIEGNE TODAY":** *New York Times,* June 21, 1940, p. 1.

Page 42 **"... FULL FRENCH SURRENDER":** *New York Times,* June 22, 1940, p.

Page 42 **"... HALF OF FRANCE":** *New York Times,* June 24, 1940, p. 1.

5. The Accidental Tourist

Page 44 **"... who can *get* them out":** Donald Carroll, interview with Anna Caples-Hagen.

Page 45 **On June 4, Mann, in California:** See Anthony Heilbut, *Exiled in Paradise,* p. 40.

Page 46 **... best novelists in the world:** Ernest Hemingway, *Selected Letters,* p. 531.

Page 47 **... never mind "Jews and Communists":** see Henry L. Feingold, *The Politics of Rescue,* p. 132.

Page 47 **... membership in polite society:** Otto Friedrich writes most vividly of this in *City of Nets,* pp. 47–48.

Page 47 **... to petition her for help:** Cynthia Jaffee McCabe, "Wanted by the Gestapo: Saved by America," in *The Muses Flee Hitler,* p. 80.

Page 47 **"... political persecution to land":** Mary Jayne Gold, *Crossroads Marseille, 1940,* p. xv.

Page 48 **Fry had told Hagen confidentially:** Fry, draft MS (*Fry Papers,* Box 11).

Page 49 **... uninvolved and rigidly neutral:** For a good account of contemporary frustration with the isolationists and the Monroe doctrine, see Clare Booth (Luce), *European Spring,* p. 305.

Page 50 **... its director there, Richard Allen:** See letter to Fry from James T. Nicholson, assistant to the chairman of the Red Cross (*Fry Papers,* Box 10).

Page 50 **Thus armed, Fry's next task:** See *Fry Papers,* Box 1, Box 10.

Page 50 **... BRIEF APPOINTMENT?:** Fry, undated cable to Ambassador William C. Bullitt (*Fry Papers,* Box 10).

Page 50 **... already in a rocky state:** The best description of these hateful conditions is to be found in Benjamin Welles, *Sumner Welles, F.D.R.'s Global Strategist,* esp. p. 263. A broader and very enlightening account of interdepartmental and international tensions involving the State Department at this time is in *A Man Called Intrepid,* by William Stevenson.

Page 51 **... twelve submachine guns:** Benjamin Welles, *Sumner Welles, F.D.R.'s Global Strategist,* p. 260.

Page 51 **... Monday morning, July 29:** See *Fry Papers,* Box 10.

Page 51 **... Secretary of the Navy:** Benjamin Welles, *Sumner Welles, F.D.R.'s Global Strategist,* p. 263.

Page 52 **... one-way ticket:** the envelope on which Fry scribbled down his answers survives in the *Fry Papers,* Box 10.

Page 52 **... act as agents for the Emergency Rescue Committee:** ERC contract of employment, *Fry Papers,* Box 8.

Page 53 **"... the pleasure that they had given me":** Varian Fry, *Surrender on Demand,* p. xiii.

Page 53 **... out of Bordeaux:** See Fry's notes (*Fry Papers,* Box 11).

Page 53 **... until Heiden had arrived:** *New York Times,* September 20, 1960 (Heiden's obituary).

Page 54 **Heinrich Mann was even more well known:** See John Russell Taylor, *The Hollywood Emigrés,* p. 53. "Too bad we can't get our hands on the writers themselves," Golo Mann remembered hearing at the time of the book burnings (*Reminiscences and Reflections,* p. 307).

Page 55 **... uprooting his life:** See Fry's notes (*Fry Papers,* Box 8).

Page 56 **... some gray flannel pants:** See Fry's notes (*Fry Papers,* Box 11).

Page 56 **"... in September—I hope":** Fry, letter to Miss Chase, August 4, 1940 (*Fry Papers,* Box 10).

Page 56 **Late Friday evening:** Fry, draft MS (*Fry Papers,* Box 11).

Page 58 **He didn't know if it would fool:** Fry, draft MS (*Fry Papers,* Box 11).

PART 2: EXILES

6. On the Road

Page 61 **Many years ago:** The poem was "Der Erkennende" (see Susanne Keegan, *The Bride of the Wind,* p. 214).

Page 62 **... a love fetish:** (in the anthropological sense of the term) Mary Jayne Gold, *Crossroads Marseille, 1940,* p. 181. For Kokoschka's own account, see his autobiography, *My Life,* p. 117.

Page 62 **"... Alma will be booked up there, too":** Alma Mahler Werfel, *And the Bridge Is Love,* p. 170.

Page 63 **Luckily for him, Werfel:** See Alma Mahler Werfel, *And the Bridge Is Love,* pp. 218–23.

Page 63 **The year before at the PEN Congress:** See Lothar Kahn, *Insight and Action: The Life and Work of Lion Feuchtwanger,* p. 216.

Page 63 **They moved to a small fishing village:** John Russell Taylor, *The Hollywood Emigrés,* p. 53.

Page 64 **... Alma's endless entertaining:** See Alma Mahler Werfel, *And the Bridge Is Love,* p. 226.

Page 64 **Suddenly, after the declaration:** See Alma Mahler Werfel, *And the Bridge Is Love,* p. 233.

Page 67 **... a "crazy contagion":** Antoine de St. Exupéry, *Flight to Arras,* p. 76.

Page 67 **As their train made its way:** See Alma Mahler Werfel, *And the Bridge Is Love,* pp. 234–41.

Page 68 **... repel the invaders:** *New York Times,* June 14, 1940, p. 1.

Page 68 **... surrender or resign:** Benjamin Welles, *Sumner Welles, F.D.R.'s Global Strategist,* p. 262.

Page 68 **Realizing that at any moment:** See Alma Mahler Werfel, *And the Bridge Is Love,* p. 234.

Page 69 **For hundreds of years:** See V. S. Pritchett, *The Spanish Temper,* pp. 13–14.

Page 70 **After Paris, he had been drawn back:** Constance Regnier Carroll, interview with Hertha Pauli, mid-seventies.

Page 71 **... the chase was on:** See Walter Mehring, *The Lost Library: Autobiography of a Culture,* pp. 255–56.

Page 73 **... hanged himself in his New York hotel room:** See Lewis A. Coser, *Refugee Scholars in America,* p. 230.

Page 75 **. . . they decided to carry on:** Arthur Koestler mentions this ship in *Scum of the Earth*, pp. 211–12 (he arrived twenty-four hours after Mehring and Hertha Pauli had left).

Page 76 **. . . now heading for Montauban:** Varian Fry, *Surrender on Demand*, p. 32.

7. A Cold Mecca

Page 77 **It was hot midday:** This account is based on an unpublished draft MS of Varian Fry, pp. 104–6, 136, and records what Albert O. Hirschman (then Otto Albert Hirschmann) told him in 1940 (*Fry Papers*, Box 11).

Page 78 **. . . They never thought to look:** Albert O. Hirschman, interview with Donald Carroll, mid-seventies.

Page 78 **In Italy, he found himself:** Albert O. Hirschman, *A Propensity to Self Subversion*, p. 119.

Page 80 **When they went into battle:** Varian Fry, p. 245 of draft MS account of conversation with Stéphane Hessel, in *Fry Papers*, Box 11.

Page 80 **". . . look out for number one":** Varian Fry, *Surrender on Demand*, p. 25.

Page 81 **. . . "It's okay. Get in":** Lisa Fittko, *Solidarity and Treason*, pp. 48, 54.

Page 82 **. . . essentials they should each take:** Lisa Fittko, *Solidarity and Treason*, p. 9.

Page 83 **spontaneously aborted:** Anthony Heilbut, *Exiled in Paradise*, p. 35.

Page 83 **In the old days:** Lisa Fittko, *Solidarity and Treason*, p. 73.

Page 84 **She had to register:** Lisa Fittko, *Solidarity and Treason*, p. 85.

Page 86 **. . . "Destination: Marseille":** Lisa Fittko, *Escape Through the Pyrénées*, p. 87.

Page 86 **It was one o'clock:** The following account is from Charles Fawcett, interview with the author, 1998.

Page 89 **". . . stare out of the windows":** Varian Fry, letter to Eileen written aboard the Yankee Clipper en route to Lisbon, August 5, 1940 (*Fry Papers*, Box 3).

Page 89 **He took the risk:** Varian Fry, draft MS, (*Fry Papers*, Box 11).

Page 89 **. . . "I have been smothered in kindness":** Varian Fry, letter to Eileen, August 12, 1940 (*Fry Papers*, Box 3).

Page 91 **The train from Barcelona:** Varian Fry, draft MS account (*Fry Papers*, Box 11).

8. Pagaille

Page 92 **. . . without being arrested:** Marta Feuchtwanger, interview with Constance Regnier Carroll, mid-seventies; Lion Feuchtwanger, *The Devil in France*, p. 175.

Page 93 **. . . Fatalism alone:** "My fatalism is not so primitive as all that. It is, rather, the logical consequence of bitter experiences upon which I later brought my reason to bear" (Lion Feuchtwanger, *The Devil in France*, p. 15).

Page 93 **When Feuchtwanger arrived:** See Otto Friedrich, *City of Nets*, p. 96; Lothar Kahn, *Insight and Action*, p. 150.

Page 94 **. . . never see Germany again:** See Lion Feuchtwanger, *The Devil in France*, p. 13: he had publicly declared Hitler meant war "ever since 1933" (see also *New York Times*, March 2, 1933: "Dr. Feuchtwanger Sails").

Page 94 **. . . he left for the United States:** John Russell Taylor, *Strangers in Paradise*, p. 142.

Page 95 **". . . atmosphere of the Soviet Union":** From *Moscow*, by Lion Feuchtwanger, quoted in *Time* magazine, November 11, 1940.

Page 95 **. . . put out his pipe:** See Lothar Kahn, *Insight and Action*, pp. 208–9.

Page 95 **. . . even more unpopular than Hitler:** Anthony Heilbut, *Exiled in Paradise*, p. 35.

Page 96 ... **ominously rejected:** See Lion Feuchtwanger, *The Devil in France*, p. 36; for Muenzenberg, see Lothar Kahn, *Insight and Action*, pp. 219–21, and Arthur Koestler, *The Invisible Handwriting*, p. 198).

Page 96 ... **an overdose of sleeping pills:** See Lion Feuchtwanger, *The Devil in France*, pp. 89, 93–94 (Feuchtwanger is plainly guilt stricken at the part he played in Hasenclever's death).

Page 96 **There were those who criticized:** see Donna Ryan, *The Holocaust and the Jews of Marseille*, p. 105, and also Franz Schoenberner's own book, *The Inside Story of an Outsider.*

Page 96 ... **in the camp guards:** See Lion Feuchtwanger, *The Devil in France*, p. 31.

Page 96 **". . . those fourteen books".** Lion Feuchtwanger, *The Devil in France*, p. 86.

Page 97 **At the start of the German invasion:** Lisa Fittko, *Escape Across the Pyrénées*, p. 22.

Page 98 **After fleeing Germany in 1933:** see John Russell Taylor, *Strangers in Paradise*, p. 53.

Page 99 ... **at the house of a Mme. Behr:** Thomas Mann, *Selected Letters*, p. 271.

Page 100 **They waited nearly all day:** See Lion Feuchtwanger, *The Devil in France*, p. 182.

PART 3: THE SECRET CITY

9. The Secret City

Page 103 **Marseille, self-absorbed:** See especially Joseph Conrad, *A Personal Record*, p. 134.

Page 103 ... **or even nearby Toulon:** Varian Fry, draft MS, (*Fry Papers*, Box 11).

Page 103 **". . . a questionable but picturesque quarter":** "Winter in Marseille, 1941," American *Vogue*, April 1, 1941.

Page 104 ... **A disorienting experience:** Varian Fry, draft MS (*Fry Papers*, Box 12).

Page 105 ... **the hovering porter:** See *Surrender on Demand*, p. 3. We know the desk clerk at the Splendide was Jewish, because Fry harangued a Vichy minister about the man's racially motivated dismissal in mid-1941 (see "Last conversation with René Gillouin," *Fry Papers*, Box 11).

Page 105 **". . . as they take everything":** Fry, letter to Eileen, September 7, 1940 (*Fry Papers*, Box 3).

Page 105 ... **an "unnatural sparkle":** *Surrender on Demand*, p. 4.

Page 105 ... **the Noilly Prat fortune:** Martica Sawin, *Surrealism in Exile*, p. 121.

Page 106 **". . . wait your turn!" he shouted:** *Surrender on Demand*, p. 5.

Page 106 ... **the lawns of the Château Pastré:** Today that building is the *Musée de la Faïence.*

Page 107 **In fact, he did have papers:** *Surrender on Demand*, p. 18.

Page 108 **At the gendarmerie:** There are several versions of Mehring's arrests: Fry has only the one, later incident in his book, but Donald Carroll remembers being told in detail about this earlier one, and I have decided to include it because it seems true to Mehring's overall behavior, not to mention his bad luck. Miriam Davenport Ebel recalls Mehring being arrested as he left Fry's offices (interview with the author, 1998).

Page 108 **As it was:** See Michael R. Marrus and Robert O. Paxton, *Vichy France and the Jews*, pp. 5, 13.

Page 109 ... **Then they arrested him:** See Fry's notes (*Fry Papers*, Box 11).

Page 109 **The head of the new Vichy government:** See Michael R. Marrus and Robert O. Paxton, *Vichy France and the Jews*, Chapter 1.

Page 110 ... **one American who witnessed their actions:** Mary Jayne Gold, *Crossroads Marseille, 1940*, p. 66.

Page 110 ... **brought some unforeseen consequences:** Michael R. Marrus and Robert O. Paxton, *Vichy France and the Jews,* p. 67.

Page 110 ... **7 percent of the mainland population:** Michael R. Marrus and Robert O. Paxton, *Vichy France and the Jews,* p. 35.

Page 111 **Laws had already been passed:** Michael R. Marrus and Robert O. Paxton, *Vichy France and the Jews,* pp. 55–56.

Page 112 ... **a fluttering tricolor:** A photograph taken of this poster by Varian Fry is in the *Fry Papers,* Box 16.

Page 113 ... **I have met one person who does":** Fry to Eileen, September 7, 1940 (*Fry Papers,* Box 3).

Page 113 **Reality had certainly shrunk Werfel:** *Surrender on Demand,* p. 6.

Page 114 ... **"the shock of my own inadequacy":** Fry to Eileen, September 7, 1941, (*Fry Papers,* Box 3).

Page 115 ... **"the least desirable elements":** Quoted in David S. Wyman, *Paper Walls: America and the Refugee Crisis, 1938–1941,* p. 143.

Page 115 **". . . interpret them too strictly":** Varian Fry, note of conversation with Herbert C. Pell, American Minister to Portugal (*Fry Papers,* Box 11).

Page 115 **". . . Even in the enemy countries we have friends":** Varian Fry, article in *New Leader,* January 10, 1942.

Page 115 ... **"postpone and postpone and postpone":** Quoted in Kassof, *Intent and Interpretation: The German Refugees of Article 19 of the Franco-German Armistice 1940–1941,* p. 63. For a detailed portrait of Long, his background and motives, see Richard Breitman and Alan M. Kraut, *American Refugee Policy and European Jewry, 1933–45,* Chapter Six, "Breckinridge Long and the Jewish Refugees," pp. 126–45.

Page 117 **Fry learned from Bohn:** Fry mistakenly reports in *Surrender on Demand* that it was Harry Bingham who rescued Feuchtwanger.

Page 117 ... **she called Bohn "an unctuous ass":** Eileen to Fry, March 29, 1941 (*Fry Papers,* Box 3).

Page 117 **"Or maybe Harry Bingham was out":** *Surrender on Demand,* p. 10.

10. An American in Marseille

Page 118 **Later, another refugee:** Fry was later unsure of the original route, but it seems certain that this was it (see Fry's notes, *Fry Papers,* Box 10).

Page 119 ... **"settle in with them like bedbugs":** Lisa Fittko, *Escape Through the Pyrénées,* p. 94.

Page 119 **". . . you couldn't tell one from another":** *Surrender on Demand,* p. 10.

Page 120 **"He looked like an attractive person":** Albert O. Hirschman, interview with the author, 1998.

Page 121 **". . . this American had a list":** Hans Natonek, *In Search of Myself,* quoted by Cynthia Jaffee McCabe, "Wanted by the Gestapo: Saved by America," p. 83.

Page 121 ... **really a leftish German Jew:** The story of the murder of Madame Delapré's husband was told to the author by Charles Fawcett, 1998.

Page 123 ... **they got along "beautifully":** See Fry's notes (*Fry Papers,* Box 11).

Page 123 ... **He heard about Willi Muenzenberg's murder:** For an account of Meunzenberg's death, see Arthur Koestler, *Scum of the Earth,* p. 262. Mehring's disgusted appraisal of Muenzenberg (nameless but likely) can be found in *The Lost Library,* pp. 157–58.

Page 124 **". . . ought to have been on."** *Surrender on Demand,* p. 31.

Page 124 ... **they had thought only of death:** See *Memoirs of a Revolutionary,* p. 362.

Page 125 **". . . the pain of having to turn others down":** Fry to Eileen, September 7, 1940 (*Fry Papers,* Box 3).

Page 126 **". . . little better than death":** Fry to Eileen, September 7, 1940 (*Fry Papers,* Box 3).

Page 126 **". . . almost twenty thousand dollars a month:** Undated cable from Eileen to Fry, December 1941 (*Fry Papers,* Box 3).

Page 126 ... **gross domestic product:** See Ousby, *Occupation,* p. 66.

Page 127 **". . . always ready for the police":** *Surrender on Demand,* p. 36.

Page 127 **Oppy's work:** Danny Bénédite, confidential financial report for the Centre Américain de Secours, 1941 (*Fry Papers,* Box 7).

Page 127 **The Montagues and Capulets:** See Mary Jayne Gold, *Crossroads Marseille, 1940,* p. 203, and Donna Ryan, *The Holocaust and the Jews of Marseille,* p. 193.

Page 127 ... **It was really the Dorade:** The restaurant still exists at the same location (its name is now spelled "Dourade").

Page 127 ... **black market goods, and *coco:*** See *Surrender on Demand,* p. 46.

Page 127 **Vinciléoni's competitor, Sabiani, on the other hand:** See note in *Fry Papers,* Box 7 (and also Victor Serge, *Memoirs of a Revolutionary,* p. 361, where Serge mentions Sabiani by name).

Page 128 ... **between 1926 and 1934:** see Donna Ryan, *The Holocaust and the Jews of Marseille,* p. 19.

Page 129 ... **"felt like an empty glove":** *Surrender on Demand,* p. 47.

Page 129 ... **fired for stealing money:** Letter from Fry to Beamish November 30, 1940 (*Fry Papers,* Box 8).

Page 129 **"You seem to have disappeared . . .":** Eileen to Fry, August 16, 1940 (*Fry Papers,* Box 3).

11. Irreversible

Page 131 ... **kicked him onto the street:** Charles Fawcett, interview with the author, 1998.

Page 132 **". . . utterly crazy youngster":** Fry, letter to John Graham, June 22, 1942 (*Fry Papers,* Box 6).

Page 132 ... **High Commissioner for Refugees:** Not the Jewish Joint Distribution Committee, as Fry says (see *Surrender on Demand,* p. 35).

Page 132 **It worked every time:** Donald Carroll, interview with Lena Fischman, mid-seventies.

Page 132 **She never told anybody this:** Lena finally told Fry in a letter of April 4, 1966 (*Fry Papers,* Box 4).

Page 132 ... **"Il ne faut pas exagérer":** See *Surrender on Demand,* p. 35.

Page 133 **She said Mehring had sent her:** Miriam Davenport Ebel, interview with Donald Carroll, mid-seventies.

Page 134 ... **"I very badly need help":** Fry, letter to Miriam Davenport, August 27, 1940 (*Fry Papers,* Box 3).

Page 135 ... **"C'est de la blague":** *Surrender on Demand,* p. 90.

Page 135 **". . . fascism is neither":** Fry to Eileen, 7 September, 1940 (*Fry Papers,* Box 3).

Page 135 ... **the Prefecture in Marseille:** See Fry's notes (*Fry Papers,* Box 7).

Page 136 **". . . very frigid":** *Surrender on Demand,* p. 34.

Page 136 **". . . better English than you think":** Charles Fawcett, interview with the author, 1998.

Page 136 ... **Heiden was top:** See *Fry Papers,* Box 11.

Page 136 ... **how long even he would be safe:** Walter Meyerhof, interview with the author, 1998.

Page 138 **add his name to the list:** Donald Carroll, interview with Albert O. Hirschman, mid-seventies.

Page 139 **. . . refused to issue exit visas:** *Surrender on Demand,* p. 37.

Page 139 **. . . a fraction of its value:** See Donna Ryan, *The Holocaust and the Jews of Marseille,* p. 33, for a good description of this law.

Page 139 **. . . a number of meal coupons:** Miriam Davenport Ebel, interview with Donald Carroll, mid-seventies.

Page 139 **. . . where he was well known:** Varian Fry, draft MS, p. 104 (*Fry Papers,* Box 11).

Page 139 **Charlie in Marseille:** Charles Fawcett, interview with the author, 1998.

Page 140 **. . . Fry's Scottish ancestors:** Miriam Davenport Ebel, interview with the author, 1998.

Page 141 **. . . Aix-en-Provence to the north:** *Surrender on Demand,* p. 42.

Page 141 **He also tracked down:** Lisa Fittko, *Escape Through the Pyrénées,* p. 98.

Page 141 **His real coup:** This information comes from Donald Carroll, interviews with Bill Spira (Bill Freier), mid-seventies.

Page 142 **When he had finished:** Charles Fawcett, interview with the author, 1998.

Page 142 **There were other, less savory:** *Surrender on Demand,* p. 42.

Page 143 **. . . appearances in Marseille:** *Surrender on Demand,* p. 44.

Page 143 **. . . "a woman who will someday be famous":** Albert O. Hirschman, interview with Donald Carroll.

Page 144 **". . . a knight in overalls":** *Surrender on Demand,* p. 53.

Page 144 **. . . "Without his pleading":** Letter to Fry from Otto Meyerhof, September 18, 1945 (*Fry Papers,* Box 4).

Page 144 **". . . the ordinary relief agencies":** Fry to Eileen, October 31, 1940 (*Fry Papers,* Box 3).

Page 145 **. . . worthy of saving:** Miriam Davenport Ebel, interview with the author, 1998.

Page 145 **For all the staff:** For a discussion of the "LPC" clause, its prehistory and consequences, see Arthur D. Morse, *While Six Million Died: A Chronicle of American Apathy,* Chapter VII, "Likely to Become a Public Charge," pp. 130–49.

Page 146 **. . . allowance for food and accommodation:** Fry, *Journal,* p. 535 (*Fry Papers,* Box 13).

Page 146 **. . . a typical comment:** Quoted in Kassof, *Intent and Interpretation,* p. 124.

Page 146 **". . . we are bored and are going home":** Report to the Emergency Rescue Committee in New York, for the period of September to December 1940 (*Fry Papers,* Box 7).

12. Trouble

Page 147 **Late one evening:** Albert O. Hirschman, interview with Donald Carroll.

Page 147 **. . . "no sign of indignation":** Fry, notes, September 23, 1940 (*Fry Papers,* Box 7).

Page 147 **. . . On the other hand:** Article in *Le Gringoire,* "It Is Too Easy to Escape from Internment camps!" February 20, 1941.

Page 148 **Ration cards had been introduced:** Fry, notes (*Fry Papers,* Box 7).

Page 149 **. . . camps in France:** *Surrender on Demand,* p. 48.

Page 149 **. . . the first glass of wine:** See Walter Mehring, *The Lost Library,* p. 265.

Page 150 **Saturday came:** *Surrender on Demand,* p. 54.

Page 150 **That was not the end:** From a Confidential Report on the activities of the Centre Américain de Secours, submitted by Marcel Verzeano, summer 1941 (*Fry Papers,* Box 7).

Page 151 **... all the way to Lisbon if necessary:** *Surrender on Demand*, p. 53.

Page 151 **Probably it had been Kershner's:** *Surrender on Demand*, p. 49.

Page 152 **Barellet's father owned:** see Donna Ryan, *The Holocaust and the Jews of Marseille*, p. 95.

Page 152 **The setup was a lucrative cash cow:** See Fry's notes, in *Fry Papers*, Box 11.

Page 153 **Barellet was not about to suffer:** *Surrender on Demand*, p. 50.

Page 153 **"... tentacles of a totalitarian regime":** Albert O. Hirschman, quoted by Cynthia Jaffee McCabe, "Wanted by the Gestapo: Saved by America," p. 83.

Page 153 **Fry already knew:** See Fry's notes in *Fry Papers*, Box 11; Fry, letter of May 15, 1945, to Hedwig Wachenheim of the German Labor Union in New York (*Fry Papers*, Box 6).

Page 154 **"... sons of bitches":** Charles Fawcett, interview with the author, 1998.

Page 154 **So was Giuseppe:** *Surrender on Demand*, p. 23.

Page 154 **"It worked beautifully":** *Surrender on Demand*, pp. 49, 51.

Page 155 **After the disturbances:** *Surrender on Demand*, p. 51.

Page 155 **"... He was Gestapo":** Bill Spira, interview with Donald Carroll, mid-seventies.

Page 155 **... Mann went on his way:** see Nigel Hamilton, *The Brothers Mann*, p. 313.

Page 156 **... coming in the front:** Charles Fawcett, interview with the author, 1998.

Page 156 **"... all the way to Port-Bou":** See Fry's notes (*Fry Papers*, Box 10).

Page 156 **... It was a longer crossing:** Lisa Fittko, *Escape Through the Pyrénées*, p. 101.

Page 156 **... shapely young model, Dina Vierny:** See Fry's notes (*Fry Papers*, Box 10).

Page 157 **"They've got it, old man":** *Surrender on Demand*, p. 54.

13. Going Underground

Page 158 **"It wasn't a very brilliant idea":** The dialogue on this page is as reported by Lisa Fittko, *Escape Through the Pyrénées*, p. 118.

Page 160 **After the debacle:** *Surrender on Demand*, p. 56.

Page 160 **The following day:** *Surrender on Demand*, p. 57.

Page 162 **Fry had instinctively:** *Surrender on Demand*, p. 59.

Page 163 **He gave Fry the map:** *Surrender on Demand*, p. 60.

Page 165 **One French army officer:** Danny Bénédite, Report on Internment Camps, winter 1940 (*Fry Papers*, Box 9).

Page 165 **... Snow Whites and the Seven Dwarfs:** Information supplied by Donald Carroll.

Page 167 **The plan was to catch:** *Surrender on Demand*, p. 62.

Page 168 **"... we heard no more from her":** *Surrender on Demand*, p. 64.

Page 169 **"... nothing but thistles to hold onto":** Alma Mahler Werfel, *And the Bridge Is Love*, p. 245.

Page 170 **"It was a long, hot climb":** *Surrender on Demand*, p. 67; Alma Mahler Werfel, *And the Bridge is Love*, pp. 244–6.

Page 170 **... Over the centuries:** See V. S. Pritchett, *The Spanish Temper*, p. 15.

Page 170 **All eyes were on:** *Surrender on Demand*, p. 68, 69.

PART 4: FRIENDS

14. Ursula

Page 176 **... "He's not a very pleasant chap":** *Surrender on Demand*, p. 70.

Page 177 **"You can never be too careful":** *Surrender on Demand*, p. 72.

Page 177 **Captain Darling, the British vice-consul:** Letter from Darling to Fry, December 4, 1967 (*Fry Papers,* Box 3).

Page 178 **Lisbon, too, had its rumor factories:** This information comes from recently declassified ULTRA intercepts of Spanish and German communications now held in the Public Records Office, Kew, London (first reported in *The Sunday Telegraph,* December 28, 1997).

Page 179 **If the Germans controlled Africa:** for an excellent summation of the situation, see William Stevenson, *A Man Called Intrepid,* p. 272.

Page 180 **Fry went straight from the airport:** *Surrender on Demand,* p. 74, 75.

Page 181 BABY PASSED CRISIS: *Surrender on Demand,* p. 74.

Page 182 **". . . rubbing them on stones to get them clean":** Fry, draft MS, pp. 407–8 (*Fry Papers,* Box 14).

Page 182 **. . . pair of socks:** *Surrender on Demand,* p. 75.

Page 182 **Fry demurred:** *Surrender on Demand,* p. 78.

Page 183 **. . . Ernst and Rosi Scheuer:** Fry, *Journal,* p. 459 (*Fry Papers,* Box 13).

Page 183 **. . . clandestine entry and smuggling:** See *Surrender on Demand,* p. 78.

15. The Fall

Page 185 **". . . our days of grace were over":** *Surrender on Demand,* p. 94.

Page 186 **. . . mercifully uneventful:** Constance Regnier Carroll, interview with Marta Feuchtwanger, mid-seventies; see Lothar Kahn, *Insight and Action,* p. 241, for a slightly different account of this last incident.

Page 186 **Lena had positioned herself:** Donald Carroll, interview with Miriam Davenport Ebel.

Page 187 **This entertaining tale:** See *Surrender on Demand,* p. 80.

Page 187 **Fry soon met:** See Fry's notes (*Fry Papers,* Box 8, Box 11).

Page 187 **. . . regardless, but with care.:** See *Surrender on Demand,* p. 98.

Page 188 **". . . with Hitler's government":** Howard L. Brook, *Prisoners of Hope* (uncorrected galleys in *Fry Papers,* Box 18).

Page 188 MUST REQUEST YOUR RETURN: Cable passed on from General Frank R. McCoy to Consul Hugh Fullerton and then to Fry, October 3, 1940 (*Fry Papers,* Box 8).

Page 189 **". . . disowning me now?":** See Fry's notes for draft MS (*Fry Papers,* Box 11).

Page 189 THIS GOVERNMENT DOES NOT REPEAT NOT: Undated cable from the State Department to Consuls in France—approximately September 1940 (*Fry Papers,* Box 11).

Page 189 **. . . "The truth is, of course":** Fry to Eileen, October 1, 1941 (*Fry Papers,* Box 3).

Page 190 MR FULLERTON HAS JUST COMMUNICATED ME: Cable from Fry to the American Embassy at Vichy, September 25, 1940 (*Fry Papers,* Box 8).

Page 190 MILDRED FRANK PAUL ALL BELIEVE: Cable from Eileen to Fry, date from internal evidence very probably October 3, 1940 (*Fry Papers,* Box 3).

Page 190 **Fry wrote back:** Fry to Eileen, October 31, 1940 (*Fry Papers,* Box 3).

Page 190 **". . . the American Embassy in Vichy":** Fry to Jacques Lipchitz, June 6, 1965 (*Fry Papers,* Box 1).

Page 191 **Coming on top:** See Michael R. Marrus and Robert O. Paxton, *Vichy France and the Jews,* pp. 3–4, 199.

Page 192 **. . . "So am I," he replied evenly:** Charles Fawcett, interview with the author, 1998.

Page 193 **. . . went safely to Cuba on them:** See Fry's notes (*Fry Papers,* Box 11).

Page 193 **Two or three times a week:** Fry, from phone conversation with Maurice Verzeano, February 27, 1967 (*Fry Papers,* Box 10).

Page 193 **They would begin early:** See Lisa Fittko, *Escape Through the Pyrénées*, p. 124.

Page 194 **A stroke of good fortune:** See Lisa Fittko, *Escape Through the Pyrénées*, p. 127.

Page 194 **". . . beginning of the tunnel":** Albert O. Hirschman, interview with Donald Carroll, mid-seventies.

Page 194 **". . . they'd go by foot":** Fry, note, March 1, 1967 (*Fry Papers*, Box 10).

Page 194 **Lisa reported:** See Lisa Fittko, *Escape Through the Pyrénées*, p. 127.

Page 195 **. . . or didn't care:** See *Surrender on Demand*, p. 105.

Page 195 **. . . the Geneva Conventions:** Fry, from phone conversation with Maurice Verzeano, February 27, 1967 (*Fry Papers*, Box 10).

Page 195 **" . . . questioned by the police":** *Surrender on Demand*, p. 124.

Page 196 **". . . in similar circumstances":** *New York Times*, October 5, 1940.

Page 197 **". . . the bigger the blinders":** Lisa Fittko, *Escape Through the Pyrénées*, p. 153.

Page 197 **". . . rescue work in France":** *Time*, November 11, 1940.

Page 197 **". . . marooned in France":** *New York Post*, January 24, 1941.

Page 197 **". . . the broadcast declared":** *New York Sun*, November 23, 1940.

Page 198 **There were tragedies:** For this story, see Lisa Fittko, *Escape Through the Pyrénées*, Chapter 7, "Old Benjamin" (pp. 106–15).

Page 199 **That night, in a hotel:** The owner of the hotel "Fonda de Francia," Juan Suñer Jonama, had well-known connections with the German Nazis, and this has given rise to several (implausible) murder theories. See Momme Broderson, *Walter Benjamin: A Biography*, pp. 250–54.

Page 199 **Charlie Fawcett believed:** Charles Fawcett, interview with the author, 1998.

Page 199 **The truth is:** Benjamin had previously divided up his morphine pills with his friend Arthur Koestler, and had been worried that he was left with an insufficient dose. See David Cesarani, *Arthur Koestler, The Homeless Mind*, p. 217.

Page 199 **. . . "Papers of unknown content":** Lisa Fittko, *Escape Through the Pyrénées*, p. 114. Broderson agrees that Benjamin's MS was probably destroyed straight after the cursory autopsy (see *Walter Benjamin: A Biography*, p. 260).

Page 200 **. . . its office on the Canebière:** Lisa Fittko, *Escape Through the Pyrénées*, p. 95.

Page 200 **What all this means:** Fry, letter to Mildred Adams, September 1940 (*Fry Papers*, Box 2).

Page 201 **. . . "It would be just the sort of trick":** *Surrender on Demand*, p. 95.

16. Happy Birthday, Varian

Page 203 **. . . a Rockefeller Foundation fellowship:** See Lewis Coser, *Refugee Scholars in America*, p. 163.

Page 204 **". . . the puckish smile":** Mary Jayne Gold, *Crossroads Marseille, 1940*, p. 158.

Page 204 **". . . little rich girl":** Fry, letter to Daniel Bénédite, September 22, 1941 (*Fry Papers*, Box 2).

Page 204 **. . . south of France:** Fry, *Journal*, p. 485 (*Fry Papers*, Box 13).

Page 206 **". . . cypress trees":** Fry, draft MS, p. 243 (*Fry Papers*, Box 9).

Page 207 **. . . Utopia for Fry:** See Fry, draft MS, p. 244 (*Fry Papers*, Box 9).

Page 208 **". . . thirty-two degrees above zero":** Arthur Koestler, *Scum of the Earth*, p. 103.

Page 208 **". . . our enemies":** Letter from Lion Feuchtwanger printed in the *New York Times*, April 27, 1942.

Page 209 **. . . their visa applications:** See Mary Jayne Gold, *Crossroads Marseille, 1940*, p. 223.

Page 209 **It was a leaky:** See *Surrender on Demand*, p. 90.

Page 210 **". . . hesitated to expel me":** Unaddressed letter from Fry written in Marseille, 1941 (*Fry Papers*, Box 7).

Page 211 **And the *maddening* thing:** Fry to Eileen, October 17, 1940 (*Fry Papers*, Box 3).

Page 211 **"If you really want . . .":** Fry, letter included with report to Emergency Rescue Committee, period of September to December, 1940 (*Fry Papers*, Box 7).

Page 212 MODERATE YOUR TELEGRAMS: Eileen to Fry, undated cable, late 1940 (*Fry Papers*, Box 3).

Page 212 **I have no hope:** Eileen to Fry, November 10, 1940 (*Fry Papers*, Box 3).

Page 212 PLEASE MAKE THEM REALIZE: Fry, cable to Eileen, November 10, 1940 (*Fry Papers*, Box 3).

Page 213 **". . . undercover work":** *Surrender on Demand*, p. 100.

Page 214 **". . . best of terms with":** Fry to Eileen, November 29, 1940 (*Fry Papers*, Box 3).

Page 214 **. . . "When I first met him":** *Surrender on Demand*, p. 102.

Page 215 **It was genuine bad luck:** See *Surrender on Demand*, p. 92.

Page 216 **. . . a wrecking ball:** See *Surrender on Demand*, p. 108.

17. That Sinking Feeling

Page 217 **Standing in his tattered:** Charles Fawcett, interview with the author, 1998; we can be sure of the date because of a letter Fry wrote to Eileen en route to Tarascon on October 27, as he was making himself scarce.

Page 218 **. . . allow her passage:** See *Surrender on Demand*, p. 110.

Page 218 **. . . would not agree:** Charles Fawcett, interview with the author, 1998.

Page 219 **Taking refuge in poetry:** See *Surrender on Demand*, p. 113.

Page 220 **rethink his position:** See Martica Sawin, *Surrealism in Exile*, p. 132.

Page 220 **On the day:** See Fry, draft MS, p. 256 (*Fry Papers*, Box 9).

Page 221 **". . . carried shrieking off":** Fry to Eileen, October 27, 1940 (*Fry Papers*, Box 3).

Page 221 **. . . the Val d'Enfer:** See Fry, draft MS, p. 257–8 (*Fry Papers*, Box 9).

Page 222 **". . . I don't want them anymore":** Fry to Eileen, November 29, 1940 (*Fry Papers*, Box 3).

Page 222 **It was Miriam:** Miriam Davenport Ebel, interview with the author, 1998.

Page 223 **The broad gravel terrace:** Fry, letter to Théo Bénédite, December 18, 1941 (*Fry Papers*, Box 3).

Page 224 **. . . a typical Fry rejoinder:** See Fry, letter to Daniel Bénédite, May 12, 1942, p. 8 (*Fry Papers*, Box 2).

Page 224 **Breton brought with him:** See Mark Polizzotti, *Revolution of the Mind: The Life of André Breton*, p. 484.

Page 225 **The rest of that autumn:** See Martika Sawin, *Surrealism in Exile*, p. 130; *Surrender on Demand*, p. 184.

Page 225 **everybody's existence a little:** See Peggy Guggenheim, *Out of This Century: Confessions of an Art Addict*, pp. 135–36.

Page 226 **One of the most beautiful:** See Martika Sawin, *Surrealism in Exile*, p. 132; Mark Polizzotti, *Revolution of the Mind*, p. 494.

Page 228 **. . . a lethal cartoon:** See Fry's notes, Box 3, *Fry Papers*.

Page 228 **The other thing:** See Fry's notes, Box 11, *Fry Papers*.

Page 230 **. . . dying like flies:** See "Report from Casablanca, June 17th, 1941" (*Fry Papers*, Box 11).

Page 230 **Les femmes de France:** See Fry's notes (*Fry Papers*, Box 11).

Page 231 **. . . some cognac after all:** *Surrender on Demand*, p. 147.

Page 231 **". . . wonder where you are":** See Fry's notes (*Fry Papers*, Box 3).

Page 232 FRY AND MISS GOLD: Cable from the American consulate in Marseille to the State Department in Washington, D.C., at the time of the *Sinaia* episode, which Fry found in ERC files on his return to New York (*Fry Papers,* Box 11).

Page 232 "... apologies from the authorities": Fry, letter to ERC in New York, January 21, 1941 (*Fry Papers,* Box 2).

Page 232 Luckily he made it: Charles Fawcett, interview with the author, 1998.

18. The Turning Year

Page 234 "The women in the camps": Fry, *Journal,* p. 522 (*Fry Papers,* Box 13).

Page 234 There were 17,000 people: See "Internment Camps" (*Fry Papers,* Box 9).

Page 236 "... he knows so many people there": Fry to Eileen, November 29, 1940 (*Fry Papers,* Box 3).

Page 236 flee the county for Switzerland: See Michael R. Marrus and Robert O. Paxton, *Vichy France and the Jews,* p. 205, and Richard H. Weisberg, *Vichy Law and the Holocaust in France,* p. 69–70.

Page 237 ... dumped them in France: See Michael R. Marrus and Robert O. Paxton, *Vichy France and the Jews,* p. 172.

Page 237 "... worse than they are": Fry, communication with ERC in New York, February 1, 1941 (*Fry Papers,* Box 2).

Page 237 ... the runaround everywhere: *Surrender on Demand,* p. 127.

Page 238 ... asking formally for an interview: Fry, letter to American Chargé d'Affaires at Vichy, November 17, 1940.

Page 238 ... "Que ces gars là": *Surrender on Demand,* p. 149.

Page 239 He had been sitting: Charles Fawcett, interview with the author, 1998.

Page 240 ... subsequently left alone: Mary Jayne Gold, unpublished monograph, 1965 (*Fry Papers,* Box 18).

Page 241 ... no guarantee of identity: Lisa Fittko, *Escape Through the Pyrénées,* p. 149.

Page 241 ... a "bitter *parvenu*": From a review by Fry in *New Masses* of a book called *The Gravediggers of France,* October 16, 1944.

Page 241 ... "I have a rope": Fry, draft MS, p. 352 (*Fry Papers,* Box 9).

Page 242 "... his best girlfriend": *Surrender on Demand,* p. 151.

Page 242 When Beamish reached Banyuls: See Lisa Fittko, *Escape Through the Pyrénées,* pp. 137–41.

Page 243 "'... are against you'": Fry to Eileen, November 29, 1940 (*Fry Papers,* Box 3).

Page 244 "... dangerous because justified": Quoted in Michael R. Marrus and Robert O. Paxton, *Vichy France and the Jews,* p. 171.

Page 244 ... dwindling supply of fuel: See letter from Albert O. Hirschman to Fry, July 31, 1942 (*Fry Papers,* Box 11).

Page 245 ... "All human acts involve": Gide, *Journals,* pp. 265, 269, 273.

Page 245 ... "If all the talented people": *Newsweek,* March 1, 1942.

Page 245 "... surrounded himself with": *Surrender on Demand,* p. 157.

Page 245 The day after: Lisa Fittko, Albert O. Hirschman, interviews with Donald Carroll, mid-seventies.

Page 246 "You get better stories here": Fry, draft MS, p. 351 (*Fry Papers,* Box 11).

Page 247 ... in serious trouble: See Fry, letter to Jacques Lipchitz, June 6, 1965 (*Fry Papers,* Box 1).

Page 247 FIELDING ESPECIALLY WORRIED: Fry, cable to Eileen's sister, January 3, 1941 (*Fry Papers,* Box 7).

PART 5: ENEMIES

19. The Friend

Page 251 **When Fry went:** See Fry's notes (*Fry Papers*, Box 11).

Page 251 **. . . "Serious trouble":** U.S. Consul Fullerton, letter to Fry, January 21, 1941; Fry to Lipchitz, June 6, 1965 (*Fry Papers*, Box 7, Box 1).

Page 252 **. . . the second Mrs. Hemingway:** See Ernest Hemingway, *Selected Letters*, p. 491.

Page 252 **. . . watery-eyed admiration:** See letter from Fry to Eileen, February 15, 1941 (*Fry Papers*, Box 3).

Page 252 **Allen said:** See *Surrender on Demand*, p. 154.

Page 253 **". . . *in charge* as on January 1":** Jay Allen, memorandum to Fry, January 20, 1941 (*Fry Papers*, Box 2).

Page 253 THIS MESSAGE SENT: Lena Fischman, cable to her fiancé Melvyn Hagen, December 18, 1940 (*Fry Papers*, box 2).

Page 253 **. . . "FUNDAMENTALLY INCORRECT":** Melvyn Fagen, cable to Centre Américain de Secours, December 1940 (*Fry Papers*, Box 2).

Page 253 **. . . the Fittko route:** See contribution to administrative report, early 1941, by Marcel Verzeano (*Fry Papers*, Box 7).

Page 254 **. . . brief imprisonment on the SS *Sinaïa*:** See Fry's notes in Box 11, *Fry Papers*, Victor Serge, *Memoirs of a Revolutionary*, p. 364.

Page 255 **". . . qu-il est malade":** See Fry's notes (*Fry Papers*, Box 11).

Page 255 **"The truth is":** Letter from Fry to Eileen, January 5, 1941 (*Fry Papers*, Box 3).

Page 255 **. . . daily hour of lucidity:** See Ian Ousby, *Occupation*, p. 37.

Page 255 **". . . because you didn't":** Letter from Eileen to Fry, January 15, 1941 (*Fry Papers*, Box 3).

Page 256 **In late January:** See "Confidential Financial Report" by Daniel Bénédite, 1941 (*Fry Papers*, Box 7).

Page 256 **. . . "I will moreover":** Jay Allen, memorandum to Fry, January 20, 1941 (*Fry Papers*, Box 2).

Page 256 **". . . dig up something big":** Harold Oram, letter to Fry, January 22, 1941 (*Fry Papers*, Box 5).

Page 257 **". . . unjustified and insulting":** Fry, report to ERC in New York on Jay Allen's activities, January 21, 1941 (*Fry Papers*, Box 2).

Page 257 **"COMMITTEE FULL CONFIDENCE":** Albert O. Hirschman, cable to Fry, January 29, 1941.

Page 257 ALL I KNOW OR HEAR: Dr. Charles Joy, cable to ERC in New York, January 31, 1941 (*Fry Papers*, Box 2).

Page 258 **". . . piddling that job was":** Letter from Fry to Eileen, February 2, 1941 (*Fry Papers*, Box 3).

Page 258 CABLES SIGNED KINGDON: Ingrid Warburg, cable to Fry, January 30, 1941.

Page 258 **". . . some very substantial ones":** Fry, report to ERC in New York on Jay Allen's activities, January 21, 1941 (*Fry Papers*, Box 2).

Page 260 **. . . Casablanca and Dakar:** See *Surrender on Demand*, p. 165.

Page 261 **On the last day:** See Fry, draft MS, p. 377 (*Fry Papers*, Box 11).

Page 261 **Fry had planned:** See *Surrender on Demand*, p. 170.

Page 263 **"'Partez!'":** Walter Mehring, letter to Fry, December 22, 1941 (*Fry Papers*, Box 7).

Page 263 **Breitscheid and Hilferding:** See written report by Frau Breitscheid submitted to Fry, February 20, 1941 (*Fry Papers*, Box 11).

Page 264 **". . . over his face":** See *Surrender on Demand*, p. 77.

Page 264 **". . . telling the truth":** See letter to Fry from Major Maurer of the Historical Studies Branch, U.S.A.F. Historical Division, March 22, 1967, where it is explained that an American air raid (August 24, 1944) took place on a radio factory and SS offices close to the concentration camp barracks where Breitscheid was held. Some of the bombs fell astray on the barracks themselves (*Fry Papers*, Box 3).

20. Full Steam Ahead

Page 265 **"He said he would like":** Letter from Fry to Eileen, February 15, 1941 (*Fry Papers*, Box 3).

Page 266 **". . . as for your opponents":** Letter from Eileen to Fry, February 16, 1941 (*Fry Papers*, Box 3).

Page 266 **. . . or even impossible:** Fry, *Journal*, p. 462 (*Fry Papers*, Box 13).

Page 266 **"How do they expect":** Letter from Fry to Eileen, April 29, 1941 (*Fry Papers*, Box 3).

Page 267 **. . . "severely repressed spinster":** See Fry's notes (*Fry Papers*, Box 15).

Page 267 **. . . "Suppose they torture":** Fry, *Journal*, p. 472 (*Fry Papers*, Box 13).

Page 268 **. . . "Oh France":** Fry, *Journal*, p. 458 (*Fry Papers*, Box 13).

Page 268 **"I cabled you":** Eileen to Fry, February 18, 1941 (*Fry Papers*, Box 3).

Page 269 **. . . "Do you ever think about me":** Eileen to Fry, March 6, 1941 (*Fry Papers*, Box 3).

Page 269 **. . . not come at all:** Fry, *Journal*, p. 493 (*Fry Papers*, Box 13).

Page 269 **The Bretons were:** Fry, *Journal*, p. 480 (*Fry Papers*, Box 13).

Page 269 **. . . buy a ticket:** See Claude Lévi-Strauss, *Tristes Tropiques*, p. 24.

Page 269 **. . . They in turn:** See Martica Sawin, *Surrealism in Exile*, p. 136.

Page 270 **". . . Good luck":** See *The New Yorker*, March 7, 1964.

Page 271 **"I hope you're not helping Jews":** Fry, notes (*"VICHY, NOVEMBER 1940"*) in *Fry Papers*, Box 11. See also David S. Wyman, *Paper Walls*, p. 163.

Page 271 **Fry also recalled:** See Fry, notes (*Fry Papers*, Box 11).

Page 271 **". . . within the gates":** Letter from Fry to Daniel Bénédite, November 25, 1941 (*Fry Papers*, Box 2).

Page 271 **". . . too good to be true":** Fry, *Journal*, p. 460 (*Fry Papers*, Box 13).

Page 272 **. . . with Himmler in genocide:** See Michael R. Marrus and Robert O. Paxton, *Vichy France and the Jews*, p. 76.

Page 272 **". . . because of the race":** Clark Husted to Fry, March 1, 1941 (*Fry Papers*, Box 7).

Page 272 **". . . persons of other faiths":** Letter from Fry to Husted, April 10, 1941 (*Fry Papers*, Box 7).

Page 272 **. . . "They have never":** Fry, *Journal*, p. 460 (*Fry Papers*, Box 13).

Page 273 **". . . death to a refugee":** Fry, *Journal*, p. 461 (*Fry Papers*, Box 13).

Page 273 **". . . independent of the Committee":** Daniel Bénédite, Administrative Report (*Fry Papers*, Box 7).

Page 274 **". . . job to someone else":** Marcel Verzeano, interview with the author, 1998.

Page 274 **Wolff's anger:** Report submitted by Marcel Verzeano to files of Centre Américain de Secours, summer 1941 (*Fry Papers*, Box 7).

Page 274 **. . . He soon discovered:** Marcel Verzeano, interview with the author, 1998.

Page 274 **. . . escort of Garcia's men:** Fry and Lisa Fittko present different accounts of this, but Verzeano is adamant that it was Garcia's men who undertook the trip (personal communication with the author, 1998). See further evidence in Daniel Bénédite, *La filière marseillaise: Un chemin vers la liberté sous l'occupation*, p. 203 (Paris, Editions Clancier Guenaud, 1984).

Page 275 **. . . his boss was out:** Fry, *Journal*, p. 466 (*Fry Papers*, Box 13).

Page 275 **. . . watch them watching him:** Fry, *Journal,* p. 482 (*Fry Papers,* Box 13).

Page 276 **". . . he gets away with it":** Letter from Fry to Eileen, March 18, 1941 (*Fry Papers,* Box 3).

Page 276 **". . . not excepting butter":** Fry, *Journal,* p. 482 (*Fry Papers,* Box 13).

Page 276 **. . . antagonism toward women:** See *Surrender on Demand,* p. 116.

Page 277 **The day after the riot:** Fry, *Journal,* p. 489 (*Fry Papers,* Box 13).

Page 277 **". . . good for him":** Letter from Eileen to Fry, March 24, 1941 (*Fry Papers,* Box 3).

Page 277 **. . . "Will you tell me":** Letter from Eileen to Fry, April 2, 1941 (*Fry Papers,* Box 3).

Page 278 **". . . especially today":** Letter from Fry to Eileen, May 1, 1941 (*Fry Papers,* Box 3).

Page 278 **. . . Ah, love:** Fry, *Journal,* p. 494 (*Fry Papers,* Box 13).

Page 279 **"That's the way":** Fry, *Journal,* p. 497 (*Fry Papers,* Box 13).

Page 279 **" '. . . that file on Dobos' ":** Mary Jayne Gold, *Crossroads Marseille, 1940,* p. 334.

Page 279 **Peggy Guggenheim:** See letter from Fry to Eileen, May 3, 1941.

21. Betrayals

Page 281 **The incident had occurred:** Fry, *Journal,* p. 503 (*Fry Papers,* Box 13).

Page 281 **It was also a plan:** Danny Bénédite called it "a plan so lacking in prudence that it seemed quite mad" (see comment in *Fry Papers,* Box 7).

Page 281 **. . . straight into a trap:** Fry, *Journal,* p. 503 (*Fry Papers,* Box 13).

Page 282 **. . . "Naturally I was kinda":** Fry to Eileen, April 21, 1941 (*Fry Papers,* Box 3). This entire saga is politely referred to and ignored by Fry in two or three sentences in *Surrender on Demand* (see p. 191).

Page 283 **. . . "Danny, thank God":** *Surrender on Demand,* p. 199.

Page 283 **. . . Prado for nearly a week:** Marcel Verzeano, interview with the author, 1998; Fry, *Journal,* p. 514 (*Fry Papers,* Box 13).

Page 283 **At Banyuls:** See Lisa Fittko, *Escape Through the Pyrénées,* p. 154.

Page 283 **". . . our game will be up":** Fry, *Journal,* p. 514 (*Fry Papers,* Box 13).

Page 284 **After the interview:** Fry, *Journal,* p. 518 (*Fry Papers,* Box 13).

Page 284 **". . . only thing we have left":** Fry, *Journal,* p. 540 (*Fry Papers,* Box 13).

Page 285 **". . . or back on Lipari":** *Surrender on Demand,* p. 204.

Page 285 **On top of all this:** See Fry, *Journal,* pp. 534, 539 (*Fry Papers,* Box 13).

Page 285 **". . . anti-Semite himself":** Fry, *Journal,* p. 538 (*Fry Papers,* Box 13).

Page 286 **". . . amazingly heavy":** Fry, *Journal,* p. 510 (*Fry Papers,* Box 13).

Page 286 **Kourillo, as a trusted agent:** See Fry, *Journal,* pp. 541 (*Fry Papers,* Box 13).

Page 286 **". . . *all* of them":** Eileen to Fry, May 1, 1941 (*Fry Papers,* Box 3).

Page 286 **". . . not so sure myself":** Fry, *Journal,* p. 496 (*Fry Papers,* Box 13).

Page 286 **". . . at the same time":** Daniel Bénédite, Confidential Financial Report on "L'Affaire Kourillo" (*Fry Papers,* Box 7).

Page 287 **". . . She looks so reproachful":** Fry, *Journal,* p. 552 (*Fry Papers,* Box 13).

Page 287 **". . . Gestapo rise, in fact":** Fry, *Journal,* pp. 555, 561; Fry, letter to Albert O. Hirschman, November 30, 1941 (*Fry Papers,* Box 13, Box 8).

Page 287 **". . . I couldn't help crying":** Fry, *Journal,* p. 563 (*Fry Papers,* Box 13).

Page 288 **. . . people to persecute:** See Michael R. Marrus and Robert O. Paxton, *Vichy France and the Jews,* p. 92; Fry, *Journal,* p. 568 (*Fry Papers,* Box 13).

Page 288 **THE LAST TEN YEARS:** Fry, cable to Eileen, June 1, 1941 (*Fry Papers,* Box 3).

Page 288 **. . . "Evidently there is":** Letter from Eileen to Fry, June 3, 1941 (*Fry Papers,* Box 3).

Page 289 **". . . confidence in you":** Letter from Eileen to Fry, March 6, 1941 (*Fry Papers,* Box 3).

Page 289 **". . . knew it anyway":** Letter from Eileen to Fry, May 9, 1941 (*Fry Papers,* Box 3).

Page 289 **". . . but resurrected":** Letter from Fry to Eileen, May 31, 1941 (*Fry Papers,* Box 3).

Page 289 **". . . just *aren't,* you know":** Letter from Eileen to Fry, March 14, 1941 (*Fry Papers,* Box 3).

Page 289 **. . . studio bosses and producers:** See Thomas Mann, *Selected Letters,* p. 287.

Page 290 **". . . we advanced him":** Danny Bénédite, letter to Fry, December 17, 1941 (*Fry Papers,* Box 5).

Page 290 **". . . relief organizations":** Fry, letter to Danny Bénédite, January 20, 1942 (*Fry Papers,* Box 2).

Page 290 **". . . pay for things there":** Letter from Fry to Eileen, May 31, 1941 (*Fry Papers,* Box 3).

Page 290 **Eileen was unimpressed:** See letter from Eileen to Fry, May 16, 1941 (*Fry Papers,* Box 3).

Page 290 **". . . look at their pictures":** Letter from Fry to Eileen, June 6, 1941 (*Fry Papers,* Box 3).

Page 290 **". . . a small oil":** Letter from Fry to Eileen, July 16, 1941 (*Fry Papers,* Box 3).

Page 291 **". . . I guess she's right":** Letter from Fry to Eileen, May 2, 1941 (*Fry Papers,* Box 3).

Page 291 **". . . Well, *hardly* ever":** Fry, letter to Danny Bénédite, October 7, 1942 (*Fry Papers,* Box 2).

Page 291 **. . . unwelcome at Forty-second Street:** See letter from Fry to Eileen, October 11, 1941 (*Fry Papers,* Box 3).

Page 291 **"'. . . frying out here'":** Letter from Eileen to Fry, May 3, 1941 (*Fry Papers,* Box 3).

Page 291 **Donald Ogden Stewart:** He was head of the Anti-Nazi League in the United States, and later one of the "Hollywood Ten" (see Otto Friedrich, *City of Nets,* p. 47 passim).

Page 291 **". . . not one jot to them":** Letter from Fry to Eileen, May 31, 1941 (*Fry Papers,* Box 3).

Page 291 **". . . confusion and inefficiency":** Letter from Fry to Eileen, February 23, 1941 (*Fry Papers,* Box 3).

Page 292 **". . . supreme contempt officially":** Letter from Fry to Eileen, May 1, 1941 (*Fry Papers,* Box 3).

Page 292 **"This all makes me think":** Eileen to Fry, August 5, 1941 (*Fry Papers,* Box 3).

Page 292 **. . . his German identity:** See Fry, *Journal,* p. 544 (*Fry Papers,* Box 13).

Page 292 **". . . increasingly nervous":** See Fry, *Journal,* p. 562 (*Fry Papers,* Box 13).

Page 293 **. . . leave the Villa Air-Bel:** Mary Jayne Gold, *Crossroads Marseille, 1940,* p. 354.

Page 293 **". . . I only saw their backs":** Mary Jayne Gold, *Crossroads Marseille, 1940,* pp. 357, 370.

Page 294 **. . . "I begin to suspect":** Letter from Eileen to Fry, May 9, 1941 (*Fry Papers,* Box 3).

Page 294 **". . . so sissy about it":** Letter from Eileen to Fry, May 31, 1941 (*Fry Papers,* Box 3).

Page 295 **". . . or else let me know":** Letter from Eileen to Fry, May 25, 1941 (*Fry Papers,* Box 3).

Page 295 **". . . such beautiful gardens":** Letter from Fry to Eileen, May 31, 1941 (*Fry Papers,* Box 3).

Page 295 **. . . "I have been sorry":** Letter from Eileen to Fry, June 3, 1941 (*Fry Papers,* Box 3).

Page 296 **"They are even trying to 'frame' me":** Letter from Fry to Eileen, May 31, 1941 (*Fry Papers,* Box 3).

Page 296 **". . . paid attention to them":** Letter from Eileen to Fry, June 26, 1941 (*Fry Papers,* Box 3).

Page 296 **"Have they continued":** Letter from Fry to Eileen, May 31, 1941 (*Fry Papers,* Box 3).

Page 296 **". . . however unsatisfactory":** Letter from Fry to Eileen, July 16, 1941 (*Fry Papers,* Box 3).

Page 296 ... **"What sort of stories":** Letter from Fry to Eileen, July 17, 1941 (*Fry Papers*, Box 3).

Page 297 **". . . made under this rubric":** Letter from Fry to Eileen, July 31, 1941 (*Fry Papers*, Box 3).

Page 297 **". . . hurt feelings and suspicions":** Letter from Eileen to Fry, July 8, 1941 (*Fry Papers*, Box 3).

Page 297 **". . . unworthy of your intelligence":** Fry to Eileen, July 31, 1941 (*Fry Papers*, Box 3).

Page 298 ... **Danny told Fry:** See Fry, *Journal*, p. 616 (*Fry Papers*, Box 13).

Page 298 **Then in mid-June:** See Fry, *Journal*, p. 583 (*Fry Papers*, Box 13).

Page 298 **The truth:** See Fry, *Journal*, p. 599 (*Fry Papers*, Box 13).

Page 298 ... **Fullerton replied:** See Fry, *Journal*, p. 596 (*Fry Papers*, Box 13).

Page 299 **". . . what will become of them":** See Fry's notes (*Fry Papers*, Box 11).

Page 299 **". . . the man can't get his":** See Fry's notes (*Fry Papers*, Box 11).

Page 300 **". . . so thoroly [sic] disgusted":** Miriam Davenport, letter to Dr. Charles Joy, November 3, 1941 (*Fry Papers*, Box 3).

Page 300 ... **"We believe":** See Fry, *Journal*, p. 610 (*Fry Papers*, Box 13).

Page 300 **". . . Jews and anti-Nazis":** *Surrender on Demand*, p. 224.

Page 300 **It was there that Dohrn discovered:** See Klaus Dohrn's account of his escape across the Pyrenees and his imprisonment by the Spanish Fascists (in *Fry Papers*, Box 8).

Page 301 ... **help him escape to England:** See Mary Jayne Gold, *Crossroads Marseille, 1940*, p. 380.

Page 301 **". . . infinite possibilities":** See Fry, *Journal*, p. 580 (*Fry Papers*, Box 13).

Page 301 ... **"Perhaps, after all":** Fry, letter to Lilian Fry, July 4, 1941 (*Fry Papers*, Box 3).

Page 301 **". . . Germany cannot win this war":** See Fry, *Journal*, p. 604 (*Fry Papers*, Box 13).

22. Fugitive Fry

Page 302 ... **"You don't need":** Fry, *Journal*, p. 617 (*Fry Papers*, Box 13).

Page 302 ... **the Carbone-owned *Midi*:** See Fry, *Journal*, p. 600 (*Fry Papers*, Box 13).

Page 303 ... **"There is no hostility":** See "Proposal for a Resettlement Project" by Paul Schmierer (*Fry Papers*, Box 8).

Page 304 ... **"pimping slavies":** Fry to Eileen, October 22, 1941 (*Fry Papers*, Box 3).

Page 304 **Railway coaches:** See Fry, *Journal*, p. 626 (*Fry Papers*, Box 13).

Page 305 **". . . as much as the next fellow, even":** Fry to Eileen, July 31, 1941 (*Fry Papers*, Box 3).

Page 305 **On his travels:** See Fry to Eileen, August 14, 1941 (*Fry Papers*, Box 3).

Page 306 ... **How about *you*:** Eileen to Fry, September 9, 1941 (*Fry Papers*, Box 3).

Page 306 **". . . apologize and surrender":** Fry to Eileen, October 1, 1941 (*Fry Papers*, Box 3).

Page 306 **". . . fulfillment of obligations":** Antoine de St. Exupéry, *Flight to Arras*, p. 129.

Page 306 ... **"I find it difficult":** Albert O. Hirschman, letter to Eileen Fry, February 1941 (*Fry Papers*, Box 3).

Page 306 **"Whom did Otto marry":** Fry to Eileen, July 31, 1941 (*Fry Papers*, Box 3).

Page 306 **At Vichy nothing happened:** See Fry to Eileen, August 17, 1941 (*Fry Papers*, Box 3).

Page 307 ... **"If you had taken":** Fry, letter to Danny Bénédite, October 2, 1941 (*Fry Papers*, Box 2).

Page 307 ... **"No, my pet":** Fry to Eileen, August 5, 1941 (*Fry Papers*, Box 3).

Page 308 "... a mental hospital": Fry, *Journal,* pp. 636–637 (*Fry Papers,* Box 13).

Page 308 "... until X gets here": Fry to Eileen, August 28, 1941 (*Fry Papers,* Box 3).

Page 308 ... "Everyone is convinced": Fry, *Journal,* p. 637 (*Fry Papers,* Box 13).

Page 308 "Friday, August 29": Fry, *Journal,* p. 641 (*Fry Papers,* Box 13).

Page 308 "Remember": See Lucie Heymann's report on Fry's arrest (*Fry Papers,* Box 8).

Page 308 The previous day: See Ian Ousby, *Occupation,* pp. 218, 225.

Page 309 ... "thirty momentous days": Lucie Heymann, report on Fry's arrest, p. 2 (*Fry Papers,* Box 8).

Page 310 "Nous ne sommes pas": Fry, letter to Albert O. Hirschman, November 30, 1941.

Page 310 "'We pinched them'": Fry, *Journal,* p. 644 (*Fry Papers,* Box 13).

Page 310 ... "Those fools": Letter from Fry to Eileen, October 1, 1941 (*Fry Papers,* Box 3).

Page 310 For the next week: See Fry, letter to Albert O. Hirschman, November 30, 1941.

Page 310 ... like a Goya painting: See Fry, *Journal,* p. 651 (*Fry Papers,* Box 13).

Page 311 Fry also had the last laugh: See letter from Fry to Eileen, September 7, 1941.

Page 311 "for what will the Vichysois think": Letter from Fry to Eileen, October 1, 1941 (*Fry Papers,* Box 13).

Page 312 "... with all my heart": Fry, letter to Danny Bénédite, October 28, 1941 (*Fry Papers,* Box 2).

Page 312 "Forgive me, then": Letter from Fry to Eileen, September 7, 1941 (*Fry Papers,* Box 3).

Page 312 "... new work ahead": Fry to Théo Bénédite, September 14, 1941 (*Fry Papers,* Box 3).

Page 312 ... "Shall I gradually return": Letter from Fry to Eileen, September 7, 1941 (*Fry Papers,* Box 3).

Page 313 "... to make sure we weren't dreaming": Letter from Fry to Théo Bénédite, September 14, 1941 (*Fry Papers,* Box 3).

Page 313 ... "Something is happening": Fry, Notes, "September 1941" (*Fry Papers,* Box 11).

23. The Homecoming

Page 314 His reunion with Eileen: See Fry, letter to Jean Gemahling, January 9, 1945 (*Fry Papers,* Box 4).

Page 314 "... beyond belief": Fry, letter to Danny Bénédite, January 20, 1942 (*Fry Papers,* Box 2).

Page 315 "... no one can stand": Fry, letter to Danny Bénédite, May 12, 1942 (*Fry Papers,* Box 2).

Page 315 "Any American official": Fry, notes, (*Fry Papers,* Box 17).

Page 315 "... doesn't do as an explanation": Fry, letter to Théo Bénédite, November 14, 1941 (*Fry Papers,* Box 3).

Page 316 "... an enemy alien": Peggy Guggenheim, quoted by Mary Jayne Gold in unpublished monograph, 1965 (*Fry Papers,* Box 18); see also Serge Guilbaut, *How New York Stole the Idea of Modern Art: Abstract Expressionism, Freedom, and the Cold War,* p. 73 ("Max Ernst was the darling of museums and society matrons alike").

Page 316 "... some of his pictures": Fry, letter to Jean Gemahling, January 9, 1945 (*Fry Papers,* Box 4).

Page 316 Breton, on the other hand: The art historian Martika Sawin says that at this time Jacqueline Breton was involved with another Surrealist named Esteban Frances, but Fry's reference to Matta is contemporary (from above letter to Jean Gemahling).

Page 316 . . . **internment on Martinique:** See Claude Lévi-Strauss, *Tristes Tropiques, p.25.*

Page 316 . . . **"The Committee felt":** Fry, letter to Victor Chernov, June 29, 1944 (*Fry Papers,* Box 3).

Page 316 **". . . certain refugee circles":** Fry, letter to Danny Bénédite, May 12, 1941 (*Fry Papers,* Box 2).

Page 317 **". . . explicit as I do":** Frank Kingdon, letter to Fry, February 13, 1942 (*Fry Papers,* Box 4).

Page 317 . . . **"Will you be good enough":** Fry, letter to Kingdon, February 14, 1942 (*Fry Papers,* Box 4).

Page 317 . . . **"That's that":** Fry, letter to Danny Bénédite, January 20, 1942 (*Fry Papers,* Box 2).

Page 317 **Under Fry's leadership:** See Howard L. Brook, *Prisoners of Hope.*

Page 317 . . . **"I am not very gay":** Lucie Heyman, letter to Fry, October 7, 1941 (*Fry Papers,* Box 13).

Page 318 . . . **"As far as I can see":** Fry, letter to Danny Bénédite, November 20, 1942 (*Fry Papers,* Box 2).

Page 318 **Fry was unprepared:** Danny Bénédite, letter to Fry, December 8, 1941 (*Fry Papers,* Box 13).

Page 319 . . . **"details of my sexual life":** Fry, letter to Danny Bénédite, May 12, 1942 (*Fry Papers,* Box 2).

Page 319 **I am sorry that:** Jean Gemahling, letter to Fry, April 1, 1942 (*Fry Papers,* Box 2).

Page 319 **"I want you to know":** Fry, letter to Jean Gemahling, June 9, 1942 (*Fry Papers,* Box 4).

Page 320 **Fry was now entering:** See Fry, letter to Jean Gemahling, January 9, 1945 (*Fry Papers,* Box 4).

Page 320 . . . **surveillance by the FBI:** Mentioned in Walter Meyerhof, letter to Donald Carroll, December 19, 1996. Fry's FBI file is a matter of fact.

Page 320 . . . **"It is irritating":** Fry, letter to Théo Bénédite, July 14, 1941 (*Fry Papers,* Box 3).

Page 320 . . . **a peaceful idyll:** See Fry, letter to Jean Gemahling, January 9, 1945 (*Fry Papers,* Box 4).

Page 320 . . . **gone into hiding:** For an account of the court's decisions, see Danny Bénédite's farewell letter to his staff at the Centre Américain de Secours, October 4 1942 (*Fry Papers,* Box 2).

Page 321 **Here are the latest:** Transcript of *Daily News* radio news broadcast, November 11, 1942.

Page 321 **". . . singing in my ears":** Fry's notes (*Fry Papers,* Box 11).

Page 321 . . . **He learned that Berthold:** See Miguel Vidal Guardiola, letter to Fry, January 26, 1942 (*Fry Papers,* Box 4).

Page 321 . . . **He heard that little Frederic:** See Fry's notes (*Fry Papers,* Box 11).

Page 321 **". . . where they belong":** Letter from Fry to Eileen, October 22, 1941 (*Fry Papers,* Box 3).

Page 322 **Fry was cheered:** Paul Elbogen, letter to Fry, August 4, 1942 (*Fry Papers,* Box 3).

Page 322 **". . . safe shore of America":** Charlotte Feibel, letter to Fry, March 23, 1945 (*Fry Papers,* Box 3).

Page 322 . . . **"I am sure you would":** Erich Lewinsky, letter to Fry, May 4, 1945 (*Fry Papers,* Box 3).

Page 323 **"I spoke to Mr Jaeger":** Fry, "The Massacre of the Jews", in *The New Republic*, December 21, 1942, p. 817. For an excellent account of when and what was known in the West, see David S. Wyman, *The Abandonment of the Jews*, Chapter 3, "The Worst Is Confirmed," pp. 42–58. According to Wyman, news of exterminations had been received officially (and kept secret) only two months earlier.

Page 323 **... Clovis's new "wife":** See Fry, letter to Jean Gemahling, January 9, 1945 (*Fry Papers*, Box 4).

Page 323 **In May 1941:** The authoritative account of this meal is to be found in Salka Viertel, *The Kindness of Strangers*, pp. 250–51, is repeated with additional material in Otto Friedrich, *City of Nets*, p. 99, and is quoted by Lawrence Weschler in his essay, "Paradise," in *Exiles & Emigrés*, p. 342, and by John Baxter in *The Hollywood Exiles*, p. 216.

Page 324 **... a coronary in August 1945:** See Alma Mahler Werfel, *And the Bridge is Love*, p. 266.

Page 324 **... "I never come to these things":** Thomas Mann, *Dr. Faustus: The Genesis of a Novel*, pp. 110–11.

Page 324 **... "He stayed in his cabin":** See Nigel Hamilton, *The Brothers Mann*, p. 314.

Page 325 **... One dinner guest recalled:** See Nigel Hamilton, *The Brothers Mann*, p. 328.

Page 325 **Hardly a day passed:** See Salka Viertel, *The Kindness of Strangers*, p. 272.

Page 325 **... forbidden to climb stairs:** Otto Friedrich, *City of Nets*, p. 410.

Page 326 **In May of 1949:** See Nigel Hamilton, *The Brothers Mann*, pp. 355–58; Otto Friedrich, *City of Nets*, pp. 410–13.

Page 326 **The Feuchtwangers arrived:** Constance Regnier Carroll, interview with Marta Feuchtanger, mid-seventies.

Page 327 **When Hertha Pauli landed:** See Fry's notes (*Fry Papers*, Box 17).

Page 327 **... "I have tried":** See Fry's abandoned Foreword to *Surrender on Demand* (*Fry Papers*, Box 11).

Page 328 **WE ALRIGHT NOW:** Danny Bénédite, cable to Fry, December 22, 1944 (*Fry Papers*, Box 2).

Page 328 **... "embauchage illicite":** Anna Gruss, letter to Fry, September 25, 1944 (*Fry Papers*, Box 4).

Page 328 **"DANNY AFTER MIRACULOUS":** Théo Bénédite, cable to Fry, January 9, 1945 (*Fry Papers*, Box 3).

Page 328 **... and surrendered:** See Fry, letter to Anna Gruss, October 1, 1944 (*Fry Papers*, Box 4).

Page 329 **"... biggest surprises of my life":** Théo Bénédite, letter to Fry, March 16, 1946 (*Fry Papers*, Box 3).

Page 329 **Also came:** See Fry, letter to Victor Serge, April 2, 1945 (*Fry Papers*, Box 5).

Page 329 **But there were shreds:** Donald Carroll, interview with Bill Spira.

Page 330 **"So many things":** Jean Gemahling, letter to Fry, December 22, 1944 (*Fry Papers*, Box 4).

Page 330 **... *Liberté*, and *Verité*:** Statement by Jean Gemahling, August 12, 1967 (*Fry Papers*, Box 4).

Page 330 **... "In the meanwhile":** Jean Gemahling, letter to Fry, March 21, 1945 (*Fry Papers*, Box 4).

Page 330 **This proportion:** Jean Gemahling, letter to Fry, May 12, 1945 (*Fry Papers*, Box 4).

Page 331 **"... progressed in my analysis":** Fry, letter to Jean Gemahling, January 9, 1945 (*Fry Papers*, Box 4).

Page 331 **... "What really puzzles me":** Jean Gemahling, letter to Fry, March 21, 1945 (*Fry Papers*, Box 4).

PART 6: EPILOGUE

Epilogue

Page 335 "... history of migration": Laura Fermi, *Illustrious Immigrants*, p. 3.

Page 336 **Those artists:** See Martica Sawin, *Surrealism in Exile*, pp. 196, 294, 413.

Page 337 **"It is the most interesting":** Fry, letter to Jean Gemahling, January 9, 1945 (*Fry Papers*, Box 4).

Page 337 **"The peace would":** Thomas Keneally, *Schindler's Ark*, p. 421.

Page 338 **The pioneering sexual researcher:** See Fry, letters to Kinsey, January 21 and February 6, 1946 (*Fry Papers*, Box 6).

Page 338 **Any hormonal:** See Alfred Kinsey, "Homosexuality: Criteria for a Hormonal Explanation of the Homosexual," in *The Journal of Clinical Endocrinology*, 1, no. 5 (May 1941), pp. 424–28 (*Fry Papers*, Box 6).

Page 339 **... judicial murders:** See *Fry Papers*, Box 9.

Page 339 **Fry joined and left:** See Fry's correspondence with the Creative Age Press during August 1946 (*Fry Papers*, Box 6).

Page 339 **It was around:** See correspondence in *Fry Papers*, Box 10.

Page 339 **... colors to the mast:** See *Fry Papers*, Box 7.

Page 340 **"... satisfied with that":** Fry, letter to Jean Roumilhac, March 20, 1946 (*Fry Papers*, Box 5).

Page 340 **... "I sell practically":** Fry, letter to a young writer, "Russel," December 21, 1943 (*Fry Papers*, Box 6).

Page 340 **"... a bureaucrat at heart":** Fry, letter to Danny Bénédite, June 3, 1942 (*Fry Papers*, Box 2).

Page 340 **"... his old friend Max Ascoli":** See Fry, letter to Ascoli, May 7, 1946 (*Fry Papers*, Box 2).

Page 340 **"... selling anything":** Fry, letter to Danny Bénédite, January 20, 1942 (*Fry Papers*, Box 2).

Page 340 **... buy him out:** See addendum by Annette Fry to a commentary by Martin Braun on the television documentary, "The Artists' Schindler," p. 5 (personal communication).

Page 341 **"... a complete disaster":** Fry, letter to Anna Gruss, July 14, 1967 (*Fry Papers*, Box 4).

Page 341 **Dear Eileen:** Quoted by Donald Carroll in unpublished monograph.

Page 341 **"... an unruly adolescent":** Miriam Davenport Ebel, letter to Annette Fry, June 27, 1983.

Page 341 **By coincidence:** Annette Fry, interview with the author, 1998.

Page 342 **We saw a perfect madman:** Mary McCarthy, letter to Hannah Arendt, *Between Friends*, p. 6.

Page 342 **... went too far:** See Annette Fry, "Mary McCarthy and Varian Fry" (personal communication).

Page 343 **"... Communist Party activities":** Norman Thomas, letter to Colonel Phelps of October 12, 1951, in which he quotes the colonel's accusations against Fry (*Fry Papers*, Box 1).

Page 343 **"... the democratic system":** Statement by the American Committee for Cultural Freedom, read by Senator Paul Douglas of Illinois into the Congressional Record, March 8, 1954 (*Fry Papers*, Box 7).

Page 343 **Fry had set about:** See J. Edgar Hoover, letter to Fry, November 19, 1951 (*Fry Papers*, Box 1).

Page 343 ... **"I am beginning":** Fry, letter to Colonel Phelps, November 6, 1951 (*Fry Papers,* Box 9).

Page 344 ... **his corporate clients:** Addendum by Annette Fry to Martin Braun's commentary, p. 5 (personal communication).

Page 345 **". . . the right approach":** Stéphane Hessel, letter to Fry, May 8, 1963 (*Fry Papers,* Box 2).

Page 345 **". . . his many hobbies":** Addendum by Annette Fry to Martin Braun's commentary, p. 5 (personal communication).

Page 345 ... **"Varian, don't feel unhappy":** Dr. Alex Makinsky, letter to Fry, January 11, 1962 (*Fry Papers,* Box 2).

Page 345 **". . . father of three children":** Article on twenty-fifth anniversary staff reunion of the Centre Américain de Secours, *Parade* magazine, February 13, 1966.

Page 346 ... **period of decades:** Fry's essay is in the *Fry Papers,* but the story of his sacking is told in a letter to Sam Heppner, September 10, 1965 (*Fry Papers,* Box 4).

Page 346 **". . . your classes":** See Annette Fry, "Varian Fry Chronology" (personal communication).

Page 346 ... **The problem was:** See Annette Fry, open letter, June 1993 (*Fry Papers,* Box 9).

Page 346 **Chagall kindly lent:** See Fry, letter to Jacques Lipchitz, February 4, 1965; André Malraux, letter to Fry, November 13, 1964 (*Fry Papers,* Box 1, Box 4).

Page 347 **". . . the first shock":** Max Ernst, letter to Fry, October 6, 1966 (*Fry Papers,* Box 1).

Page 347 ... **"Breton says":** In Hanne Benzion, letter to Charles Sternberg at the International Rescue Committee offices in Paris, January 31, 1966 (*Fry Papers,* Box 3).

Page 347 ... **"He's an old dear":** Fry, letter to a young sculptor, "Charlie," in London, January 19, 1967 (*Fry Papers,* Box 4).

Page 347 **An unexpected bonus:** See Fry, letter to Anna Gruss, July 14, 1967 (*Fry Papers,* Box 4).

Page 348 **Did you have pain:** Fry, letter to Max Ernst, 1966. See also Fry, letter to Albert O. Hirschman, March 6, 1967 (*Fry Papers,* Box 10).

Page 348 **". . . Look at me":** Fry, letter to Annette, September 18, 1966 (*Fry Papers,* Box 3).

Page 348 ... **"He was so terribly depressed":** Chris (Kerstin) Brown, quoted by Annette Fry in her "Varian Fry Chronology" (personal communication).

Page 349 ... **In 1940 and 1941:** See Fry, letter to Anna Gruss, July 14, 1967 (*Fry Papers,* Box 4); André Malraux, *Anti-Memoirs,* p. 117.

Page 350 ... **"His health was rotten":** Miriam Davenport Ebel, letter to Annette Fry, April 27, 1993.

Page 351 **"At the same time":** Marcel Verzeano, letter to Tom Fry, January 8, 1968.

Page 351 **"It was endlessly fascinating":** Albert O. Hirschman, introduction to *Assignment Rescue,* p. vii.

Page 351 ... **Fry, "obstinately virtuous":** Alfred Kazin, "Homage to Varian Fry," in *The New Republic,* February 9, 1998, pp. 27–30.

Page 352 ... **"a magnificent man":** Quoted in Martica Sawin, *Surrealism in Exile,* p. 140.

Page 352 **"I did not want to go":** Jacques Lipchitz, letter to Annette Fry, September 22, 1967 (*Fry Papers,* Box 1).

BIBLIOGRAPHY

Baker, Carlos, ed. *Ernest Hemingway: Selected Letters* (London: Granada, 1981).

Barron, Stephanie, ed. *Exiles and Emigrés: The Flight of European Artists from Hitler* (Los Angeles County Museum of Art/Harry N. Abrams Inc., 1998). See esp. Elizabeth Kessin Berman's essay, "Moral Triage or Cultural Salvage?" pp. 99–112. Also Lawrence Weschler, "Paradise."

Baxter, John. *The Hollywood Exiles* (New York: Taplinger, 1976.

Booth, Clare. *European Spring* (London: Hamish Hamilton, 1941).

Breitman, Richard, and Alan M. Kraut. *American Refugee Policy and European Jewry, 1933–45* (Bloomington: Indiana University Press, 1987).

Brightman, Carol, ed. *Between Friends: The Correspondence of Hannah Arendt and Mary McCarthy 1949–1975* (London: Secker & Warburg, 1995).

Broderson, Momme. *Walter Benjamin: A Biography.* Ed. Martina Dervis. Tr. Malcolm R. Green (London: Verso, 1997).

Brooks, Howard L. *Prisoners of Hope* (New York: L. B. Fischer, 1942).

Cesarani, David. *Arthur Koestler: The Homeless Mind* (William Heinemann, 1998).

Coser, Lewis A. *Refugee Scholars in America: Their Impact and Their Experiences* (New Haven, Conn.: Yale University Press, 1984).

Feingold, Henry. *The Politics of Rescue: The Roosevelt Administration and the Holocaust 1938–45* (New Brunswick, N.J.: Rutgers University Press, 1970).

Fermi, Laura. *Illustrious Immigrants* (Chicago: University of Chicago Press, 1968).

Feuchtwanger, Lion. *The Devil in France* (London, Hutchinson, 1942).

Fittko, Lisa. *Escape through the Pyrénées* (Evanston, Ill.: Northwestern University Press, 1991).

———. *Solidarity and Treason* (Evanston, Ill.: Northwestern University Press, 1995).

Fleming, Donald, and Bernard Bailin, eds. *The Intellectual Migration: Europe and America 1930–1960* (Cambridge, Mass.: Harvard University Press, 1969).

Friedrich, Otto. *City of Nets* (London: Headline, 1986).

Fry, Varian. *Assignment Rescue* (New York: Scholastic, 1997).

———. *Surrender on Demand* (Colorado: Johnson Books, 1997).

Gide, André. *The Journals of André Gide.* Volume II (New York: Vintage, 1960).

Gildea, Robert. *France Since 1945* (Oxford: Oxford University Press, 1997).

Gold, Mary Jayne. *Crossroads Marseilles, 1940* (New York: Doubleday, 1980).

Guggenheim, Peggy. *Confessions of an Art Addict* (London: André Deutsch, 1980).

Guilbaut, Serge. *How New York Stole the Idea of Modern Art: Abstract Expressionism, Freedom, and the Cold War* (Chicago: University of Chicago Press, 1983).

Hamilton, Nigel. *The Brothers Mann: The Life and Times of Heinrich and Thomas Mann, 1871–1950 and 1875–1955* (London: Secker & Warburg, 1978).

Heilbut, Anthony. *Exiled in Paradise: German Refugee Artists and Intellectuals in America from the 1930s to the Present* (New York, Viking, 1983).

Jackman, Jarrell C., and Carla M. Borden, eds. *The Muses Flee Hitler: Cultural Transfer and Adaptation, 1930–45* (Washington, D.C.: Smithsonian Institution Press, 1983). See esp. Cynthia Jaffee McCabe, p. 72: "Wanted by the Gestapo, Saved by America: Varian Fry and the Emergency Rescue Committee").

Kahn, Lothar. *Insight and Action: The Life and Work of Lion Feuchtwanger* (Rutherford, N.J.: Fairleigh Dickinson University Press, 1975).

Kassof, Anita. "Intent and Interpretation: The German Refugees of Article 19 of the Franco-German Armistice 1940–1941." Master's thesis, United States Holocaust Memorial Museum, Washington D.C.).

Keegan, John. *The Second World War* (London: Penguin, 1989).

Keegan, Susanne. *A Bride of the Wind: The Life and Times of Alma Mahler-Werfel* (London: Secker & Warburg, 1991).

Keneally, Thomas. *Schindler's Ark* (London: Hodder & Stoughton, 1993).

Kirstein, Lincoln. *Mosaic: Memoirs* (New York: Farrar, Straus and Giroux, 1994).

Koestler, Arthur. *The Invisible Handwriting,* (New York: Macmillan, 1954).

———. *Scum of the Earth* (London: Hutchinson, 1968).

Kokoschka, Oskar. *My Life* (London: Thames & Hudson, 1974).

Kurth, Peter. *American Cassandra: The Life of Dorothy Thompson* (New York: Little, Brown, 1990).

Lévi-Strauss, Claude. *Tristes Tropiques* (London: Jonathan Cape, 1973).

Lowrie, D. A. *The Hunted Children: The Dramatic Story of the Heroic Men and Women Who Outwitted the Nazis to Save Thousands of Helpless Refugees in Southern France During World War II* (New York: Norton, 1963).

Mahler Werfel, Alma. *And the Bridge Is Love* (London: Hutchinson, 1959).

Malraux, André. *Anti-Memoirs* (New York: Bantam, 1970).

Mann, Golo. *Reminiscences and Reflections* (London: Faber & Faber, 1990).

Mann, Thomas. *Dr. Faustus: The Genesis of a Novel* (London, Secker & Warburg, 1961).

———. *Selected Letters* (London: Penguin, 1970).

Marrus, Michael R., and Robert O. Paxton. *Vichy France and the Jews* (New York: Schocken Books, 1983).

Martin, Gilbert. *The Second World War* (London: Weidenfeld & Nicholson, 1989).

Mehring, Walter. *The Lost Library: The Autobiography of a Culture* (London: Secker & Warburg, 1951).

Monson, Karen. *Alma Mahler, Muse to Genius* (Boston: Houghton Mifflin, 1983).

Morse, Arthur D. *While Six Million Died: A Chronicle of American Apathy* (New York: Overlook Press, 1998).

Ousby, Ian. *Occupation: The Ordeal of France, 1940–1944* (London: John Murray, 1997).

Paldiel, Mordecai. *The Path of the Righteous* (New York: KTAV, 1993).

Paxton, Robert O. *Vichy France: Old Guard and New Order, 1940–44* (New York: Alfred A. Knopf, 1972).

Pimlott, John. *The Viking Atlas of World War II* (London: Viking, 1995).

Polizzotti, Mark. *Revolution of the Mind: The Life of André Breton* (London: Bloomsbury, 1995).

Ryan, Donna F. *The Holocaust and the Jews of Marseilles: The Enforcement of Anti-Semitic Policies in Vichy France* (Urbana: University of Illinois Press, 1996).

Sahl, Hans. *In Search of Myself* (New York: Putnam, 1994).

St. Exupéry, Antoine de. *Flight to Arras* (London: Heinemann, 1942).

Sawin, Martika. *Surrealism in Exile and the Beginning of the New York School* (Cambridge, Mass.: MIT Press, 1995).

Schoenberner, Franz. *The Inside Story of an Outsider* (New York: Macmillan, 1949).

Serge, Victor. *Memoirs of a Revolutionary 1901–1941* (Oxford: Oxford University Press, 1963).

Spalek, John H., ed. *Lion Feuchtwanger: The Man, His Ideas, His Work: A Collection of Critical Essays* (Los Angeles: 1972).

Steinman, Lionel B. *Franz Werfel: The Faith of an Exile: From Prague to Beverly Hills* (Wilfrid Laurier University Press, 1985).

Stephenson, William. *A Man Called Intrepid* (New York: Ballantine, 1977).

Tashjian, Dickran. *A Boatload of Madmen: Surrealism and the American Avant-garde, 1920–1950* (New York: Thames & Hudson, 1995).

Taylor, John Russell. *Strangers in Paradise: The Hollywood Emigrés 1933–1950* (London: Faber & Faber, 1983).

Taylor, Telford. *The Breaking Wave: The Second World War in the Summer of 1940* (New York: Simon & Schuster, 1967).

Toller, Ernst. *I Was a German: The Autobiography of Ernst Toller* (New York: New York University Press, 1979).

Weisberg, Richard H. *Vichy Law and the Holocaust in France* (New York: New York University Press, 1997).

Wyman, Davis S. *The Abandonment of the Jews: America and the Holocaust, 1941–1945* (New York: New Press, 1998).

———. *Paper Walls: America and the Refugee Crisis, 1938–41* (Amherst: University of Massachusetts Press, 1968).

Viertel, Salka. *The Kindness of Strangers* (New York: Rhineholt & Winston, 1969).

Zuccotti, Susan. *The Holocaust, the French, and the Jews* (New York: Basic Books, 1993).

INDEX